MONETARY AND FISCAL THOUGHT AND POLICY IN CANADA, 1919-1939

T0313911

CANADIAN STUDIES IN ECONOMICS

A series of studies sponsored by the Canadian Social Science Research Council, and edited by V. W. Bladen.

1. International Cycles and Canada's Balance of Payments, 1921-33. By Vernon W. Malach.

2. Capital Formation in Canada, 1896-1930. By Kenneth Buckley.

3. Natural Resources: The Economics of Conservation. By Anthony Scott.

4. The Canadian Nickel Industry. By O. W. Main.

5. Bank of Canada Operations, 1935-54. By E. P. Neufeld.

6. State Intervention and Assistance In Collective Bargaining: The Canadian Experience, 1943-1954. By H. A. Logan.

7. The Agricultural Implement Industry in Canada: A Study of Competition. By W. G. Phillips.

8. Monetary and Fiscal Thought and Policy in Canada, 1919-1939. By Irving Brecher.

Monetary and Fiscal Thought and Policy in Canada

1919–1939

IRVING BRECHER

UNIVERSITY OF TORONTO PRESS: 1957

TO MY FAMILY

PREFACE

IN the field of economic policy--and, indeed, over the whole range of social experience--ample support can be found for the generalization that old ideas die hard; they typically display a tenacity which far exceeds the limits justified by their intrinsic merit. To a considerable degree, this persistence is a reflection of the success with which vested interests pursue rationally conceived objectives. But it would be an unbalanced view of history which overlooked the fact that, with the passage of time, general absorption of a system of thought often becomes so deep as to make the acceptance of new ideas, however simple and sound, a slow and arduous psychological process. By the same token, it would seem reasonable to expect a close causal connection between prevalent ideas and attitudes on the one hand and the evolution of economic policy on the other. Against the background of these observations, the present study traces the course and interrelationships of Canadian "stabilization" thought and policy during the period 1919-39. Primary attention is devoted to monetary and fiscal thinking, and to their impact on public policy in the federal sphere.

At any stage of a country's development, it is not difficult to be overwhelmed by contemporary events, and to dismiss historical experience as inapplicable to current circumstances. This is especially true now for a country like Canada, where a decade of rapid and sustained economic growth since World War II has been accompanied by impressive gains in economic understanding and knowledge. The inquiry which follows, however, is rooted in the conviction that, while the magnitude of these changes warrants a healthy optimism over prospects for preventing a repetition of inter-war business-cycle experience, the problems associated with cyclical fluctuations remain sufficiently complex to make a "sense of history" an indispensable condition for effective stabilization policy.

I have been the fortunate recipient of generous assistance from numerous sources in both Canada and the United States. Several of these are particularly worthy of specific acknowledgement. Very much in the forefront is the contribution made by Professor B. H. Higgins, who first suggested the topic for analysis, and whose critical comment and advice were invaluable throughout the work. I am also grateful for the constructive research guidance provided by Professors A. H. Hansen and J. H. Williams. To Professor V. W. Bladen and the Editors of the University of Toronto Press go my sincere thanks for their helpful editorial suggestions, and for so efficiently seeing the manuscript through to ultimate publication. A generous grant-in-aid of publication was made by the Canadian Social Science Research Council. Finally, I owe a profound debt of gratitude to my wife. The completion of this study is a tribute to her monumental patience and her unflagging encouragement at every stage of the research.

CONTENTS

TABLES

CHARTS

MONETARY AND FISCAL THOUGHT AND POLICY IN CANADA, 1919-1939

CHAPTER I

THE PROBLEM IN ITS GENERAL SETTING

MUCH of the ground covered here has been surveyed before, and significant studies beyond the interwar period have been made. Indeed, the present Dominion-wide acceptance of the Keynesian "income-expenditure"
approach[1] to economic stability is the culmination of the economic thinking of the two decades preceding World War II, and, even more, the
product of the powerful stimulus to increased understanding of economic
principles and the functioning of the Canadian economy provided by the
need for preserving economic balance in the prosecution of the war.[2]

As will be subsequently shown, the decade of the twenties was distinguished only for the superficial and imperfect diagnoses of, and remedial suggestions for, unemployment made chiefly by the relative handful
of thinkers associated with the Progressive and United Farmer movements then springing up in the West. It was the thirties which, under the
impact of the Great Depression, witnessed the first real stirrings of
careful economic analysis in cyclical terms, and of statistical techniques
for measuring the value of annual productive activity and income receipts
in the Dominion. But even the latter development, by the end of the decade, had reached a stage which still left much to be desired;[3] while the
former comprised studies which lacked thoroughness, did not emphasize
the income-expenditure aspects of stability, or were concerned mainly
with equity and efficiency rather than stability.[4] As for the war and postwar periods, they have brought forth an unprecedented outpouring of
books, pamphlets, journal articles, government documents, and parliamentary pronouncements directly involving problems of war finance, employment prospects, the measurement of income-employment variables,
and alternative policy routes to full employment. But again, these publications have either excluded the interwar period from their terms of reference or have analysed only particular "stability" aspects of that
period.[5]

Thus, the writer has selected the interwar period as the unit for
comprehensive treatment; and has attempted to appraise the evolution
of the Canadian policy of monetary and fiscal stabilization against the
"thought environment" in which it was conceived and implemented, and
against the standards set by modern income-employment theory.[6] That
is to say, the major effort is in the nature of synthesis of what appears,
in the present context, to have been the piecemeal approach to the interwar stability problem in Canada, with the emphasis on the content of
"stabilization thinking" and on its implications for policy. The difficulties associated with this task are compounded of the specific procedural
techniques used in the investigation, and the inherent characteristics of
the subject matter being investigated. With these difficulties, and with

the over-all cyclical pattern of the interwar period, the remainder of these introductory remarks is concerned.

I. PROBLEMS OF METHODOLOGY

Problems Posed by Choice of the Interwar Period
     The choice of the interwar period as the object of analysis would seem to have ample basis in economic fact, quite apart from any difficulty of obtaining reliable "stability" data for the pre-1914 period of Canadian development. The two decades between the wars mark the first clear appearance of a pattern of economic thought and policy relating to cyclical fluctuations in employment and income. It will be seen that this pattern reflected, in general, the most primitive notions and policies; that it was partly moulded by previous Canadian experience, especially during World War I; and that it contained the seeds of growth for attitudes towards, and for methods of handling, economic problems during and after World War II. Moreover, both world wars bring to light many of the "stability" problems which arose during the interwar period, and the latter becomes fully comprehensible only through comparison with wartime and post-World War II experience. But the twenties and thirties remain unique in terms of their striking projection of both the domestic and external aspects of economic stability into a peacetime historical setting.

     Concentration on the interwar period, nevertheless, has important procedural consequences. It is evident, for example, that the relative briefness of the period renders impossible any precise distinction in time between economic thought and economic policy. The general difficulties encountered in the formulation of a cause-effect relationship between thought and policy will be elaborated in the concluding section of this investigation. Special attention should now be drawn to the fact that many of the views recorded below were expressed after the implementation of the policy upon which they had a bearing. In the nature of the case, this had to be so; that is, the surge of events frequently occurred with such swiftness as to make after-the-fact crystallization of attitudes a common feature of interwar experience. But the writer envisions the main object of the survey of ideas to be the description of the "thought milieu" in which Canadian stabilization policy evolved, and, in that sense, distortions of any preconceived chronological thought-policy pattern cannot be regarded as a crucial defect of the analysis.

     The other point worth noting in connection with the period selected is the overwhelmingly important role played by the controversy over the establishment of a central bank in Canada. No student of Canadian interwar experience can fail to be impressed by this fact. In part, it reflected the contemporary foreign emphasis on the monetary approach to stabilization theory and policy; and in part, the relatively advanced stage of development which Canadian banking institutions (as contrasted, say, with the

fiscal and labour-management structures) had reached by the end of
World War I. But whatever the reasons, the fact is that virtually the
entire "stability" sphere of economic policy in Canada takes its form
through the ideas inspired by the "central bank controversy." This will,
indeed, become apparent from an examination of the necessarily disproportionate amount of analytical effort directed by the writer at the nature
and implications of this controversy.

Topical vs. Chronological Analysis

Closely allied to the problem of selecting the period for investigation
is the question whether the general approach to the subject should be
topical or chronological. The former approach has much to commend
it when applied to historical studies of a long period of time, and to
studies whose purpose is to underscore the distinctiveness of change in
a wide variety of economic fields. This inquiry, however, is designed
to provide a basis of comparison for both the pre-1919 and post-1939
experience with the relatively brief but highly significant interwar period;
and to bring to light the interrelationships of all those factors (ideas on
the causes of unemployment, monetary and fiscal thought and policy, etc.)
impinging upon cyclical fluctuations in Canada during that period. The
chronological approach, therefore, is deemed preferable in the present
context.

But the topical question is not thereby eliminated from consideration.
For the great concern here with economic thinking means that a decision
must also be made as to whether, within each decade, the analysis should
proceed topically or in terms of the contribution to thought made by each
of the regional, political, and occupational groups in the Canadian economy. The basis for this decision is the desire to emphasize, not the
special characteristics of each group's thinking on all "stability" problems, but rather the marked differences of attitude towards, and their
policy implications for, each problem. Thus the analysis for each decade is topical, as represented by the chapter headings throughout. The
topical-chronological decision actually made will now be seen to involve
the admixture of topics, as compared with the admixture of groups involved in a topical-group decision.

Other Procedural Problems

The emphasis on economic thinking gives rise to other problems
which are not resolvable through a choice between topical and group approaches. There is, first, the problem of adequacy of coverage. A
truly comprehensive survey of thought must include bibliographical
material ranging all the way from (1) highly technical books and articles
through (2) governmental and parliamentary publications to (3) newspapers
and the great variety of non-technical literary media for group expression. The author has attempted, wherever feasible, to satisfy this criterion, but he is forced to acknowledge its frequent violation with respect

to the third-mentioned category of data. This is partly the result of the sheer physical impossibility of coping with the hundreds of popular and semi-popular publications throughout the Dominion. But there is the further consideration that such an undertaking would be beyond the scope of this inquiry; and that, even if it were assumed possible to select a small representative number of these publications for analysis, the results of that analysis probably would serve only as a means of confirming the "thought" cleavage already explored. In any case, evidence of such confirmation is often cited in those parts of the study where it is particularly relevant.

Secondly, there is the related problem of the permissible degree of mixture of scientific economic analysis and popular "journalese." The latter is not unique to newspapers and non-academic periodicals, but is also a characteristic feature of parliamentary debates, royal commission proceedings, and the pronouncements of leaders in industry and finance. In other words, exclusive preoccupation with technical analysis would make little sense, since it would involve the omission of what has to be viewed as an integral part of Canadian economic thought and policy during the interwar period. On the other hand, the question remains as to how best achieve the combination of both elements. Obviously, no precise operating guide to action is available. The writer conceives his task, in general terms, as one of effecting that combination which will be broad enough to reflect reality, and yet narrow enough to allow maximum scope for applying analytical tools and economic principles to all facets of the subject under investigation.

A third problem, or rather set of problems, posed by the emphasis on economic thinking is that of the frequency of quotation, the possibility of distorting views through quotation, and the possibility of confusion between the views surveyed and the author's analysis. The latter two difficulties call for the greatest care in the selection of quotations and in the use of paraphrasing respectively. The degree of difficulty, in this connection, will, of course, vary directly with the frequency of quotation. But the problem of frequency is important in its own right. Moderately used, the technique of quoting gives meaning and substance to a study of thought; overdone, it reduces such a study to a mere collection of unintegrated statements. The author, again, has attempted to steer a careful course between shallowness and over-quotation. If he has erred in the latter direction, his only defence is the inherent difficulty of achieving a fully satisfactory compromise, and his preference for error in this latter direction to error in the former.

In the fourth place, there is the problem of artificiality--in its two main forms of regional-occupational division and topical division. Various aspects of this problem will be alluded to throughout the inquiry. It should be especially noted here, however, that hard and fast lines of distinction among regions and occupations cannot possibly be drawn. This is true even of the basic East-West division in economic thinking. It is true, also, of the division among bankers, businessmen, economists, government officials, and other occupational groups; for such a division immediately creates problems of overlapping for, say, those economists who are bankers or governmental officials as well, and those government officials with strong business backgrounds.[7] Cutting across regional and occupational lines are the numerous instances of individual thinkers whose ideas cannot easily be associated with those of the political or class grouping to which they belong.

But the problem of topical division is more complex than these regional, occupational difficulties, which can, after all, be remedied through proper qualification. That is to say, the writer's separation for analytical treatment of the general approach to economic stability, monetary thought, and fiscal thought, is not strongly rooted in the Canadian thought processes which actually evolved during the interwar period. There was no such neat separation of concepts by the individuals and groups that gave expression to their views. On the contrary, the loose combination of essentially different, often mutually inconsistent, ideas stands out as one of the prime characteristics of interwar Canadian economic thinking.[8] In that sense, the author's comparative appraisal represents a distortion of the actual "thought" pattern--a transplanting of ideas from their original context so as to achieve conformity with the pattern sketched for purposes of this investigation. However, there are at least two cogent reasons for pursuing this course of action. One is that it provides a practical and coherent framework of analysis, to which the only alternative would be the "group" approach (as contrasted with the topical approach) already rejected on grounds of misplaced emphasis. The other reason is that it has doctrinal validity and facilitates the critical examination of interwar thought against the background of contemporary economic analysis.

The Conceptual Framework: Problems of Scope and Definition

It remains only to give precision to the writer's conceptual system, with attention being centred on the nature of, and relationship between, monetary and fiscal problems. The first point worthy of emphasis is that, to the extent that this study concerns itself with the evolution of policy, its scope is limited, for the most part, to the federal sphere. This limitation creates no special problems for Canadian monetary policy, which has always been under federal jurisdiction, but the implementation of fiscal policy in the Dominion takes place in a federal-provincial-local setting. For full comprehension of such policy, it therefore becomes essential to examine the fiscal operations of subsidiary governments and their impact upon federal policy. A "stability-oriented" study of this kind has yet to be undertaken for Canada. The sole reason for its neglect by the author is the pragmatic one of manageability for a single investigation.

Secondly, there is the limitation of exclusive concern with the "stabilization" aspects of monetary and fiscal problems. The great importance of economic fluctuations as a separate branch of economic science would appear to provide adequate justification for this procedure. It means, however, that, on the monetary side, there will be little treatment of institutional and organizational problems in the commercial banking field; and that, on the fiscal side, the analysis will not be conducted in terms of income distribution, resource allocation, or economic growth. In the latter connection, it is, of course, neither possible nor desirable to separate completely fiscal policy in the "stability" sense from fiscal policy aimed at other socio-economic objectives. Nevertheless, the major effort must be devoted to the former type of policy, with the latter being of interest here only by way of its implications for economic stability.[9]

The construction of the entire study on a monetary-fiscal base suggests, finally, a specific approach, on the part of the writer, to the terms, "monetary policy," and "fiscal policy"--allowing for the two limitations already noted--and to the rationale for the distinction made between them. Monetary policy is defined, then, as conscious central bank and/or governmental action designed to achieve high-level economic stability by influencing the supply of money;[10] that is, action designed mainly to influence interest rates by changing the composition (or cash proportion), not the over-all size, of assets held by economic units.[11] Among central bank instruments of monetary policy would be included "moral suasion" applied to commercial banks, variation of rediscount rates, open market operations, and changes in commercial bank reserve requirements.[12] As for treasuries and finance departments, they would employ such techniques as sterilization and de-sterilization of gold, devaluation, and shifts in deposits as between central and commercial banks.[13]

Fiscal policy is here defined as revenue-expenditure-debt policy consciously pursued by government, with the objective of directly influencing aggregate demand and so maintaining economic stability at high levels of employment and income. Consequently, three distinguishing features of fiscal policy manifest themselves: (1) its directness in changing the over-all size, rather than the composition, of assets; (2) the possibility of its implementation with or without a change in the money supply; and (3) its administration through the budgetary process. Each of these features calls for some clarification.

The first is, perhaps, the most fundamental, since it uncovers the prime economic difference in the operation of monetary and fiscal policy, namely, the fact that the former acts indirectly, through interest rates, on the consumption and investment components of aggregate demand, while the latter brings about the direct variation of these components. Thus, analysis of the stimulative effects of, say, central bank purchase of government securities in the open market must proceed in two stages, one involving the question as to whether, and the extent to which interest rates would be reduced; and the other involving the question as to the relationship, if any, between low or declining interest rates and levels of consumption and investment activity. On the other hand, analysis of the stimulative effects of, say, government transfer expenditures directed towards the lower-income groups takes as its starting point the fact of stimulus, and proceeds from there to determine the strength of the stimulus through consideration of such factors as the size of the transfer, multiplier

effects, and the elasticity of labour supply.[14] There is an element of
directness and precision in the fiscal analysis--various items of uncertainty notwithstanding--which no monetary analysis can provide.

The second unique feature of fiscal policy, involving the role of the
money supply, is also of real importance in that it drives home the fact--
seldom understood by Canadians during the interwar period--that changes
in aggregate money demand are not synonymous with changes in the supply of money; account must also be taken of hoarding and dishoarding,
that is, of additions to, and reductions in, the supply of idle balances.
Indeed, this fact goes to the heart of the inadequacy of the "quantity-
theory" approaches to the value of money, and it points up the essence of
the contribution made by Keynesian income-expenditure theory.[15] The
general prevalence of quantity-theory notions in the decades between the
two world wars had the broadest ramifications. It meant not only preoccupation with monetary policy almost to the point of exclusion of fiscal
policy; but also the failure to realize that government outlays can have
an expansionist effect (through progressive taxation) even if they are not
deficit-financed,[16] and (through tax reductions and borrowing from idle
balances) even if the deficit is not financed by new money. The consequences of this lumping together of monetary and fiscal expansion are
twofold: (1) it is seldom possible for the economic analyst to determine
precisely whether Canadians were advocating one or the other, or some
combination of both; and (2) proposals for fiscal expansion encountered
far stronger resistance from orthodox groups in the Canadian economy
than would otherwise have been the case.

The third unique feature of fiscal policy, namely its execution through
the budgetary process, has the most direct bearing upon the problem of
whether to characterize exchange depreciation (and devaluation) in monetary or fiscal terms. It is, in reality, an important hybrid case which
partially satisfies the first two criteria while violating the third. Through
its impact upon price levels expressed in domestic and foreign currency,
depreciation alters real incomes in the depreciating country and in the
countries with which it carries on transactions in goods, services, and
capital. Both consumption and investment are, therefore, likely to be
affected; moreover, changes in the money supply of the countries involved are not a necessary condition of such effects.[17] The fact remains,
nevertheless, that the immediate effects of depreciation are real (in
terms of prices), not monetary (in terms of money incomes); that depreciation therefore provides a non-selective policy instrument whose results cannot be precisely determined and will depend upon prevailing
conditions of supply and demand for the wide array of items moving in
international trade; and that changes in monetary reserves are of the
essence, and changes in the money supply a characteristic feature, of
depreciation. The writer's decision to consider depreciation as one aspect of monetary policy rests, then, on more than the absence of budgetary techniques. That depreciation traditionally has been the concern
of the central bank--operating alone or in conjunction with the government

treasury or finance department--is, indeed, merely the manifestation of the two more fundamental factors outlined above.[18] In any case, it matters less whether depreciation is discussed in terms of monetary or fiscal policy than whether the analysis proceeds in such a manner as to emphasize both the monetary and fiscal implications of depreciation. It is this latter emphasis which the author (in chapters VII and IX) has particularly endeavoured to achieve.

II. THE INTERWAR CYCLICAL PATTERN

In the broadest sense, the interwar period in Canada can reasonably be viewed as comprising a decade of rapid and widespread economic expansion followed by a decade of painful experience with, and slow adjustment to, severe economic depression. The increasing industrialization and urbanization of the twenties, and the all-pervasiveness of the Great Depression of the thirties--these are, without doubt, the major characteristics which emerge from any study of Canadian development during those years.

The Over-all Picture

Analysis in terms of cyclical fluctuations, however, sheds light on other aspects of the interwar period. A clear cyclical pattern-- common, indeed, to most industrialized countries in most postwar periods[19]-- reveals itself in the Canadian economy between the first and second world wars. This pattern comprises, in sequence, minor recession, primary postwar boom, primary postwar depression, recovery, secondary postwar prosperity, and deep prolonged secondary postwar depression. It is useful, also, to describe the pattern in terms of three major and six minor cyclical phases;[20] in the latter category, the recessions of early 1919, 1920-2, and 1937-8, the 1919-20 boom, and the 1922-5 and 1938-9 recoveries; and in the former category, prosperity from 1925 to 1929, the downswing from 1929 to 1933, and the recovery from 1933 to 1937.[21]

A wide array of statistical evidence can readily be submitted in support of these cyclical groupings. Such evidence is contained in Table I, which serves mainly to illustrate the following facts: (1) the swiftness and severity of the 1920-2 recession, as underscored by (a) the 68 per cent fall in the value of commodity exports from December 1919 to April 1921,[22] (b) the 52 per cent collapse in grain prices between 1920 and 1922,[23] and (c) the 43 per cent decline in wholesale prices between May 1920 and September 1922;[24] (2) the intensity and long duration of the Great Depression, as strikingly shown, for 1929 to 1933, by (a) the 89 per cent drop in gross domestic investment,[25] (b) the 83 per cent fall in the volume of output, and the 72 per cent contraction in employment, in the construction industries,[26] (c) the 64 per cent collapse in prices of common stock, (d) the 53 per cent decline in grain prices,[27] and (e) the 49 per cent reduction in the value of exports of goods and services;

TABLE I

Economic Fluctuations in Canada, 1919-1939

Year	(1) Index of industrial production 1935-39=100	(2) Index of employment 1926 = 100	(3) Index of wholesale prices 1926 = 100	(4) Index of cost of living 1935-39=100	(5) Index of security prices 1935-39=100	(6) Gross national product $mm
1919	56.0	-	134.0	126.5	59.2	3,816
1920	59.7	-	155.9	145.4	60.3	4,598
1921	51.6	88.8	110.0	129.9	52.1	3,507
1922	65.7	89.0	97.3	120.4	56.4	3,671
1923	71.6	95.8	98.0	120.7	61.7	3,847
1924	70.4	93.4	99.4	118.8	63.6	3,865
1925	76.7	93.6	102.6	119.8	72.7	4,239
1926	85.5	99.6	100.0	121.8	90.1	5,294
1927	90.3	104.6	97.7	119.9	111.2	5,647
1928	100.7	111.6	96.4	120.5	143.8	6,105
1929	108.9	119.0	95.6	121.7	171.8	6,166
1930	92.3	113.4	86.6	120.8	122.7	5,546
1931	77.0	102.5	72.1	109.1	76.8	4,560
1932	63.2	87.5	66.7	99.0	50.1	3,767
1933	65.6	83.4	67.1	94.4	61.8	3,552
1934	80.0	96.0	71.6	95.6	77.2	4,034
1935	88.5	99.4	72.1	96.2	83.6	4,345
1936	97.8	103.7	74.6	98.1	108.9	4,701
1937	108.0	114.1	84.6	101.2	115.8	5,355
1938	102.1	111.8	78.6	102.2	94.9	5,233
1939	109.3	113.9	75.4	101.5	91.6	5.707

(1) D.B.S., Economic Fluctuations in Canada during the Postwar Period, Supplement to Monthly Review of Business Statistics, Jan. 1938 (Ottawa, 1938), pp. 1, 2; and Canadian Statistical Review, XXIII (Jan. 1948), p. 1.

(2) D.B.S., Canada Year Book, 1947 (Ottawa, 1947), p. 613. No figures are available for 1919 and 1920. The index for 1926 shows a slight deviation from 100, since it applies to the twelve months Jan. 1 to Dec. 1, 1926; while the average for the calendar year 1926, which is the base used in computing all the employment indexes, include figures up to Dec. 31, 1926.

(3) D.B.S., Prices and Price Indexes, 1944-1947 (Ottawa, 1948), p. 8.

(4) Ibid., p. 59.

(5) Ibid., p. 87; and D.B.S., Economic Fluctuations in Canada during the Postwar Period, pp. 27, 28. Figures are for common stock prices.

(6) C.Y.B., 1945, p. 905; and D.B.S., National Accounts: Income and Expenditure, 1926-1950 (Ottawa, 1951), pp. 26, 27. No figures on gross national product are available for the years prior to 1926. The above 1919-25 figures represent net national income at market prices (that is, gross national product less depreciation). Even these, however, cannot be regarded as accurate. It is only during the past decade that the national-income concept and its implications have come to be thoroughly understood. The Dominion Bureau of Statistics, employing new techniques, is now engaged in an extensive revision of past statistics on the national income of Canada. This revision has so far been carried back to 1926.

The Bureau now distinguishes between "gross national expenditure" (comprising the "expenditure" components of the market value of goods and services produced annually) and "gross national product" (comprising

TABLE I (Continued)

Economic Fluctuations in Canada, 1919-1939

Year	(7) Personal consumption expenditure $mm	(8) Gross domestic investment $mm	(9) Government expenditure $mm	(10) Exports of goods & services $mm	(11) National debt $mm	(12) Bank clearings $mm
1919	-	1,015	697	1,499	1,575	16,681
1920	-	970	786	1,565	2,249	20,251
1921	-	325	528	1,071	2,341	17,443
1922	-	655	464	1,151	2,422	16,227
1923	-	951	435	1,310	2,454	17,333
1924	-	836	371	1,354	2,418	17,008
1925	-	1,124	351	1,592	2,417	16,762
1926	3,687	897	521	1,650	2,390	17,715
1927	3,919	1,167	567	1,618	2,348	20,568
1928	4,194	1,293	597	1,773	2,297	24,555
1929	4,393	1,391	682	1,632	2,226	25,105
1930	4,204	900	767	1,286	2,178	20,092
1931	3,646	403	738	967	2,262	16,828
1932	3,108	146	643	804	2,376	12,914
1933	2,887	157	526	826	2,596	14,721
1934	3,077	376	568	1,018	2,730	15,964
1935	3,243	425	603	1,143	2,846	16,927
1936	3,457	419	600	1,428	3,006	19,203
1937	3,777	741	671	1,591	3,084	18,850
1938	3,815	595	720	1,356	3,102	17,264
1939	3,904	936	735	1,451	3,153	17,743

the costs of producing this aggregate). Cf. D. B. S., National Accounts: Income and Expenditure, 1926-1950, pp. 9, 10. Throughout this study, the term "gross national product" is used in its broadest sense to embrace both D. B. S. concepts; though the focal point of interest here lies in the "expenditure" field (see note 1, chapter I).

(7) D. B. S., National Accounts: Income and Expenditure, 1926-1950, pp. 26, 27. No figures are available for years 1919-25.

(8) D. B. S., National Income of Canada, 1919-1938, part I (Ottawa, 1941), p. 113; and National Accounts: Income and Expenditure, 1926-1950, pp. 46, 47. The accuracy of the 1919-25 figures is doubtful for the reason noted above. "Gross domestic investment" for 1926-50 comprises capital expenditures by (a) private and government business enterprises, (b) private non-commercial institutions, and (c) individuals (on residential construction; that is, all such capital outlays on new durable physical assets, and to replace existing assets.

(9) Ibid.; and C.Y.B., 1941, p. 753. Figures for the 1919-25 period apply to fiscal years and represent expenditure of the Dominion government only.

(10) F. A. Knox, Dominion Monetary Policy, 1929-1934, A Study Prepared for the Royal Commission on Dominion-Provincial Relations (Ottawa, 1939), p. 91; and D. B. S., National Accounts: Income and Expenditure, 1926-1950, pp. 26, 27. Professor Knox' earlier figures (1919-25) differ from the later figures of D. B. S. (1926-39), in that the former exclude all gold transactions, while the latter include shipments of non-monetary gold.

(11) C.Y.B., 1947, p. 972. Figures apply to fiscal years.

(12) D. B. S., Recent Economic Tendencies in Canada, 1919-1934, Supplements to Monthly Review of Business Statistics, June 1935 (Ottawa, 1935), pp. 49, 50; and C.Y.B., 1940, p. 905.

(3) the Canadian economy's great interwar dependence on exports, ranging from one-fifth to one-third of gross national product; (4) the relatively important economic role played by government in, and the consequent strong governmental fiscal impact exerted (whether wittingly or
unwittingly) upon, income-employment fluctuations, as measured (approximately) by the 10-15 per cent ratios of government expenditure to gross
national product, and the 50-440 per cent ratios of government expenditure to gross domestic investment, throughout most of the interwar
period; [28] and (5) a relatively unimportant national debt, which at no
time during this period exceeded 73 per cent (the 1933 ratio) and frequently fell short of 50 per cent, of gross national product. [29]

Charts 1 and 2 provide further illustration of the first two--of the
above five--descriptive facts concerning the two most serious interwar
downswings. Several additional significant points clearly emerge from
Chart 2. First, there is the comparatively stable pattern traced out by
personal expenditure on consumer goods and services during the 1926-
39 period; the maximum rise over 1926 was 19 per cent (in 1929), while
the greatest drop was 22 per cent (in 1933), as compared with the 55 per
cent increase and the 84 per cent fall in the case of gross investment
activity (in 1928 and 1933, respectively). There are, in the second
place, the markedly cyclical, rather than countercyclical, fluctuations
in the level of government expenditure, with peaks occurring in 1920
and 1930, and troughs in 1925 and 1933. [30] A third prominent feature of
Chart 2 is the time lead displayed by the "gross investment" series in
the upswing, and by the "exports" series in both the upswing and downswing of the Great Depression: [31] for the two variables, the upturn occurred not in 1933 but in 1932, and the downturn for exports in 1928
rather than 1929; this fact, taken in conjunction with that of the extreme
volatility of the two series, justifies the prime causal role now attributed
to these items in Canadian cyclical fluctuations. Precise determination
of the relative importance of gross investment and exports is quite impossible, but there can, finally, be no doubt about the greater instability
of the former throughout the interwar period: while between 1926 and
1939 (using 1926 as the base year) the index of gross investment rose
to 155 (in 1929), fell to 16 (in 1932), and rose again to 104 (in 1939),
the major high and low points for exports were 107, 49, and 88 (in 1928,
1932, and 1939, respectively). [32]

Regional and National Comparisons
Great importance attaches, also, to two other features of the
Canadian interwar cyclical pattern: the regional impact of the economic
fluctuations, and their degree of intensity by comparison with the patterns shown by other countries. In both cases the statistical picture
is clear. Thus, in regional terms, analysis of income, production,
and prices points to: (1) the particularly severe incidence in the
Prairie Provinces of all the interwar downswings; (2) the extensive
sharing in expansion by the Prairie Provinces, British Columbia,

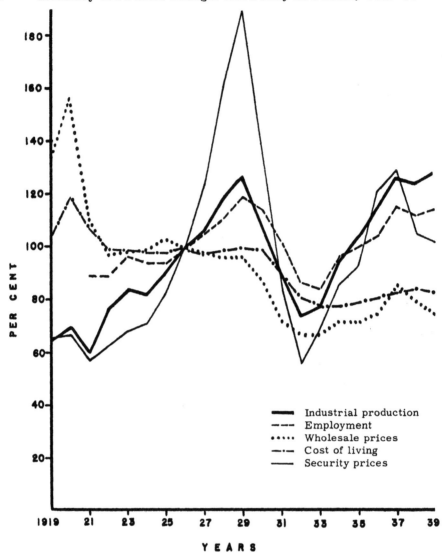

CHART 1. Indices of prices, production, and employment in Canada, 1919-39. 1926 = 100.

The year 1926 is used as the base for all five series so that direct comparisons of their fluctuations may be made. This was not done in Table I, where the intention was to emphasize each series separately and where, therefore, the latest base years available--either directly or through conversion--were presented. The choice of 1926 in preference to 1935-39 was made on grounds of the former's more central time position in the period under review.

Source: Computations made from figures in Table I.

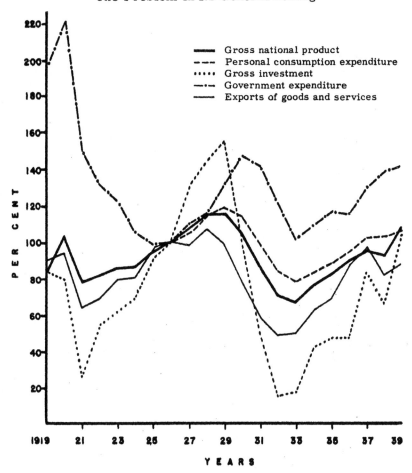

CHART 2.   Indices of gross national product and its components, 1919-39.   1926 = 100.

Since personal consumption expenditure is calculated inclusive of goods and services purchased both domestically and from other countries, exports are a component of gross national product or expenditure only when considered net of imports.   In this way, account is taken of the leakage from gross national product due to consumption of externally produced goods and services.

Because of discrepancies (already noted) in statistical procedure for the periods before and after 1926, each of the curves showing gross national product, gross investment, government expenditure, and exports, is regarded as two curves with 1926 as the dividing line; and the pre-1926 figures are calculated from the 1926 estimates made in terms of the earlier statistical approach.   The reason for selecting 1926 as the base was stated in Chart 1.

Source: Computations made from figures in Table I.

Ontario, and Quebec; and (3) the economic stagnation characterizing the Maritime Provinces.[33]

In international comparative terms, the basic fact emerges that Canadian interwar economic fluctuations ranked in severity with those of the most cycle-sensitive countries in the world. This can be most easily observed through comparisons with the Great Depression as it affected, first, the United States,[34] and, second, other countries throughout the world. Taking gross national product, gross domestic investment, the volume of industrial production, and wholesale prices as indices of cyclical change, one finds 1929-33 declines for Canada amounting to 42 per cent, 89 per cent, 40 per cent, and 30 per cent, respectively, as compared with 46 per cent, 92 per cent, 37 per cent, and 31 per cent for the United States.[35] The comparison between Canada and other countries (also in relative terms) is similarly impressive, yielding: (1) for the 1929-33 period, a drop in wholesale prices exceeding those of the United Kingdom, Germany, Australia, Argentina, and many other countries; (2) for the same period, a collapse of agricultural prices greater than the declines in those countries and, indeed, second only to that of the United States; (3) for the years 1929-32, a fall in the volume of industrial production exceeding, among others, those of the United Kingdom, Germany, France, and Sweden; and (4) for the 1929-32 period, a decline in the dollar value of exports greater than those of Germany, Australia, and New Zealand, and only slightly less than those of the United Kingdom, Sweden, and Argentina.[36]

PART I

THE DECADE OF THE TWENTIES

CHAPTER II

EAST AND WEST IN CANADIAN ECONOMIC THOUGHT

THE CANADIAN ECONOMY emerged from World War I stronger and more mature than at any time since Confederation. And even while Canada had been making an important contribution to the Allied war effort,[1] remarkable economic advances had been taking place, greatly speeding up the transformation of the entire economic structure of the country.

Although the figures are sketchy and not fully accurate, the following broad statistical picture will serve to illustrate the nature of Canada's economic growth during World War I:[2] The acreage in field crops had risen from 35 million in 1913 to 53 million in 1919, an increase equal to that which had taken place during the twenty years prior to 1913. In 1919 the national income stood at $4.2 billion, as compared with $2.4 billion in 1913, an increase of over 70 per cent. During that same period, the money value of primary production had risen 99 per cent, and manufacturing production 155 per cent. Between 1914 and 1918, the volume of Canadian exports had more than doubled, and the value more than quadrupled.[3] Largely responsible for this development was a combination of physical separation from the European battlefronts, an abundant supply of undeveloped natural resources, and vigorous--if not always economically sound--pursuit of clearly defined war objectives.[4]

I. THE EAST-WEST DIVISION

There were, however, serious shortcomings in the Canadian position, aside from those rooted in the wartime excesses of public policy, and in the crucial problem of balance between the extractive and manufacturing sectors of the economy. One of the great sources of weakness lay in the realm of ideas--in the rather primitive Canadian conceptions of the role of government in the economic sphere, of the workings of the Canadian economy, and of the reasoning processes applied to economics in general; though it is of particular interest to note, in this connection, that the fundamental issue of economic stability--or of cyclical fluctuations in production, employment, and income--provides whatever unifying thread there is in the field of Canadian economic thought.

While physically untouched by war, Canada began early to feel the effects of nation-wide social and political rumblings.[5] By the end of the war, sectional groups had already begun to solidify in western Canada, in the Central Provinces, and in the Maritime Provinces. Such groupings were by no means a new phenomenon in Canadian history. More than once had they threatened to shatter the unity so precariously achieved in 1867. But the impact of the war--bringing, as it did, such sudden and far-reaching economic changes in regional structure as even an expanding economy like Canada would find difficult to absorb--was to give Canadian sectionalism a hardness and an inflexibility which it had probably never possessed before, and which inevitably exerted a vital influence on the country's economic development during the interwar period.

These regional differences do not, however, constitute a satisfactory basis for classification and analysis of the cleavage in economic ideas following upon World War I. In the latter case, it seems quite appropriate to distinguish merely between the "conservative East" (extending from western Ontario through the Maritimes) and the "radical West."[6] Obviously, such a generalization cannot be fully valid and requires qualification. There was, in the first place, French Canada--a closely knit homogeneous national entity centred mainly in the province of Quebec, and comprising, in 1921, over one-third of the population of the country.[7] One hundred and ninety-three years ago, a French, Catholic, and rural community was conquered by an English, Protestant, and commercial power. Since that time, the races have evolved side by side without either of them yielding its culture, with little assimilation, and with little understanding. It is this aspect of Canadian history that conditions everything about the Dominion. The truth, as clearly expressed by Professor A. R. M. Lower of Queen's University, is that:

> The French have always ... mistrusted what the Anglo-Saxon has been pleased to call progress. It is only within the last few years that the results of the English Industrial Revolution-- low wages, slums, unemployment, and, among the elite, the strong consciousness of being second-class citizens--have provoked stirrings of revolt. These have taken, among the intelligentsia, the form of an intransigent nationalism; among the labouring masses a recourse to unionism.... Some of the church authorities and others have looked kindly on the conception of the "corporate state", ... and the future may yet see attempts to build such a structure in French Canada.[8]

Secondly, there were, within each major "thought class," numerous subclasses whose existence is attributable to sharp disagreement over important policy questions. The tariff controversy, for example, might well be considered the essential distinguishing feature between the Liberal and Conservative parties, both of which were drawing their chief support from the East. Lines of division crystallized, also, around such issues as railroad policy, agricultural policy, and Anglo-Canadian relations. There was, thirdly, considerable overlapping of views with respect to East and West, so that no hard and fast separation can be made. This was true not only of economists--who, imbued to some extent with a sense of scientific objectivity, might be expected to be unamenable to rigid classification--but of politicans and government officials as well.

But when all this is said by way of refinement, the basic fact remains
that the story of the development of economic ideas in Canada during the
decade of the twenties is primarily a story of East-West evolution.[9]
More significant, however, is the fact that, for the most part, those individuals and institutions representing the so-called "radical" point of
view demonstrated a greater capacity for understanding economic principles and problems than those following the "conservative" approach.

II. GOVERNMENT AND THE ECONOMY

The decade of the twenties ushered in a new era in Canadian economic
history. The Dominion was gradually coming of age as an industrial
nation, and one of the important manifestations of this trend was the
growing intensity of political agitation directed at such problems as unemployment, inequality of income distribution, and monopolistic control
of industry. As early as 1920, this agitation achieved formal and co-
ordinated expression through the establishment of the Progressive party
by politically conscious rural groups in Western Canada.[10] Ostensibly,
it was demands by the farmers for low rail rates and drastic tariff reductions which formed the basis for the new party. In this respect, it was
not unlike the sectional economic reform movements which other young
and expanding countries, such as the United States, had experienced.
But the Canadian Progressive movement went deeper and embodied, for
the first time, a strong challenge against the traditional conceptions of
government and the economic system held by the Liberal and Conservative parties. This, in essence, is the interpretation advanced, only two
years after the Progressive party's formation, by Professor W. A. Mackintosh of Queen's University:

> Curious parallels can be drawn between the sectionalism of
> the American West, with its Granger movements, its advocacy
> of cheap money, its suspicion of the "money" power, and its
> hatred of the East, and the farmers' movements, the denunci-
> ations of Eastern banks and "Big Interests", and the whole
> anti-Eastern attitude of our own West. Such analogies must
> not be pushed too far. The Canadian farmers' movement has
> attained a power, a sanity, a constructive program, and seem-
> ingly a permanence never achieved in the United States.[11]

The course of economic thought and policy during the twenties--and perhaps even more during the thirties--cannot be comprehended outside
this framework.

Individual and Group Sentiment on Governmental Functions

Fundamental, too, is an understanding of the divergent attitudes in
Canada, at that time, towards the role which government should play in

the economy. Such understanding is important, not only for its own sake, but also because it helps to explain the general scarcity of profound analysis of economic theory and policy, as well as the consequent difficulty of carrying through any systematic survey of contemporary economic thought.

One can agree with Professor J. A. Corry of Queen's University that:

> Canadians have never had any fear of, or prejudice against, state action as such. Great numbers of them have always been able, thus far, to recall the origin of the state. Having seen it constructed and having watched it grow, they had that familiarity which at least dispels fear.... Thus the state has lacked the awe and mystery with which age and ceremonial surrounded it in other countries, and it has never had the record of bad behaviour which made men fear it in England. Furthermore, the opening up of a new country requires more than individual initiative; it requires highly organized co-operative effort to overcome natural obstacles.... "Laissez-faire" philosophy, as interpreted in Canada, has never objected to the principle of state action in the name of national development, however much opposition might be aroused against particular expedients which were subsumed under it.[12]

And yet, while Canada's "laissez-faire" philosophy may have been less extreme than that of Great Britain or the United States, it was, after all, a difference in degree rather than in kind. The prevalent Canadian attitude was one in which were combined a firmly held belief in the smooth, automatic functioning of the Canadian economy, and strong misgivings about so-called "bureaucratic inefficiency" and governmental interference with private enterprise and "essential liberties."

This approach to the role of government had appeared early in World War I, and by the end of that conflict had become almost universal.[13] Its further development can be traced through the twenties, when its impact upon both economic theory and policy was very powerful. The views expressed in 1926 by Dr. R. J. Manion, a cabinet member in two Bennett Administrations, and subsequently national leader of the Conservative party, were quite typical:

> I think we have too much government at the present time.... There are certain lines of endeavour which a government alone can properly handle--the mails, for instance, hygienic and sanitary questions, the supplying of cities and towns with a safe water supply, and other lines of endeavour of that nature affecting the whole community of a city or province or the citizens of the whole country.... But there are other lines of endeavour which should be left to private initiative. Most of us believe ... that practically everything that is done

by government is done more extravagantly [and less efficiently] than if the same service were performed by a private corporation. This is true, I believe, from a municipal, provincial, and Dominion standpoint.[14]

More concretely, the general conception of the role of government in the maintenance of economic stability finds what is perhaps its clearest expression in the following extract from a parliamentary address made in 1922 by Mr. H. H. Stevens, then a prominent Conservative in the House of Commons, and Minister of Trade and Commerce in the Bennett Government of 1930-5:

> The suggestion has been repeatedly made ... that it is the duty of government to supply employment for its citizens. I challenge that statement.... It is not the function of government to find employment for individuals. If [this] is the function of government, ... then it is the duty of every individual so employed to go and do as he may be instructed by such government.... But that is the exact reversal of what humanity has been struggling against from the dawn of history to the present time.... If it is possible for the government or for Parliament to find some temporary method of ameliorating the conditions of today, by all means let it be employed. But I warn Parliament and I warn the government against assuming responsibility for finding employment for all who happen to be unemployed.[15]

The Prime Minister, Mr. Mackenzie King, was similarly cautious, though apparently somewhat less reluctant to assign a role to government in combating unemployment. In the course of a parliamentary address made one month after that of Mr. Stevens, he spoke as follows:

> I do not think the Government can admit that it is primarily a federal obligation to look after the unemployed. I think that there is a national significance to the problem of unemployed, but the problem primarily is ... a matter for individuals in the first instance; between municipalities and the people living within their bounds, in the second instance; next, between the provinces and the citizens of the respective provinces; and only finally a matter of concern in the federal arena.... [Unemployment] only becomes a federal problem when both the municipalities and the provinces have found it impossible to cope with a situation that is completely beyond their control.[16]

Only by the Progressives, and by the Labour representatives affiliated with them, was any substantial emphasis placed upon the importance of governmental responsibility in the economic affairs of the country.[17] Demands from this minority group, both in and out of Parliament, ranged from government intervention designed to ease the tight credit situation in rural areas, all the way to large-scale nationalization of industry. This being the case, many of these demands went, and have since gone, unheeded; but others, many of which were at first greeted with contempt--notably in the fields of monetary and fiscal policy--have been incorporated into the law of the land. Indeed, this long embittered struggle in the evolution of economic ideas from the radical or "crank" stage to ultimate fruition in accepted policy is one of the supremely important features of Canadian economic history after World War I.

Economic Over-Optimism

Two other points remain for consideration. First, there is the widespread spirit of unbounded optimism which prevailed throughout the Dominion. This was not unconnected with the negative approach to government already discussed. As a matter of fact, each undoubtedly served to intensify, and was stimulated by, the other. Confidence in Canada's recuperative and self-stabilizing powers was everywhere to be seen--in the press, in parliamentary debates, in official Government pronouncements such as the budget speeches of the Minister of Finance. Thus, during the depression of 1920-2, vague platitudes about Canada's abundant natural resources, and pious wishes for speedy recovery, were the order of the day. During the ensuing upswing, on the other hand, the mood changed rapidly from one of subdued faith to one of overwhelming confidence in the future course of Canadian economic development. Even so acute an observer as Professor Mackintosh seems to have become entangled in this web of over-optimism. In an article written less than three years before the Great Depression of the thirties, he predicted that: "For the next decade the general trend of prices in gold standard countries is likely to be a slightly upward one. In other words, the probability is that we will not experience the long decline of prices which was the sequel to the wars of the nineteenth century."[18]

It must, of course, be acknowledged that political considerations, rather than well-reasoned economic analysis, were often the driving force behind the cautious and pessimistic outlook of the radicals.[19] Moreover, they held no monopoly over accuracy in forecasting, for many Canadians from all walks of life were well aware of impending danger in the late twenties.[20]

General Neglect of Economic Analysis

The second point involves the low esteem in which economists, both Canadian and foreign, were held by the public. This was, no doubt, partly owing to the relative immaturity of economic science at that time, and, consequently, to the limited scope for policy recommendations based on economic analysis. It was owing even more to what was apparently a deep-rooted Canadian aversion towards new economic theories or new doctrinal conceptions of society or the state.[21]

Ironically enough, it was the Progressive and Labour groups that

relied most heavily on the writings of economists, most of whom were
staunch defenders of capitalism, and that envisioned an important function
for economists in the policy field. Thus it was a generally unsympathetic
Parliament to which the following plea was directed by Mr. W. C. Good,
an Ontario farmer and Progressive, during the depression of the early
twenties: "What about our experts in political economy? Are these men
of no value? Is it not possible that we may get some suggestions from
them which may assist us in meeting the present need?"[22]

III. BEGINNING STAGES IN THE DEVELOPMENT OF IDEAS ON THE CAUSES OF UNEMPLOYMENT

The problem of economic instability is one which antedates the capitalist system, and which has engaged the attention of economists for cen-
turies. It is however, in one important sense, a new problem. For the
partial shifting of emphasis from questions of resource allocation and income distribution to that of cyclical fluctuations in employment and income--
largely under the inspiration of the Keynesian analytical system--is a relatively recent phenomenon which can hardly be traced beyond the nineteen-
twenties--if, indeed, that far back. [23]

Since Canada was a comparatively underdeveloped country, the swings
marked out by business fluctuations were not as clearly observable as in
more advanced industrial nations like the United States, Great Britain,
and Germany. It is, therefore, all the more understandable that, within
the Canadian and Anglo-American intellectual atmospheres described
above, little attention should have been paid to the analysis of business
cycles.

The Economists on Unemployment[24]

During the twenties, Canadian economists tended to adopt a cautious
approach to the question of business cycle causation and to avoid sweeping generalizations. Their explanations, however, were not always
clear, nor were they exhaustive by current standards. The most thoroughgoing analysis was probably that of the first postwar depression made by
Dr. W. C. Clark, then Professor of Economics at Queen's University.[25]

This study was essentially, as Dr. Clark himself stated, an application of the analytical tools and phraseology of Professor W. C. Mitchell
to the Canadian economy. In other words, according to Dr. Clark, the
depression was "the result not so much of an industrial reaction as of a
price collapse following a period of unprecedented credit inflation."[26]
Wholly neglected was the question whether the changes in cost-price relationships so lucidly outlined constituted the basic causal factor, or
were merely symptomatic of, and acted to intensify, the more fundamental changes introduced into the income flow by way of the savings-
investment process. Unmistakably clear, moreover, are traces of the
"economic fatalism" which had taken hold in the country during the first
World War.[27] Thus Dr. Clark wrote that "it would be madness to imagine

that we can escape paying a high price for our follies of the last few years. If much has already been paid on the account, less remains to be paid. A dark picture of the past or immediate present is the only real ground for optimism. "[28]

It was only natural, in a country so dependent on international trade, that considerable causal influence should have been assigned to external factors. Discussing the recession of 1920-2, Professor G. E. Jackson of the University of Toronto argued that "Canada seems to have been in a large measure the victim of external forces. It was not a series of crop failures--though local failures did occur--but ... a too plentiful world harvest which combined with forces raising the price of manufactured goods to destroy the purchasing power of the farmer. "[29] Professor H. Michell of McMaster University gave substantially the same explanation: "The great decline of 1920-21 ... was caused by a miscalculation on the part of the commercial world of the buying capacity of Europe after the war."

Seven years later, Professor Michell seems to have shifted his emphasis to the concept of "velocity of money, " though failing to distinguish precisely--that is, as precisely as possible in a necessarily complex business cycles analysis--between cause and effect. The following quotation illustrates this point: "The business cycle ... is marked by [the] acceleration of the velocity of turnover of money up to that point where the amount of money available is unable to stand the strain; it collapses under the cumulative stresses of the weight placed upon it. Such, in brief, we may venture to suggest, is the underlying cause of the 'economic cycle. '"[31]

To the extent, then, that Canadian economists wrote about cyclical instability--the amount of relevant literature was small--they showed a keen awareness of the problem, and a reasonable measure of understanding of the economic forces at work. For their failure to grasp the significance of the income flow in terms of consumption, savings, and investment, they were no more to blame than other economists throughout the world.

The Radicals on Unemployment

As for the views of other groups and individuals on unemployment, a curious and striking fact must be recorded. During the entire decade, the only discussion worthy of analytical treatment was that carried on by the two Labour members of Parliament, Mr. J. S. Woodsworth and Mr. W. Irvine. There was, it is true, some recognition of the problem in the East, notably among the politicians, but it was really of the nature of speculation--superficial, sweeping, and conspicuously lacking in understanding of basic economic processes. The views expressed by Mr. T. L. Church, Conservative member of Parliament, provide one example among many--perhaps extreme but not unique--of the kind of economic reasoning which predominated: "Unemployment is caused by the failure of this country to develop its natural resources and to protect its native industry adequately.... In my opinion, a proper allocation of the principle of protection will solve all the economic ills of every province in the Dominion from Vancouver to Halifax. "[32]

The economic theories of Mr. Woodsworth and Mr. Irvine are important, not because of their great accuracy--for this was not the case--but because they represent what was probably the earliest Canadian attempt to construct a general body of doctrine to explain cyclical fluctuations in employment and income; and because they provide the rationale for the radical monetary and fiscal thinking of the decade of the twenties. The new doctrine, however, was little more than an "underconsumptionist" view of economic development. To the two radicals, the fundamental cause of unemployment was the inadequacy of consumer purchasing power.

In the tradition of Malthus, Hobson, and Foster and Catchings--and, indeed, frequently citing the latter three as authorities--Mr. Woodsworth argued:

> We have so-called "overproduction"; that is, more goods are being produced than can be bought back with the resources at the disposal of the consumers. Indeed, many economists of high standing have suggested that one trouble with the world today is that there has been ... too much thrift; that on account of the unequal division of wealth the people who so very largely control the processes of manufacture, distribution, and exchange, are able to retain in their own hands a great part of what is produced; that, not being able themselves to consume this large quantity, they are forced to ... plough it back into the business. The result is that they develop still greater plant equipment which, in turn, produces an increasing volume of goods, and today we are suffering from overdevelopment of plant equipment, of facilities for producing. On the other hand, we have not adequate buying power on the part of the masses of the people.[33]

Mr. Irvine's diagnosis of the ills of the Canadian economy was quite similar: "We must find some way of placing our people in a position to purchase the necessaries of life. Put an end to the underconsumption, ... and industry will soon be humming. Make consumption possible, and production will look after itself. "[34]

But there was one important difference between the two approaches. Whereas Mr. Woodsworth's analysis ran mainly in terms of the progressive decaying and ultimate collapse of the whole capitalist system, Mr. Irvine, at this stage in the development of his thought, [35] apparently incorporated into his analysis the Douglas theory of Social Credit; that is, for Mr. Irvine the root of the underconsumption difficulty was a deficient financial machinery which could be corrected, under the existing economic system, by monetary manipulation designed to increase the flow of purchasing power to Canadian consumers. Thus, in discussing the depression following World War I, Mr. Irvine had this to say:

> Clearly, the present paralysis of industry in Canada is . . . due
> to a lack of finance, to a lack of financial credit, if you wish. . . .
> At present, prices include cost of plant and overhead, materials,
> dividends, wages, etc. These expenses are charged and are
> paid always by the consumer--there is no one else to pay them.
> Prices, therefore, could be reduced by the amount of capital
> expended in production, which expenditure could be made good
> to the capitalists by an issue of government treasury notes. . . .
> There is a way by which Canada can borrow from herself on
> the strength of her own credit, and a way to regulate the prices
> so as to prevent inflation, which, if adopted, will be a . . . way
> in which we could increase the purchasing power of the nation,
> stimulate industry, do away with unemployment, and bring a
> prosperity that will only be limited by our utmost power to
> produce.[36]

Shortcomings in this Canadian variant of the underconsumption theory
are not far to seek. First, it was, like most theories of underconsumption, "a theory of the crisis and depression, rather than a theory of the
cycle."[37] Little attempt was made to apply the tools of economic analysis to the other phases of the business cycle. Second, the failure to
stress external factors and foreign markets--indeed, the conscious
minimization of their importance--was particularly serious in the case
of Canada. Third, the approach was highly abstract, with little analysis
or testing in the light of actual experience. Fourth, and most important,
while there was a considerable element of truth in the Hobson-Foster-
Catchings analysis of saving expounded by Mr. Woodsworth and Mr.
Irvine, it did not strike at the heart of the unemployment problem.
Hobson and his fellow-underconsumptionists regarded saving as being
done primarily for the purpose of capital accumulation, and failed to
acknowledge the problem of making savings flow into investment as the
crux of the difficulty. A high rate of saving which is offset by investment
provides a net stimulus to the economic system, but the underconsumptionists implied that such offsets had deflationary effects in both depression and prosperity. Thus, the main difference between their theory and
the Keynesian analysis was that "they looked upon savings as deflationary,
whether they are offset by investments or not, while Keynes considered
as deflationary only savings which do not get invested."[38]

Finally, there were the fallacies associated specifically with the
social credit version of underconsumption. Chief among these was the
famous "A + B theorem." Major Douglas and his followers divided total
factory payments into two parts, A and B; in group A were included all
payments made to individuals, that is, wages, salaries, and dividends;
and in group B all payments made to other organizations, that is, for
raw materials, cost of plant and machinery, bank charges, etc.[39] Hence
A represented purchasing power distributed to consumers and A + B represented the total entrepreneurial charges required for profitable busi-

ness operation. It followed, according to Douglas, that A, purchasing power, would never be able to purchase A + B, the market value of output, unless additional purchasing power equal to the value of B were distributed. Economists have long agreed that this crude proposition collapses to the ground when it is realized that only the "value added" by each producing unit is included in the national product; and that the productive process is continuous, in the sense that consumer goods and producer goods are produced simultaneously throughout the system. In other words, there is no reason why total A payments of the entire system should be less than the A + B payments of the retailer; in fact, except for time lags, they must be equal.[40]

But the most destructive criticism cannot alter the fact that to men like Mr. Woodsworth and Mr. Irvine belongs the distinction of having been among the first Canadians to attempt, however imperfectly, to fill the gap left by the failure of the classical economists to formulate a theory of "effective demand." In this attempt, the Canadian radicals became a part of the slowly expanding world group determined to solve a fundamental problem which previously had either been totally ignored or considered automatically solvable within a competitive system. No more appropriate evaluation can be applied to the contribution made by Mr. Woodsworth and Mr. Irvine than Keynes's comments on the writings of some of the most famous underconsumptionists:

> Major Douglas is entitled to claim, as against some of his ortho-
> dox adversaries, that he at least has not been wholly oblivious
> of the outstanding problem of our economic system. Yet he has
> scarcely established an equal claim to rank--a private, perhaps,
> but not a major, in the brave army of heretics--with Mandeville,
> Malthus, Gesell, and Hobson, who, following their intuitions,
> have preferred to see the truth obscurely and imperfectly rather
> than to maintain error, reached indeed with clearness and con-
> sistency, and by easy logic, but on hypotheses inappropriate to
> the facts.[41]

CHAPTER III

THE IMPACT OF MONETARY THOUGHT ON POLICY

DURING THE TWENTIES, questions of monetary theory and policy became a focal point in the economic literature of the Western world.[1] Although central banking machinery had long since been in operation in England, France, and Germany, and the Federal Reserve System had been established in the United States about six months prior to the outbreak of the First World War, it remained for the postwar world to see the emergence of centralized monetary control in a recognized and accepted form.

The wartime experience in the techniques and dangers of large-scale financial operations, together with the unprecedented postwar currency inflation in Germany, could not help but leave a vivid impression with economists, bankers, politicians, and businessmen. The result was years of lively controversial discussion of both the workings of monetary and banking systems and their implications for policy, with sides being taken mainly on the questions of adherence to, and dissent from, the philosophy of "monetary orthodoxy."

To some extent, it was a continuation of the split which had grown out of the English Bullion Report of 1810 and had centred around the Banking and Currency Schools. There was, indeed, much debate over issues which had previously inspired the high-quality analysis of such pioneers as Thornton, Tooke, and Overton. But there was a great deal more than that. Investigation was directed towards the deepest problems of monetary theory, and policy recommendations took on a sense of urgency matched only by their infinite variety.

Only among the leading theoretical economists was there anything approaching agreement and understanding. Fisher's "equation of exchange" ($MV = PT$) and Keynes's "cash-balance" ($n = pk$) and "fundamental" equations represented analyses of the relationship between money and the level of prices which, on close examination, did not prove to be fundamentally dissimilar. With Hawtrey and others, Fisher and Keynes believed that the quantity of money was one of the major determinants of the price level, and that central bank action through manipulation of the rediscount rate, open market operations, and variations in reserve requirements of commercial banks could, by controlling the volume of the circulating media (currency and bank credit), control the price level, and so virtually eliminate economic fluctuations.[2] A corollary of this view was a lack of the reverence with which the international gold standard was widely regarded.

Canadian monetary thought was a direct reflection of that of the Western world. In Canada there were the same imperfections in the understanding of monetary processes and the same controversial debates over the issue of monetary orthodoxy. The essential points of difference lay in the fact that there was no central bank in Canada, and that, by and large, the most conspicuous advances in monetary theory were being made not by Canadian economists but by a handful of politicians whose sympathies lay with the Progressive and Labour groups in the House of Commons.[3]

I. THE CANADIAN MONETARY STRUCTURE[4]

During the twenties, banking in the Dominion was conducted by a comparatively small number of banks commanding large capital resources with their head offices concentrated in the large cities, and a network of branches throughout the country and abroad.[5] It was a system which had the important advantages of mobility of funds within a wide territorial expanse, and of ability to muster considerable financial strength in times of adversity. On the other hand, it had the disadvantage of rigidity or slowness in, and strong power to resist, adaptation to changing conditions; and the danger that the outstanding executive leadership required might not be forthcoming. The major powers of Canadian banks were specified in a series of decennially revised Bank Acts the first of which had been passed in 1871.[6]

Second only to branch banking as a distinctive feature of the Canadian banking system was the Canadian Bankers' Association, set up in 1892 as a voluntary organization for the common benefit and protection of the banks. Although it was primarily concerned with making the routine operations of banking more efficient, the general influence of the Association in matters of banking policy should not be overlooked. It was an indirect, partly unconscious kind of influence and, therefore, one which does not lend itself readily to any precise evaluation. It was, nevertheless, inevitable that within the closely knit banking system of the Dominion even the most informal contacts between the leading bankers should have important effects on policy.[7]

The Canadian currency system comprised (in addition to subsidiary coinage) legal tender Dominion notes and the notes of the chartered banks. While frequent changes were made in the conditions determining the volume of notes outstanding, the Dominion note issue was based essentially on the Bank of England principle of a limited uncovered (fiduciary) issue and a covered issue with 100 per cent gold backing; while the bank note issue was governed by the "banking principle" that the notes of a commercial bank should be permitted to the extent of the bank's capital, with a penalty for excessive use except on such occasions as the crop-moving season.[8]

The basic operating principle of the system was the gold standard. Adopted even before Confederation (1853) by the United Provinces (now Ontario and Quebec), this standard had been maintained uninterruptedly until shortly after the outbreak of war in 1914. Gold had been freely bought and sold at a fixed price, and had been regarded as the chief instrument for the settlement of Canada's international accounts:

> An active or passive balance, accompanied by an inflow or out-
> flow of gold, was normally supposed to result in an expansion
> or contraction of the domestic money supply, and this expansion
> or contraction was expected to bring about a rise or fall in the
> level of domestic costs and prices, tending in the former case,
> to stimulate imports and discourage exports, or, in the latter,
> to discourage imports and stimulate exports. Gold flows,
> changes in the quantity of money, and changes in relative price-
> levels thus appeared as the principal factors in the mechanism
> of adjustment.[9]

Canada first abandoned the gold standard on August 22, 1914, with
the passage of the Finance Act following heavy withdrawals of gold from
banks in the large cities.[10] What the Act did, in essence, was (1) to sus-
pend the redemption of Dominion notes in gold, and (2) to authorize both
past and future issues of such notes in excess of previous statutory provisions. The Minister of Finance was empowered to make advances of
Dominion notes to the banks upon the pledge of satisfactory collateral.
Administrative responsibilities--that is, the prescription of the terms
of loans, the conditions of repayment, and the rate of interest--were
vested in a Treasury Board consisting of the Minister of Finance as
Chairman, and five other ministers nominated from time to time by the
Governor-in-Council, with the Deputy Minister of Finance acting as secretary. In 1923 a new Finance Act gave permanent authority to the Department of Finance to make advances of Dominion notes to the banks, gave
the Treasury Board full control over the rediscount rate, and, in general,
elaborated upon the earlier statute.[11]

With the resumption, on July 1, 1926, of the obligation to buy and
sell gold freely at a fixed price, Canada returned to the gold standard.
The Canadian authorities had, in fact, originally abandoned that standard
under conditions of extreme duress, and with every intention of restoring
it when more favourable circumstances returned. The "gold-standard
mentality"[12] was very strongly entrenched, and persisted even after a
combination of ill-conceived domestic financial policy and international
developments beyond the control of Canada had precipitated the second
abandonment of gold at the close of the twenties.

II. NOTIONS OF MONETARY AND BANKING PROCESSES

Such theoretical views as were expressed in this field during the
decade after the First World War really belong within the larger context
of the central bank controversy. They are, however, of sufficient importance to merit separate consideration.

The Credit System

Perhaps the clearest impression of the spirit of Canadian monetary thought at that time can be gained from an examination of conflicting attitudes towards the process of expansion and contraction in the mechanism of commercial credit. As was so often the case in the monetary sphere, the controversy involved chiefly the bankers and the radicals. The economists, the businessmen, and the Liberal and Conservative politicians were, with few exceptions, more conspicuous for the lack of effective participation in the debate than for any profound insight into, or misconceptions with respect to, this crucial problem.

The gradual displacement of notes and metallic coin by commercial credit in the form of book deposits with the banks had been a natural and necessary consequence of the Industrial Revolution. This technological upheaval could hardly have exerted the fullest effect if, in response to the growing interdependence and specialization in the economies undergoing industrialization, there had not been developed a highly flexible and intricate machinery designed to facilitate and enlarge the circular flow of exchange. The need for the utmost clarity with respect to the workings of this machinery had therefore been one of long standing.

But the Canadian bankers responded with the muddled thinking characteristic of the approach taken by most bankers in other countries. There was, first, a great reluctance to admit that demand deposits withdrawable by cheque were just as much a part of the money supply of Canada as notes and coin. Second, there were the rather pointless denials, extending into the realm of philosophy, that bank credit--or anything else for that matter--could be "created"; the real issue was not whether commercial credit is created out of nothing, but whether, as a result of bank lending, changes in the volume of the circulating medium can be effected. Third--and most significant--there was the general failure to distinguish between the individual bank and the banking system as a whole; and, consequently, the failure to realize what is now standard textbook doctrine, namely, that, under any form of fractional reserve system, whereas the individual bank can ordinarily lend or invest only what it receives, less the amount of its required or customary reserves, the banking system as a whole can make loans and investments amounting to some multiple of any addition to its reserves; the actual magnitude of this increase, and, therefore, of the increase in bank deposits, depending on the reserve ratio, the demand for funds in the money market, and the willingness of the banks to employ their funds.[13] That is to say, the loans of one bank are usually deposits in, and sources of new loans by, other banks (or possibly the same bank), and it is this chain relationship between loans and deposits which accounts for the multiple and, by the same token, highly unstable aspects of any fractional reserve credit system.

There was, indeed, some understanding of these monetary factors among responsible public officials. Thus, Sir Henry Drayton, the Conservative Minister of Finance in the Meighen Administration, made the following comments in regard to the postwar boom of 1920:

> Inflation of credit has more to do with increased buying power, and therefore to do with affecting the cost of commodities, than currency circulation. It is true that in part these credits are increased by an inflated circulation, but the circulation deposited in banks from time to time plays but a small part of the total deposits. Every credit transaction, every advance made by a bank to a customer inevitably produces a corresponding deposit in the banks of the customer's creditor or creditors. The net result is to increase bank deposits by the extent of the credit, and to increase the liabilities of the bank granting the credit without any corresponding increase in its cash assets.[14]

The most vigorous discussion of these problems, however, was concentrated within the group of radical politicians in the federal sphere. This was, in reality, but one facet of an intensity of interest shown by them in the whole range of problems involved in monetary theory and policy. An important conditioning influence was, of course, the fact that many of those individuals represented constituencies containing emigrants from the western regions of the United States, where preoccupation with monetary panaceas and the "dangerous money power of the East" had long played a major role in national political and economic affairs. Nevertheless, there is good ground for the contention that the monetary theories and proposals of the radicals demonstrated a perception of economic problems unique among Canadians in public life.

The view that the banking system creates credit had many enthusiastic supporters in the radical group. An excerpt from a parliamentary address made in 1926 by Mr. Woodsworth points up the general line of argument followed by this group:

> We have today three principal kinds of money: first, gold money, which is practically not in use in this country; second, money which we call bank-note money; and third, cheque-money. About 96 per cent of the entire business of Canada is carried on by means of the cheque system. . . . The only way of increasing the quantity of gold is by digging it out of the earth. The quantity of bank notes may be increased by putting the printing presses to work, but either directly or indirectly the government controls the quantity of bank-note money in circulation. It is, however, an altogether different matter with credit money--or bank deposits drawable by cheque. To a very large extent, the control of the amount of this class of money that is in circulation is in the hands of the banks, and this without any supervision or regulation whatever by the government. In that sense, then, it may be said that we have handed over to private corporations the right to make money or to destroy money.[15]

Here was a process of reasoning highly coloured by monetary objectives ranging from the establishment of a central bank to the nationalization of the banking system. Consequently, the analysis of the credit system was defective in that it exaggerated the banks' capacity for expanding credit, The radicals assumed, or at least implied, that the Canadian banking system enjoyed full freedom in the scope of their lending and investing operations. Consistently lacking was acknowledgment of the fact that, while banks can create their own resources, they cannot do so "at will, " but only on the basis of increased cash reserves, and then only within the limits of public readiness to borrow, legal or customary reserves, and cash payment to depositors. This was, in fact, the element of truth in the bankers' argument. Without it no analysis of the credit mechanism could be complete or accurate. But the radicals were moving in the right direction. Through their extensive references to the views of prominent writers in the field, and through their attempts to apply careful theoretical analysis to economic phenomena, they were making a significant contribution to the clarification of a complex problem.

Money and Prices

Even more interesting, from the standpoint of monetary theory, are the important beginnings made in the development of ideas about the role of money in the determination of the level of prices. Here again the "intellectual battle" was joined by the radicals and the bankers; the economists, businessmen, and Eastern politicians, if they had any theoretical conceptions along these lines, for the most part kept their silence.[16]

Actually, the controversy involved little more than inadequate exposition of, and general expression of faith in, the contemporary Fisher-Keynes versions of the "quantity theory" of money by the Labour and Progressive members of Parliament, and denial of the validity of that theory by the bankers. Thus Mr. Woodsworth contended: "The amount of money in circulation, together with the rapidity of the circulation [have] a very decided effect upon the value of money itself. The accepted theory of the economists is that the value of money varies inversely to the quantity in circulation. ... Those who control the quantity of money in circulation ... [therefore] control the value of all other things, since all other things are measured in terms of money. "[17] In a similar vein, Mr. W. C. Good[18] argued that, when the government increased the supply of money with its own promises to pay, it thereby reduced the purchasing power of the money already in the hands of the public. Therefore, as Keynes had pointed out in his Tract on Monetary Reform, the government taxed the public to that extent. But inflation was not always brought about by governments; banks also expanded the money supply and so exercised the taxing power. "According to Mr. Keynes, 'the internal price level is mainly determined by the amount of credit created by the banks. ' That is a clear statement of a fact which is not generally recognized or admitted."[19]

The general attitude of Canadian bankers towards monetary theory was one of distrust,[20] mingled with a frankness in the admission of ignorance which was largely the reflection of contempt. It was no less a figure than

Sir John Aird, General Manager of the Canadian Bank of Commerce and
Vice-President of the Canadian Bankers' Association, who, testifying in
1923 before the House of Commons Select Standing Committee on Banking
and Commerce, declared that he had never heard of the quantity theory,
and that "we do not want theories [like the quantity theory] introduced into banking. If you get into theories, you are on dangerous ground."[21]
On the same occasion, Mr. H. O. Powell, General Manager of the Wey-
burn Securities Bank, made the following acknowledgment: "I am not a
theoretical chap, I am practical; I cannot go into these theoretical questions, because they are too deep for me."[22] Sir Frederick Williams-
Taylor, General Manager of the Bank of Montreal, made it quite clear to
Mr. Irvine, during the course of his testimony, that "we entirely differ
in one notable respect, that I am just a plain banker, and you are a student, I should judge, with a technical knowledge of things that I do not
happen to possess."[23]

In the light of these general statements, it is hardly surprising that
the bankers' dismissal of the quantity theory was not based on such valid
objections as its over-emphasis on the quantity of money, its over-
simplification of the role of what Fisher called the "velocity of circulation" and the "volume of transactions," and its failure to consider the
factors governing the flow of expenditures from private, business, and
governmental sources. The bankers' argument, instead, took the form
of unqualified adherence to the "banking principle" that the supply of
money is purely passive, adjusting itself automatically to the "needs of
trade." Since this view was, during the twenties, such an important
part of the bankers' case against the establishment of a central bank, it
will be more fully examined in that context.

The "Gold-Standard Mentality"

There were, finally, the very similar lines of division which were
beginning to develop over the nature and functions of the gold standard.
The Canadian "gold-standard mentality" has already been noted. It im-
plied--in addition to the conventional notions of commercial bank operations described below--full acceptance of the assumption that the maintenance of stability in the foreign exchanges (within the limits set by the
gold points) was an essential prerequisite to a strong system of international trade. The loss of autonomy in internal monetary policy which
this assumption entailed (by requiring national "price" and "income" responses to gold movements between countries) either was not recognized
or was not considered too high a price to be paid. The plain fact is that,
to the extent that such recognition did exist, "any alternative to a policy
of maintaining rigid exchange rates was a heresy without political support."[24]

The Labour and Progressive politicians dissented sharply from this
general point of view. With Keynes and the other "unorthodox" economists, they shared the conviction that national autonomy in the economic
sphere must not be sacrificed on the altar of foreign-exchange stability.

Their contention was that, in any case, the gold standard was only a "fair-weather" standard--that, in Mr. Irvine's words, "this gold basis, which is more required, if it is going to function, when the country is really facing a crisis, is not to be found there when the crisis comes; ... gold is only a basis when people do not want it, when confidence can be retained even without it."[25]

The significance of the two opposing schools of thought did not really manifest itself during the greater part of the decade of the twenties, when definite ideas on these matters were only beginning to take shape, but rather during the Great Depression of the thirties, when Canada found itself confronted with basic issues of foreign economic policy. This much, however, can be said by way of appraisal of the earlier period: neither group showed appreciation of the possibility that the way out of Canada's and the world's international-trade difficulties might be, not through strict enforcement of the "rules of the gold-standard game," or adoption of a system of unlimited freedom of the exchanges, but through some institutional arrangement (such as the International Monetary Fund set up at Bretton Woods in 1944) designed to preserve the advantages, and eliminate the disadvantages, of both extremes.

The orthodox position did, nevertheless, have one important source of strength, though its actual realization can hardly be attributed to those who supported that approach. "While trade was expanding and capital imports flowed freely, the advantages of this policy of [maintaining rigid exchange rates], which was essentially one of leaving decisions of monetary policy to the great creditor nations, were overwhelmingly preponderant for a small country with rudimentary machinery for monetary control."[26]

III. THE CENTRAL BANK CONTROVERSY

Undoubtedly, the discussions and writings related directly or indirectly to the central bank question shed the greatest light on the economic thinking which pervaded the decade of the twenties. There is an abundance of interesting and important information, provided chiefly by the debates in the Dominion Parliament and the House Committee on Banking and Commerce (meeting in 1923, 1924, and 1928), and in part by those Canadian books and journals dealing with economic problems.

Although there had been some consideration, before and during World War I, of the feasability of establishing a central bank in Canada,[27] the decade of the twenties served as the formative stage in the evolutionary process which culminated in the central bank legislation of the thirties.

Canadian Bankers and the Central Bank

There were two main issues in the central-bank controversy: first, the purpose and significance of commercial banks in the economy; and second, the adequacy of the then-existing Canadian banking system. Extension of the line of inquiry in these two directions provides the basis for an understanding of the many "pro" and "con" judgments made with respect to the establishment of a central bank in the Dominion.

The banking function. Canadian bankers were the first to admit that their conception of the banking function was a narrow one. Each banker confined himself to the operations of his own particular bank, with little or no awareness of, or interest in, the repercussions of his actions and those of his fellow-bankers on the economic system as a whole. Mr. A. E. Phipps, General Manager of the Imperial Bank of Canada, and President of the Canadian Bankers' Association, gave the following description of this attitude: "The banker is primarily and mainly concerned about the safety of his advances and the certainty that the advances will be returned within a reasonable time with adequate interest. He is not thinking about the volume of credit in the country nor the effect which the granting or withholding of credit in the particular instance will have upon the price level of commodities in the country."[28]

It was quite natural that this indifference towards the broader aspects of banking should have expressed itself in the actual belief that the banking function is performed solely in response to the "needs of trade" and is therefore perfectly neutral in so far as its effects on the economy are concerned. This general advocacy of the banking principle of note issue was, as already indicated, the bankers' basis for rejection of the quantity theory of money.

Thus Sir Frederick Williams-Taylor declared, in 1923, that the only relation which fluctuations in the supply of money have to the price level is that, "if the prices of commodities rise, then more money is required."[29] Discussing the depression of the early twenties, he expressed the bankers' appreciation of the trying conditions which the Canadian farming community had been experiencing. He was convinced, however, that those conditions were "not due to inadequacy of Canadian banking facilities, but to the rapid deflation which has taken place in the prices of agricultural produce compared with other commodities, deflation over which the banks certainly had no control."[30]

In the opinion of Sir Edmund Walker, President of the Canadian Bank of Commerce, "under the Canadian banking system there is never too much or too little money in circulation, because it falls and rises exactly as the transactions of the country fall and rise";[31] so that the bankers had no control over production. The chartered banks were not responsible for the misfortunes which had befallen many people in Canada. Those misfortunes would be eliminated only by "years of economy and hard work. I do not know how the banks can do anything more than to preach annual sermons and give objurgations as to the necessity for doing that."[32]

Clearly, then, Canadian bankers were advocates of the banking principle of note issue. They stressed only the demand side of credit, that is, that the state of business determined the amount of credit and therefore rendered impossible the exercise of control from the supply side. Apparently, they failed to perceive the fact of complex interaction between the volume of credit and the volume of business, each variable being both cause and effect of fluctuations in the other. Mr. Irvine's early (1923) critical evaluation of the Canadian bankers' position would seem to have been a harsh, but not inappropriate, expression of the truth: "[The bankers] know their own business as it now exists. They are good book-keepers. They understand what good security is for credit. They know the mechanics of banking, but, through the confession of ... some of the bankers, ... they do not know what money is and they do not know what money should do in the industrial system, nor have they any idea of the banks' action upon the industrial system."[33]

    The Canadian banking system. Closely interwoven with this general approach to banking was the bankers' virtually unanimous expression of satisfaction with the Canadian banking system as it existed during the twenties. Sir Frederick Williams-Taylor argued that there was no necessity for a central bank in Canada. "Under the Finance Act ... banks in need of temporary assistance can and do obtain from the Dominion Government that assistance, while our branch bank system insures an ample supply of currency at all times and places where it is needed for crop movement or other purposes."[34] Sir Edmund Walker was convinced that Canadian banks were "serving the people of Canada as well as any banking system in the world."[35] According to Sir John Aird, the time had not yet arrived for the establishment of a central bank; it would entail too great a cost and would be too risky in a sparsely populated and undeveloped country like Canada.[36] Mr. C. E. Neill, General Manager of the Royal Bank of Canada, was firm in the belief that, "as far as the needs of Canada, the Canadian banks, and the Canadian public are concerned, the re-discounting facilities granted by the Finance Act are quite satisfactory--all we need."[37] Mr. Phipps's view was that, in the Finance Act, Canada had "in effect a central bank of rediscount with scarcely a dollar of additional cost and without any of the elaborate machinery which characterizes such institutions in other countries"; [38] and that there was no difference between the central bank functions of the Federal Reserve System of the United States and those provided by the machinery of the Finance Act.[39]

The Civil Servants and Eastern Politicans: A Common Outlook

    Such responsible civil servants as did take a definite stand were in accord with the bankers on the issue of the adequacy of the Canadian banking system. Thus Mr. G. W. Hyndman, Assistant Deputy Minister of Finance in 1928, identified the functions of the Treasury Board with those performed by the Federal Reserve System in the United States.[40] And Mr. C. E. S. Tompkins, Inspector-General of Banks at that time, contended that a central bank was unnecessary in Canada; and that "the banking system as it prevails meets the needs of the country adequately, and while improvements might be necessary from time to time, I cannot see that there is anything radically wrong with it at the present time."[41]

    Although not as extreme, the attitude of the Liberal Government (as well as that of most Liberal and Conservative politicians) did not differ markedly from that of the bankers.[42] Furthermore, it underwent little or no change throughout the entire decade during which the Liberal party

was in power. The statement of policy made in 1923 by Mr. W. S. Fielding, Minister of Finance, came, perhaps, as close as any other, during
the early twenties, to suggesting the point of view of a government apparently reluctant to commit itself on this question: "I have given no particular consideration to [the] theory [of the government issuing all notes]. I
think the present system is working very well, and ... I cannot say that
I have ever thought it would be at all a desirable thing to deprive the banks
of this privilege."[43]

Economists and the Central Bank

Among the professional economists, there were differences of opinion
with respect to the central bank issue, though most of them seemed to
share in common a tendency towards caution in the expression of their
views. Dr. W. C. Clark was a notable exception. As early as 1918, he
had been arguing in favour of a central bank. As time passed, the western
members of Parliament became heavily indebted to his ideas in their agitation for such an institution, though he was not the source of many of the
"home-grown" radical notions which they espoused.

Professor Mackintosh, too, made his position reasonably clear during the early stages of the controversy, at least hinting at some of the
implications of central banking.[44] What he did emphasize was the view
that the Finance Act had been adopted as a war measure and should, therefore, have no place in the Canadian banking system when the effects of
the war had passed; and that the problem of economic fluctuations could
no longer be ignored.

Professor Jackson showed a keen appreciation of the broader aspects
of monetary policy, and of their significance for the Canadian banking
system. He recognized the limitations of that system, but he seems to
have remained non-committal as far as recommendations for improvement were concerned:

> Any man was a heretic some years ago who questioned the fitness
> of gold for use as a monetary standard. But not so today, when
> a school of thought ... comprising J. M. Keynes, J. F. Darling,
> etc., ... is growing rapidly, which would stabilize the price level
> by control of bank credit, irrespective of gold supply. Tomorrow
> this may be the doctrine of economic orthodoxy. Who knows?
> But the proposal to make stable business conditions and stable
> markets the goal of banking policy presupposes the existence of
> a central bank in the country which is to follow this plan. We
> have no central bank in the Dominion. Though the chartered
> banks of Canada have the privilege of rediscount with the Treas-
> ury, the Finance Minister seems never to have attempted to con-
> trol their credit policy by changing the rate of discount ... or
> otherwise.[45]

Appearing before the House Banking and Commerce Committee in

1923, the eminent Dr. Adam Shortt combined a high degree of economic understanding with an anti-central-bank approach.[46] He criticized Professor Fisher's proposal for a "compensated dollar,"[47] on the ground that the index numbers required were merely averages and therefore subject to the same possibilities of distorted measurement as all averages; and that the proposal reflected a superficial analysis of the economic system. On this latter point, Dr. Shortt's analogy is of special interest: "This adjusting of the dollar every now and again is impossible; ... you are looking to your thermometer and trying to regulate the thermometer by holding a match under it to adjust it, or cooling it down with an ice jacket when it is the temperature outside; it is the wave from the north that you want to get rid of; it is this question of unadjusted production and consumption. The desirability is absolute, but you can easily see you have to go far more fundamentally than that."[48] Dr. Shortt, however, advanced only one remedial suggestion, namely, the extension of the powers of the Canadian Bankers' Association: "that... would be far better than any superimposed scheme of a Federal Reserve Board or anything of that sort."[49]

The most outspoken--if not the most clearly formulated--views among the Canadian economists were those outlined to the Banking and Commerce Committee in 1923 by Professor W. W. Swanson of the University of Saskatchewan. At one point in his testimony, he declared that it was absurd to blame the chartered banks for the 1921 collapse of prices.[50] Yet later, in the course of questioning, he admitted that, "insofar as [the banks] contracted credit at the time when prices were falling, and compelled producers, farmers, and others, to throw their products on the market, of course to that extent they were a factor in the price decline";[51] and that he could hardly conceive that Canada had bankers in a position of power, trust, and responsibility who did not realize that banks and bankers can and do affect the price level.[52] In Professor Swanson's opinion, there was no urgent need for a central banking system in Canada; moreover, it would be "a very dangerous thing ... for the government, or any semi-official banking authority representing the interest of the government, to go into the control of credit."[53]

The Radical Stimulus to Central Banking
Virtually every year after 1921, when the first two Labour members and the first small group of Progressives sat in the House of Commons, they repeatedly brought before Parliament the issue of a central bank for Canada.[54] There can be no doubt, however, that all during the twenties: (1) the matter of securing an additional supply of funds was uppermost in the minds of most of them; (2) many of the more radical "social credit" types of proposals, such as those of Mr. George Bevington, rested on very shaky foundations;[55] (3) there was a wide diversity of views as to the nature of the agency which should be established; (4) the central bank agitation in the West was beclouded and rendered less effective by its frequent and indiscriminate combination with what was essentially a political

objective, namely, the nationalization of the whole banking system;   and
(5) the radical group (along with a growing number of professional economists in other countries) committed the grave error of looking to more
comprehensive results from monetary policy than it could reasonably be
expected to produce.

But notwithstanding these defects, it remains true that the radical
politicians won for themselves a unique and vital role in the development
of Canadian central banking in particular, and of Canadian monetary
thought in general. It was in response to their pointed, persistent questions, and their repeated affirmations of the important causal role of
money in the price system and the consequent need for parliamentary
investigation leading to the establishment of central bank machinery, that
the bankers, eastern politicians, and other opposition groups stated and
elaborated upon their views.[56]

The radical group was noteworthy for the scale of its members' participation. Special mention, however, must be accorded Mr. Woodsworth,
Mr. Good, and Mr. G. G. Coote, not so much for the vigour of their advocacy of a central bank--for in this respect they had no monopoly of ac-
tion--as for their efforts, however imperfect, to outline concretely the
functions of the proposed institution.[57]

Mr. Woodsworth envisaged these functions as comprising the issue of
currency, the protection of the weaker portions of the country and the
weaker industries against the strong concerns allegedly working in close
co-operation with the banks, the control of credit and therefore of prices,
and the facilitation of the process of government financing.[58] Mr. Coote
set forth the functions of issuing notes, rediscounting, control exchange
rates, handling government deposits, and receiving private deposits like,
and so competing with, the chartered banks.[59]

Probably the clearest ideas were those expressed by Mr. Good. It
was his belief that:

> We have at the present time ... all the necessary elements for a
> Federal Reserve or a central bank. We have our discount facili-
> ties under the Finance Act, we have our Central Gold Reserve,
> we have the Bankers' Association, we have practically a centrali-
> zation of financial power in this country in this private organiza-
> tion. ... Now ... we should link up these elements in a co-ordinated
> scheme under the supervision of a board of experts, and they do
> not need to be very many. Here is something that can be established
> in Canada in the near future at practically no expense because it
> means substantially nothing in addition to what is now in existence
> or in immediate prospect.[60]

The Deputy Minister of Finance had admitted that he had never contemplated changing the rate of interest, that the matter had never been discussed by officials of his Department. And yet, Mr. Good argued, it was
recognized by English and American monetary authorities--as well as by

the world's leading economists--that rediscount rate variation was the instrument best adapted for stabilizing the price level; this was particularly true for conditions then existing in Canada. Managed currency achieved through central bank machinery was, therefore, essential for the prevention of "alternative periods of boom and depression--what is known now among economists as the business cycle"; [61] and, indeed, for the survival of the economic and industrial world.

The radicals, apparently, gave no consideration to open market operations, or to variations in the reserve requirements of the chartered banks. But apart from the fact that there was then no Canadian legal stipulation as to reserve ratios, these were, after all, rather advanced monetary techniques which were still in the experimental stages even in those countries where central banks had already been established. At any rate, the realization was beginning to arise--despite the frequently exaggerated impressions of the efficacy of monetary policy--that such policy represented only one of many ways of attacking the problem of economic instability.

IV. MONETARY EXPERIENCE

The provisions of the Finance Acts altered the whole structure of the Canadian banking system. They introduced, for the first time, machinery through which the banks could materially and rapidly increase their cash reserves. Such increase had previously been possible only by resort to foreign sources, that is, by liquidation of foreign call loans, by borrowing abroad, or by sale of securities in other countries. The real significance of the change was that the system lost its automatic inflexible features without at the same time acquiring that measure of central control which alone could have secured monetary stability.

Boom and Collapse: 1920-2

It would be unreasonable to attribute to the Canadian banking system prime responsibility for the boom of 1920 and the downswing which followed in 1921. Although selection and appraisal of the causal factors operating in any particular business cycle is extremely difficult, there is little question that the fundamental causes were, rather, (1) the instability of postwar European demand for Canadian exports, (2) highly volatile business expectations, (3) inventory accumulation and liquidation, (4) cyclical (as against countercyclical) fiscal policy, (5) inadequate price control in the upswing, and (6) the piling-up of a great "backlog" of demand in the construction industry during the downswing.[62] It is equally clear, however, that faulty monetary policy, at the very least, intensified both the upward and downward phases of the postwar cycle.

Thus, during the upswing, "the combined actions of the banks and the Ministry of Finance led to monetary expansion. The bankers' role was a passive one, in accordance with the universal 'needs of trade' conception of banking policy."[63] The monetary expansion had begun during the war, and the early postwar period saw a further projection of the wartime trend. In November 1916, bank borrowings of Dominion notes under the Finance Act amounted to $4.4 million; in November 1918 they stood at $116.5 million, and in November 1920 at $123.7 million. Moreover, total bank credit increased by $784.5 million--from $1,187.3 million in October 1916, to $1,971.8 million in October 1920--by far the largest part being due to an increase in loans rather than investments. Monetary policy became distinctly deflationary early in 1921, as shown by the reduction of both call and current loans at that time.[64] And although there is no direct evidence of action actually taken by the banks to raise loan rates or to restrict credit at prevailing rates, the fact that by 1920 most bankers were convinced that prices had to be forced down would indicate the strong likelihood that such independent action from the supply side of the credit mechanism did take place.[65]

Recovery and Expansion until 1929[66]

From 1923 to the end of 1927, amounts borrowed under the Finance Act rarely exceeded $25 million and at one time (February 1926) were as low as $2 million. As business improved, however, the banks used the facilities of the Finance Act more extensively, with the result that from 1927 until the end of 1929 the amount so borrowed, as well as the bank credit which it supported, showed a phenomenal increase. Advances under the Finance Act rose from $8.7 million in May 1927 to $111.4 million in November 1929. Current loans, which were below $1 billion in 1925 and 1926, increased to a maximum of $1,473.4 million in October 1929. Call loans in Canada, which were about $100 million in 1925, rose to a high of $280.8 million in September 1929.[67]

This credit expansion did not materially affect the domestic price-cost structure, but it did upset the equilibrium in the Canadian balance of payments, since much of the newly created credit flowed across to the United States. The adverse movement of the foreign exchanges which appeared late in 1928 was caused chiefly by large-scale Canadian buying of securities in New York.[68]

When the United States-Canadian exchange rate reached the gold-export point, Canadian banks began to present Dominion notes for redemption at the Finance Department, and to get gold from the government's reserve. During December 1928 and January 1929, some $45 million in gold was obtained and exported from Canada to the United States, mainly in order to meet the increasing Canadian demand for funds in New York. As this continued, the banks found it necessary to replenish their reserves by borrowing other Dominion notes from the government under the provisions of the Finance Act. In the words of Professor C. A. Curtis of Queen's University, "the Department of Finance was in the position of paying out Dominion notes with one hand and cashing them for gold with the other."[69] The result was little change in the volume of Dominion notes, continued expansion of bank credit, and a drop of 22 per cent in the ratio of government gold holdings to Dominion notes outstanding between November 1927 and December 1928.[70]

Thus, the Finance Act was unwittingly being converted into an effective instrument for violating the rules of the gold standard game: "The loss of gold did not reduce bank reserves and restrict credit. Although gold was exported, bank reserves in the form of Dominion notes were not reduced on account of the rediscounting operations under the Finance Act. Thus the normal influence of gold exports was never exerted on the credit structure. The only check on credit expansion, apparently, was the ability of the banks to place further loans to their satisfaction."[71] Naturally, this situation could not continue much longer. By the end of 1928, the government's gold reserve had fallen so low that the banks were unofficially requested to abstain from demanding gold under the Dominion Notes Act. Although it was not generally realized at the time, this action signified the de facto Canadian abandonment of the gold standard. Legal abandonment, in the form of an official embargo on gold exports, did not occur until October 19, 1931.[72]

In appraising this unimpressive record of Canadian monetary experience during the late twenties, one must be careful to stress the fallacy of attributing all responsibility for the excesses of that period either to the commercial banking system or to the Treasury Board's administration of the Finance Act. "The fact remains, however, that public policy was lacking in providing restraints to excessive capital expenditure and speculation, and banking policy was deficient in its extraordinary recourse to the Finance Act as a source of bank cash, and in its failure, until the boom was well advanced, to restrain the expansion of bank credit, even though such restriction was not implied in the crude operation of the Finance Act."[73] More specifically, the errors of Canadian commercial bank policy--in no small measure the product of "economic ignorance"-- would have been minimized if there had been an intelligent centralized control over monetary policy.[74] The Treasury Board did have the power to conduct rediscount operations, but there the parallelism with central bank control ends. By their own admission, neither the Board nor the Department of Finance within which it functioned had the personnel, the knowledge, or the techniques required for controlling the monetary system.[75]

To be sure, the available historical evidence does not afford a basis for definitive judgment as to the causal relations among the three major variables analysed, namely, structure, thought, and experience. In the light of the inherent complexity of their interaction, this negative view should not be an unexpected one. But it does not preclude the contention-- which is, in fact, made here--that the adverse impact of cyclical instability upon Canada during the twenties was substantially aggravated by the shallowness of the environment of monetary thought in which public policy was implemented.

CHAPTER IV

THOUGHT AND POLICY IN FISCAL DEVELOPMENT

AS World War I came to a close, the nineteenth-century economic philosophy of laissez-faire remained strongly entrenched in Western countries. In the fiscal sphere, it was therefore quite natural that public revenue and expenditure should have been widely regarded as wholly unproductive--as necessary evils resulting from the need to keep internal order and to provide for defence against foreign aggression. The French economist, J. B. Say, had clearly set forth this attitude more than a century before the war in his famous "golden maxim" that "the best scheme of finance is to spend as little as possible; and the best tax is always the lightest. "[1]

The concept of a "neutral" fiscal policy had rested primarily on this premise. Nor had the view that public revenues and expenditures should be as neutral as possible in their effects on the economic system been inconsistent with a socio-economic framework in which the total revenues and expenditures collected and disbursed by the state did not exceed approximately 10 per cent of the national income. Within this framework, the aggregate of public levies had not been so large as to be a major factor in the level of costs and profits, nor had the aggregate of public expenditures been sufficiently large to exert an important influence on the level of employment. Thus, there had been some cogency in the argument that, on practical grounds, the simple principle of "neutrality of effect" in public finance management constituted a salutary guide for fiscal authorities, "since at the best society stood to gain little from an abandonment of that principle in favour of a more complicated formula, while it might possibly lose much were there fiscal mismanagement. "[2]

Acceptance of this argument had led, in turn, to the widespread advocacy of the principle that budgetary equilibrium should be achieved annually. The balancing of governmental revenues and expenditures, regardless of general economic conditions, had become a fundamental objective of fiscal policy. Although the operation of this rule of thumb had accentuated depressions (booms) by requiring decreased (increased) public outlays or increased (decreased) taxes, or both, during such periods, the adverse consequences of these policies had been minimized by the relatively small amounts involved; and in practice, these effects had tended to be offset by the fact that, so long as budgets were balanced, there was no danger that investment incentives, already weakened by a low current rate of profit, would be further undermined by fears over the soundness of the public credit.

This, then, was the philosophy of "sound, orthodox finance" which the English classical economists had been so instrumental in constructing, and which the postwar world adopted completely and without question. In essence, it was but a reflection of the firm belief that the competitive private enterprise system functioned in such an automatic compensatory fashion as to forestall any large-scale fluctuations in employment and income, and so to remove the problem from the realm of public policy.

What responsible men in the postwar world failed to grasp was that the smoothly operating, automatic, highly fluid economy postulated by the classical economists--however appropriate it may have been for nineteenth-century conditions--was fast ceasing to exist. Indeed, the tendency towards economic instability had been the inevitable concomitant of the rising standards of living growing out of the Industrial Revolution. But it was not until the early years of the twentieth century that the factors making for this instability assumed serious proportions.[3]

Concentration on the "expenditure" basis of cyclical fluctuations would have pointed clearly to the desirability of a "compensatory" fiscal policy. Since economic stability was primarily dependent upon the level of income-generating expenditure, and since the non-governmental components of such expenditure were subject to violent change, then public policy in the field of taxation, expenditure, and debt had to be carried out in such a way as to "compensate" for these fluctuations and so stabilize aggregate expenditure. That is to say, clearly implied by the "expenditure" approach was: (1) governmental action aimed at balancing the budget not annually but over the business cycle, the budget deficits incurred in the downswing phase of the cycle being offset by the surpluses achieved in the upswing phase; (2) the stimulation of aggregate demand during depression by reduced tax rates and/or increased government expenditures; and (3) the curbing of inflationary expansion through a carefully chosen combination of increased tax rates, reduced government expenditures, and repayment of the public debt.

But this approach to business cycles had never met with any substantial degree of acceptance. During the nineteen-twenties, it continued to live on in the underworld of monetary cranks and heretics. For most of the decade, it remained wholly outside the framework of analytical techniques then familiar to professional economists; while politicians, government officials, and other policy-makers seemed typically hardly aware of the fact that such problems existed. This intellectual narrowness in fiscal matters was to no small extent due to the gradual and recent character of the institutional economic change which had necessitated the reorientation of views. It was, nevertheless, one outstanding aspect of early twentieth-century economic thought.

Canadian postwar attitudes conformed closely to this general pattern of fiscal thought. Clear thinking about fiscal problems was very much the exception rather than the rule--a fact which unquestionably made its mark in the policy field. Before turning to this phase of the inquiry, however, it will be instructive to examine the postwar fiscal structure within which Canadian thought and policy evolved.

I. THE CANADIAN FISCAL STRUCTURE AT THE END OF WORLD WAR I

Significant changes in the Canadian fiscal system, particularly in taxation, had been achieved during the First World War.[4] It was at this time that the Dominion had adopted many of the basic components of present-day federal tax structures.

Wartime Tax Changes in the Federal Structure

In 1914 the Canadian tax system was a primitive one in which customs and excise duties comprised about 99 per cent of total tax revenues.[5] This lack of machinery for directly taxing the net incomes, profits, and wealth of individuals and business enterprises meant that the sudden introduction of such tax measures on the scale required for waging war would be too drastic to be practical on political or economic grounds. Furthermore, the government apparently believed that heavy direct taxation would be a serious deterrent to investment and private initiative in the under-developed, expanding Canadian economy.[6] Finally, public sentiment throughout the country was quite definitely opposed to any substantial increase in the tax burden. The consequence of this set of factors was that, during the war and immediate postwar periods, taxation and other revenues failed in most instances to provide sufficient cash even to take care of the government's non-war outlays, including capital expenditures; and that almost the entire cost of the war was met by borrowing. Table II illustrates these aspects of the Dominion government's war finance.

The relatively minor wartime role of taxation contributed significantly to the phenomenal inflationary expansion which characterized the war period.[7] The fact remains, nevertheless, that important changes in the tax structure did occur, though they were the product of necessity rather than conscious planning. By 1916 the growing financial burden produced by the gradual intensification of the Canadian war effort and by the cessation of British war loans to Canada had reached serious proportions. Thereafter, attempts were made to supplement domestic borrowing with increased tax revenues.

Early in 1916 a business profits war tax, retroactive to the beginning of the war, was imposed. It covered only business enterprises with a paid-up capital of more than $50,000, and absorbed one-fourth of all net profits in excess of 7 per cent for corporations and 10 per cent for individually owned businesses and partnerships. The tax was obviously limited in scope; in the first fiscal year of operation, 1917 (that is, 1916-17), it produced only $12.5 million or 7 per cent of total tax revenue.[8] Moreover, it was abolished as of December 31, 1920. But it did increase steadily in importance during the latter part of the war; and it did establish a vital precedent in Dominion tax legislation, namely, the taxation of business.

In 1917 Parliament imposed a personal income tax for the first time in Canadian history. The tax was then regarded as a considerable burden, but, judged in terms of present standards, the rates were very light. The Income War Tax Act levied a normal tax of 4 per cent on incomes exceeding $2, 000 in the case of single persons, and on incomes exceeding $3, 000 in the case of married couples; a "super-tax" was also imposed, progressing from 2 per cent on the amount by which an income exceeded $6, 000 but did not exceed $10, 000, up to only 25 per cent on the amount by which an income exceeded $100, 000. In 1918 a fundamental extension of the tax was made, with the levying of a tax of 6 per cent on corporate incomes exceeding $3, 000; there was no stipulation regarding a super-tax or surtax. At the same time, the personal income tax was altered by reduction in exemptions, and by increased rates in the higher income brackets. Income tax collections did not begin until fiscal 1919, when only $9. 3 million, or 4 per cent of total tax revenue,[9] accrued to the federal government. It was an unimpressive beginning for a source of revenue which was to become a permanent and major component of the federal tax structure.[10]

TABLE II

Revenue and Expenditure of the Dominion Government,
Fiscal Years Ending March 31, 1915-20

(millions of dollars)

Revenue and Expenditure	1915	1916	1917	1918	1919	1920
Ordinary expenditures	136	130	149	178	233	304
Capital expenditures and investment	87	45	73	128	47	232
Total excluding war	223	175	222	306	280	536
Less current revenues	133	172	233	261	313.	350
Deficit (-) or surplus (+) excluding war	-90	-3	+11	-45	+33	-186
Expenditures on war and demobilization						
Overseas	9	38	125	191	158	75
In Canada	52	128	182	153	289	272
Total	61	166	307	344	447	347
Total deficit (financed by borrowing	151	169	296	389	414	533

Source: J. J. Deutsch, "War Finance and the Canadian Economy, 1914-20, " C. J. E. P. S. , VI (Nov. 1940), p. 540.

Thus, as indicated in Table III, the Dominion tax system, by the end of the fiscal year 1919, was broader and deeper than it had been before the war. Relative to both total revenue and national income, tax revenue had changed little during the war; in fiscal 1914, it amounted to 78 per cent of total revenue, and in fiscal 1919, 75 per cent. The corresponding figures obtained on the basis of national income are 5.4 per cent and 6.3 per cent, respectively.[11] While not enormous, however, the shift from the prewar dependence on customs and excise duties was significant. Both taxes had increased in absolute terms, but had declined--particularly the former, from 82 per cent to 63 per cent--in comparison with other taxes. The important structural changes were therefore due to the tax innovations that had been made during the war; in 1919, the business profits tax alone accounted for 14 per cent of all taxes, and, together with the other war taxes, for 24 per cent.

TABLE III

Revenue of the Dominion Government,
Fiscal Years Ending March 31, 1914 and 1919

Revenue	1914		1919	
	Amount $1000	Per cent of total taxes[1]	Amount $1000	Per cent of total taxes[1]
Customs duties	104, 691	82.1	147, 169	63.0
Excise duties	21, 452	16.8	30, 342	13.0
Income taxes Individuals	-	-	7, 973	3.4
Corporations	-	-	1, 377	.6
Business profits tax	-	-	32, 970	14.1
Miscellaneous taxes	1, 335	1.1	13, 858[2]	5.9
Total taxes	127, 478	100.0	233, 689	100.0
Total revenue	163, 174		312, 947	

(1) Figures rounded to total 100 per cent.
(2) This figure includes manufacturers', transporation, and stamp taxes, and other war taxes.
Sources: C.Y.B., 1938, pp. 848, 851; Report of Royal Commission on Dominion-Provincial Relations, book III, p. 30; Department of National Revenue, Taxation Statistics (Ottawa, 1946), p. 11.

Federal Expenditure Changes

The prodigious wartime growth in debt charges and pensions was the most important development in the field of federal expenditure. Between the fiscal years 1914 and 1919, the net national debt had risen from $336 million to $1.6 billion, an almost fivefold increase.[12] As a result, in 1919 interest paid on the debt stood six times as high as the 1914 level, having increased from $12.9 million to $77.4 million, and accounted for no less than one-third of total ordinary expenditures.[13] Debt charges together with pension payments, which showed an even greater increase during the war--from only $311.9 thousand to $18.3 million--amounted to 41 per cent, as compared with 10 per cent before the war.[14] Most of the other "expenditure" items had declined in importance. This was particularly true of capital expenditures, which had dropped sharply in both relative and absolute terms--from $74 million or 40 per cent of total expenditures in 1914, to $47 million or 7 per cent of total expenditures in 1919.[15]

The Provinces and Municipalities[16]

The financial capacity of the provinces and municipalities was far more limited than that of the Dominion government. The subsidiary authorities had no right to issue currency. They did not have the same ready market for borrowing, either among the general public or in the banking system. Both before and after the war, corporation taxes, succession duties, and taxes on real property yielded most of the provincial tax revenues; while licences, public domain, and Dominion subsidies were among the major sources of non-tax revenue. The real property tax was the only municipal revenue source of any consequence. Because of the more regressive nature of this provincial and municipal taxation, efforts by these governments to finance increased outlays by taxation would have still more depressing effects on private spending than corresponding attempts on the part of the federal government.

Thus, even in the early twenties, there were beginning to appear, among the provincial and local governments, structural revenue problems which were not encountered by the federal government.[17] Moreover, the rapid wartime expansion in Dominion expenditure (much of it completely or partially uncontrollable) and debt was accompanied by similar changes at the other two governmental levels.

Here then, was the fiscal system within which Canadian fiscal thought and policy were to develop. In that institutional setting, even the most profound understanding of financial problems would have rendered difficult the execution of economically sound policies. That such understanding was not generally forthcoming, is one of the most salient features of the decade of the twenties.

II. FISCAL THOUGHT IN CANADA

It is of considerable interest to note that the Canadian tariff occupied

the centre of the stage in postwar fiscal discussion--so much so that, by
and large, debate over other economic issues, particularly in parliamentary circles, was purely secondary, real importance being attached to
such debate only in so far as it impinged upon the "tariff controversy."[18]
It was not as though extensive tariff changes were being effected. Admittedly, "the strength of Western opinion in 1918 and 1919, and the subsequent winning of the balance of power by the Progressives, gave impetus
to the enactment of tariff reductions by the Liberal Administration from
1922 to 1925, contrary as they were to world--and expecially United
States--tariff trends of the times."[19] Moreover, during the next five
years, reductions were made on some articles of capital equipment--
automobiles, coal, and textile products--along with an extension of the
intermediate tariff to a large group of countries with which trade agreements were negotiated by Canada and Britain.[20] But despite these Liberal
reductions, the situation was one of relative stability, with "freer-trade
preachments and protectionist practices"[21] characterizing both major
political parties.

It was, rather, the dependence of Canadian expansion upon external
markets and sources of supply which made foreign trade and tariff policy
an issue of the first magnitude. The truth is, of course, that for purposes
of fiscal policy, a clear distinction should have been drawn between the
"revenue" and "protectionist" aspects of the Canadian tariff. To the extent that the latter type of consideration was paramount, questions of both
commercial and stabilization policy were involved. But the impact of tariff policy on economic stability was of little concern throughout the Dominion; the tendency was to lump together all tariff questions in the term
"fiscal policy, " which came, however, to be virtually synonymous with
"commercial policy." And coupled with this terminological distortion
were the far more serious, widely held misconceptions with respect to
the countercyclical role of government fiscal policy.

Orthodox Parliamentary Views
The deepest insight into prevailing fiscal attitudes during the twenties
can be gained from a perusal of official policy pronouncements by Canadian
Government leaders, both Conservative and Liberal, in the House of Commons. Basic to the entire approach was the concept of the "balanced budget. "
All financial problems were viewed in the light of the universally declared
objective of, whenever possible, financing government expenditures out of
current revenues, and keeping the public debt down to a minimum. The
inflationary and deflationary implications of taxation were generally not
understood, and important tax proposals received consideration only when
consistent with the achievement of this "sound finance" objective. Government expenditure was accepted as unavoidable, but only in minimum proportions. "Debt management" signified "debt reduction" and nothing more.
And the general framework within which these ideas were fitted, and from
which was derived their justification, was, as already indicated, the
strong faith in laissez-faire capitalism, in the abundance of Canadian

resources, and in the stimulating influences associated with proximity to the United States.

In his 1921 budget speech, Sir Henry Drayton, a Conservative, ex-, pressed the following fiscal views in connection with the depression which Canada was then experiencing: "The country's revenues have [undergone a]... marked increase [over the last fiscal year]. In a year of deflation, [this] can only be regarded as satisfactory.... The policy of the government is to pay at least all current expenses, including capital expenditure for canals, public works, etc., out of current revenue."[22] Commenting a year later on the same situation, Mr. W. S. Fielding, the Liberal Minister of Finance, deemed two thoughts to be fundamental:

> The first is as to the need, the deep and earnest need, of economy.... The second thought is that, with all the economy that we can practise, there will still be need of [increased] taxes.... [As yet] we have not only made no reduction in the public debt, but we have to acknowledge a steady increase in the public debt ever since the war.... If we cannot reduce our debt, we should at all events make strenuous efforts to guard against increasing it. We should endeavour to balance our budget, i.e., to pay all classes of our expenditure.... We must accept the responsibility of additional taxation [along with a drastic reduction in all government expenditures].[23]

Similar fiscal appraisals were made by Mr. J. A. Robb, the Liberal successor to Mr. Fielding as Minister of Finance, and by Mr. C. A. Dunning, who later replaced Mr. Robb in the Liberal Government. These views were accurately summarized and sanctioned in the following excerpts from parliamentary addresses of the then Prime Minister, Mr. W. L. Mackenzie King:

> What did we find when we came into charge of the administration of the country's affairs? We found the depressed condition that Canada was then in. We had before us the record of [the Conservatives], where year after year deficits were exhibited in the public accounts.... We put on some extra taxation so that we might be able to balance the budget and restore public confidence in the public finances of the country.... [And we made] persistent and vigorous efforts ... to retrench in matters of expenditure.... For the last few years [since 1925], ... we have been following a consistent line of policy which, year after year, has resulted ... in surpluses, in reduction of the public debt, in reduction of taxes, and with them has come a general increase in prosperity throughout the Dominion.[24]

Mr. King's observations came down, in essence, to the highly dubious proposition that the Canadian recovery from the postwar depression occurred largely because of, and not in spite of, the orthodox financial policies carried out by the federal government.

The fiscal approach adopted by these national leaders was quite representative of the views expressed by the rank-and-file members of the two major political parties in the Dominion. The Liberal member of Parliament, Mr. L. T. Pacaud, for example, was one of the early advocates of the strictest economy as the keynote of anti-depression policy: "There should be elimination even of those expenditures which in ordinary times might be considered legitimate, but which should be discarded today or deferred at all costs. Why? The better to relieve the taxpayers of Canada.... Without [such] economy, all our hopes of rapid recovery [from the collapse of 1921] would be quickly shattered."[25] Dr. R. K. Anderson, a Conservative, also believed that economy in government was absolutely necessary to insure postwar recovery: "We should balance our budget and endeavour in addition to have a small surplus with which to start a sinking fund for the purpose of paying off the national debt. If we go on adding to the debt each year the interest charges will increase so that it will become an intolerable burden to the people. Why should we pass that burden on to future generations?"[26] No attempt was made by Dr. Anderson (or his parliamentary colleagues) to analyse (1) the interest burden in terms of changing national income, (2) the "income distribution" aspects of the debt, (3) the proportions of domestically and foreign owned debt, or (4) the effects of debt retirement on the economy.[27]

Radical Fiscal Thought

It would be an exaggeration to contend that the entire Progressive-Labour group took a united stand on fiscal issues. There were some who believed--with Mr. R. Forke, House leader of the Progressives--that the utmost government economy was essential at all times, and--with Rev. A. J. Lewis--that it was both imperative and practical to reduce the national debt to zero in the not-too-distant future.[28] In this respect, there was little to choose between the Liberal-Conservative and Progressive-Labour ideas. It is a fact, however, that, in broad outlines, the latter group did put forward a representative point of view, defective in much of its reasoning, but notable for its originality and for its utilization of the methods of economic analysis.

A close Canadian approach to a Keynesian basis for fiscal policy was that provided by Mr. Irvine in 1922. His remarks pertaining to the Dominion budget for that fiscal year merit detailed quoting:

> A budget statement is incomplete which does not embody our total national assets as well as our total national liabilities.... When the Prime Minister speaks, I urge that he tell the country what the total national production amounts to annually in money value and what the total annual national consumption amounts to, in terms of dollars.... Now if our total production in Canada be $6 billion, and our annual consumption only $2 billion, then we have a differ-

ence of $4 billion between our consumption and our production. . . .
What is the value of strict economy when you are not able to consume much more than one-third of what has been produced? [29]

Here was a fiscal-policy guide which was oversimplified and predicated
upon an unduly narrow underconsumptionist view of economic fluctuations.
Nevertheless, it stands as one of the earliest statements of principle to
capture the spirit, if not the letter, of the "national employment budget, "
the concept of "gross national product, " and the role of government in the
achievement of high and stable levels of employment and income.

One important facet of the radicals' attack on government economy
during the twenties was the strenuous effort which they made to implement
federal social-security legislation.[30] Led by Mr. Woodsworth and his
Labour colleague, Mr. A. A. Heaps, they repeatedly emphasized the urgency of unemployment, old age, sickness, and disability insurance.[31]
Their supporting arguments centred on the "social welfare, " rather than
the "stabilization." aspects of social security. But they were not unaware
of the potentialities and limitations of social security policy in combating
unemployment; [32] and they were, after all, advocating the incorporation
into the Dominion fiscal structure of a class of expenditures which necessarily had major implications for economic stability. In any case, despite their persistence, and despite their frequent embarrassing references
to early policy pledges made by both the Liberal and Conservative parties,[33]
most of the radical demands went unheeded.[34] The struggle for national
recognition of the principles of social-security policy had yet to be won.

Considerable interest was also evinced in questions of taxation and
public debt. In 1922 Mr. Irvine condemned the sales tax as a strong impediment to increased consumer purchasing power, and, consequently,
to business recovery.[35] Mr. Good declared, in 1924, that:

> The basic principle of sound taxation is payment for service
> rendered; it is logical and necessary, however, that this prin-
> ciple should be modified, to a limited extent by that of "ability
> to pay. " Also, . . . a sound system of taxation should be such
> as cannot easily be evaded and shifted, and whose cost of collec-
> tion is a minimum. I submit that the taxation of land values,
> above all other systems of taxation, is the one which conforms
> most closely to the above requirements. . . . [Support for this
> contention can be found in the writings of J. S. Mill, F. Walker,
> Ricardo, Seligman, and J. R. Commons, among others.][36]

At the same time, Mr. T. A. Crerar, who until 1922 had been national
leader of the Progressives, called for an intensive study of the whole
question of taxation, with particular reference to the incidence of federal
and provincial taxes, and to overlapping in the imposition of taxes.[37]
Four years later (1928), Mr. Coote urged that the Advisory Board on
Tariffs and Taxation report on: (1) the application and administration

of the income tax--whether its schedules were equitable as between different incomes, and whether it acted as a greater brake on the wheels of business than a tax on commodities (such as the sales tax or the tariff); and (2) the advisability of changing the application of the income tax, so that taxpayers would be assessed on their incomes over a period of three years.[38]

By the end of the twenties, the Progressives were making impressive contributions to the understanding of debt management techniques. Mr. Irvine, for example, emphasized the fact that debt repayment is an operation which requires a great deal of skill and caution in its performance:

> There are times when debts should not be paid even if the government were in a position to pay them. There are times when to pay debts would very materially interfere with the business and industrial success of the country. If, for instance, the Minister of Finance, because he happens to have a few millions in the treasury, rushes off to pay debts at a time when we are passing through industrial depression, it is altogether unlikely that such amounts of money as he paid would find opportunity for re-investment, and the result would be that, through removing from circulation the amount of the debt he paid, he would force us into further depression.[39]

And Mr. H. E. Spencer (among other radicals) was equally emphatic in pointing out that Canada needed a more systematic way of dealing with the public debt than by chance surpluses shown in the budget:

> If the Minister of Finance tries to pay off large debts in dull times, he reduces the purchasing power of the people [through taxation and hoarded "repayment" funds] and drags down prices, making times so much harder; on the other hand, it is essential that we should try to raise as much money by way of taxes as the people will stand in prosperous times, when the effect of paying off amounts owned by the government will not be nearly so harmful. ... Therefore, it is the business of any Minister of Finance to watch both the payments of bonds coming due and the issuing of new ones, so that he can act according to the necessities of an inflation or deflation period.[40]

Meanwhile, Mr. Heaps was proposing an 18 per cent reduction (about $405 million) in the national debt as of 1920--that reduction corresponding to the relative decline in retail prices between 1920 and 1926. The debt retirement would not be effected through taxation or borrowing, but through the issue of Dominion currency, equivalent to the amount of the reduction, over a period of three years. Such a retirement procedure would not have deflationary tendencies, as in the case discussed by Mr. Irvine and Mr. Spencer; it would, on the contrary, exert inflationary pressure. In Mr.

Heaps's words: "It would mean a policy of limited inflation of the currency of the country.... In place of creating any difficulty, ...this limited increase in money...would be an advantage, because, in the first place, it would mean a huge annual saving which, of itself, could finance the entire cost of the old age pension scheme for this Dominion. It would mean, further, that this extra money so created would have to find an outlet, and this, in turn, would stimulate commercial activity."[41]

These observations on the public debt were hardly in the classical tradition. They amounted, in fact, to a reiteration and expansion of the heretical views which Keynes had publicly expressed--probably for the first time--only a few years previously (1925), before the English Colwyn Committee on National Debt and Taxation. On that occasion, he had warned the country against premature or excessive repayment of public debt, arguing that repayment policy should be cognizant of effects on expenditures and savings; that if the demand for gilt-edged securities was large, repayment might well be unwise; and that "repayments in order to conform to sound budgetary principle ... or in order to produce an aesthetic balance sheet ... should be restricted, [since an] exchange of cash for government securities [might] merely encourage conservative investment at the expense of risk taking."[42]

Other Fiscal Views

The analysis of fiscal problems carried on outside the political arena was of a minor nature. Only a few isolated journal articles by economists appeared during the entire decade.

In 1923 Mr. H. R. Kemp of the University of Toronto subjected the sales tax to careful examination, on the basis of which he stressed its regressive features, as well as the even greater regressiveness of the so-called "universal turnover tax"[43] then being widely advocated.[44] Writing in 1924, also a year of low business activity for Canada, Professor Mackintosh apparently chose to follow the orthodox approach to fiscal policy. Thus he argued that "clearly the present is a time when no extravagance should be tolerated and when government expenditures should be pared to the bone (indeed it would have been well had this movement been inaugurated three or four years ago)."[45]

In 1928 Professor W. B. Hurd of Brandon College concluded, from a thoroughgoing statistical survey of trends in federal taxation and expenditure, that the federal tax burden was not nearly so heavy as generally assumed, and that, if the then prevailing rate of activity in trade and industry were to continue and be accompanied by a moderate increase in population, the tax burden would soon drop back to the prewar level.[46] In an atmosphere in which each politician was usually striving to outdo the other in the advocacy of tax reduction, it was quite natural, even at a time of great prosperity, that such tacit theoretical support for maintaining or increasing tax rates should be ignored.

Similarly overwhelmed by the sound-finance misconceptions permeating the Dominion at that time was one of the few Keynesian fiscal proposals made by civil servants during the twenties. According to Mr. J. B. Alexander, Chief of the Division of Timber Mechanics in the federal Department of Mines and Resources, business depressions could be minimized by: (1) "governments, municipalities, and large corporations postponing their construction programs when prosperity is at its zenith and costs are high, and placing such contracts in times of depression when labour is cheap and efficient and material costs are low"; and (2) the practice of thrift by the public during good times so that they might spend more freely when business conditions were unfavourable.[47]

III. THE POLICY IMPLICATIONS OF "SOUND FINANCE"

The preponderance of Canadian opinion, then, adhered unequivocally to the orthodox principles of public finance. The fiscal policies pursued by the federal government during the twenties clearly reflected this sentiment.

The 1919-20 Boom

While total tax revenue increased from $236 million to $294 million during the inflationary period from 1919 to 1920,[48] and virtually all categories of taxes shared in the increase,[49] the heavier yields were due more to rising national income than to upward revision of tax rates. Indeed, there is reason to believe that federal tax policy had inflationary effects.

In 1919 the business profits war tax, which in the previous year had been extended to companies with capital between $25,000 and $50,000, was limited, for these companies, to 25 per cent of profits in excess of 10 per cent; the previous tax-free portion of their profits had been only 7 per cent. Thus, despite the enormous profits amassed during the postwar boom, the yield of the profits tax rose only $11 million in 1920.[50] Against this tax reduction must be set the increased rates on personal and corporate incomes. In 1919 the personal income tax was amended by the levying of steeper, more progressive rates, and all corporations were required to pay 10 per cent of their net incomes in excess of $2,000, as against 6 per cent of net income over $3,000 in the previous year. These increases, however, could hardly be considered burdensome: in 1920 the total income tax yield was only $20 million.[51]

On the expenditure side, the general picture has been accurately summarized as follows:

> The immediate aftermath of war proved more costly for the Canadian government than the war itself. Both outlay and deficit were at their highest levels in fiscal 1920, a period roughly the same as the upswing. Monthly expenditure reached a peak of $60 million ... from March to November 1919, when the most violent boom developed. ... In addition, the composition of expenditures changed once again. War expenditures were down slightly for the fiscal year as a whole, but increased

enormously from April 1919 to January 1920. Public works expenditures, including outlays on railways and canals, were more than double their level for the preceding fiscal year.... These expenditures unquestionably provided an enormous stimulus to expansion.[52]

The Recession of 1920-2

Federal fiscal policy in 1920-2 was well designed to bring about deflation, or, at best, to intensify the downswing. Tax collections swelled from $294 million in 1920 to $369 million in 1921; in 1922 they were still $320 million and the drop had occurred more because of lower incomes than of the few tax-rate reductions made in 1921.[53] Total revenues amounted to $350 million in 1920, $436 million in 1921, and $382 million in 1922.[54]

The changed composition of tax revenue also must have had depressing effects on the Canadian economy. In 1920 all tax and surtax rates on personal incomes of $5,000 or more were raised 5 per cent; by 1921, income taxes had increased from 7 per cent of total taxes (in 1920) to 13 per cent.[55] Of greater significance were the new excise taxes on monetary instruments and so-called "luxuries"[56] and the introduction in May 1920 of a general sales tax of one per cent.[57] The result was a fivefold increase in the yield from this tax source in 1921--equivalent to a shift from 5 per cent to 21 per cent of total tax revenue.[58]

There was, on the other hand, a further reduction in the business profits war tax in 1920, involving exemption for all business firms earning profits amounting to less than 10 per cent of paid-up capital in fiscal 1921; a 7 per cent decline in yield occurred.[59] The business profits tax was abolished in 1921, although progressively smaller revenues continued (with the exception of 1928) to be received until fiscal 1933; the revenue drop between 1921 and 1922 amounted to 44 per cent.[60]

On balance, the Dominion Government's tax policy of 1920-2 probably acted in a deflationary manner:

> Payment during 1921 of [the] higher rate on the relatively large incomes earned in the previous year must certainly have operated as a limiting factor on both consumption and investment. The previous boom having been based partly upon actual or expected increases in consumption, a tax policy which penalized consumption would have serious repercussions. ... A general sales tax tends to raise prices and so to restrict demand. The effects upon investment would be neutral at best, lower profits taxes counterbalancing higher income taxes. In the depression as in the boom, [the tax] policy actually adopted was a far cry from what was necessary to maintain stability.[61]

Federal expenditures were reduced from $786 million in 1920 to $528 million in 1921, and to $464 million in 1922; the deficit was therefore narrowed from $436 million in 1920 to $92 million in 1921, and $81 million in 1922.[62] All items likely to have strong secondary stimulative effects on private investment were sharply reduced in 1921 and 1922: war and demobilization expenditures from $347 million (in 1920) to $17 million to $2 million; railway subsidies from $335 million to zero; expenditures on railways and canals from $30 million to $12 million to $6 million; and expenditures on public works from $48 million to $38 million to $21 million.[63] During the two-year period 1921-2, total capital expenditures fell from $232 million to $60 million; as a result of this 74 per cent decline, capital expenditures amounted to only 13 per cent of total expenditures, as compared with 30 per cent in 1920.[64] Thus, the evidence pointing to the cyclical character of federal spending is clear.[65]

The 1922-5 Recovery

Nor is the Dominion fiscal record for the recovery period 1922-5 much more impressive. Tax collections were relatively stable, rising from $320 million in 1922 to $335 million in 1923 and $342 million in 1924, and falling to $294 million in 1925; total revenue followed a similar course.[66] In 1922 the normal rate of sales tax was increased from 4 per cent to 6 per cent. The tax on checks and bills of exchange was also increased; minor downward revisions were made in the income tax; and both upward and downward changes in excise taxes.[67] The year 1923 gave rise to a series of minor rate reductions in virtually all components of the tax structure.[68] More significant cuts were made in 1924,[69] particularly in terms of: (1) increased income tax exemptions; and (2) a one per cent sales tax reduction on most commodities, a 3 1/2 per cent reduction on certain goods, and complete exemption for still others.[70]

The expenditure-debt trend begun during the depression continued throughout the recovery period. By 1925 federal expenditures had been reduced from the $464 million level in 1922 to $351 million, and the $436 million deficit had become a surplus of $346,000.[71] Again it was particularly the important categories of expenditure, from the point of view of secondary effects, which fluctuated in a cyclical manner, though with an occasional lag. The drop in public works expenditures from $21 million in 1922 to $13 million in 1923 was immediate and pronounced; expenditures on war and demobilization[72] rose from $2 million in 1922 to $4 million in 1923, but declined once more to $446,000 in 1924; expenditures on canals, which were more than doubled between 1922 and 1925, constitute the lone significant exception to the general cyclical trend.[73]

The Period of Prosperity 1925-9

It was not unreasonable that tax collections and total revenues should have undergone only a moderate rise during the early stages of the 1925-9 prosperity period. Indeed, some reduction in federal receipts probably would have been even more appropriate at this time. That such an overall reduction did not occur between 1925 and 1928 was not the result of rate increases--for there were relatively few of these--but, in the main, of a 21 per cent rise in the national income.[74]

In 1925 minor changes, largely in a downward direction, were made in sales and income taxes.[75] The reductions effected in 1926 were more substantial: (1) the exemption limit of the personal income tax was raised from $2,000 to $3,000 for married persons or those with dependents, and from $1,000 to $1,500 for other persons; (2) personal income tax rates were reduced all along the line, those with incomes of $5,000 or less paying only 2 per cent instead of 4 per cent or more of their taxable income; and (3) the rate of taxation on corporate incomes was reduced from 10 to 9 per cent.[76] In 1927 the general rate of the sales tax was reduced from 5 to 4 per cent; the income tax was amended to the extent that each taxpayer had to pay only 90 per cent of the amount due on the same income in the preceding year; and reductions were made in excise taxes and taxes on the media of exchange.

As the expansionary development began to assume boom proportions, there should have been a realization of the urgent need for higher tax rates, or, at the least, for rate stability. Instead, an intensification of the previous downward trend occurred in 1928: (1) the general rate of the sales tax was reduced from 4 to 3 per cent; (2) the personal income tax was further lowered so as to make each taxpayer liable for only 80 per cent of what he would have paid on the same income two years before; and (3) the rate of taxation on corporate incomes was reduced to 8 per cent on incomes in excess of $2,000.[77] By 1929 the income tax had fallen to 15 per cent of total taxes, and the sales and special excise taxes to 21 per cent, compared respectively with 19 and 29 per cent in 1925.[78] The downward tax revision continued on into 1929, the most notable change being the further sales tax reduction from 3 to 2 per cent.

At no time during the 1925-9 period did the annual rise in total Dominion expenditures exceed $20 million.[79] Again, however, it seems reasonable to argue that the mere fact that the direction of change was continually upward--and, consequently, that the highest surplus attained amounted to only 16 per cent of the peak deficit of 1920--must have had inflationary repercussions in the advanced stages of the upswing. More striking is the statistical evidence relating to "public investment."[80] Between 1926 and 1930, direct investment outlays by the Dominion government increased from $46 million to $99 million, while during the 1926-9 period the investment expenditures of federally owned public utilities (chiefly the Canadian National Railways) rose from $120 million to $198 million; direct Dominion investment comprised 28 per cent of total expenditure on current and capital accounts in 1930, as compared with only 16 per cent in 1926.[81] To this near-doubling of such a powerful source of income generation and aggregate demand, there is ground for attributing fundamental causal importance in the Great Depression of the thirties-- or, at least, a role fraught with destabilizing dangers.

Provincial and Municipal Fiscal Policy

Such factual data as are available suggest that the fiscal policies carried out during the twenties by the provincial and municipal governments did not differ markedly from those of the Dominion government. The public investment field affords one important source of corroboration for this conclusion. Between 1926 and 1930, direct investment outlays by provincial governments increased from $49 million to $112 million, a 129 per cent rise, as compared with the 117 per cent rise for the Dominion government; the corresponding change for municipal governments was from $73 million to $111 million, or 53 per cent.[82] There was more than a doubling of investment (from $15 million to $36 million) by provincially owned public utilities, and a 57 per cent increase (from $21 million to $33 million) for public utilities owned by the municipal governments. Finally, direct investment by provincial governments increased from 31 to 43 per cent of total provincial expenditures, while the rise for municipal governments was from 28 to 36 per cent.

Table IV summarizes the course of investment expenditures at all three governmental levels during the boom of the late twenties. In addition to the factors already emphasized, this tabular presentation shows that municipal expenditures for investment purposes were more stable than those of the federal and provincial governments. This relative stability arose, not from any deeper conviction at the municipal level that government should play an active role in offsetting fluctuations in private spending, but largely from the relative stability of municipal revenues throughout the twenties. In other words, it was the overwhelming importance of the "income-inelastic" real property tax in the municipal tax structure--one of the significant institutional accidents of Canadian economic history--which appears to have made municipal spending a somewhat milder destabilizing influence in the first postwar decade.

All things considered, it seems clear that, "in the timing of their fiscal actions, the various Canadian governments tended to aggravate, rather than smooth, the disturbances imposed on the Canadian economy"[83] during the decade of the twenties. Fiscal positions were dictated mainly by the economic conditions ruling from year to year, and fiscal actions limited to what prevailing economic conditions seemed to permit.

It is the fundamental proposition of this chapter that Canadian fiscal evolution could hardly have been otherwise in the kind of economic milieu pervading the Dominion at that time. More concretely, the policy pattern which emerged from the twenties had its roots in a fiscal philosophy which might be described as follows: "Tax as little as possible at all times; tax even less than usual when the budget is balanced or a surplus appears; maintain spending at a minimum, particularly when revenues are low and budget deficits are incurred; accumulate a minimum of debt, and carry out debt retirement whenever funds are available or can be obtained." On the basis of this interpretation, it is submitted that those relatively few deviations from cyclical fiscal policy which did take place are to be explained mainly in terms of public officials reluctantly making temporary modifications in their "sound finance" principles; and in terms of the accidental fact of the appropriateness of these principles during certain phases of the cyclical process.

TABLE IV

New Investment and Maintenance by Governments on Own Account
and Publicly Owned Public Utilities
1926, 1929, 1930

Governments	Direct investment						Investment by publicly owned public utilities					
	1926		1929		1930		1926		1929		1930	
	Value $mm	% 1	Value $mm	% 1	Value $mm	% 1	Value $mm	% 2	Value $mm	% 2	Value $mm	% 2
Dominion	45.5	15.6	79.9	24.7	98.7	27.7	119.7	72.5	197.7	71.2	155.6	61.2
Provincial	49.1	31.4	87.4	38.6	112.2	43.1	15.4	23.9	29.9	25.5	36.3	24.4
Municipal	72.8	28.3	103.5	34.8	111.3	35.5	20.7	22.1	32.0	23.6	32.6	22.7
TOTAL[3]	167.4	22.8	270.8	30.7	322.2	33.0	155.8	48.2	259.6	48.9	224.5	41.1

[1]Per cent for each level of government is expressed in terms of total government expenditure (excluding public utilities) at that level.

[2]Per cent for each level of government is expressed in terms of total investment expenditure of all government departments and publicly owned public utilities at that level.

[3]Per cent for all governments is expressed in terms of total expenditure of all governments (excluding public utilities).

Source: Department of Trade and Commerce, Private and Public Investment in Canada, 1926–1951 (Ottawa, 1951), pp. 147, 166, 167, 187, 190, 198.

PART II

THE BACKGROUND OF THE GREAT DEPRESSION

CHAPTER V

CANADA IN THE WORLD ECONOMY

WHILE THE CIRCUMSTANCES of the decade of the twenties were favourable to Canadian expansion, they also increased the vulnerability of the economy.[1] Primarily responsible for the rising standard of living was a heavy reliance on narrow specialization geared to a maximum of international trade.

I. THE SOURCES OF CANADIAN INSTABILITY

The major sources of instability were threefold. First, there was the fact that the chief Canadian product, wheat, in addition to being subject to the incalculable vagaries of nature, was subject also, along with most of the other Canadian export staples, to a relatively inelastic demand; that is to say, a substantial increase in the supply of these staples, unaccompanied by any increase in world requirements, was apt to bring about a drastic fall in price, which, however, was not likely to increase consumption to any appreciable extent.[2] Secondly, there was the high degree of rigidity of Canadian natural resources: "Large parts of Canada are amazingly endowed for the production of some one thing, but one thing only. Over a great part of the West, it is "wheat or nothing." In large areas of the northern parts of Central Canada, it is "pulp and paper or nothing," or "copper or nothing." And so it goes on. Vast areas of Canada, which under a happy conjunction of economic events are great sources of wealth, have simply no alternative economic activity."[3] In the third place, a large part of the capital invested in Canadian business and in government securities during the twenties was directly concerned with increasing the capacity and efficiency of the export industries; and one-half of this capital in 1930 took the form of bonded debt, of which about two-fifths was held abroad.[4] In other words, the inherent instability of the capital goods industries was particularly acute in Canada, where the substantial fixed-interest foreign claims on the national income could be met only by a sustained heavy flow of exports of goods and services the prices of which would determine the weight of the burden.[5]

But the Canadian economy was plagued with other structural rigidities at that time. Many of its manufacturing industries were seriously lacking in real flexibility of internal organization. This was largely the consequence of the marked trend towards concentration in the large-scale industries, in which a small group of corporations frequently controlled from 75 to 95 per cent of the total output.[6] Moreover, the typical large manufacturing company maintained an expensive coast-to-coast selling and distributing organization, with its resultant overhead costs and internal or managerial rigidity. The price-fixing arrangements frequently entered into by Canadian manufacturers added a further element of rigidity to the price structure for manufactured goods, and for many imported goods.[7]

Again, with the exception of certain naturally sheltered branches, and that portion engaged in the processing of export staples, the Canadian manufacturing industry grew up behind a protective tariff. In this sector of the economy, therefore, prices would be, and were, adjusted to costs; whereas the exporters were obliged to make the opposite kind of adjustment, that of costs to the prices which they could get on the world markets. And since the prices of the protected industries partly determine the costs of the exporters, the latter were clearly in an unenviable position.

The federal budgetary structure also helped to rigidify the Canadian economy. Although federal expenditures during the twenties were consistently maintained at far higher levels than those of prewar years, by 1929 they amounted to only about 20 per cent of gross private investment;[8] and the latter had expanded so rapidly that it was almost 26 per cent of gross national product.[9] This meant that, at the very time when the "investment" source of instability could no longer be discounted by comparison with external trade, off-setting changes in federal spending could not be effective unless, on a relative basis, they greatly exceeded the fluctuations in private investment. Even assuming governmental readiness to make the necessary changes, their realization would, therefore, have been difficult enough with a highly flexible structure of federal expenditure. But there was no such flexibility in 1929. Rigid outlays like interest charges on the national debt, war pensions, and routine government expenditures, were predominant; while direct public investment comprised only one-fourth of total federal spending.[10] Thus, there were serious practical limitations on the Dominion government's scope for action in this field.

The federal tax picture gave less cause for concern. The major instruments of tax control over aggregate demand--personal and corporate income taxation and sales taxation--had been incorporated into the revenue structure during and immediately after the First World War. Between the fiscal years 1919 and 1929, they increased respectively, from about $9 million and $12 million to $59 million and $83 million.[11] In 1929 their combined total amounted to approximately 36 per cent of all federal tax revenue, as compared with 9 per cent in 1919.[12] Consequently, an alert and willing Government would have had more "tax" than "spending" leeway in pursuing a policy of compensatory fiscal variation. But even by 1929, income and sales taxation had not yet matched customs and excise duties in importance, the latter comprising 63 per cent of total tax revenue; while total tax revenue, in turn, amounted to only 25 per cent of gross private investment.[13] There is, furthermore, the vital problem of time lags--extreme in, but not unique to, the case of expenditure policy--between the need for fiscal action and public recognition of this need, between fiscal planning and fiscal action, and between the use of fiscal techniques and their reflection in economic change.

Still other rigidities stemmed from the following set of considerations;

(1) considerable immobility of labour existed in Canada, though the obstacles to mobility were not fundamentally economic or psychological in nature--as in advanced industrial countries like Great Britain--but were, instead, obstacles of geography, race, and language; (2) heavy "social overhead costs" were necessarily incurred in building a nation in Canada-- a country which, by virtue of its great length, little depth, and extremes of climate, demanded a quantity and quality of capital works in transportation that were fully utilized for only a small part of each year; (3) in a country of huge territorial expanse and main centres of population separated by hundreds of miles of uninhabited land, highly rigid transportation costs naturally bulked large in the calculations of all producers.

II. THE TRIANGULAR INTERNATIONAL PATTERN OF CANADIAN TRADE AND FINANCE

An important distinction should be drawn between two major policy determinants--what may be called the "objective economic environment, " and the "subjective responses" of men's minds to this environment. The internal institutional aspects of the former have already been outlined. The Dominion's international economic position, vaguely but none the less widely perceived by Canadians, was the other "objective" factor which provided a unifying thread for the whole body of thought and policy evolving in the thirties. General reference has been made to the international economic orientation and vulnerability of Canada. It remains to analyse this problem in more precise quantitative terms.

One of the remarkable facts of the twenties is the status which Canada attained in international trade. By 1929 the Dominion had become the fifth-ranking trading nation, with a merchandise trade amounting to 3. 7 per cent of the world total.[14] In the same year, Canadian exports of goods and services represented approximately 26 per cent of gross national product, this proportion having fluctuated between 26 and 31 per cent during the 1926-9 period.[15]

But the Canadian position assumes significance only when considered in relation to that of the United States and of the United Kingdom, the leading and second most important trading nations, respectively, at that time.[16] It was during the twenties that this triangular economic relationship became clearly defined.

Relative National Roles in the Triangular Pattern

The first point to be noted in this connection is that Canada's commodity trade with the United States and the United Kingdom was far more important to Canada than to either of the latter two countries. Thus, in each of the three years 1926-8, only 5 per cent of all United Kingdom imports came from Canada, and in 1929 only 4 per cent; for exports from the United Kingdom to Canada, the proportions were 4 per cent in 1926 and 1927, and 5 per cent in 1928 and 1929.[17] American dependence on Canadian sources of supply and demand was considerably greater during this

TABLE V

Canadian Commodity Trade, 1926-9[1]

(millions of dollars)

Item	Year			
	1926	1927	1928	1929
Total exports	1,272	1,215	1,341	1,178
Exports to United Kingdom	315	271	288	224
Per cent of total	25	22	21	19
Exports to United States	476	489	507	519
Per cent of total	37	40	38	44
Total imports	973	1,057	1,209	1,272
Imports from United Kingdom	148	171	194	188
Per cent of total	15	16	16	15
Imports from United States	652	690	810	875
Per cent of total	67	65	67	69

[1]Excluding gold.
Source: D. B. S., The Canadian Balance of International Payments, 1926-1945, pp. 48-50.

four-year pre-depression period, the import ratio varying between 11 and 12 per cent, and the export ratio between 15 and 18 per cent.[18]

Table V reveals the sharp contrast between these sets of figures and the corresponding ratios for Canadian external trade. The United Kingdom and the United States combined took an average of about 62 per cent of all Canadian goods exported annually, while the average annual proportion of Canadian imports coming from both countries was no less than 82 per cent.[19] In the case of both exports and imports, the United States played the predominant role. In 1929, for example, Canadian exports to, and imports from, the United States were valued, respectively, at more than twice, and more than four times, Canadian exports to, and imports from, the United Kingdom. Nor are the ratios appreciably different for total Canadian transactions on current account (excluding gold movements), as can be seen in Table VI, the greater inclusiveness of which derives largely

TABLE VI

Canadian Transactions on Current Account, 1926-9[1]

(millions of dollars)

Item	Year			
	1926	1927	1928	1929
Total current credits	1,635	1,601	1,748	1,609
Credits with United Kingdom	352	305	323	256
Per cent of total	22	19	18	16
Credits with United States	757	789	827	862
Per cent of total	46	49	47	54
Total current debits	1,538	1,643	1,820	1,957
Debits with United Kingdom	294	324	344	355
Per cent of total	19	20	19	18
Debits with United States	1,018	1,069	1,216	1,336
Per cent of total	66	65	67	68

[1]Excluding gold.

Source: D. B. S., The Canadian Balance of International Payments, 1926-1945, pp. 48-50.

from two items, one (the tourist trade) highly volatile and income-elastic, and the other (interest and dividends) relatively stable and an important source of rigidity and cycle-sensitivity in the Canadian economy.[20]

Commodity Distribution of Canadian Trade

The second important observation relates to the actual distribution, by commodities, of Canadian trade with the other two "sides" of the "economic triangle" during the four-year period preceding the Great Depression. The patterns of distribution, which would, of course, determine the severity and direction of Canadian effects consequent upon any dislocation in international trade are illustrated in Tables VII and VIII.

In both the export and import fields of trade between Canada and the United Kingdom, particularly the former, one finds a heavy concentration on a relatively small group of commodities. More concretely, Canada's

TABLE VII

Principal Canadian Commodity Exports to United Kingdom and
United States as Percentage of Total Exports to These Countries[1]
Fiscal Years 1926-9

Items	United Kingdom				United States			
	1926	1927	1928	1929	1926	1927	1928	1929
Barley	4	4	4	4	(.001)	(.005)	(.002)	(.006)
Wheat	53	56	60	60	3	2	2	4
Milled products	4	6	5	4	1	(.4)	1	1
Whiskey	(.01)	(.03)	(.03)	(.02)	3	3	4	4
Cattle	2	1	(.03)	(.01)	1	1	3	3
Fishery products	1	1	1	1	3	3	3	3
Furs	1	2	2	2	2	3	3	3
Hides and skins	(.01)	(.01)	0	(.003)	1	2	2	2
Meats	6	5	3	2	1	2	2	2
Milk and its products	8	6	5	6	2	3	2	2
Wood and wood products	3	3	3	3	29	29	25	22
Newsprint	(.2)	(.2)	1	2	20	23	25	25
Iron and its products	2	2	2	2	2	2	2	2
Non-ferrous metals	3	3	4	4	12	8	9	13
Non-metallic minerals	(.2)	(.4)	(.5)	(.5)	4	4	3	4
Chemicals and allied products	1	1	1	1	1	2	2	2
Other products	12	9	8	8	15	13	12	10
Total	100.	100.	100.	100.	100.	100.	100.	100.

(1) Excluding gold.
Source: Rounded percentages calculated on the basis of figures in C.Y.B., 1930, pp. 494-513.

TABLE VIII

Principal Canadian Commodity Imports from United Kingdom and
United States as Percentage of Total Imports from These Countries(1)
Fiscal Years 1926-9

Items	United Kingdom				United States			
	1926	1927	1928	1929	1926	1927	1928	1929
Agricultural and vegetable food products(2)	5	6	5	5	8	8	8	7
Whiskey	13	15	20	21	(.002)	(.001)	(.001)	(.001)
Rubber	1	(.4)	(.4)	(.4)	5	4	3	2
Animals and animal products	4	3	3	3	5	5	6	5
Cotton	10	9	8	7	7	5	6	5
Flex, hemp, and jute	4	4	4	4	1	(.4)	(.4)	(.2)
Wool	22	24	20	21	1	(.4)	(.4)	(.5)
Mixed textiles	4	4	4	4	1	1	1	1
Wood, wood products, and paper	2	2	2	3	6	6	6	6
Rolling mill products	5	2	3	4	5	6	5	6
Engines and boilers	(.4)	(.5)	1	1	2	2	2	2
Farm implements and machinery	(.1)	(.1)	(.1)	(.1)	2	3	4	5
Non-agricultural machinery	2	2	3	2	4	5	6	6
Automobiles and parts	(.2)	(.3)	(.3)	(.2)	6	8	9	11
Non-ferrous metals	3	4	3	4	6	6	7	7
Coal and coal products	4	1	4	2	9	10	8	7
Petroleum, asphalt, and products	(.03)	(.1)	(.2)	(.2)	6	7	6	6
Chemicals and allied products	2	3	2	3	3	3	3	3
Other products	18	20	17	15	23	20	19	20
Total	100.	100.	100.	100.	100.	100.	100.	100.

(1) Excluding gold.
(2) Includes minor non-food items, and chiefly fruits, grains, and sugar.
Source: Rounded percentages calculated on the basis of figures in C.Y.B., 1930, pp. 514-45.

annual sale of wheat to the United Kingdom constituted, on the average, about 57 per cent of total Canadian exports to that country; the corresponding ratio for all important food exports--wheat, barley, milled products, cattle, fishery products, meat, and milk and its products--was 78 per cent. On the import side, wool alone varied between 20 and 24 per cent of all imports from the United Kingdom, and whiskey between 13 and 21 per cent; the average annual ratio for all fibres and textiles (including wool, cotton, silk, mixed textiles, flax, hemp, jute, etc.) was 42 per cent.[21]

With respect to the United States, there was a similar concentration-- though centred around a different group of commodities--in the export trades, together with a striking diffusion and heterogeneity in the import trades. The highest single-commodity concentration for such Canadian exports was that of newsprint, which rose from 20 per cent in 1926 to 25 per cent in 1929. For all wood, wood products, and paper, the average annual ratio was 50 per cent,[22] and for these wood products and the non-ferrous metals together, 60 per cent. The statistical picture of Canada's imports from the United States completes the justification for the contention that, while Canadians exported a great deal of a few things, they imported almost everything. At no time between 1926 and 1929 did any single commodity import from the United States exceed 11 per cent of the total of such imports. This was the proportion attained by automobiles and automobile parts in 1929; it was approached only by (1) coal and coal products, (2) non-ferrous metals, and (3) petroleum, asphalt, and their products. The only concentration of any significance is obtained when American goods are subsumed under some such broad collective category as that of basic sources of mechanical energy (coal and oil), capital goods, and durable consumers' goods (mainly automobiles); this type of classification yields an average annual ratio of upwards of 40 per cent.

Impact of Capital Movements into Canada
        There was, in the third place, Canada's large-scale dependence upon capital inflows from the United Kingdom and the United States as a supplement to domestic savings. This was not a new process. It had been occurring at intervals for at least forty years prior to the outbreak of World War I. Thus, the years from 1900 to 1913 had been a period of enormous growth in Canada. It is clear that neither the physical resources nor the productive capacity of the Dominion itself could have met the demand for expansion. The consequence was that no other country in the world had absorbed external capital as rapidly as Canada.[23]

        The decade of the twenties was also a period of notable externally financed capital expansion, though the pace was less rapid and the investment less concentrated in the Western plains. The distinctive features of this second stage of development was the increasing importance of capital imports from the United States. From a marked secondary position, with an investment in Canada that was less than $1 billion in 1914, the United States had surpassed the British investment of $2.8 billion in 1929 by about $1.2 billion.[24]

TABLE IX

Canadian Transactions on Capital Account and
External Capital Invested in Canada, 1927-9

(millions of dollars)

	Year		
Item	1927	1928	1929
Total capital imports	365	326	434
Per cent from United Kingdom	16	11	8
Per cent from United States	82	84	91
Total capital exports	369	408	266
Per cent to United Kingdom	20	19	19
Per cent to United States	63	67	79
Total external capital invested	6,184	6,499	6,836
Per cent by United Kingdom	42	41	40
Per cent by United States	55	56	57

Source: D. B. S., The Canadian Balance of International Payments,
pp. 174-6, 218-22.

Table IX sets out the triangular pattern with regard to annual capital
inflows and outflows, as well as total external capital invested in the Dominion, in the 1927-9 period. It can be seen that the annual net import or
export of capital was not large. The explanation is quite simple. At the
same time that Canadians were floating hundreds of millions in securities
in other countries, they themselves were investing substantial sums
abroad, and were participating in the speculative boom which had engulfed
the New York stock market. Gross capital inflows, however--particularly
those from the United States, which in 1929 comprised 91 per cent of the
total from all countries--were of the utmost importance, in terms of their
contribution to Canadian development. The ownership of all external capital invested in Canada, as of December 31, 1929, was more evenly divided
between Great Britain and the United States, the former's share amounting
to 40 per cent, and that of the latter to 57 per cent.

Recognition must be accorded the powerful stimulative influence exerted by this external capital investment on the Canadian economy. Indeed,
as already noted, such investment was the only practical instrument for
the achievement of the spectacular industrial growth actually experienced
by the Dominion. But this process was not costless; it had serious potentialities for intensification of industrial fluctuations in Canada. With so

TABLE X

Canadian Balance of International Payments, Net Balances of Transactions
All Countries, the United Kingdom, and the United States, 1927-9
(millions of dollars; net receipts or credits, +; net payments or debits, −)

Items	1927 All countries	1927 U.K.	1927 U.S.	1928 All countries	1928 U.K.	1928 U.S.	1929 All countries	1929 U.K.	1929 U.S.
Current account									
1. Merchandise	+158	+100	−201	+132	+94	−303	−94	+36	−356
2. Non-monetary gold[1]	+32	−	+32	+40	−	+40	+37	−	+37
3. Tourist trade	+63	−10	+76	+79	−10	+91	+90	−11	+103
4. Interest and dividends	−216	−99	−135	−229	−98	−149	−261	−111	−172
5. Freight and shipping	−12	−1	−15	−20	+1	−24	−38	−4	−35
6. Miscellaneous	−35	−9	−5	−34	−8	−4	−45	−9	−14
7. Balance on current account	−10	−19	−248	−32	−21	−349	−311	−99	−437
Long-term capital account									
8. New issues and retirements of Canadian securities	+141	−16	+156	+7	−43	+50	+147	−15	+163
9. Other security transactions	−184	−5	−118	−188	−5	−124	−105	−3	−97
10. Other capital movements	+23	+6	+11	+12	−1	+15	+39	+4	+34
11. Balance on long-term capital account	−20	−15	+49	−169	−49	−59	+81	−14	+100
12. Balance on current and long-term capital account	−30	−34	−199	−201	−70	−408	−230	−113	−337
Balancing items[2]									
13. Canadian bank assets abroad	+16	−1	+16	+87	+9	+63	+88	+3	+92
14. Monetary gold[3]	−7	−	−7	+49	−	+49	+37	−	+37
15. Total	+9	−1	+9	+136	+9	+112	+125	+3	+129
16. Residual item[4]	+21			+65			+105		

Source: D. B. S., The Canadian Balance of International Payments, pp. 240-2; and D. B. S., The Canadian Balance of International Payments, 1926-1945 (Ottawa, 1947), pp. 48-50.

TABLE X (Continued)

(1) Before 1949 the practice of the Dominion Bureau of Statistics was to omit exports of non-monetary gold to the United Kingdom, and to countries other than the United States, from the total current credits with those countries; that is, to include all exports of non-monetary gold in the current account with the United States. The main reason given for this procedure was that the United States traditionally had been the principal market for the world's gold production; and that a current account with other countries which excluded such gold exports to those countries as did arise through temporary market conditions would, therefore, be more representative of normal commercial trade between them and Canada than an account which included that item. In any event, for the period summarized statistically in Table X, this problem does not arise, since all Canadian exports of non-monetary gold went to the United States.

But for the D.B.S. technique, since 1949, of excluding nearly all gold movements from the commodity account, see: D.B.S., The Canadian Balance of International Payments, 1926-1948 (Ottawa, 1949); D.B.S., The Canadian Balance of International Payments in the Post War Years, 1946-1952 (Ottawa, 1953); and P. Hartland "The Treatment of Gold in the Canadian Balance of International Payments," C.J.E.P.S., XXI (Feb. 1955).

(2) The above classification of "balancing items" is made by Professor Knox (Dominion Monetary Policy), but not by the Dominion Bureau of Statistics--apparently, in the latter case, on the ground that "the distinction between long and short-term capital transactions is not always clear-cut" (D.B.S. The Canadian Balance of International Payments, p. 108). It appears to the writer that, while this is undoubtedly true, the "balancing items" classification has conceptual usefulness; as well as being operationally helpful in terms of the role played by long-term capital inflows in Canadian economic development, and of the destabilizing aspects of short-term capital movements. It is assumed here, then, that short-term capital movements and monetary gold provide a measure of the balancing factor in the payments mechanism. This assumption is valid only when these capital movements occur in the same direction as the gold movements; that is, in opposition to the balance on current and long-term capital account as against all countries. Otherwise--as was the case during the thirties for both Canada and the United States, particularly the latter--the short-term capital movements are "autonomous" and "disequilibrating"; and, by partially, completely, or more than offsetting the monetary-gold item, they understate or distort the balancing factor. Of course, to the extent that the disequilibrating short-term money flows are effected through gold transfers--American experience during the early thirties may be cited--the latter also act to aggravate, rather than to ameliorate, balance-of-payments difficulties. (Cf. chapter IX; also, United States, Department of Commerce, The United States in the World Economy, Washington, 1943, Table II.)

(3) Statistics on the Canadian balance of international payments do not classify by countries the movement of monetary gold into and out of Canada. In the above Table, all such gold flows are placed in the "United States" category, on the assumption that, in terms of the great excess of Canadian-American deficits on current and long-term capital account over Canadian-United Kingdom deficits, the bulk, if not all, of these gold flows occurred between Canada and the United States.

(4) This is the amount required to balance the whole account because of errors and omissions.

large a proportion of Canadian capital imports taking the form of fixed-
interest-bearing loans with rigid amortization provisions, the result of
a depression abroad might well be, not only a contraction in Canadian export markets, but also the virtual cessation of foreign capital inflows in
conjunction with the obligation to meet unchanged money charges in foreign
currencies on account of debt service. This vulnerability was rendered
all the more acute by Canada's increasingly marked movement out of the
British, and into the American, trade and financial orbit--a movement
away from a country which apparently was becoming less cycle-sensitive,
and towards a country which was highly susceptible to cyclical disturbance.

The Pattern of Payments
     The three-year Canadian balance-of-payments position summarized
in Table X is, in a sense, the statistical expression of the observations
made thus far in relation to the triangular nature of Canada's foreign
trade. In reality, however, it is more than that, for it illustrates the
final major point to be made in connection with Canada's position in the
world economy: the triangularity of the Canadian payments mechanism.
     Actually, it had not yet become customary for Canada to settle large
current account deficits with the United States out of large surpluses with
Britain and Western Europe. The deficiency in Canadian transactions
with the United States was substantial, reaching $437 million in 1929;
but it was not until the thirties--and even then not to any great extent--
that the Dominion developed any surplus in its transactions with the United
Kingdom.
     In the late twenties, while Canada's commodity trade with the latter
showed a surplus, Canadians made substantial payments for interest and
dividends on British investments, and for the use of British shipping,
with the result that the current balance ran consistently in favour of Britain. Canadian "transactions with the rest of the world, particularly con-
tinental Europe and to a lesser degree the British Dominions and colonies,
did, however, result in a substantial surplus. It averaged some $280 mil-
lion in the late twenties and was the main offset to the trading deficit with
the United States."[25] The pattern of payments, then, was a triangular
one, with Britain playing a minor role in the triangle; and with a trading
system characterized by advanced development along multilateral lines,
and by maximum convertibility of currencies.[26]
     The delicate nature of this framework of international payments, and
the dangers of its weakening or breaking down are immediately apparent.
Two considerations are involved: first, the possibility of complete collapse of the multilateral, convertible currency system, bringing with it
the gravest long-run problems of readjustment in Canada's entire trading
position; and second, the possibility of foreign-exchange instability,
with the consequent intensification of those Canadian "payments" difficulties precipitated by economic contraction in the United States. The latter
possibility became one of the grim realities of the Great Depression,
while the former emerged from World War II as one of the basic economic
problems facing Canada.

CHAPTER VI

CHANGING CANADIAN VIEWS ON "STABILITY" PROBLEMS

IT HAS BEEN DEMONSTRATED that at the end of the twenties "Canada had attained a high level of prosperity, but the increased specialization, the great dependence upon raw material exports, large overheads, stubborn rigidities, and a relatively high per capita income greatly enhanced her vulnerability to economic fluctuations."[1] In those circumstances, and in an environment characterized by non-receptiveness to bold remedial action by government, the great economic collapse of the early thirties was bound to have the most severe repercussions on all phases of Canadian activity.[2] Attention is now turned to this environmental setting. Some preliminary recognition of developments in the realm of federal politics is warranted, however, since so much of the economic thought and policy then evolving had its basis in the political stirrings uniquely associated with the Great Depression.[3]

I. CANADA'S CHANGING POLITICAL STRUCTURE

Canada entered the decade of the thirties with the two-party system of federal politics still intact. The view of most political writers had been that the party system, particularly under cabinet government, would find the best conditions for its operation where there were only two parties, or, at least, two parties sufficiently large to provide, as a rule, a clear majority in the legislature; that such a system ensured firm executive leadership, stable legislative action, and the predominance of long-run, semi-permanent policies over short-term considerations; that additional parties might come into being from time to time and provide a desirable freshness of approach, but, in the long run, the best interests of government would be served by their absorption by the major parties, or, as an alternative, the absorption of one of the major parties by a newcomer.[4] But whatever the theoretical justification of the two-party system, the Canadian people had clearly endorsed it at the polls until the end of the First World War. The previous role of the minor parties had been the limited--though by no means insignificant--one of formulating issues before the major parties were ready to take them up, agitating and educating, presenting new points of view, and leaving to the major parties the great responsibility of adjusting conflicts and working out national policy.

The Rise and Decline of the Progressive Movement

In 1919, however, the Progressive movement had sent sixty-five members to the House of Commons, and had seemed likely for a time to become the second party of Canada (displacing the Conservatives), without even undergoing the "third party" phase of development. But the Progressives had never been able to decide definitely whether they were a party or not--that is, whether they were prepared to assume the responsibilities of public office, or wished to remain only a populist movement of protest. They had never succeeded in becoming national in the sense of drawing support from all geographical sections of the Dominion. Moreover, if a new movement was to challenge the Liberal-Conservative monopoly and produce a new alignment in federal politics, it would have required as its base a degree of organization in agriculture and labour which did not yet exist in Canada. Lacking internal cohesion and breadth of purpose, the Progressives had fallen easy prey to the unremitting efforts of the Liberals to absorb them, both by direct attack and by infiltration. By 1930, with only twenty Progressive and Labour members left in the House, Canadian politics had apparently resumed its old prewar status.[5]

But this impression was more apparent than real. Notwithstanding their temporary appearance on the political stage, the Progressives had unquestionably sown the seeds of strong discontent with the prevailing political machinery, and of a general approach to economic problems which not only was radical and new but probably came closer than any other to appreciating and utilizing the analytical techniques gradually being developed by professional economists. The Progressive movement was, in fact, the foundation upon which was built the deep "depression" penetration of the classical two-party system in the thirties.

C. C. F. Origins

In the summer of 1932, there was formed the first national Canadian party to take the social question for its programme. Some of the radical elements of the Progressive movement joined with the urban labour organizations of the West to found the Co-operative Commonwealth Federation (C. C. F.), headed by Mr. J. S. Woodsworth.[6] From the very beginning, too, the C. C. F. had gathered up support from eastern labour (though failing to secure the adherence of organized labour as a whole), from the small Canadian group of doctrinaire Socialists and from many intellectuals rapidly becoming dissatisfied with the orthodox conceptions of society.[7]

The general purpose of the new party was stated in the original platform adopted at its first national convention in 1933:

> We aim to replace the present capitalist system, with its inherent injustice and inhumanity, by a social order from which the domination and exploitation of one class by another will be eliminated, in which economic planning will supercede unregulated private enterprise and competition, and in which genuine democratic self-government, based upon economic equality, will be possible .... This social and economic transformation can be brought about by political action, through the election of a government inspired by the ideal of a Co-operative Commonwealth and supported by a majority of the people.[8]

More explicitly, among the C. C. F. proposals for a "planned economic system" were: (1) the setting up of a National Planning Commission; (2) the socialization of all financial institutions, transportation, communications, and public utilities; (3) the restoration by government of prosperity in agriculture; (4) the regulation of foreign trade in accordance' with the "National Plan"; (5) the formulation of a national labour code guaranteeing freedom of association, state regulation of wages, and the right to work or to maintenance through stabilization of employment and unemployment insurance; (6) comprehensive social insurance against sickness, death, industrial accidents, and old age, and limitation of hours of work and protection of health and safety in industry; (7) socialized health services; (8) broad extension of graduated income, corporation, and inheritance taxes, and "the cessation of the debt-creating system of Public Finance"; (9) depression relief through an extensive programme of federal public spending financed by "the issuance of credit based on the national wealth"; and (10) the amendment of the British North America Act so as to give the federal government adequate powers to deal effectively with economic problems essentially national in scope.[9]

The seven-member C. C. F. group elected to the House of Commons in 1935 made a parliamentary contribution which was quite disproportionate to both the party's vote and its popular influence, even at that early stage in the movement's growth. It would be difficult to refute the observation of Mr. D. Lewis, then National Secretary of the C. C. F., to the effect that this little group surpassed all others in the House: "This is true not only of their intelligence and debating ability but also of their alertness and industry. Every question discussed is carefully followed by some, at least, of the C. C. F. members, and no opportunity of voicing the demands of workers and farmers alike is let slip."[10]

The Abortive Reconstruction Party Revolt

Socialistic groups of the C. C. F. and other varieties coalesced with Canada's increased industrialization.[11] But it should not be overlooked that Canada was still predominantly a land of farmers and small townsmen; and that, as such, it would inevitably breed protest movements designed to curb the steadily increasing powers of "big business." One such outburst was the 1935 rebellion against the Conservative party, headed by Mr. H. H. Stevens, erstwhile Minister of Trade and Commerce in the Bennett Administration, and Chairman of the Royal Commission on Price Spreads.[12]

The immediate cause of the Conservative split was Mr. Stevens' growing sense of dissatisfaction and frustration over the Government's ineptitude in combating the glaring imperfections discovered in the Canadian competitive structure by the Price Spreads Commission.[13] The new Reconstruction party founded by Mr. Stevens made a strong appeal to the small retailers and manufacturers of the towns and cities caught in the deflationary process and anxious to maintain their position in the face of deep "big-business" inroads. But the Reconstruction candidates everywhere failed of election, and Mr. Stevens became a party of one--until he quietly found his way back to the Conservative fold.

The Stevens movement was, nevertheless, something more than a passing political fad. It stirred up considerable popular feeling, and provided further clear indication of the fact that the traditional approach of the major parties to basic economic issues would have to be drastically modified if those parties were to retain their hold on the Canadian electorate.

Social Credit Beginnings

More important was the Social Credit upheaval that came out of Alberta as a result of the Great Depression and spilled over into the federal arena:

> Alberta has been Canada's "last frontier," a stronghold of sturdy agrarianism. It contains a large population of American immigrants from states such as Nebraska which as semi-frontier communities had provided support for William Jennings Bryan in his free-silver campaigns of 1896 and 1900; these men and their children have been ultra-susceptible to cheap-money doctrines, as have all frontier communities throughout the history of the continent. They had formed the most vigorous contingent of the Progressive party and the fighting nucleus of the United Farmers of Alberta, who had governed that province from 1920 to 1936. But the United Farmers had crystallized in office, they had no more novelties left to offer a population that was determined to "try anything once," and so they could not weather the hard times. In the elections of 1935, their representation in Parliament fell before a campaign based on as fantastic a program as had ever appeared in Canadian public life. [14]

The fact is, nevertheless, that, for the untrained economic mind, the main Douglas-Aberhart concepts--deficient purchasing power, "monetizing the national credit," and the "national dividend"--had enough plausibility to arouse strong popular sentiment in their favour. The surprising thing, therefore, is not so much that the new gospel made so many converts as that it failed to emerge from its local habitat. [15]

Liberal-Conservative Dominance

The Liberal and Conservative parties which dominated the political field in 1930 cannot be differentiated by consistent divergence of political principles; that is to say, it is virtually impossible to examine the course pursued by either party, and from that to deduce any one philosophy or set of ideas which had been steadily espoused throughout the years. [16] Not only did the two parties have in common a deep-rooted faith in private enterprise and the liberty of the individual, but both also displayed a totally empirical approach to economic and social problems--this approach, in the past, having manifested itself repeatedly in a strange readiness, on the part of each group, to support or carry out ideas which the other had sanctioned at some other time, or even at the same time. Nevertheless, the contention frequently made by radical thinkers--that the major parties were so completely similar as to make political rivalry meaningless--is an exaggerated one:

> The truth which lies buried in [the] confusing record is that although there [was] no rigid consistency to be found in either party's performance, certain broad tendencies and attitudes can be traced as fairly indicative of each party's general position. It may, for example, be asserted with some confidence that the Liberals [desired] a lower tariff than the Conservatives; that they [were] more inclined to favour the primary producers, especially in Western Canada; that they [were] more nationalistic and less Imperialistic; that they [were] generally more tolerant of sectional or racial differences. In short, Liberals and Conservatives [approached] a new or old problem not with a predetermined philosophy behind them, but with a certain leaning or bias which, however, each [was] prepared to modify--and sometimes to modify substantially--should the circumstances seem to warrant it. [17]

II. CANADIAN GENERAL ATTITUDES TOWARDS GOVERNMENT AND THE ECONOMY

This general party alignment symbolized, in part, the continuation of the "East-West division" which had prevailed during the twenties. But, with the newly enforced focussing of attention on broader social and economic questions, there gradually appeared an increasing amount of economic sense and balanced judgment, not unmixed with a recognition of the "political facts of life." The result was a further blurring of the East-West dividing line, and the beginnings of a process of intellectual "give-and-take" which reached its full fruition during and after the Second World War.

And yet, for the most part, the people of Canada were no better prepared, psychologically or intellectually, to cope with the Great Depression which struck in the latter part of 1929 than they had been at the time of the first postwar deflation. There was, indeed, the same negative approach to the economic role of government, the same feeling of generous optimism, the same contempt for the advice of professional economists, and much of the superficiality of views relating specifically to the causes of unemployment.

The Scope of Governmental Economic Activity

In the course of a parliamentary address made soon after the downswing began, the Prime Minister, Mr. Mackenzie King, gave expression to what was doubtless the prevailing inclination to underestimate the gravity of the "unemployment" problem.[18] He could see nothing arising out of the recognition of unemployment as a national problem which obliged the federal government--in terms of the Canadian constitution and the division of powers there set out--"to collect taxes from the people generally in order to meet a situation which affects only a certain group of people in some municipalities in this country, but which does not adversely affect the country as a whole."[19] Mr. King's general reasoning was, in fact, such as to suggest that even the recognition of employment as a national problem was a principle which he was coming to accept slowly, and then only with the greatest reluctance.[20]

However, within the relatively small groups comprising the professional economists and political scientists, and the radical politicians, there was a growing awareness of the potentialities of economic planning by government in an economy subject to violent business fluctuations.[21] Both groups were agreed that the essence of the case for planning lay in the recurring breakdowns of the capitalist system; differences arose chiefly over the question as to whether or not such planning could and should be carried on within the existing political framework.

In 1931 Dr. O. D. Skelton gave a lucid exposition of what may be termed the intellectually advanced, pro-capitalist Canadian view regarding the role of government in the economy.[22] The state could play its part adequately only if it confined its efforts to the limited field where private initiative was weakest. The tasks which governments could and should undertake in this sphere were wide enough and growing wider:

> They have their part to do in finding and providing, for their own and the public use, information as to the facts of production and marketing, the trends of home and foreign trade. They can seek to advance industrial peace and industrial justice. They can counteract the swing of private industry; theoretically a simple task, politically difficult, for it is as hard to restrain the demands on a full treasury as to embark on greater construction programs on an empty one; but it is not insoluble; whether by preparing reserves in good times or by courageous borrowing in bad ones, it can be done.... To fill the gaps in work that will still remain by some form of contributory insurance, ... is a task full of difficulties and dangers, but a task with which all progressive governments must grapple. Governments, again, ... must recognize that the present currency and credit mechanism is out of gear, that sudden changes in the price level are a material factor in our present discontents, and that unremitting study, nationally and internationally, must be given to this most difficult but most essential [governmental responsibility]. And finally, governments ... must strive for world peace and world co-operation.[23]

In a similar vein, Professor Alexander Brady of the University of

Toronto[24] argued that the belief of the eighteenth- and nineteenth-century thinkers in the providential guidance of natural law was outworn;   that little further reliance could be placed on the "invisible hand" extolled by Adam Smith as the guarantor of economic prosperity.   "We are inexorably forced to place dependence upon collective action by, or under the aegis of, the state for the mastery over economic forces.   We have all become collectivists in some degree."[25]   Professor Stephen Leacock of McGill University also condemned the theoretical system constructed by the English classical economists, though his convictions on remedial anti-depression policy were vague and involved little more than the avoidance of Socialism at all costs.[26]

Far more radical and outspoken were the views set forth by Professor F. H. Underhill of the University of Toronto.[27]   In his opinion, two and a half years of world depression had made everyone conscious that Western civilization must face the task of political control of its economic activities or perish:

> Our absurd North American party system has worked well enough hitherto, because it had no very important tasks to perform.   We all took for granted that the real work of developing the country was being done elsewhere than in Parliament;   It was being done by private profit-seeking business concerns, and the function of politics was merely to distribute in a haphazard happy-go-lucky way the privileges and special opportunities sought by business. This carefree planless era has gone forever.   If democracy cannot organize its economic life, the necessary task of organization will be taken over by other forms of government....   The challenge of our times is whether parliamentarism as a method of organizing the political and economic life of a people can survive.[28]

It was this broad concept of national economic planning which the Progressives--with little apparent consideration for procedural techniques and difficulties, or for political and economic implications--were vigorously advocating in the early thirties.[29]   And it was this type of planning--with its attendant ambiguous theoretical support[30]--which became the basic objective of C. C. F. policy.[31]

The Outlook on Economic Recovery

In the spring of 1931, approximately two years before the trough of the depression was reached, Senator G. D. Robertson, the Conservative Minister of Labour, went on record as stating that the Canadian unemployment problem was diminishing: "We have experienced the most distressing winter in many years, but we emerge into the sunlight of hope at the beginning of another season, and it is within the realm of reason to say that, before the snow falls again, our worries will have largely disappeared."[32]   One year later, the Conservative Minister of Finance, Mr. E. M. Rhodes, expressed his firm conviction that "we are not far removed

from events which will herald the dawn of better days; that those qualities
of courage, resourcefulness, and thrift which characterized our forbears
are not lost to the present generation."[33]

As early as July 1930, Mr. R. J. Hutchings, President of the Canadian
Manufacturers' Association, was telling his fellow-members that encouraging signs of improvement were already visible, and that "this depression,
like all previous depressions, will pass."[34] In the opinion of his successor,
Mr. E. Davis, too much importance was not to be attached to temporary
depressions of the kind in which Canada then found itself; these depressions, after all, had come periodically in the country's history, and although trying while they lasted, all such depressions in the past had been
followed by periods of prosperity.[35]

Addressing the Annual Shareholders' Meeting in February 1931, Sir
James Woods, Vice-President of the Canadian Bank of Commerce, contended that it was the common opinion, and one with which he was in agreement, that the bottom of the depression had been reached, and that a turn
for the better should not be far off; with great material resources and a
varied industrial life, the future of the Dominion was assured.[36] According to Mr. W. G. Gooderham, President of the Bank of Toronto, "from
the fact that business has been depressed for fifteen months, and from the
knowledge that constructive factors are again at work, we can reasonably
hope for better things in the near future."[37] Mr. S. H. Logan, General
Manager of the Canadian Bank of Commerce, believed that no scheme of
things was perpetual, and that prosperity would inevitably come again to
those who earned it by thrift and persistent efforts to improve efficiency.[38]
Sir John Aird, President of the Canadian Bank of Commerce, was confi-
dent that Canada would surge forward as "natural forces" triumphed over
all governmental attempts to defeat them.[39] Sir Herbert Holt, President
of the Royal Bank of Canada, argued that, since Canada was in a relatively
satisfactory position, and since economic history showed that the interval
required for recovery after every previous depression had been distinctly
shorter than the period of decline, Canadians were justified in looking to
the future with confidence.[40]

The Skeptical Approach to Economic Analysis

The fact, also, that little change had come about in the previous attitude of Canadian politicians towards the writings of professional economists
is clearly shown in the heated parliamentary controversies which raged
over the establishment of a central planning agency for the purpose of co-
ordinating economic research, and, more generally, for eliminating, or
at least mitigating, business depressions. Of particular interest is the
proposal made in 1931 and 1932 by Mr. Alfred Speakman for the appointment of a National Council of Social and Economic Research.[41] Mr.
Stevens' reply constituted the main line of reasoning on which the Government's rejection of this suggestion was based: "Choose from the universities of Canada the most outstanding economists, gather them together, and
ask them to tackle this problem, and what would be the result? ... They

would labour for months, possibly for years, without bringing forward a practical solution of the problems with which we are confronted."[42] The Prime Minister, Mr. Bennett, apparently shared this point of view, as did Mr. Henri Bourassa, the eminent Independent.[43] The former, in fact, never got far beyond the stage of restricting his sources of advice to practical business men and bankers who continued to believe in a favourable balance of trade, and to think that banks lend out only the money that is deposited with them.[44]

The criticism levelled by Mr. F. J. Pouliot, a Liberal, and Mr. T. L. Church, a Conservative, against the National Economic Council created towards the close of the Bennett Administration was not unrepresentative of the general outlook. The former considered this legislation a farce, the only purpose of which was "to give a sinecure to some people who like to split hairs, who are not serious but are dreamers and cranks.[45] In the latter's opinion, if Canadians wished to do something practical, they would have to rely on others than economists: "Political economy is not an exact science like physics, chemistry, or biology. These scientists can argue from facts, but our professors and political economists cannot do that. They give their opinions ... [which] are as far apart as the poles."[46] Nor did Mr. Mackenzie King, on assuming the premiership, consider it in the public interest to maintain the Council in operation: the legislation was "superfluous, " and it was prodigal to add to public expenditures to the extent required by it.[47]

III. ATTITUDES TOWARDS CAUSATION IN UNEMPLOYMENT

The extreme severity of the Great Depression gave the issue of the causes of unemployment an urgency hitherto unknown in Canada and many other countries. The discussion of causal factors--though by no means always illuminating--had at least emerged from its isolation in the radicalism of the twenties, and proceeded to point up some of the basic elements in the highly complex unemployment problem.

Government Views
The prevailing notions were, in fact, still quite primitive in certain respects. This was no less true of the top policy-makers in the federal Government than of any other Canadian group. Although Prime Minister Bennett, for example, thought that "there must be something in business cycles, "[48] he told the 1930 Special Session of the House of Commons, convened to combat the unemployment crisis, that the Government was "dealing with a condition and not a theory; we are not concerned at all ... with the great causes of unemployment."[49] The Minister of Trade and Commerce, Mr. Stevens, believed that the unemployment existing in 1930 was very unnecessary and easily preventable. "Were we all to practise a little intelligent discrimination in our daily buying [that is, buy Canadian, not foreign, goods], our unemployment problem would quickly and permanently disappear."[50] Mr. Mackenzie King, as Leader of the

Opposition, acknowledged that unemployment was partly due to defects and maladjustments in the capitalist system, but he attributed prime responsibility to "the greed of individuals, to human selfishness and greed.... Human greed is responsible for the conditions that we have at the present time."[51]

Mature thinking. However, there were more profound appraisals at the top policy level, though typically made after the critical depression period had passed. In the opinion, for example, of Mr. C. A. Dunning, Minister of Finance in the Liberal Government elected in 1935, the Great Depression was largely related to the fall in prices and the inequalities in various kinds of prices which resulted from that fall.[52] Mr. Dunning emphasized the vulnerability of the Canadian economy to external disturbance, and the consequent necessity for Canadians to make some kind of choice between self-sufficiency and rising standards of living based on advanced specialization and international trade; [53] he was also well aware of the crucial role of the capital goods industries in the cyclical process, and of the need for stabilizing those industries, especially construction.[54] There were, moreover, the reports of the National Employment Commission[55] and the Royal Commission on Dominion-Provincial Relations.[56]

The 1938 Final Report of the National Employment Commission[57] was among the most important official policy pronouncements that had yet been issued on the Canadian unemployment problem.[58] It was also one of the earliest applications, by government, of carefully reasoned economic analysis to this problem.[59] Economic depression was defined as:

> A state in which the national income falls below attainable levels not because of any shortcomings in the technique of production or in the bountifulness of nature, but because maladjustments of costs and prices (themselves arising from a great variety of causes) prevent the use of labour, capital, and resources to the extent that they have hitherto been used. Though crop failures and other disasters may intensify the distress arising from depression, unemployment of labour, capital, and resources is of its essence.[60]

For debtor countries like Canada, deriving a relatively high proportion of income from the sale of exports, economic fluctuations were largely external in origin and, to a degree, uncontrollable. The Great Depression, according to the Report, had been a world-wide catastrophe, explainable in terms of the great wartime distortions of prices, incomes, and production, the huge wartime increase in debt charges, and the short-sighted policies pursued by most countries in the postwar years; and communicated to Canada through the medium of its exports and imports of goods and services.[61] An important accompanying depression factor, the Report continued, had been the sharp decline in Canada's capital goods industries. The fluctuations in national income occasioned by unstable export incomes would be much less severe in the absence of wide swings in the volume of investment:

> The sluggish rise in the rate of interest under the rising demand for capital during the boom period becomes a sharp rise in the

> period of crisis. This, in conjunction with an existing or pros-
> pective unprofitable relationship between costs and prices, pro-
> motes a stoppage in the processes of investment and, in a severe
> depression such as we have experienced, investment may give
> place to disinvestment, that is the wearing-out and using-up of
> capital goods more rapidly than they are replaced. It is only thus
> that a country's consumption may actually exceed its income in a
> depression. As the depression proceeds, and as through liquida-
> tion and the revaluing of assets the demand for capital falls off,
> the rate of interest declines to low depression levels.... Only,
> however, as unprofitable relationships between costs and prices
> throughout the economy are removed, and as confidence in the
> future is re-established will low interest rates promote renewed
> investment and recovery. [62]

The other intensifying factors noted in the Report were (1) structural
rigidities in the Canadian economy, and (2) the weak market position to
which wheat and newsprint, Canada's two chief exports, had shifted by
1929.

  In breadth of coverage and quality of analysis, the survey of the
Canadian economy carried out by the Royal Commission on Dominion-
Provincial Relations set an important precedent in the field of governmentally initiated research into problems of economic policy. For the
first time, Canadian fiscal problems were subjected to intensive study
in the broadest possible context, and, despite the inevitable shortcomings
of an investigation of such scope, [63] it did have the overwhelming advantage of viewing this maze of problems as an orderly, unified whole.
While theoretical questions of business cycle causation were not the major concern of the Commission, [64] they received more detailed consideration than had hitherto been accorded them in official government publications. The analytical system closely resembled that which had been
adopted by the Report of the National Employment Commission and, indeed, in the earlier writings of Canadian economists; [65] that is, the approach, as already indicated, was mainly in terms of Canadian vulnerability to external shock, structural rigidities, and the decline in capital
investment. [66] New insights into Canadian economic fluctuations were
nevertheless, provided by the extensive historical and statistical analysis
applied to economic development in the Dominion.

The Liberal and Conservative Politicians

  Private members of the major parties in the House of Commons expressed an incredible variety of views on the unemployment question.
with causes ranging from the breakdown of ethical values, at one extreme,
to malfunctioning of the savings-investment process, at the other; no
uniform pattern can be discerned. Under such circumstances, it was
highly probable that certain politicians would touch upon important causal
factors. But even where this was the case, the discussion was usually
fragmentary and narrow.

The chief controversial issue was the tariff, with the Conservatives convinced that free trade policies were the root cause of the depression, and the Liberals equally vehement in arguing that trade relations were not free enough. Thus, along with many of his party colleagues, Col. T. Cantley, a Conservative, saw the only depression cure in "the inauguration and vigorous application of a national policy which will protect the Canadian producer on the farm and in the mine, and the workers in our manufacturing establishments, by damming back the flood of products coming in from other lands where the workers are not enjoying [our] standard of living.[67] On the other hand, Mr. E. J. Young, a Liberal,[68] contended, characteristically, that world prosperity would return if, first, the problem of war reparations were solved, and, second, tariffs were reduced.[69]

Non-tariff questions received scattered recognition from the private members. Mr. M. N. Campbell, a Liberal,[70] placed responsibility for the downswing on (1) the stock-market crash and the consequent great reduction of purchasing power, (2) the reduction in wheat prices, (3) the large immigration into Canada, and (4) the efficiency of machines.[71] In the opinion of Mr. C. Bourgeois, a Conservative, the main causes could "be summed up as follows: (1) the World War which upset everything; (2) overproduction; (3) the credit crisis."[72] According to Mr. J. A. Barrette, a Conservative, the main cause of the depression was "the lack of trust among nations as well as among individuals. It belongs to a moral order rather than to a material one."[73] The Liberal member, Mr. R. J. Deachman, had an explanation which, if less lofty, was certainly more in line with what contemporary economists were thinking. He joined with the Liberal, Dr. H. R. Fleming,[74] and others, in pointing to the wide discrepancy between the prices of agricultural and manufactured products, and the resultant maldistribution of purchasing power throughout the Dominion.[75] In addition, he argued, among the higher-income groups, income usually "goes back not into consumers' goods but into investments, into bonds or savings. While it ... would in normal times be employed in the production of capital goods, it does not now go back into the production of capital goods because money is invested in capital goods for the production of consumer goods, and if there is no demand for consumer goods, then the money will not flow in capital production."[76]

Bankers' and Businessmen's Attitudes

The pattern of bankers' thought reflected a wide array of impressions--some of them directly contradictory--regarding the causal factors operating in the Great Depression. Whatever consistency these impressions had, was to be found in the solidly entrenched philosophy of the inevitability of depression as an aftermath of inflationary expansion, and the certainty of recovery from low levels of economic activity.

Addressing the shareholders of the Royal Bank of Canada at the end of the year 1930, Mr. C. E. Neill, Vice-President and Managing Director of the Bank, [77] attributed the downswing to the "easy money" policy pursued in Canada and the United States during the middle twenties; and to the substantial rise in interest rates in the latter part of 1928, when the boom had already assumed dangerous proportions and the economy had, therefore, become highly vulnerable to rapid and marked changes in the price of credit. Of special interest here, however, is the rationale for Mr. Neill's rejection of all those explanations of causal forces framed in terms of deficiency of aggregate demand: "The fact is overlooked that total purchasing power of the world is governed by total volume of production valued at current prices, and purchasing power can be increased only by increased production. Commodities pay for commodities. Money is only a medium of exchange, and all exchange is ultimately barter. Demand and supply are therefore reciprocal."[78] Mr. Neill, then, in the tradition of Say, Ricardo, and J. S. Mill, was unqualifiedly applying the principles of barter to the money exchange economy; that is, treating money as a neutral intermediary in trade and so identifying supply with demand and making general overproduction impossible by definition.

But there was no unanimity on the issue of overproduction. Some of the bankers were moving towards a concept of aggregate demand. For example, the General Manager of the Royal Bank of Canada, Mr. M. W. Wilson, made the following causal interpretation of the Great Depression and those economic disturbances which had preceded it:

> In general, the difficulties which were confronted in the distant past were the outcome of shortages. Supplies of food were not sufficient to meet the requirements of expanding population. At the present moment, the major difficulties have to do with the distribution of an increasing surplus which tends to exceed purchasing power. Increasing attention must be given to measures which will provide for a freer and move even flow in the exchange of goods and services.[79]

Sir John Aird seems to have had much the same idea in mind in contending that "the increase in capacity for production during the last period of prosperity outstripped that in world population."[80]

Perhaps the most noteworthy of all such bankers' pronouncements was that of Mr. J. P. Bell, Manager-in-Chief of the Western Ontario Division of the Canadian Bank of Commerce--by way of taking note of the theory of employment set forth in an English Labour Party Policy Report:

> The national income equals the expenditure on consumption plus national savings. These savings ought to be invested to create further wealth so that next year's income will be larger, then there will be more goods consumed and more savings available.... When savings do not go into capital goods, there is less income to spend on the consumption of goods next year, a fall in prices, and a decline in employment.... If the opposite occurs and more money is spent on capital goods and at a rate faster than savings

accrue, then the demand for immediate consumption is greater
than the supply and there is a rise in prices, profits, and employment.[81]

Here, obviously, was the basis for the more elaborate attempt, made two
years later by Keynes,[82] to steer a difficult course between the long-run
over-optimism of the classical economists and the short-run over-pessimism
of the underconsumptionists. The implications of this approach, however,
were by no means obvious to contemporary Canadians. Indeed, the curious
fact is not this general lack of recognition, but rather that the Labour Report should have been cited at all.

A substantial group of financial and industrial leaders did find a basis
for agreement in the serious monetary disturbances, both domestic and
international, which had characterized the decade of the twenties.[83] Sir
Thomas White, then on the Board of Directors of the Canadian Bank of
Commerce,[84] argued, in general terms, that "in a period of boom... there
is an overexpansion of credit and there must be ultimately a collapse."[85]
The appraisal by Mr. S. R. Noble, Assistant General Manager of the Royal Bank of Canada,[86] was more specific. It was his view that "the main
factor in bringing about and continuing the present world-wide depression
has been the disastrous fall in the commodity price level, and this has
been brought about not by overproduction, tariffs, war debts, stock market collapse, or any of the usual causes assigned, but by a thoroughly-
stupid central-bank policy, with France and the United States as the principal villains in the piece."[87] These comments should have given rise to
grave doubts concerning the passive role traditionally assumed by the
commercial banks in the economic process; but no such inference was
drawn by the bankers and businessmen.

The Crystallization of Radical Thought

In a sense, radical thinking on the causes of unemployment did not
reveal any sharp break with that of the decade of the twenties. The concept of the inadequacy of aggregate demand continued as the major focal
point of all radical discussion. But the thirties did have a claim to uniqueness, in the much wider diffusion of the unorthodox approach among the
Western parliamentary representatives, as well as in the great variety
of interpretations which found favour within the "aggregate demand"
framework.

It would, therefore, be quite misleading to suggest that radical thinking in the thirties encompassed a consistent, uniform, vigorously analytical body of economic doctrine. It was, instead, a rather loose admixture
of generalities, which were traceable to such sources as Marx, Douglas,
and Hobson, and which were often indiscriminately combined in the over-
all attitudes of a single political group or an individual.[88] Nevertheless,
within this realm of confused and conflicting ideas, one can readily ob-
serve a definite consolidation of thought on the unemployment question;
and the real beginnings of the struggle towards an understanding of the

savings-investment process.

The C. C. F. (and Labour and Progressive) members of Parliament.
The views of Mr. Woodsworth on the causes of economic breakdown remained substantially unchanged. The pillar of his whole argument still
took the form of the Hobson version of underconsumption, "the phenomenon of a great deal more being produced than the people can purchase, of
a very large amount being put back into fixed capital so that the fixed capital is out of all proportion to the commodities produced."[89] To the C.C.F.
leader, furthermore (though not to Hobson), this was an inherent defect of
capitalism, which was responsible for increasingly frequent and progressively more severe crises, and which would lead ultimately to the complete collapse of the capitalist system. But of greater significance and
validity was Mr. Woodsworth's attempt, before an unsympathetic House
of Commons, to crystallize the concept of "involuntary unemployment":

> In western Canada, . . . we have got past the stage where we attri-
> bute unemployment to the laziness or shiftlessness of the indivi-
> dual. . . . There are undoubtedly a few people who will not or can-
> not work, but the great majority of those out of work today are
> people who have been working and who have helped to build up
> Canada, and they ought to be seen through these difficult periods.
> The idea that being out of a job is a man's own fault, is an inheri-
> tance of the pioneer days when it was largely true.[90]

There was nothing precise or technical in these statements, but it is their
novelty which is striking, particularly in the light of the fact that contemporary professional economists had not even begun to recognize involuntary unemployment as a theoretical possibility, and so had failed to incorporate it into their analytical structure.

The ideas advanced by Mr. Irvine clearly exemplify the loose, poorly
integrated thinking which characterized the radical approach to economic
problems. The "A plus B theorem," enunciated in social credit doctrine
and espoused by Mr. Irvine in the early twenties, apparently remained as
the basis of his attack on unemployment.[91] And yet, in sharp contrast
with Major Douglas, he believed "that unemployment cannot be cured under
the present economic system, and that the first step towards a cure is a
definite decision by the government and Parliament that a new system
must be introduced. . . . That reformation must and will come either by
legislation or by revolution."[92] Indeed, one of the most interesting aspects
of Mr. Irvine's thinking involved the two "Marxist-Keynesian" reasons advanced by him for the inevitable collapse of capitalism. In the first place,
"capitalism. . . cannot go on without foreign markets, and there are not sufficient foreign markets in the world to take delivery of all the goods which
the industrialized world is capable of producing."[93] And secondly, "already the field for the investment of capitalistic surplus has narrowed almost to the vanishing point. . . . Now what happens when you cannot find
profitable investments for surplus capital? Simply this: capitalism stops."[94]

This causal interpretation is still another instance of radical generalization unsupported by rigorous analysis as to countries, time periods, and other variables. But there is the characteristic radical groping towards the formulation of important economic principles and concepts--in this case, the role of "net foreign investment" as a component of aggregate demand, and the "secular-stagnation thesis."

Full expression to this reasoning was given also by Mr. A. MacInnis, though his analysis was even more strongly couched in Marxist "surplus value" terms.[95] The history of capitalism had always been a series of recurring ups and downs in business; and analysis of those cycles revealed that the periods of prosperity were continually getting shorter, and the periods of depression continually getting longer:

> Every time profits are created unemployment is also created, because profits are made out of the surplus values that the working class produce, the surplus value over and above what they receive in wages, and because over a cycle of time these surplus values accumulate to such an extent that industry has to slow down in order that they may be consumed when production is not taking place .... There are two things absolutely essential to capitalism; first, foreign markets; and secondly, an ever-expanding field for new capital investment. These are not to be found anywhere on earth today.... The capitalist system we maintained has reached the limit of its usefulness, and it should now be replaced by Socialism, just as it replaced another economic system.[96]

This kind of attack on established institutions was, as has already been noted, the main point of departure between the two important schools of radical thought--the C. C. F. and Social Credit parties--emerging in Canada during the thirties. That is to say, the latter group was radical only in the same restricted sense in which Keynes was radical, namely, the conviction that unemployment could and should be eliminated or minimized, not by a fundamental change in the pattern of property ownership, but by careful manipulation of monetary and fiscal machinery within the existing institutional structure.[97]

Social Credit thought. The Social Crediters became especially articulate in the federal sphere after the Dominion and Alberta elections of 1935. Fundamentally, their analysis of the causes of unemployment involved a highly concentrated exposition of the Douglas theories already examined in connection with some of the radicals in the C. C. F. movement. Apart from this, however, two aspects of Social Credit thinking should be recorded because of the significant light which they shed on the evolution of Canadian economic thought during the thirties.

One of these relates to the critical comments applied by Mr. J. H. Blackmore, then Social Credit leader in the House of Commons, to the federal budget brought down in 1937. It was, he contended, a budget whose basis was to be found in the classical approach to stability problems:

> The guiding principle of the old economics, or the economics of scarcity, was this: ... "Supply creates its own demand." These are ... the words of an eminent authority [J. S. Mill]. ... That was sound enough until we got into the era of overproduction; but everybody recognizes now [as Keynes has shown] that it is no longer sound. ... We simply cannot understand existing conditions, because our conceptions were framed on the theories of the old economics; and as long as we continue to keep those old theories, we shall be unable to explain the facts of the existing situation, and we shall never find a solution. ... The new economics can be put in these words: Demand creates its own supply. Just the reverse of the old definition. ... The goods are here in abundance; what is needed is effective demand.[98]

This statement would not have constituted an inappropriate preface to Keynes's General Theory, which had been published less than a year before.

The second interesting aspect of social credit thinking is its apparent absorption of the Foster-Catchings interpretation of the savings-investment relationship, that the act of investment has undesirable employment consequences because of the general overproduction associated with funds being spent more than once in succession on capital goods.[99] Thus, Mr. N. Jaques[100] argued:

> Savings create a shortage of purchasing power. When a man saves, he refrains from consuming, and to that extent goods are not sold. We are told that money saved is an investment which eventually will be paid out in wages and salaries. That may be true, but when the money is paid out again in wages and salaries, it is paid out with respect to another cycle of production. We have two lots of goods and one lot of money, and it is impossible for one lot of money to buy two lots of goods. ... [Therefore, although] saving is the only individual remedy for financial insecurity, at the same time it is, I believe, a social evil of the worst kind. ... I suggest that the mere fact of saving is one of the causes of unemployment and poverty.[101]

Mr. V. Quelch's approach was much the same, though somewhat more comprehensive in the sense of allowing for dishoarding:

> If ... total payments equal total prices, then when any portion of these payments is saved goods to that extent will be left unsold. On the other hand, if savings of the past are being spent at the same rate as savings of today, then the two will balance each other. Nevertheless, it is generally conceded that the practice of saving today is going ahead at an accelerated rate, and therefore a deficiency of purchasing power is caused to that degree. ...

[Moreover,] the reinvestment of savings today causes a permanent
deficiency of purchasing power, equal to the amount of the reinvestment where it is used as working capital.[102]

That spending sequence may be a matter of considerable importance in the
business cycle has already been acknowledged. But from such a concession
to the underconsumptionists it by no means follows that the act of saving
per se must be regarded as deflationary. In the last analysis, Foster and
Catchings, and with them Social Credit observers like Mr. Jaques and Mr.
Quelch, "fell into the same trap which caught most of the underconsumptionists; that is, they thought that oversaving is evidenced by the investment of too much savings, instead of the failure to find investments for
all the savings which people desire to create."[103]

    The League for Social Reconstruction. As regards the problem of
unemployment, then, the radical approach continued, throughout the decade of the thirties, to be underconsumptionist in one form or another.[104]
The most thorough elaboration of the radical approach came, however,
not from the politicians, but from Socialist sources outside Parliament.
Prominent among these was the League for Social Reconstruction,[105]
whose analysis represents the most sophisticated of all contemporary
formulations of radical doctrine--not only with respect to cyclical causal
forces, but also in terms of appraising the operation and policy significance of monetary and fiscal processes.[106]

    Although the League did not probe deeply into the determinants of
employment and income (not even Keynes had as yet done so), it did demonstrate quite clearly an understanding of the causal role of the savings-
investment relationship in cyclical fluctuations. The League realized, in
other words, that business depression was the necessary consequence of
distortion in the "balance between the output of consumption goods and the
portion of income which is spent on consumption, on the one hand, and between the production of capital goods (buildings, plant, machinery, etc.)
and the amount of income which is saved, on the other."[107] Specific form
was given to this generalization by means of the League's reform proposals in the investment field,[108] and by its refutation of the Social Credit
thesis.

    In the latter connection, critical attention was centred on the "A plus
B theorem" purporting to show, in quasi-mathematical fashion, that "the
fundamental trouble with the present system ... is that the purchasing
power available is less than the collective prices of the goods for sale;
that there is not enough money to buy what we produce."[109] For one
thing, according to the League, the "A plus B" classification was concep-
tually incorrect in omitting interest from the A payments: "Even if we
admit that some interest goes to the banks, the mass of interest payments
made by Canadian producers is paid in respect of bonds and mortgages
which accrue to individuals in the same way as dividends (which Major
Douglas includes among the A payments). This surely is a serious omis-
sion--unless the intention is to confuse such payment with bank interest,

in which case it is smart play, but not evidence."[110] But the fundamental source of error in the Douglas scheme was the "ambiguous" and "unsatisfactory" explanation offered for the alleged failure of the B payments to become available as consumers' income. To state that these were in the nature of the repayment of a bank loan by all the organizations to which they were made, was stating as a fact what had yet to be proved. "If it could be shown that a large part of all business receipts were used to pay off bank loans Major Douglas would have proved something--though not as much as he thinks. But he does not attempt to prove it."[111] The truth, reasoned the League, was that anyone with enough patience and endurance to follow the payments process through to completion could discover that, somewhere or other, sooner or later, the B payments became payments made to individuals, in other words, A payments. "Indeed, all costs of production can be finally resolved into A payments, provided you trace them far enough. That is to say, all costs of production are, ultimately, incomes."[112]

The League drew attention, finally, to two plausible variants of the "A plus B theorem." One of these apparently acknowledged that the B payments eventually became income to consumers, but argued that the economic system would break down anyway, because the "rate of flow" of purchasing power was vital and there would be a net loss of purchasing power if the "outflow" were less than the "inflow." This contention, according to the League, ought to have suggested to Major Douglas the possibility that the "velocity of circulation" of money was just as important a determinant of employment as the quantity of money. The second variant emphasized the time lag between the distribution of incomes involved in the earlier stages of production and the offer for sale of the finished product; for this reason, consumers' incomes would be inadequate to buy all the goods currently offered for sale at prices which covered their costs of production. But it was obvious to the League that:

> This argument omits to take into account the simple fact that, taking economic activity all round, the production of goods at all stages is roughly continuous. This is to say, incomes are always being earned in the course of producing raw material and intermediate goods which will not be ready for final sale to consumers for some time. Such incomes, however, are likely to be spent partly on goods produced in an earlier cycle of production, and will tend to counter-balance the deficiency of purchasing power to which the theory refers. There may be a lack of balance at certain times, but to point out that, in fact, production in general is discontinuous is to beg the question. What we have to discover is the reason for the ups and downs of capitalist production.[113]

Canadian Economists and the Problem of Unemployment

Canadian professional economists cannot be deemed to have made a vital contemporary contribution to the understanding of the Great Depression in particular or of business cycles in general. One probes the economic journals and other published sources in vain, in search of thoroughgoing discussion of the economics of employment. Such analysis as can be discovered either emerged after economic recovery was well under way[114] or was fragmentary, fatalistic, and confused.[115]

Some typical examples. The appraisal of the Great Depression made by Professor A. B. Balcom of Acadia University is cited in support of the latter generalization:

> The present depression does not differ from others so far as the nature of the immediate cause is concerned. In no period of expansion were those uneconomic and antisocial practices which inevitably lead to reaction more clearly present than during the months immediately preceding the break in 1929. We are now suffering the consequences. The elimination of the unfit practices and industries, the disposal of accumulated surpluses where overproduction occurred, and the redistribution of misdirected productive effort so that it shall most effectively satisfy human desires, must go on until the body economic is thoroughly purged. When that is consummated, we shall again be ready for the upswing. An earlier recovery is improbable and certainly undesirable.[116]

Another case in point is the terminology by which Professor Leacock characterized the 1929 downswing.[117] In his view, Canada's power to produce goods had outstripped its power to absorb production. "Mass production, machinery, standardization, the desire to invest money rather than to 'blow it in', has created a situation which of itself tends to run to a full stop. . . . If people did 'blow in' their money instead of saving it, the situation would be at once relieved."[118] Miss I. M. Biss of the University of Toronto took issue with this interpretation, though her position was neither typical nor clear.[119] She pointed out that there was still a division of opinion between such authorities as Hobson and Keynes on the question of underconsumption. "It may be, as the latter suggests, that so long as investment keeps pace with saving, all is well and there is no danger of depression. But Hobson [may be] right [in arguing] that investment does proceed too fast for consumption and precipitates depression."[120] Professor Leacock's "confused heresy" was, finally, in sharp contrast to the "classical orthodoxy" bluntly espoused by Professor Swanson of the University of Saskatchewan:

> The so-called "new economics, " as I understand this teaching which we now [1933] find being applied in the United States and in European countries, . . . is not new at all. It is merely a return to the seventeenth and eighteenth centuries of mercantilism. You can sum it up all in one phrase that it is based on the belief that the technological improvements that have been made, and the advancement of science, have proceeded so far that now we have

to be afraid of over-production. On the other hand, the orthodox
economist [such as I] believes that there is no such thing as general over-production, that what is wrong with the world today is unbalanced production.[121]

   Mr. Parkinson. The analysis of Mr. J. F. Parkinson of the University of Toronto--strikingly Keynesian and unorthodox in 1933--provides
one of the few notable exceptions to the general rule enunciated above.[122]
The most important cause of business cycles, he contended, lay in the
spasmodic and fluctuating character of the rate of new investment outlays,
and in the unbalanced and uneconomic direction so frequently given to
such expenditures:

> The development of the economic system ... is speeded up or re-
> tarded by the disturbances to the normal processes of real invest-
> ment in new capital equipment. These disturbances are produced
> by a rapid and extravagant expansion in all directions at one period,
> out of proportion to the real savings of the people, initially stimu-
> lated by a rising price level, a condition which over-investment
> aggravates. The ultimate consequence is an apparent excess of
> commodities and capital equipment unable to find markets and
> steady use, resulting in falling prices, falling values, and in gen-
> eral economic recession.[123]

The most common reaction to such a disturbance--and that experienced in
Canada during the early thirties--was the virtual stagnation of capital development, "with new borrowing and new investment falling far short of
the generally-manifested ability on the part of the economy as a whole to
save, a condition which is complicated by the high rates of interest to be
earned from savings accounts."[124] Mr. Parkinson attributed the frequent
instability and excessiveness of investment chiefly to the high degree of
integration and the abusive practices of the investment market; and to the
rigidity of the capital structure in terms of the transfer of so large a portion of an internationally vulnerable national income to the rentier, "the
least capable of making effective use of the purchasing power available."[125]
   Mr. Burton. A second exception was the business cycle analysis
made a year later by Mr. F. W. Burton, a graduate student in economics
at the University of Toronto.[126] The main lines of his analysis stemmed
from the theoretical "innovations" scheme which had been set out by Professor Schumpeter.[127] Thus, the cause of the business cycle, Mr. Burton
argued, had to be sought among the dynamic forces impinging upon the
static system conceived by economic theory, and constantly thrusting that
system out of equilibrium:

> [The cause itself] is the process of economic evolution [which is,
> in turn] the result of that part of the activity of business men which
> is concerned, not simply with carrying on their businesses in a

routine way, but with innovation. Innovation means the introduction of new commodities or of new and more economical ways of
producing commodities already known. The process of evolution
is the series of such innovations which emerges in the course of
time. The effect of this process is to provide constantly-new sat-
isfactions and more efficient ways of obtaining accustomed satis-
factions; it therefore increases steadily the total real income of
the economy.[128]

Mr. Burton went on, however, to point out that these successive innovations had to be regarded as an "autonomous" force, "bound together in
groups partly by extensive copying, partly through a borrowing of techniques, and partly as a result of the pressure of overhead costs; ...[and]
operating upon the price-economy from without and disturbing it constantly
by changing the conditions of equilibrium."[129] In the bunching of innovations, it was possible to find the true primum mobile of the business cycle.

If, then, the causal forces in depressions operated in that way, it followed that there would be depressions as long as there were innovations.
Nevertheless, it might be possible, by the adoption of intelligent public
policies, to make the necessary adjustments smooth and rapid, and so
minimize social distress. That is to say, although the original cause of
the business cycle phenomenon was technological--the fact of innovation--
and therefore inherent in the capitalist system, it had to be conceded that,
once the original cause of disturbance had arisen, psychological and monetary reactions would develop which would have further effects upon one
another and upon technology, until the secondary causes of disturbance
might, in the short run, outweigh the primary. In the monetary sphere,
according to Mr. Burton, lay the greatest hope for an effective policy of
mitigating depressions.[130]

Applying his analysis to Canada, Mr. Burton noted the disturbing effect on the Canadian economy of fluctuations in the world's demands for
its staples,[131] and the intensification of this effect through the rigidities
of the national cost-price structure. But in Canada particularly, it was
necessary to think of business fluctuations not simply as "credit cycles,"
that is, as rhythmic and purely monetary phenomena, but also as important phases of Canadian national development. One reason for such an interpretation was the vulnerable and rigid aspects mentioned above. More
significant, however, was the fact that the cause of Canadian expansion
was not European capital, but the rise of new forms of production in other
countries; and that world depression was not an irrelevant disturbance
originating in the money markets of Europe and the United States to inter-
rupt the peaceful process of Canadian expansion, but was, rather, a phenomenon of world development which Canadian development had had a share
in creating. With those limitations, substantially the same case could be
made out for Canadian application of monetary anti-depression policy as
for the application of such policy to any industrialized country.

Like Professor Schumpeter, Mr. Burton did not incorporate into his exposition any analysis in terms of savings-investment equilibrium and income flows; nor was he sufficiently clear as to the inevitability of recurring economic breakdowns through innovations, even under conditions of continuous production. But viewed in historical perspective, such deficiencies are of secondary importance, as compared with the fact that it' was a university graduate student who made one of the few careful contemporary attempts at analytical treatment of the problem of business cycle causation.

Professor Inman. Of particular interest, finally, are the efforts made in this direction, in 1938 and 1939, by Professors M. K. Inman and A. F. W. Plumptre of the Universities of Western Ontario and Toronto respectively. The former sought to show close conformity between the incidence of the Great Depression in Canada and the Austrian--or, more specifically, Hayekian--theory of business cycles.[132] He demonstrated that from 1926 to 1929 there had been in Canada both a substantial increase in the money supply and a rise in the velocity of circulation. During the same period, industrial production had expanded, while the level of wholesale prices had declined only slightly; this development he cited as evidence of the "relative inflation" emphasized in the Austrian theory.[133] The prices and output of capital or "higher-order" goods had increased relative to those of consumer or "lower-order" goods, an indication that the "money" rate of interest was depressed below the "natural" rate.[134] Technological advances and other non-monetary factors had helped to initiate the expansion from the "goods side" (as against the "money side"). The boom, moreover, had been accompanied by a wave of security speculation, brought on not by chartered bank reduction of call-loan interest rates but by other factors, particularly the intense speculative activity in American stock markets. With the speculation under way, however, the inflexibility of short-term interest rates, on both "call" and "current" loans, had played a catalyzing role.

As for the precipitation of the downswing, Professor Inman held that the rise in long-term interest rates had been an important contributing factor, but that, apart from changes in the maximum customary rates on call and current loans, there was little ground for believing that the commerical banks employed the raising of short-term interest rates as a means of restricting credit and thereby curtailing economic expansion. "Nor is there any conclusive evidence that labour costs rose sufficiently to act as a brake upon industrial growth, although there are some indications that such costs in the capital goods industries increased, relative to those in industry as a whole."[135] The implication was that the differential between the capital goods and consumer goods sectors supported the Hayekian hypothesis that the depression phase of the cycle is characterized by--is, in fact, to be defined as--a "shortening of the structure of production."[136]

In basing his analysis on Austrian cycle theory, Professor Inman was on relatively safe ground in the sense that this explanation, in its variety of forms, commanded a wide area of acceptance among professional economists during the interwar period. In endeavouring, also, to give empirical significance to the theory, he went much further than contemporary Canadian economists--and much further, indeed, than some of the leading proponents of the theory. But it seems equally necessary to recognize that: (1) the theory itself rested on shaky foundations;[137] (2) the evidence presented by Professor Inman can hardly be considered as adequate corroboration of the theory; and (3) such facts as did seem reasonably clear would have been compatible with many of the business-cycle theories prevalent at that time.

Professor Plumptre. Professor Plumptre's analysis probably represents the earliest comprehensive incorporation of the Keynesian income-expenditure approach into Canadian cycle theory.[138] He took as his starting point the observations that personal consumption expenditure varied relatively little, changing more or less passively in response to income changes;[139] and that fluctuations in investment activity were among the most important sources of instability in the general level of income.[140] He divided income disposal into three main categories: (1) importation of goods and financial claims from abroad; (2) expenditure on domestically produced goods and services; and (3) domestic accumulation of financial claims to wealth and income. These he proceeded to consider in detail--the first in terms of the "marginal propensity to import"; the second through the "marginal propensity to consume" and the "multiplier"; and the third on the basis of the factors governing the supply of and demand for investment funds.

The significance of the marginal propensity to import, Professor Plumptre argued, was that it tended to be high for an industrially underdeveloped country like Canada which imported high-grade manufactures and luxury goods; and that such a country, therefore, would probably experience acute foreign exchange difficulties as a result of any spontaneous internal change in incomes.[141] This was "an important obstacle...to the success of various controls which the authorities might otherwise impose upon cyclical fluctuations of business and prosperity while still retaining the traditional stability of the foreign exchange rate."[142]

As for the multiple effects on income produced by successive consumption spending of any autonomous injection of purchasing power,[143] these had to be carefully qualified before being used as a guide to changing conditions in the real world. First, there were the difficulties associated with statistical estimation of the multiplier for all time periods. Second, there was the question of time lags between spending periods. And third, the multiplier appropriate to some injections of income was not appropriate to others in the same country or even at the same time. The first qualification involved a process of improvement and refinement of statistical techniques; while the second was probably less important in such countries as Canada, where agriculture was a major branch of economic activity, than elsewhere. The most serious problem centred around the actual existence of a whole series of multipliers rather than any single coefficient. There were two reasons for this phenomenon: (1) the pro-

pensity to consume was different in different industries, varying inversely
with the proportion of income accruing to the entrepreneurial class, and
with industrial dependence on imported raw materials or capital; and
(2) the investment induced by the original stimulus varied over time and
among different industries. "We may conclude that the principle introduced
by the multiplier is a very useful one in describing and analysing economic
processes. But it has its dangers."[144]

On the investment funds question, it was clear to Professor Plumptre
that a country's capacity to finance its investment undertakings without resort to new money from local or foreign sources was the greater the lower
its propensity (1) to accumulate money (that is, to hoard), or (2) to spend
on domestic products, or (3) to import. The first of these factors would
operate through raised security prices, reduced interest rates, and easy
money generally; the second through a low multiplier, low incomes, and
the consequent availability of funds to the capital market; and the third
through the easing of pressure which would otherwise appear in the foreign-
exchange market as a result of expanding domestic investment and incomes.[145]
On the demand side, the incentives to expand were complex and lay "partly
in a vague adoration of expansion as an aspect of progress, partly in a belief that expansion is the hallmark of success, ... and partly, as some economists may have over-emphasized, in the hope or the expectation of profits."[146] Again in countries like Canada, a special consideration involving
the inducement to invest was that it might depend more on income and demand conditions abroad than on similar domestic conditions. This implied
an investment volatility even greater than the "instability potential" of
other industrialized countries. But such "incentive" differences were
diminishing; as a country emerged from economic colonialism, and as
the export market ceased to dominate its economic life, changes would
come about in the factors influencing private and governmental investment
decisions:

> More attention is paid to local events and less to foreign ones;
> more to the demands of the home market and less to the behaviour
> of buyers and creditors abroad. The decline of the propensity to
> import is accompanied by the rise of the propensity to purchase
> local products; the multiplier increases. If a new infusion of
> incomes takes place the consequent aggregate response is larger;
> and the resulting change of business opinion will also, probably,
> be larger, inducing greater local financing and greater expansion
> than would otherwise occur. In such ways does independence of
> mind, motive, and movement accompany the growing independence
> of the body economic.[147]

It remained true, nevertheless, according to Professor Plumptre,
that for countries like Canada, changes in export incomes were still the
independent variables of prime importance; that boom periods were
based on rising prices of export staples, rising volumes of exports, and

capital imports. The way in which those variables produced their effects
was determined by the extent of local industrialization, by the local structure and foreign connections of the financial system, and, above all, by
the mechanism of income disposal already discussed. Within this framework, the cyclical upswing and downswing could be readily visualized.
The former was characterized in the early stages by increasing liquidity
(through local and foreign channels) of the financial system, and by increasing demand for loan accommodation; and in the later stages by progressive deterioration of this liquid position in the face of increased imports and still-expanding demand for loan funds. The seeds of contraction
were thereby sown in the upswing phase of the cycle; and the transformation could then be easily achieved by any one of a number of factors, including a collapse of foreign lending and the projection of foreign lack of
confidence into the domestic field. There followed the cumulative decline
of incomes, operating through the multiplier, and intensified by (1) the
loss of liquidity and the restrictive practices of the financial system;
(2) foreign exchange difficulties arising from fixed-interest foreign obligations and from the failure of import demand to fall as rapidly as capital
inflows and export values; and (3) individual and institutional accumulation of liquid balances. As the economy gradually regained its liquidity,
it found itself in the stagnation stage, with conditions ripe for recovery
when a favourable change occurred in the major foreign or domestic variables.[148]

The foregoing survey was designed to set forth the general economic
environment in which the impact of the Great Depression in Canada was
felt. The Dominion, in the thirties, presents a strange combination of
swiftly growing political consciousness, deep institutional and intellectual
ferment, and glaring immaturity and inaccuracy of economic thinking.
It is in terms of such a combination that it becomes possible to construct
the rationale for the evolution of Canadian monetary and fiscal policy, and
for the attitudes which helped to shape that policy, during the momentous
decade. For the greater part of the period, these attitudes remained em-
bedded in the cautious, traditional approach which had permeated economic thought for more than a century. The resultant policy objectives were
ill-defined, and the techniques crude and seldom used in a manner calculated to achieve maximum effect.

But it was a different decade from that of the twenties. Progress in
the economic sphere, however halting and unsteady, was everywhere ap-
parent--particularly in the closing years of the decade, when the pattern
of change during the World War II and postwar periods was already discernible. It is appropriate at this stage, then, to turn to the monetary
and fiscal aspects of Canadian economic development during the thirties.

PART III

THE MONETARY REVOLUTION OF THE THIRTIES

CHAPTER VII

THE INFLATION CONTROVERSY

IN the United States and Great Britain, the Great Depression of the thirties was a testing ground for the monetary approach to economic stability. The reason for this is not to be sought so much in the strong monetary emphasis then pervading business cycle theory, as in the fact that the comprehensive institutional machinery necessary for the execution of monetary policy was already close at hand, and that the monetary control function was presumed to occasion less interference than any other with the normal workings of the private enterprise system.

For Canada there was no such opportunity to test the validity of the "monetary control" hypothesis. During the crucial first half of the decade, monetary policy was, in fact, conspicuous by its absence, with the few positive measures introduced being the outgrowth not of conscious, careful reasoning, but rather of panicky, irrational response to a desperate set of circumstances.

Again, the explanation of this fact is quite clear. At the onset of the Great Depression, Canada was utterly lacking in the elaborate formal control machinery which had evolved in the American monetary sphere; nor was there any tradition of effective informal collaboration and control, such as that which had prevailed between the Bank of England and the London money market since the beginning of the nineteenth century. Equally important was the sharp contrast between the Dominion's international economic position on the one hand, and that of Great Britain and the United States on the other. Against the towering stature of the latter countries had to be set the fact that Canada was, after all, little more than an infant in the economic family of nations. Granting the genuine Canadian contribution to an expanding world income, the relationship between Canada and the rest of the world was a one-way phenomenon, for though Canada had a relatively high standard of living, sustained through international trade, she had neither long-standing financial prestige nor predominant industrial power, but rather was dependent on, and extremely susceptible to, external change. These two factors, the absence of any control mechanism, and the international vulnerability of an economically minor country, partially shaped Canadian monetary history in the thirties. The other vital influence was exerted by contemporary thinking about monetary problems--each set of factors, indeed, bearing a reciprocal cause-effect relationship to the other. The specific quality which they imparted to Dominion monetary policy during the Great Depression can, perhaps, be appropriately expressed in terms of "what might have been," rather than of "what was."

What, then, was the revolutionary aspect of monetary development during the thirties? The term "monetary revolution" is a misnomer in

the sense that few of the individual monetary changes which occurred during the decade were "revolutionary"; they tended, rather, to be of a gradual and uneven nature. But against the background of the preceding decades, the events of the thirties do assume revolutionary proportions.
The justification for the use of this term rests, accordingly, with the
writer's intention to emphasize the significance of the real transformation
in monetary thought and policy as the forerunner of the more spectacular
developments which occurred during and after World War II.

The most stimulating and provocative discussions of monetary policy
were centred on two issues which sharply divided Canadians during the
thirties: the feasibility of monetary manipulation for achieving economic
recovery, and the establishment of a central bank. These two issues were
not unrelated, as to either time or content. Both were projections of the
monetary thinking which had developed in the decade of the twenties and,
to some extent, even earlier. And both were characterized by the enunci-
ation and formulation of monetary principles and theories which could not
logically be included within the narrow confines of the inflation or the central bank issue per se. However, a careful distinction between the two
major problems seems desirable, even to the point of separating out from
their "central bank" context certain attitudes and arguments which have a
more direct bearing on monetary theory in general and on the "policy"
road to economic recovery. It is this generality of approach--together
with the fact that the agitation for banking reform attained its greatest
momentum after the most heated debates over measures for monetary
recovery had subsided--which sets the "inflation controversy" apart from
that concerned with the central bank.

I. THE BACKGROUND OF THE INFLATION CONTROVERSY

To a considerable extent, the monetary debates of the early thirties
continued to be based on the "credit creation" and "quantity of money"
theories of the monetary and banking process.

The situation regarding the theory of credit creation was accurately
depicted by Mr. B. K. Sandwell, writing in 1933 as editor of Saturday
Night:

> There is still a profound difference of opinion between the West
> and the East as to the nature of the banking process, and few
> parliamentarians are able to discuss that difference in intelligible
> terms. The west as a political whole is imbued with the doctrine
> that the granting of a bank loan creates and maintains a corres-
> ponding bank deposit. The East holds that the securing of a depos-
> it enables a bank to make a loan. . . . Both of these views involve
> a dangerous and misleading over-simplification of description of
> what is really a highly complicated and continually-revolving pro-
> cess.[1]

On both sides, then, the fundamental misconception of credit creation persisted, namely, the failure to distinguish between the loan-deposit operations of an individual commercial bank and those of the banking system as a whole.[2] The important difference in the early thirties as against the previous decade was that more mature thinking and more vigorous discussion, together with the force of economic circumstances, provided the "clearing of the air" which in the latter part of the decade gave way to genuine understanding.[3]

The logical next step leading from this "credit" background was--as it had been during the preceding ten years--the formulation, however informally and inadequately, of a theory of the relationship between money and the level of prices. The quantity theory had been carried over into the thirties by British and American economists, with the resultant emphasis on price stabilization through monetary measures, and in Canada the development was quite similar. Canadians fluctuated between the view that the postulation of a causal role for money in the determination of prices was completely nonsensical, and the view that such a theory represented man's great hope for a future of abundance and stability. The choice of positions on this issue (as might be expected) was that of almost unqualified rejection by the bankers and virtually complete acceptance by the radicals, with the professional economist standing somewhere in between.[4]

But, despite the analytical advances made on the issues of "credit creation" and "price level" both extreme groups generally neglected or misunderstood, while the professional economists inadequately emphasized, the following set of critical observations, which by the early thirties had already begun to permeate British and American monetary discussions: (1) Commercial banks were neither neutral in, nor fully capable of controlling, the process of economic fluctuations. (2) All the equations of exchange were to be regarded as definitional truisms with no causal significance, and with magnitudes not easily measured. (3) The quantity theory expressing a long-run proportional relationship between money supply and price level was not in serious conflict with the statistical facts, although these facts provided no proof of the alleged passivity of the price level, or of the crucial role of price changes in the operation of the economy. (4) The short-run cyclical version of the quantity theory was not wholly corroborated, either by general statistical findings or by specific historical experience--again apart from the question of the alleged passiveness and overwhelming importance of price changes. And (5) the utility of the equations of exchange as tools of economic analysis was clearly demonstrated--along with the need, however, for going beyond the narrow confines of these equations in order to explain, in "income-expenditure" terms, the workings of the monetary process in particular and the economic system in general.

II. THE POPULAR CASE FOR MONETARY ORTHODOXY

The inflation controversy revolved around three main topics, all closely interrelated: the gold standard, internal currency inflation, and the depreciation of the Canadian dollar in terms of foreign currencies. The discussions generally found the politicians of the major parties and the businessmen taking their stand alongside the bankers in favour of "monetary orthodoxy, " and the professional economists ranging between this position and the "monetary heresy" of the radicals.

Monetary Orthodoxy in Government
Vigorous proposals for inflation of the Canadian price structure came out of the West during the period 1930-3, and continued, with less intensity, into the latter part of the decade. To such suggestions, those directly responsible for governmental policy were unalterably opposed.

Cabinet views. Within the Government group, no one was more emphatic in his opposition than the Conservative Prime Minister, Mr. Bennett, who believed from the outset that if the Dominion Notes Act were repealed --that is, if the gold backing for Canadian currency were removed--the dollar would depreciate to a point where it was worth about twenty-five cents at the most, and probably less:

> There is no man who has given any attention to this who has not realized that. . . . Behind what we emit as money, behind the currency that we send out from the Treasury, must not we always have something that has a fixed value? How otherwise can we manage?. . . This talk of the gold standard in theory is something about which. . . we could have very learned and lengthy discussions. . . . I am not an economist, but. . . I have been dealing with a real problem, maintaining the credit and financial integrity of Canada, and I know exactly what at least the men we owe say.[5]

At no time during the depression years did Mr. Bennett retreat from his orthodox position, based on the assumed certainty of runaway inflation, and, for him, on the overriding need for maintaining Canada's financial integrity throughout the world.

Even in those instances where policies pursued had inflationary implications, the Prime Minister took the greatest pains to assure all Canadians that such measures were carried out quite reluctantly, and that, in any case, they involved no real departure from monetary orthodoxy. Thus, with respect to the $35 million loan transaction between the government and the banks in November 1932,[6] he felt that Canada was justified-- "to the very limited degree necessary in our case--in joining other countries in the adoption of monetary measures designed to encourage recovery";[7] but at the same time he declared that "this country will not depart from the established principles of sound money."[8] And when the Dominion Notes Act was amended in June 1934, Mr. Bennett again moved swiftly to counteract the impression that he had altered his views. The Government was merely acting in accordance with the prudent recommendations (of which the reduction in gold cover against currency was one) of the 1933 World Economic Conference. The former was, in fact, "providing a margin of reserve in excess of that deemed sufficient by the Conference. I offer this comment in advance to dispel any possible doubt of those who may regard the proposed action as unorthodox or as a departure from the accepted cannons of sound monetary practice."[9]

The Minister of Finance, Mr. Rhodes,[10] acknowledged that, although economists and financial experts devoting themselves to the subject of economics disagreed on every other subject, the one subject on which they were all in agreement was the desirability of a rise in commodity prices as a necessary condition for world recovery. The means of bringing about this price rise, however, was a different question entirely. The Great Depression was an "international disease" which could be cured only by an "international remedy":

> Some of the advantages claimed for inflation may seem alluring to industries harrassed by falling prices and declining turnover. But let the sponsors of inflation never forget that, apart from the other difficulties and dangers involved in their program, one inevitable result would be a flight from our dollar, a withdrawal on a large scale of the capital invested by foreigners in this country in the form of securities and bank deposits. There are also to be considered internal reactions to any steps, which might impair confidence in a country's currency. Against policies which might lead to such dangers, this government has resolutely set its face.[11]

Strong anti-inflation pronouncements were made also by Mr. Stevens, the Minister of Trade and Commerce, and by Mr. W. A. Gordon, the Minister of Labour. Of particular interest is the latter's rationale for the Government's position, the essence of which was as follows:

> I am not going to offer much on [the] subject [of inflation], because I feel that, while I can build up a theory on both sides I am not sure that either of them is sound.... I believe I am sufficiently well acquainted with the writers on economic subjects and their works to say that I could take a dozen of the foremost authorities on the subject and find half a dozen on the one side and half a dozen on the other.... I know that there are many things that might be said in favour of inflation. At the moment, we do not think it desirable to inflate the currency of this country.[12]

These are hardly the type of considerations which one might expect from a responsible government leader on such a weighty issue. It is, of course, impossible to determine to what extent they were the consequence of an accurate appraisal of the climate of contemporary public opinion, and to what extent the result of a characteristic unwillingness or inability to examine critically the case for inflation. The fact remains, however, that careful economic arguments for monetary orthodoxy were unnecessary, so general was the support of the Government's position throughout the Dominion.

    Liberal agreement. The official Opposition in the House of Commons joined the Government in condemning any action which might lead to inflation. Mr. Mackenzie King accurately reflected the outlook of his party in his appeal to (1) extreme caution on account of limited economic knowledge, (2) the difficulty of controlling inflationary price changes, and (3) the importance of upholding Canada's reputation for credit-worthiness in the field of international finance.[13] He could not see that Canadians were sufficiently enlightened on the currency question to warrant Parliament suspending the practice of redeeming notes in gold. It was a question which was stimulating a great deal of study on the part of economists and social reformers, but there was, at that time, no generally accepted consensus. It was, indeed, quite possible that inflationary measures would further aggravate Canada's economic difficulties:

> Why should we, at this time of all times, when we are in the midst
> of a depression, ... take a step which may make things worse than
> they are?... Is it fair to those who have come forward [recently]
> and made their investments with the government of this country
> [in a conversion loan] in the belief that the government was going
> to meet its payments in gold, that, within a few days after this
> transaction had been completed, Parliament should declare that
> it has decided to pay not in gold but in inflated or depreciated cur-
> rency?... More than that, since when has in inflated or depreci-
> ated currency been a sound cure for any social ill? Much of the
> trouble which the world had experienced has arisen from curren-
> cies which have been inflated or depreciated.[14]

Canada, Mr. King continued, was fortunately anchored to a gold basis, and why should the Government--at the very time when it was seeking to expand the Dominion's foreign trade--"take the one step which, above all others, would declare to the world that we have lost confidence in our own financial and industrial position?"[15]

Monetary Orthodoxy in Finance and Business

    In their writings, general speeches, policy declarations to shareholders, and testimony at governmental hearings, Canadian bankers and businessmen left little room for doubt as to where they stood in the inflation controversy.

    The bankers' conservatism. For example, Mr. J. A. MacLeod, General Manager of the Bank of Nova Scotia, argued that it was by the application of "simple and time-honoured remedies" that Canadians would best put themselves in a position to take advantage of improved business conditions when they appeared. There was no panacea to be found, or it would have been found long before then. "Nevertheless, in this, as in previous depressions, old nostrums are loudly being advertised, and one by one the discarded monetary heresies which the world rejected on the basis of long experience in the nineteenth century are being resurrected."[16] On the other hand, governments could not solve depression problems by legislating silver (or gold) into money--the need was for the reorganization of world trade and world finance so as to relieve debtor countries from the constant drain of specie. Nor, on the other hand, could the banks of any country do what was so often demanded of them, namely, restore business activity by policies of credit inflation.

In response to the criticism then being increasingly levelled against the gold standard as a system of settling international payments, Mr. B. Leman, President of the Canadian Bankers' Association and General Manager of the National Canadian Bank,[17] advanced the contrary opinion that the defect was not inherent in the gold standard, but in the use then being made of the world's gold. "Confidence should in the not-distant future again take possession of men's minds, and the gold standard, under greater freedom of trade, can again be easily maintained in international financial markets."[18]

A helpful summary of the bankers' over-all attitude in the inflation controversy is provided by the comments of Mr. W. G. Gooderham, President of the Bank of Toronto, and Mr. J. Dodds, General Manager of the Bank of Montreal. According to the former, "theoretically, a restricted and temporary measure of currency inflation is tempting, but one dose almost invariably calls for another, and who is to say where the line should be drawn? In any event, inflation is not the remedy for depressed prices."[19] The latter reasoned that deliberate adoption of a policy of depreciation of the Canadian dollar would be both futile and expensive. It would compel the Dominion's competitors, whose currency had already been depreciated by impairment of credit, to depreciate still further, and if Canada followed this downward movement, its exports would finally be given away. Meanwhile, Canadians would be obliged to pay more for their necessary imports, such as cotton, wool, coal, petroleum, etc. Inflation "is not a way out of depression but a way in, and leads ultimately to chaos. To inflate deliberately would be to render nugatory the three years of necessary purging that business has had."[20] On behalf of the Canadian Bankers' Association, Mr. Dodds emphasized before the Royal Commission on Banking and Currency, that:

> Exchange depreciation will impair the credit of a borrowing country, disturb the flow of goods between one country and another, and exert a random and disruptive influence upon the finances of corporations, municipalities, and governments which are called upon to make interest payments in foreign currencies.... [Moreover,] any attempt to raise domestic prices... by measures designed to increase arbitrarily the volume of commercial credit

in use, is bound to disrupt the normal economic process in unpredictable directions, and to cause disequilibria difficult to eradicate
later.[21]

Business contrasts. Although predominantly "sound-money conscious, "
Canadian business interests did not reveal the same unanimity of views as
the bankers. As might be expected, the exporting groups often cut across
East-West lines to press their case for exchange depreciation;   while
those business leaders whose enterprises had a solid basis in the domestic market stated unequivocally their opposition to all potentially-inflation-
ary policies. Typical of the latter group was Mr. R. H. McMaster, President of the Steel Company of Canada:

> If experience has proven anything, it has established the fact that
> there is no royal road to, nor any painless method of, correcting
> economic mistakes. Certainly, to attempt to do so by inflation
> promises little hope in the light of the experience of those countries
> that have made such attempts or travelled this path in recent years.
> Government or other interference with the economic laws has
> everywhere served to accentuate the difficulties, rather than pro-
> vide a cure.... It has been of infinite help to the confidence pre-
> vailing throughout [Canada] that the present government has so de-
> finitely declared itself in favour of the tried principles of sound
> money.[22]

Sir Edward Beatty, Chairman of the Board and President of the Canadian
Pacific Railway Company, showed similar inclinations in attributing the
recovery which was beginning to set in during the year 1934 to "hard work
and enterprise, " and not to "the precepts of well-meaning but misguided
theorists and doctrinaires whose concepts of political economy may sound
well as short-cuts to national salvation, but are too often lacking in a basis
of hard work, economy, and individual enterprise."[23]
    What is surprising and worth noting, though more the exception than
the rule, is the fact that some businessmen, with no apparent "interest"
to advance, did approach the recovery problem with a sense of the urgent
need for bold action unhampered by orthodox restrictions and designed
not only to alleviate the depressed economic conditions but also to assure
the survival of private-enterprise capitalism. The most careful economic
analysis of this kind known to the writer was that of the Economic Reform
Association, a group of several hundred business and professional men
whose views are outlined in their appropriate heretical context.[24]

III. THE POPULAR CASE FOR MONETARY HERESY

Business Radicalism - An Exception to the Rule
    The Economic Reform Association argued that Canadians could not
hope to achieve the "golden age of economics in the stone age of economic

thought."[25] The depression was held to have been caused primarily by a maladjustment or series of maladjustments in the process of providing and distributing purchasing power. This was not meant to imply that non-monetary problems were to be ignored, but rather that the dominant and immediate problems were those of a monetary character. If a more certain and better regulated system were not achieved, the whole economic order would pass away.

The major responsibility for the maladjustment, the Association believed, lay in the "antiquated organization" of the Canadian monetary and banking system, which had failed to progress with the rapidity characteristic of the rest of the economic structure. It was therefore urged that gold be abandoned as the basis of Canada's currency.[26] Its use as a voluntary reserve, and for the adjustment of temporary balances in foreign trade, might be retained without prejudice to stability: but rigid adherence to the international gold standard would be disastrous. Moreover, if internal price stability were maintained, fluctuations in the external value of the Canadian dollar would be minimized, except in relation to currencies which themselves fluctuated in purchasing power:

> Fluctuations in the exchange value of a properly-managed currency will not constitute an additional uncertainty, but merely represent a transference of instability from the field of prices into that of exchange rates. This represents a more manageable complexity, with repercussions on foreign trade rather than the whole field of industry and commerce. The international gold standard was specifically designed to maintain a stable exchange ratio between currencies at the deliberate sacrifice of the stability of internal price levels over short and long periods. This system could only survive under conditions which may have been approximated in the nineteenth century, but, conspicuously absent since the War [of 1914-1918], are not likely to be re-established.[27]

The gold standard had never been an automatic standard. It had reached its full development only under the skilful and authoritative management of the Bank of England and the City of London. The generation of the thirties and forties was not likely to see again the favourable combination of circumstances under which England had supervised the operation of the gold standard--particularly when consideration was given to the newly dominant international economic position of an inexperienced, relatively self-sufficient, high-tariff, and poor-lending United States.[28]

With respect to internal monetary policy, the Association's proposals involved "the adoption of positive measures to raise the international price level in Canada to [the] point [1926] approximately that at which the bulk of our fixed contractual obligations were assumed."[29] For the realization of this "reflationary" objective the Association submitted the following programme:

(A) A public statement by the government that a rise in the price level of a stated extent is to be engineered for a certain set date. If presented convincingly, this would cause a rise in commodity prices and establish a premium on foreign currencies. (B) This rise would represent an opportunity to the banks to extend credit, increasing purchasing power, and establishing a foundation for the higher price level more durable than its original speculative basis.... (C) In the event that the rise in prices was not sufficient, or that the banks were unwilling or unable to effect the required increase of purchasing power, it would be initiated by the adoption of optional non-income-producing public works financed by the government through an increase in the note issue.[30]

The Monetary Heresy of the Radicals

Stated above--interestingly enough, with greater clarity and force than the radicals themselves, as a group, were able to achieve--was the crux of the radical case for inflation.[31] It was, nevertheless, the persistence of the Western politicians and farmers--acting in desperation to save the wheat economy from complete chaos, uninhibited by overworked tenets of "sound finance," and, apparently, sincerely convinced of the net advantages of an inflationary policy--which forced the issue on an otherwise apathetic public.

Mr. Coote's detailed analysis. Mr. Coote was again prominent in this phase of radical agitation. Referring, in 1931, to the immediate post-depression situation, he argued that, if Canada had not been on the gold standard, the deflation need not have been nearly as severe as it had been. Under the circumstances, the best course to follow was the complete abandonment of the gold standard at that time. Since the balance of international settlements was adverse, the Canadian dollar would soon depreciate in foreign countries, and the price of wheat and other exports in Canadian currency would be increased to the extent of that depreciation.[32] In an attempt to allay the popular fear of an increase in the cost of living commensurate with the currency depreciation, Mr. Coote quoted Mr. Plumptre's appraisal:

If we raised the price of gold one-fifth, and the exchanges moved against us to that extent, all our imports would cost us that much more. The cost of living would be raised slightly. (Not more, probably, than 3 to 4 per cent, since the cost of imports at wholesale constitutes but a small proportion of the cost of living.) This arbitrary raising of the cost of living might, in normal times, have been called an injustice, but after the year 1930, in which wholesale prices have fallen about 20 per cent and retail about 8 per cent, a plan which attempts to restore them towards their 1929 level can hardly be called "unjust." It might be called "inflation," but the proper term would be "anti-deflation."[33]

Canada's two major industries (wheat and pulp and paper), Mr. Coote continued, were in very great difficulties. Depreciation of the dollar was the easiest way of raising the prices of the goods produced by those industries, thereby insuring that production would continue. He was not suggesting that the abandonment of the gold standard would provide the solution of all the complex economic problems then facing the Dominion. "It is simply one remedy which should be applied immediately, and which, I think, would be very effective in relieving, temporarily at least, the depression from which we are now suffering."[34]

Mr. Coote acknowledged that the gold standard had some advantages. It did lend an air of respectability; and stable exchange rates were very beneficial for those having to meet commitments in the United States. In his opinion, however, the disadvantages of the gold standard more than outweighed its advantages. "It limits the amount of credit in Canada by the amount of gold in the Treasury. It puts the price level in Canada the mercy of foreign banks. Canada is a debtor country, and if we are to remain on the gold standard, we must be prepared to sacrifice internal stability of prices, wages, employment, and our whole standard of living. For what? For the sake of exchange-rate stability. Surely that is too great a price for us to pay."[35] The failure of the Government to take positive action in this sphere was particularly difficult for Mr. Coote to understand, in the light of Canadian experience during World War I. If Canada had remained on the gold standard in 1914, it would have been disastrous. Just as the Government had previously abandoned it without hesitation, so it should immediately abandon it then in the war against unemployment and poverty.

On the orthodox foreign-debt argument, Mr. Coote noted that foreign obligations were paid with exports. Those exports brought Canada the same amount of foreign exchange whether the dollar was worth 100 cents or 50 cents in New York. Canadians could meet their foreign obligations just as well whether the currency was at par or not. On the other hand, the country could not continue to meet those obligations if it bankrupted its producers through low domestic price levels. "Stability of the internal price level at a proper point is ten times more important than exchange-rate stability."[36]

Speaking in the House of Commons early in 1933, Mr. Coote was sharply critical of the Government for placing so much faith in the World Economic Conference then preparing to convene in London, and for consequently failing to apply remedial measures on a national basis. The whole internal economy was dislocated; the Canadian standard of living, incomes, and employment--all were being "sacrificed to maintain the fetish called 'sound money,' mostly sound and very little money, so far as most people can see."[37]

Several months later, in his "inflation" appeal to the Royal Commission on Banking and Currency, Mr. Coote pointed to the extraordinary situation then existing with regard to the note issue: "Dominion notes can be issued, under the Dominion Notes Act, only against gold, but Dominion

notes without limit may be issued under the Finance Act against various
classes of securities; yet until recently, under the terms of the Dominion
Notes Act, notes issued under the Finance Act might be presented for redemption in gold."[38] Consequently, there was clear justification in contemporary practice for amending the Dominion Notes Act to permit the
issue of Dominion notes without gold reserve. "Any currency becomes
inconvertible whenever the people decide to exercise their right to con-
vert.... The amount of notes should be limited only by the needs of commerce and industry, based on a stable commodity price level."[39]

Radical thought in general. Monetary agitation by other radicals took
the form, for the most part, of a reiteration of the arguments repeatedly
put forward by Mr. Coote. Important differences of emphasis persisted,
however. Thus, there were many who believed, with Mr. Woodsworth,
that monetary reform was subordinate to the need for fundamental reorganization of the entire economic structure, and that the main purpose served
by the former would be the provision of temporary assistance for Canadian
exporters, and of relief from the excessive debt burden.[40] For others,
the monetary approach, through social credit or other means, provided
the complete solution to Canada's economic problems.[41] But all appealed
strongly to the views of radical economic thinkers--such as Keynes, Fisher,
and McKenna--who had gained world prominence; and all shared the con-
viction--clearly expressed by the Manitoba Co-operative Conference (representing the United Farmers of Manitoba and other agricultural organizations)--that there were "more difficulties connected with international
stabilization [of the exchanges] than with national [stabilization of prices]",[42]
and that the circumstances demanded bold governmental action directed--
in the words of the United Farmers of Alberta--at "controlled inflation,
or 'reflation', which simply means such an expansion of currency and
credit as may be required to restore the price level to the point at which
it stood before the present great slump began."[43]

IV. CANADIAN ECONOMISTS AND THE INFLATION CONTROVERSY

By way of recapitulation, the international economic collapse of the
early thirties, particularly Great Britain's abandonment of the gold standard in 1931, made monetary policy a live issue in Canada. Previous public interest in such policy had been negligible, but now an intense verbal
struggle was being waged, as between the majority group which favoured
economic and financial retrenchment, and the minority group advocating
a radical departure from traditional practice.

The truth is, of course, that the attitudes of both government and
banking circles (which directly reflected predominant public opinion) and
the radical dissenters were, to no small extent, rooted in the objective
facts of Canada's international economic position at the onset of the Great
Depression. The statistical survey made in chapter V shows: (1) the
overwhelming United States-United Kingdom orientation of Canadian foreign trade; (2) the consequent delicateness of the Canadian dollar's inter-

mediate position between the currencies of those two countries;   (3) the
heavy concentration of Canada's exports in terms of producing groups;
(4) the extremely wide variety of goods entering into Canadian imports;
(5) the importance of sources of foreign loans in the economic development of the Dominion;   and (6) the extensiveness and rigidity of Canada's
service payments on foreign-held debt.   Given these facts, it is understandable that each "thought class"--in the emotionally charged atmosphere fostered by the suddenness and severity of the Depression--should
have sought to rationalize that line of policy which best seemed to satisfy
the conditions for its own stability, and to identify such conditions with
those required for the national welfare.   To the orthodox group it seemed
axiomatic that the only real road to recovery was that involving (1) the
preservation of Canada's world reputation for financial "soundness, "
(2) the avoidance of higher prices of the Canadian dollar for imported
merchandise, and (3) full reliance on the policy initiative of the world's
leading industrial countries.   To the radicals, on the other hand, an
autonomous monetary policy, having as its goal the raising of Canadian
prices to pre-depression levels, appeared as the basic prerequisite for
revival in all phases of Canadian economic activity.

In such circumstances, detailed comparative appraisals, by professional economists, of the implications of alternative policy measures
might well have injected the much-needed element of balance into the inflation controversy.   But the contribution of Canadian economists, with
some important exceptions, was something less than was called for by
the gravity of the problems involved.

Economists Favouring Exchange Depreciation and/or Currency Inflation

Mr. Plumptre.   From the beginning of the Great Depression, Mr.
Plumptre's major concern was with problems of monetary policy.[44]
Reference has already been made to his minimization of the increase in
the cost of living to be expected from a 20 per cent depreciation of the
Canadian dollar.   In broad terms, his approach comprised carefully--but
strongly--advanced support for unorthodox exchange rate policy, in combination with marked skepticism about the efficacy of currency manipulation directed at raising the internal price level.[45]

With regard to the former policy route,[46] Mr. Plumptre emphasized
that the gold-standard policy of fixed exchange rates was necessarily a
very difficult one in a country, such as Canada, in which there might be
large variations in the chief items of the balance of international payments.
The variable items included capital imports, but unfortunately excluded
fixed service upon past borrowing.   In order to maintain the gold standard,
much more conscious control of the balance of payments was necessary
than had been exercised in the past.   Large reserves of foreign exchange
or gold would have to be built up in "fat years" without internal credit expansion, when exports were high and borrowing easy.   These would then
be available to offset the deficits on international account which would inevitably occur in "lean years. "

In Mr. Plumptre's judgment, however, the policy of fixed exchange rates probably was not the best for a country in Canada's position. "An exchange rate which is allowed and even encouraged to depreciate in lean years would be a closer approach to an ideal credit policy."[47] There were several objections to such a line of action. First, if the monetary authority was incompetent or unduly influenced by sectional interests, it was possible that control measures might degenerate into a continuous policy of exchange rate depreciation, with resulting internal inflation. "Thus, while a conscious policy of exchange fixity may be the more difficult, a conscious policy of exchange variation may be the more dangerous."[48] A second serious objection was that there was no experience in Canada, or any other country, at that time (1932) upon which to base the policy or its execution. The third objection introduced the question of international borrowing and repayment. It was obvious, Mr. Plumptre admitted, that exchange depreciation increased the burden, in terms of Canadian dollars, of debts payable in foreign currencies. But it had yet to be proved that the Dominion government, in spite of its own debts and the assistance which it had rendered to the provinces to meet theirs, was a heavy loser on account of depreciation:

> For there must be favourable effects of depreciation upon revenues, maintained by the support which depreciation gives to prices, and the stimulus it gives to business; and other federal expenditures appearing in the recent budget, such as wheat subsidies and even unemployment-relief grants, might have been less necessary with still further depreciation. It is just possible that a thorough investigation would indicate that the Canadian governments, as a group, actually gain from some degree of exchange depreciation.[49]

But governments were not the only foreign borrowers. There were many private debtors, the vast majority of whom would be injured by depreciation. The claims of these debtors could be accommodated--granting that such accommodation was a necessary condition for continued capital movements into and out of Canada in the future--in two ways: either by maintaining a stable exchange rate with the Dominion's chief creditor (the United States), which, in effect, meant the maintenance of the gold standard; or by setting up some agency to control the volume of foreign borrowing, and to deal with demands of individual borrowers for compensation for loss occasioned by exchange depreciation. To Mr. Plumptre there appeared to be good reason for pursuit of the latter course of action.

The only alternatives, then, in a country like Canada, were "either to seize the [exchange rate] tail [of the dog of national currency] and stabilize it, perhaps under a heavy weight of gold, a policy which will necessarily result in severe oscillations of the body economic; or else we may try to influence the position of the body by gentle but firm pressure upon an exchange rate tail, the width of whose wags we hope to be able to restrain within reasonable limits."[50]

Just two years later (1934), looking back to his choice of exchange rate flexibility, Mr. Plumptre found that since 1931 the Canadian dollar probably had been higher, in terms of foreign currency, than the best interest of the country would have warranted.[51] It would have been preferable, notwithstanding many strong arguments to the contrary, to keep the Canadian dollar from any appreciation above the pound sterling. Such a policy, moreover, would have been not only preferable but also possible, for it would probably not have aroused either tariff or exchange reprisals from abroad. If, that is, in the week following the British departure from the gold standard, the Canadian dollar had found a lower international level than it actually did, the subsequent course of events outside Canada would not have been appreciably changed; whereas within the Dominion the level of prices, incomes, and tax revenues probably would have been substantially supported. That the financial position of those debtors with obligations in the United States would have deteriorated, was quite clear; but it seemed likely that "the Dominion and provincial governments would have been, on balance, better off, not to mention the majority of the Canadian people."[52]

The basis for Mr. Plumptre's over all attitude towards depreciation lay, then, in the fact that in a raw-material-exporting country the chief source of variation in the national level of prosperity was the fluctuating incomes received by the producers of such materials. Those incomes depended on the volume and prices of the exports; and the export prices depended, in turn, on world market prices converted into the exporters' currency at the prevailing exchange rate. "Thus the foreign exchange rate is and must be the monetary key to the level of prices and prosperity in a country such as Canada."[53] The Dominion stood self-condemned if, in a period of depression, it had not canvassed the possibility of utilizing the exchange rate remedy. It stood equally condemned if its previous policy of drift had so enmeshed it in foreign financial entanglements as to render the use of that remedy inexpedient.[54]

Probably because of his skepticism, Mr. Plumptre devoted relatively little attention to the question of currency manipulation.[55] His objections were twofold. First, because of the possibility of (a) panicky public reaction, (b) the policy being pushed too far, and (c) excessive resultant expansion of bank credit, he believed that, "while playing with the note issue might quite conceivably be used to good advantage, as a matter of general policy the game is not worth the candle."[56] And second, currency expansion was not likely, apart from such factors as public works or exchange rate movements, to initiate recovery, though it might serve a useful purpose by easing monetary conditions and reducing the interest burden of government debt. The peculiar weakness of currency expansion, in other words, was that, if it did not get out of hand, it was not likely to be effective.

Professor Drummond. A substantial group of Canadian economists supported Mr. Plumptre's position, though they seem to have concerned themselves more with general problems of monetary policy than with the specific issue of the desirability of unorthodox monetary measures in the early years of the Depression. Professor C. F. Drummond of the University of British Columbia was a prominent member of this group. The essence of his writings on the subject was that adherence to the gold standard in the twentieth-century world necessarily entailed severe sacrifices on the part of participating countries--sacrifices which could be avoided, without losing exchange stability, only by a combination of national intelligent monetary control and international co-operation through the technique of the equalization fund.[57] The real question, according to Professor Drummond, was not whether the countries off gold in 1933 should return to it, even under a new evaluation or coverage, but whether the gold standard, as a basis for international trade and as a reliable determinent of relative price levels, could ever be made to work efficiently again. Of that possibility he was very doubtful.

Variations in the supply of gold, in its mobility and distribution, and in its use under different banking systems, relative to the production of goods and services, brought about a random redistribution of wealth between different economic groups and between nations. Those random consequences could be avoided, and the relationships between groups made more stable, only by management and control of price levels. If all countries were to reform their banking systems with a view to control of the price level, variations of exchange rate would be negligible, violent fluctuations easily avoided, and the flow of international investments in no way impaired.

Mr. Parkinson and Professor Jackson. Referring to the years immediately following the 1929 collapse, Mr. Parkinson deplored the lack of centralized guidance for the wordy battle being fought over the depreciation issue.[58] He argued, moreover, that, "as a means of insulating the price structure of Canada from the effects of a drastic deflation abroad, some deliberate but controlled depreciation of the exchange would, on balance, be desirable."[59] Professor G. E. Jackson of the University of Toronto was similarly brief but clear in his approval of the depreciation of the Canadian dollar which had been produced by the free play of market forces; and in his declaration that he would be "by no means altogether sorry to see the depreciation carried a little further."[60]

Mr. Creighton. Citing the views of Keynes and Sir Cecil Blackett, Mr. Creighton[61] held that gold was no longer necessary as backing for notes, and that its real function--and the only one which it was, in fact, performing--was to meet an adverse balance of payments on current account; all this despite the fact that the public, which could not then get gold for notes, and bankers, who did not have the gold to give for notes, continued to imagine that gold backing was desirable. Mr. Creighton rejected all contemporary proposals for tying the Canadian dollar either to the American dollar or the British pound--the former on grounds of the destabilizing effect of American monetary policy, and the latter because Britain had failed to take the positive steps necessary to assure the stability of sterling. By that time (1933), he believed, the attention should, in any case, have been focussed on internal, rather than external, monetary policy :

The entire process of abandoning the gold standard and of watching the dollar fluctuate in terms of foreign currencies has probably caused us to think too much of the exchange side of the money problem. True, Canada is a great exporting nation, and as such, in normal times, should probably be more concerned about exchange control than most nations. However, the present depression has already gone so far, foreign exchange as a whole is so unstable, and foreign trade has decreased so greatly, that a state of emergency exists, and in that state of emergency it would seem that Canada's first duty is to set her house in order. At the present time, then, it would appear that Canadians should concern themselves less with the external value of the dollar and give their first attention to management of the internal price level.[62]

Undoubtedly, Canadians faced a serious problem in the repayment of debts which they owed abroad. But if existing conditions were allowed to continue, the country would not long be able to meet its foreign obligations regardless of what the exchange rates might be. "The government, therefore, should boldly take the responsibility of declaring that it is going to raise the internal price level to a determined level, say that of 1926. Having so determined and declared, it should resolutely administer the money and credit to that end."[63]

Mr. Goldenberg. In the opinion of Mr. H. C. Goldenberg of McGill University,[64] Canada should have followed Australia's policy by allowing the dollar to depreciate so as to maintain a higher level of internal and external prices. Indeed, to the extent that recovery was setting in, it was, in large measure, attributable to the unconscious, de facto depreciation which had occurred after 1931.

Mr. Goldenberg was critical, however, of internal governmental attempts at inflation in the early thirties. Production and trade would not be stimulated by low interest rates and abundant supplies of cheap credit in a period of falling prices. Banks would not lend, and responsible businessmen would not borrow, unless they felt relatively certain that adequate consumer purchasing power was available. That had been the experience of the United States since 1930. The faith in currency inflation alone was likewise misplaced. A policy of currency expansion would result in a rise in prices only if it was so carried out as to place the increased purchasing power in the hands of consumers who would actually spend it. That was by no means a certain consequence of the initial currency expansion. Thus, "monetary policy alone will not prevent economic disequilibrium."[65]

Mr. Burton. Much the same approach was taken by Mr. F. W. Burton of the University of Toronto.[66] In his judgment, Canadian monetary policy should aim at the following objectives: First, arrest the economic downswing, for deflation was a cumulative process to which, without a change in the monetary situation, there appeared to be no limit; it was conceivable that, if the monetary authorities failed to take stimulative action, and if public confidence were completely destroyed, "deflation might continue until there was no credit outstanding at all, and the gold was all in the hands of a few people who would be hoarding it, while all debts would have been defaulted and all production would have stopped."[67] Second, facilitate the economic system's absorption of the permanent changes brought about by the previous boom, and reduce price distortions due to world-wide price changes over which the Dominion had no control; the latter objective necessitated a policy of exchange depreciation, since "the effect of a fall in the exchange rate would be to raise the price, in Canadian dollars, of Canada's exports, and [this] would mean a reduction of Canada's internal disequilibrium."[68] And finally, to promote the resumption of the interrupted process of innovation, and so effect genuine internal recovery, by improving market conditions, lowering interest rates, and restoring confidence.

Professor Knox. Professor F. A. Knox of Queen's University[69] was another member of the "pro-depreciation" group of economists to make the point that "exchange stability, an international monetary standard, implies a nineteenth century world--it may not be worth its costs in the twentieth."[70] Concretely, he argued that Canada should not return to the gold standard, not because monetary management was in itself desirable, but rather because such management was forced on the Dominion by disunited and contradictory monetary policies throughout the world. "For the smaller countries to keep their currencies at fixed ratios of exchange to the currencies of the great powers, is to keep open the channels by which economic fluctuations are spread between countries.... One of the most important... measures [for mitigating the severity of these fluctuations] is a variable exchange rate."[71] It was desirable, then, that the Canadian dollar should be kept free of all exchange entanglements. The attempt to maintain fixed rates of exchange between it and other currencies should not be made until the advantages of such rigidity were much greater, and its dangers much less, than they were at that time.

Professor Day. Professor J. P. Day of McGill University[72] likewise devoted his attention primarily to the international sphere.[73] His analytical position, however, reflected a unique combination of radical and orthodox thinking.

Thus, he supported the Government's policy of allowing the Canadian dollar to fluctuate freely between the British and American currency units--but only as a temporary policy for minimizing the dislocations which would have resulted from rapid shifts in the exchanges in any direction. The long-run need, in his view, clearly was for exchange stability, and he often expressed the conviction that the most important monetary goal which all countries, including Canada, should strive to attain was the restoration of the international gold standard; though his grave doubts as to the likelihood of international agreement on new gold parities, and of American willingness to make substantial debt and tariff adjustments, led him to believe that this restoration was not within sight as a practical proposition. As an interim attempt at exchange stabilization, he therefore proposed the adoption, by all countries of the British Empire, of a sterling exchange standard, that is, a mechanism by which all imperial currencies would always be exchangeable at a fixed rate for sterling, and vice versa.

For Professor Day, the case for pegging all imperial rates with sterling was virtually unassailable, though he did admit that, as far as Canada was concerned, the intimacy of trade connections with the United States might well mean greater fluctuations with the American dollar than the Dominion had had before that time, as well as some credit management by the central bank (the establishment of which was so necessary in that connection), which would, when it took the form of credit restriction, be resented. The disadvantages of such fluctuations, however, were more than offset by the advantages to be derived by traders getting a stabilized currency exchange with all the countries of the sterling bloc.

Professor Day's choice of sterling as the international--or inter-imperial--currency base was dictated by the impression made on him by the contemporary respectability of the British pound, by his supreme confidence in its future stability, and by his utter lack of confidence in the stability of the American dollar. His attitude toward the role of the United States in international monetary reconstruction was particularly bitter and uncompromising:

> The idea that if you only give the people of the United States plenty of time, ... wait till this experiment has been proved futile or the next, and do not annoy them, they will co-operate intelligently in matters of world monetary reconstruction, has been falsified by experience. The policy of patience and politeness has not had any success, and, while I am far from advocating a policy of impatience or impoliteness, I think the world will do better to count the United States out in any attempts at monetary reforms, to let them go their own wild way, and to see what the rest of us can do to restore currency stability within as wide an area as possible.[74]

It would be difficult, but not impossible, for such a system to function without the United States. Granting the impossibility of that system isolating itself from the instability of the American economy, it was "better to do what is possible without their help than to continue obsequious and apparently futile efforts to lure them into a more complaisant attitude."[75]

As regards the actual machinery for promoting and maintaining the stable exchange system, what Professor Day's proposal amounted to was the planned building up and tearing down of sterling and domestic currency balances by the central banks of all participating countries; that is, the readiness of these institutions, at all times, to buy or sell sterling at a fixed price in terms of the domestic currency when the former showed a tendency, in the market, to depreciate or appreciate, respectively.[76] He rejected the proposal for the achievement of that objective by means of a single Empire central bank, on the ground that such an agency could not maintain exchange stability without having the power of controlling

credit in the various countries of the Empire, and that such interference
with their financial independence would not be tolerated.

Economists Opposing Exchange Depreciation and Currency Inflation

Arrayed against the economists whose policy recommendations contained at least some elements of monetary heresy were those who stood
fully prepared, along with most other Canadians, to sanction the monetary
orthodoxy then being preached and practised. The position taken by the
conservative economists stemmed mainly from their varying degrees of
admiration for the gold standard, and from their great concern with
Canada's debtor status in the community of nations.

Professor Michell. There is no mistaking the appraisal made, early
in the Depression, by Professor Michell of McMaster University. To his
way of thinking, the functions performed by the gold standard in world
trade were so vital that its abandonment would constitute an action "so
momentous as to confound the imagination. We need not suppose that the
genius of man is incapable of working out another system, but we can at
least say that it would present such difficulties that we may well doubt if
they could possibly be overcome."[77]

Professor Swanson. Professor Swanson of the University of Saskatchewan was equally vehement in declaring that confidence and stability
would return to the Canadian monetary system only as a result of the restoration of the gold standard at home, and of trade with the nations of the
world. His reasons for favouring this restoration of gold were that:
(1) its abandonment had had disastrous effects upon international trade;
(2) it was essential for high and stable levels of international investment;
and (3) it had the best chance of again becoming a universal standard, for
it provided the best safeguard against inflation, as well as a reasonable
stability of prices over long periods of time.[78]

As to internal change, there was, according to Professor Swanson,
"no available technique by which, even in theory, price levels can be established and maintained."[79] Furthermore, there was danger in fixing
a price level in advance, even if that could be achieved, for, if the Government "were to restore the price level of 1926, it would involve an increase
of at least 50 per cent in the price of basic commodities in this country,
which, in turn, would undoubtedly lead to a discrepancy as between cost
and price, and further demoralization of the economic structure."[80]

Professor Balcom. One of the most careful analytical treatments of
the gold standard was that undertaken by Professor A. B. Balcom of
Acadia University.[81] He began his defence of a modified gold standard by
enumerating three weighty advantages of gold. The first was that a gold
reserve promoted confidence in paper currency and thereby insured its
ready acceptance by the public; indeed, so deeply ingrained had this habit
of thought become that it was difficult to predict how much of a strain it
would stand. A second advantage of the gold standard was that it placed an
automatic control on currency expansion. And the third advantage was
that it greatly facilitated international trade and investment by automati-

cally maintaining exchange stability, that is, by automatically stabilizing exchange rates within the limits set by the gold points. Against these advantages, Professor Balcom set two basic alleged defects. First, there was no direct long-run relation between changes in the monetary supply of gold and in the credit currency derived from it, on the one hand, and the demand for money on the other. And second, the gold standard exercised no control over the volume of currency in use during the short-run ups and downs of economic activity, except automatically to limit expansion.

The first defect, according to Professor Balcom, was frequently associated with the impending failure of the gold supply to satisfy the requirements of business, and with the consequent danger of an era of falling prices. As a matter of fact, historical analysis applied to the pre-1914 period, when the gold standard was in general operation, gave little support to the contention that slowly falling prices were incompatible with economic prosperity when underlying conditions were favourable to progress. Professor Balcom also called into question the theoretical basis of the long-run criticism by arguing that, far from being dangerous or undesirable, a slowly falling price level, accompanied by a secular rise in productive efficiency, was an essential instrument for insuring the automatic sharing, by all, of the benefits of economic progress.

Professor Balcom found equally unacceptable the objection usually made in terms of the second defect--that in the gold standard lay the basic cause of economic depressions with all their attendant evils. For this criticism was derived from an inadequate analysis of the causes of depressions; that is, from the failure to realize that the phenomenon of the business cycle was not entirely, or even primarily, a problem of price stabilization through monetary control. Moreover, in so far as there was a monetary problem, attention should have been directed towards the prevention of excessive increases in the general level of prices, not towards the automatic limitations placed on currency expansion during the downswing.

The conclusion to which these arguments led Professor Balcom was that "the alleged long-run inadequacy of the gold standard has sufficient support neither in theory nor in the lessons of experience"; [82] and that, "while the price variations of the business cycle reflect a serious condition, it is not clear that this is primarily a monetary problem--a saner view locates the trouble in the shortcomings of man and in the complexities of economic life." [83] In this context, he proceeded to consider the inflationary or "reflationary" proposals made by those who held that the normal functioning of the gold standard was impossible in the postwar economic setting, and that the main cause of the Great Depression lay in the unwise efforts which had been made to restore and maintain that standard.

Admittedly, he reasoned, the arguments of the inflationists appeared plausible and attractive, but, on close examination, they revealed important shortcomings. One was that, without an active demand for funds on the part of business, any attempted credit expansion through the banking system would prove ineffective. In the second place, even assuming that the inflation had been achieved, there was the delicate problem of controlling its volume and the purposes for which it was to be used. How, for example, would the diversion of funds into all those manipulations and predatory speculations so characteristic of periods of rapidly rising prices be prevented? And by what means would the expansion be curtailed at the proper time? Professor Balcom pointed out, finally, that there was a widespread tendency among inflationists to adopt the mistaken view that economic recovery would follow automatically from the removal of the world-disturbing conditions which had been ushered in by World War I. These conditions had undoubtedly served to intensify the cyclical movements of the twenties and thirties, but even if they had been removed ten years previously the world would still have undergone recurring expansions and depressions.

Here, then, is Professor Balcom's general appraisal of the recovery problem:

> Inflation provides no short cut out of the present depression....
> [Furthermore,] monetary reform will contribute little to the solu-
> tion of exceedingly intricate and difficult problems of world read-
> justment which today challenge the intelligence and moral fibre of
> the race. These problems involve delicate questions of national
> economics and international politics, and their solution must be
> as diverse as are the problems. Those who attempt to reduce
> this confusion to a monetary basis are permitting their enthusiasm
> for their particular field of specialization to warp their judgment
> concerning larger issues. The converse contention, namely that
> the settlement of world disorder will contribute greatly to the sat-
> isfactory functioning of an automatic gold standard has more sub-
> stantial support.[84]

It could be predicted with confidence that world conditions would gradually improve, in spite of the widespread fears, jealousies, and blunderings. As the necessary adjustments occurred, the way would be clear for a return to the gold standard in full confidence that it would again function satisfactorily.

Professor Clark. Professor A. B. Clark of the University of Manitoba gave detailed theoretical consideration to both the depreciation and currency inflation problems.[85] He distinguished between two types of depreciation, on the basis of the manner in which such depreciation was brought about. If--as with the British pound and the Canadian dollar-- there was a "specific" depreciation of the currency in terms of gold before there was any "general" depreciation compared with goods, that is, a general rise in prices, then the consequence would be a stimulus to exports and a check to imports. However, if through increased currency issue, the general depreciation occurred before the premium on gold had appeared, there would actually be a stimulus to imports and a check to exports. But the effect in either case was merely transitional:

> It exists only during the process of depreciation. Once the adjustment has been brought about between prices and costs, including incomes, and equilibrium has been restored between the general and specific depreciation of the currency, the stimulus, or check, to industry vanishes. To get a continuing stimulus to exports, a process of specific depreciation of the currency must keep ahead of the general rise in prices. Further, if export industries benefit during the process of specific depreciation of the currency, those industries dependent on imports suffer; and in so far as these imports are raw materials, the rise in their prices may lessen even the temporary stimulus to the export industries. The notion of any permanent benefit to the nation as a whole ... is but a fan-fire gleam or will-o-the-wisp.[86]

On the purely domestic side, Professor Clark called special attention to the far greater severity of the collapse in farm prices than in industrial prices. To this fact he attributed, in large measure, the "variety of more or less fantastic or objectionable schemes,"[87] including compulsory debt reduction, stamp-scrip, and general inflation of prices in Canada. He acknowledged the benefit of inflation to debtors through the lessening of the burden of fixed charges in domestic currency, but in his view the injury to creditors was equally real, so that deliberate inflation might cause as many inequities as it cured. Moreover, a natural and slow rise in prices might be beneficial, but a deliberate and rapid inflation would tend to destroy that sense of security which was the basis of credit and business. If, as appeared likely, a natural rise in the price level occurred, "it would seem unwise to enter on a policy of inflation with all its risks, of which not the least is the difficulty of keeping it within bounds, with the debtor class ever claiming that money is being kept scarce."[88] A few draughts of inflation might provide an agreeable stimulus, but like other stimulants, inflation tended to excess, "with the inevitable 'morning after' and the financial headache associated with the retreat from the morass to the solid ground of the gold standard; for to that standard we must, in course of time, return."[89]

Mr. Glazebrook. The brief comments, finally, of Mr. A. J. Glazebrook of the University of Toronto echoed Professor Clark's sentiments.[90] "Inflation" had become a phrase which comforted everybody, without people knowing exactly what it meant. The whole atmosphere was full of controversial assertions and doubtful premises. It was hopeless, moreover, for the banking system to try to control the price level by regulating the volume of credit, unless that regulation was associated with a change in the mood of the public. The only sensible ultimate course of action for Canada was a return to the international gold standard.

CHAPTER VIII

THE END OF THE CENTRAL BANK CONTROVERSY

THE CENTRAL BANK CONTROVERSY, as it developed and reached its
climax during the early thirties, was an integral part of the intellectual
ferment then being stirred up in Canada by the unprecedented economic
collapse of 1929. It is no accident that the Proceedings of the Royal Commission on Banking and Currency,[1] appointed July 31, 1933, constituted
what was probably the most voluminous and representative compilation of
public testimony that had hitherto been made by an agency of the Dominion
government as a basis for the recommendation of economic policy.[2] For
these hearings, more than any other contemporary source of public expression, crystallized economic thinking on the whole range of problems associated with the alleviation of the depressed economic conditions of the time.
In more specific, more long-run terms, however, the final stage of the
central bank controversy amounted to a good deal more than this. It was
the first really comprehensive attempt made by Canadians to analyse critically the workings of their own monetary and banking system. Moreover,
this controversy provided one of the most powerful stimuli to the subsequent adoption in the Dominion of a more mature approach to both monetary and fiscal problems.

I. THEORIES OF CENTRAL BANKING, 1930-4

Despite the maze of conflicting views advanced before the Royal Commission and elsewhere--views often loosely stated and obscured through
intermixture with ideas irrelevant to the major issue--the general pattern
of thought on the central bank question is quite clear. The overwhelmingly
important fact is that by mid-1933 the position taken by Canadian bankers--
reinforced by a large segment of the business community and remaining
substantially unchanged during the fifteen years which had elapsed since
the First World War--no longer reflected the state of governmental and
public opinion; and that, in the face of the general trend towards radicalism, the battle waged by those endeavouring to maintain the status quo
necessarily degenerated into a delaying action designed to salvage as much
as possible from the approaching wreck of the control-free Canadian monetary system.

The Bankers' Position Restated
The commercial-bank function. As in the previous decade, one basic
aspect of the bankers' thinking revolved around the profit-maximizing,
"depositor-satisfying" conception of the commercial bank function in the
Canadian economy. Concrete expression of this attitude continued to take
the form of widespread adherence to the "commercial loan" theory of

banking. The proper function of the commercial bank was to provide working capital to business, and so long as the borrower was in a position to
repay the loan at maturity, the banks were justified in furnishing such
credit accomodation without limit.[3]

Role of the banks in the Depression. In these terms, and fortified
by their over-emphasis of the international basis of the Great Depression
in Canada, the bankers were quick to absolve themselves of any responsibility for the economic difficulties then besetting the country. Among the
most outspoken--and at the same time most representative--statements
depicting the bankers' general position was that made by Mr. J. Dodds,
General Manager of the Bank of Montreal:

> It is common knowledge that the depression has been world-wide,
> and that Canada has suffered along with other countries. It is not,
> however, generally appreciated that Canada has suffered less than
> most countries, and that in large measure the reason why she has
> suffered less is due to the strength of her banks and their policies
> prior to and during the depression. The conservative policy which
> the banks followed during the boom period, and the leniency ex-
> tended and constructive help given to borrowers during the depres-
> sion which inevitably followed the boom, have contributed largely
> towards preserving the country from the full impact of the shock
> suffered elsewhere.[4]

The banks' most important contribution to the depressed Dominion had
been so to conduct their affairs as to retain the confidence of their depositors. The complaint that the banks had called in loans and refused to
make new advances for business purposes was unfounded. "The truth is
that prudent businessmen have borrowed less, lacking profitable use for
money, and the banks have been even more active than usual in competing
for safe loaning business."[5]

Canada's system of monetary control. The bankers' vigorous expression of faith in the adequacy of the system of monetary control followed
logically from this conception of the role of the commercial bank in the
Canadian economy. To be sure, concessions were made in response to
the persistent attacks of the critics, but the deficiencies recognized were
invariably regarded as being of minor importance and remediable only
within the existing institutional framework. The most comprehensive
elaboration of this position is to be found in the series of memoranda presented on behalf of the Canadian Bankers' Association to the Royal Commission on Banking and Currency.[6]

The bankers were quite willing to admit that, as things stood in 1933,
Canada had no central agency specifically charged with responsibility for
controlling the volume of credit. They were emphatic, however, in citing
two offsets to this condition. First, there was the fact that, under the
guidance of their Association, the bankers had long been in the habit of
discussing important problems with one another and with high government

officials; and, consequently, that uniformity of policy prevailed among
all the banks. This necessarily implied, so the argument went, an automatic compensatory mechanism which tended to avoid both undue deple-
tion and accumulation of cash reserves. The second offset was embodied
in the machinery of the Finance Act, which had been in operation since
1914. The Act had greatly benefited Canada--first as a precaution against
panic during the war years; and secondly, as an emergency measure
during the postwar period, during the crop-moving season, and for government financing. "Based on the record of the last twenty years, the continuance of the present facilities afforded the banks under the Finance Act is
justified, and... such continuance of the Act would be of constructive value
to the Dominion. "[7]

The bankers took special cognizance of three objections raised by
critics of the Finance Act: first, that it permitted an indefinite increase
in the Dominion note issue; second, that under the Act the tendency was
towards an inflationary rise in currency; and third, that the rediscount
rates charged the banks for advances were not varied in a manner designed
to mitigate economic instability. The reply to the first criticism was that
it overlooked the provision of the Act empowering the Treasury Board to
fix the lines of credit accorded the banks, "although it is only fair to state
that the Act iself places no obligation on the Board to fix such limits nor
to control the total amount of notes outstanding by reason of advances under the Finance Act. "[8] The bankers deemed the second criticism to be
unjustified in terms of actual Canadian experience and "the natural desire
of a prudent banker to limit his Finance-Act borrowings to temporary
periods. "[9] Against the third criticism they apparently had no defence.

The Administrative Board. In effect underscoring the weakness of
their case, the bankers were ready, though reluctant, to concede the desirability of a change in the control machinery. They would go no further,
however, than to suggest: (1) the fixing of "a definite basis for the Dominion notes issue, so as to correct the anomalies in the existing legislation"; [10] and (2) the displacement of the Treasury Board by a newly constituted, independent "Administrative Board. " This Board would be "composed of experts in finance and currency and broadly representative of
the business and agricultural interests of Canada"; and it would be "endowed with authority to see that the total amount of credits granted to the
chartered banks was in keeping with the requirements of the country, and
that the rates charged on such advances fluctuate in accordance with current conditions. "[11]

Central bank techniques. Thus, for the bankers, monetary reform
meant administrative reorganization within the Finance Act. Underlying
their rejection of all more far-reaching proposals was not only their satisfaction with the existing monetary and banking structure, but also their
conviction that such proposals--particularly that involving the central
bank--would, if adopted, prove ineffective or harmful, or both.[12] In general terms, and with little supporting analysis, they denied the feasibility
of any centralized system of price stabilization through credit control: [13]

"neither the Federal Reserve System nor any other system can control prices."[14] They argued further--with respect to the Canadian economy and the sharp contrast which it presented with the economies of Great Britain and the United States--that even the control of the volume of credit by a central bank might be achieved only with the greatest difficulty,' if at all. In this connection, the bankers were well aware of, and did examine, the most important central bank techniques then in use, moral suasion, open market operations, foreign exchange operations, and changing rediscount rates.

The first of these techniques depended on the good judgment and prestige of the central bank authorities, qualities which depended, in turn, upon their acquisition of a high degree of competence. But this was, in the nature of things, a time-consuming process. It followed, therefore, that "the moral force of advice on the part of the central bank would, in all probability, be weakest in the first years of its existence, which would also be the crucial years."[15] And quite apart from this time problem, even the most effective kind of moral suasion could not, by itself, ensure adequate credit control--not to mention its limitations when applied in conjunction with positive measures.

Although they devoted no attention to the multiple expansive and contractive effects of open market operations, the bankers were reasonably clear as to the mechanics of this policy:

> The purchase and sale of bonds in the open market would, as a procedure, be very simple; for the central bank's purchase of bonds in Canada would, in the first analysis, presumably be made by means of a book entry, thus increasing the balances of the commercial banks with the central bank; and per contra, the sale of bonds in Canada, by means of a corresponding book entry, would diminish the balances of the commercial banks with the central bank. In this manner, the central bank could increase or diminish at will the cash resources of the commercial banks in Canada.[16]

But there, too, serious qualifications had to be made. One was that changes might occur in the assets of the commercial banks held abroad--these changes being independent of those brought about domestically--and so materially affect the situation in Canada. A second qualification was to the effect that securities manipulation in the open market was a complex device which could be mastered only through long practical experience, particularly by way of offsetting seasonal movements in business and in the public account. In the third place, recognition had to be accorded the limited nature of Canada's security markets. Depending upon market trends, it was at times easy to sell or to purchase substantial amounts of government obligations without disturbing prices. "But if it should happen that the central bank desired to sell when the market was unreceptive, the process would be an exceedingly slow one. On the purchasing side the situation is not so difficult."[17]

Of all the instruments of central bank policy, the bankers seem to have attached the greatest importance to foreign exchange operations. These "would have an equal or even more immediate effect than the purchase and sale of securities in the open market and would present no problems not paralleled in other markets."[18] Indeed, the bankers were willing to concede that a central bank could make a substantial contribution to the maintenance of exchange stability under the international gold standard. Central bank pressure upon, or easing of, the cash reserve position of the commercial banks would supplement the automatic compensatory action provided by gold movements in response to disturbances in the Canadian balance of international payments. Moreover, even if the gold standard were not restored, the Canadian dollar would either be pegged at a definite relationship with other currencies, or the dollar would be permitted to fluctuate freely as a means of assuring internal price stability: in the former case, the necessary action could be taken by existing agencies under governmental supervision, "although a qualified board of some kind would be required to direct any such policy";[19] and in the latter case, "a central bank would probably be essential," though Canada would meet with almost unique difficulties in attempting to perform this task.[20]

On the question of the rediscount rate, the bankers recognized the reinforcing action provided by open market operations, as well as the "moral suasion" aspect of public announcements by the central bank of changes in bank rate. They were doubtful, however, as to whether "the central bank could hope, by rate reductions alone, to effect an expansion of loans by the commercial banks."[21]

Summary. The over-all view of the bankers, then, was one of satisfaction with the main outlines of the existing control system, together with caution and scepticism towards the inauguration of central banking in the Dominion.[22] At times, the bankers did go so far as to admit that a Canadian central bank, if kept free of political influence, might be successful, "relying in the main on persuasion, rather than on the devices for controlling the domestic market that it would possess.... The prestige, foresight, and intelligence of its management would determine the extent of its accomplishments; but lacking capacity of the highest order, it could make disastrous mistakes."[23] However, the general tone of their argument, and the single impression which they desired to create, was even more conservative than this statement would indicate. As a result of their study of the entire question, their considered judgment was that:

> In the present extremely disturbed state of business, it would be most unwise to experiment with an organization entirely new to this country, namely, a central bank. On the other hand, we believe that the Administrative Board proposed...would be helpful, that it would be a careful approach to the further development of this country's financial machinery, that it would be inexpensive to operate, that it would not interfere with the ability of chartered

banks to serve the public adequately, and that in due time, as it demonstrated its competence and efficiency, it might become an institution to which perhaps greater responsibilities might be entrusted.[24]

Evaluation. There were, clearly, two elements of strength in the bankers' position: first, no one could effectively argue that the instruments of monetary policy were adequate, in themselves, for stabilizing either price levels or levels of employment and income; and secondly, the economic circumstances of Canada were such as to preclude any vigorous application of central bank techniques, at least in the early stages of the institution's development, and to reduce further the stabilization potentialities of these techniques even when they were successfully implemented. These fundamental economic truths the bankers keenly appreciated--more so than many of their radical adversaries--and used to the fullest possible extent. They were, however, on less solid ground in inferring that a central bank could not mitigate Canadian instability; and in uncritically assuming that, in any case, there were no institutional defects which could not be remedied by minor amendments of one sort or another.[25]

Divided Business Views

This was, essentially, the line of reasoning pursued by the segment of Canadian business opinion opposed to the establishment of a central bank. For it must be recorded that, among the business groups, there was nothing approaching the near-unanimity which prevailed among the bankers. Once again, differences of opinion seem to have followed geographic lines, with Eastern businessmen tending to oppose the central bank and those in the West adopting a rather favourable attitude.[26] As a matter of fact, the division was by no means as sharp as this generalization would imply. In both regions, numerous dissenting voices were raised; and, in provincial terms, Prince Edward Island actually belonged in the Western, and British Columbia in the Eastern, group.[27]

The Conservative position. Conservative business opinion was couched in generalities centring upon: (1) faith in the existing system; (2) the operational limitations placed on a central bank by the Canadian economy; (3) the excessive costs of central banking; and (4) the danger of political restraints on the freedom of central bank action.[28] A convenient summary of this general approach may be found in the brief presented to the Royal Commission on Banking and Currency by the Montreal Chamber of Commerce.[29] In its view, recent Canadian experience had demonstrated that Canadian banks were functioning soundly and rapidly. It would be extremely dangerous to alter substantially the Canadian banking system, or to deprive it of its privileges. The monetary control functions of a central bank were then being satisfactorily performed by the commercial banks and by the government itself, under the power derived from the Finance Act. A central bank would be under government control and necessarily subject to political influence. It would be an expensive institution which

would deprive the government of the important source of income which it
derived through the operations of the Finance Act;   and it also would probably involve additional expenditures.   One important function of a central
bank was the control of the money market, but since Canada had no real
money market at that time, there was no need to create special machinery
to attempt this control.   "Our lack of faith in a central bank does not mean
that our banking system has attained absolute perfection and could not be
improved upon. . . .   But we submit that amendments and modifications can
be enacted without it being necessary to effect radical changes which might
materially affect our banking system, and that, in times of depression like
these, it would not be prudent to make experiments which might disrupt or
seriously affect our national life. "[30]

Business radicalism.   More impressive and more penetrating was the
case presented to the Royal Commission by the businessmen who favoured
a central bank.   No single set of ideas was advanced;   the attack was a
many-sided one, combining detailed criticism of the existing system with
positive, if overly optimistic and frequently non-monetary, suggestions
for reform.   Two such approaches are particularly worthy of consideration
--one taken by Mr. M. Fisher, the Montreal importer of textiles, [31] and the
other by the Economic Reform Association. [32]

(1) Mr. Fisher.   The former emphasized that he had no criticism to
offer of Canadian banks on the issue of their direct relations with his firm.
He was concerned, rather, with the operation of the entire banking system
and its effects on the Canadian economy.   A great deal had been made in
the press of the fact that no Canadian bank had failed as a result of the depression, but financial solvency was, he believed, the very least that one
could expect of a bank.   Ten banks having among themselves a monopoly
of the money of ten million people acquired no merit from a comparison
of their standing with that of the five or six thousand banks which had failed
in the United States during the previous four years, and most of which
should never have been licensed to handle any of the public's money.   Sufficient tribute had not been paid to the steadiness of the Canadian people
as a factor supporting their banks.   The situation might have been different had depositors made such demands in Canada as did those of the United
States.   Moreover, the very misfortune of the United States may well have
contributed to the support of the Canadian banks through the volume of deposits fleeing from that country helping to swell the loanable resources in
the Dominion.

It was possible, then, that Canadians had paid dearly to maintain the
stability of their banks;   that, "with a properly organized system under a
central bank of issue, stability might have been maintained at far less
cost to the business community in particular and the nation at large. "[33]
There were sound liquidity reasons, from any individual banker's standpoint, for the existing tightness of credit conditions;   but from the public
standpoint, there was "something exasperatingly contradictory in the fact
that money should be tight when it is most plentiful in the banks, and borrowing should be most difficult just at a time when the people most need
money. "[34]   The fact was that, in the absence of a central bank, the indivi-

dual commercial banks could not help themselves. "They are bound to regulate their individual policies from day to day to safeguard their positions without regard to the combined effect of those policies upon the national welfare."[35] A central bank, Mr. Fisher continued, could, by means of open market operations, create additional bank money sufficient to compel the chartered banks to broaden their conception of a "sound borrower." By purchasing government securities in the open market, the central bank would be able "to create such a quantity of bank deposits in favour of those from whom it purchased them as to embarrass the chartered banks with liquid funds and to cause them to look with kinder eyes on business borrowers willing and anxious to pay 6 per cent."[36]

The world crisis had undoubtedly borne more heavily upon Canada than it need have done, by virtue of the fact that a mere association of independent banking companies did not constitute a monetary system. This, to repeat, was not the fault of the chartered banks, whose prime function as profit-making institutions was, as the bankers themselves had emphasized, to receive deposits and to lend on reasonable security to sound borrowers. The responsibility for a monetary system rested with the state. Canada had no financial policy and no economic independence, for it had no means of making a financial policy effective; and the external value of its currency, as well as the domestic purchasing power of its money, were dominated by forces outside the country.

In his concluding observations on the role of the central bank, Mr. Fisher argued that it "should have the sole right of note issue, and its notes should be legal tender for any amount throughout the Dominion. The chartered banks could relinquish their right to issue notes by a process of easy stages designed to give them time to adjust themselves to the changed order."[37] The central bank, through open market operations, would control the internal credit situation and stabilize internal values. It would also exercise a moderating influence on interest rates, facilitate government borrowing, establish the independence of the Canadian dollar, and collect and publish detailed banking statistics not then available. Canada had reached the limits of its development under its existing rigid financial system. "But the individual strength and excellent organization of the chartered banks are such that their co-operation with a modern central banking institution would bring into being as fine a monetary system as the world has known, the establishment of which would inaugurate a new erea of tremendous development in [the Dominion]."[38]

(2) _The Economic Reform Association._ In a sense, the members of the Economic Reform Association were in agreement with the case presented by those who were opposed to a Canadian central bank. That is to say, the Association, too, believed that the establishment of a central bank would be an unnecessary expense--but only on the assumption that the new central bank would be provided with no powers other than those usually accorded such institutions. The postwar experience of the Federal Reserve Banks in the United States constituted clear demonstration that the traditional indirect powers of the rediscount rate and open market operations, operating on the supply of legal tender reserves of the

commercial banks, were inadequate to control the financial structure.
Where a high degree of skill and experience existed, as in England,
these powers might carry sufficient force. But in Canada, as in the
United States, the same result could not be anticipated, because of: (1)
the power of Canadian bankers; (2) their ignorance of monetary theory:
(3) their unwillingness to co-operate in the execution of general credit
policy; (4) the limited Canadian money market which was dominated by
England and the United States; and (5) the particular ineffectiveness of
the traditional monetary instruments in the face of a falling price level.

The Association contended, therefore, that "a Canadian central bank
must have additional powers, if it is to carry out an effective and adequate
credit policy. We strongly urge that the central bank be given the power
to tax extensions of credit by commercial banks at a rate double the rate
of interest received by the commercial banks.... The invocation of this
power should be made mandatory whenever the price level of consumers'
goods in Canada rises more than 3 per cent above a predetermined norm."[39]
As a necessary complement to this provision, the central bank would be
authorized to take direct action in providing additional credit and raising
the price level if it should fall. This would involve the financing of countercyclical, "non-income-producing" public works by "permanent non-interest
bearing loans extended by the central bank."[40]

In the opinion of the Association, these extraordinary powers would
not be widely or frequently used, nor was it suggested that they should be.
The firm convication was held, however, that the provision of such powers
was essential if the central bank was to have any real authority--at least
in the private commercial banking system which the Association favoured.
Armed with the new powers, the central bank might, indeed, find that its
moral suasion alone would prove sufficient for effective control.

Unanimity among the Radicals[41]

The radicals' position on a central bank for Canada continued to stem
from their unorthodox approach to the problem of economic instability in
general, and to problems of monetary theory and policy in particular;
from their dissatisfaction with the Canadian commercial banking structure
and with the role played by the chartered banks in the cyclical process;
and from their concern with the misallocation of credit as between East
and West. The result was, again, the advocacy, often in loose terms,
of a wide range of reforms--including the nationalization of commercial
banking, and the elimination of abusive practices in the capital market--
many of which had no direct bearing on the main issue.[42] There also resulted, however, the collective formulation of an intelligent critique of
the contemporary monetary system, as well as a keen appreciation of the
scope and limitations of monetary policy.

Mr. Crowle. Special mention must be given the brief presented to
the Royal Commission by Mr. H. E. Crowle of Calgary, who based much
of his analysis on the discussion of control techniques in Keynes's Treatise
on Money.[43] Mr. Crowle rejected the idea of nationalizing the Canadian

banking system on grounds of government temptation to abuse its privileges.
He placed emphasis on control through the medium of the chartered banks'
legal cash reserves, which were to be deposited in the central bank. The
actual powers of the central bank were to include variation of legal reserve
requirements, control of the distribution of credit, and control over rediscount rates and open market operations (despite the fact that these powers, "as tried out by the Federal Reserve Banks in the United States over
a period of ten years, have not clearly demonstrated their effectiveness
there as a means of control over the price level, " and that "in Canada we
have no real money market and the market for securities is somewhat
limited").[44] The central bank would act as a depository of government
funds, would provide the government with its short-term financing requirements; and with its long-term requirements only in cases of emergency
when taxation and borrowing from the public were inadequate, or when,
"the price level being very low, a loan of reasonable proportions by the
central bank to the government might be merely corrective and be. . . what
is now called a reflation. "[45] The existence of a central bank would also
make possible Dominion co-operation "with the central banks of some
thirty or more other countries which have central banks to assist in maintaining international equilibrium of the price level as well as internal
equilibrium. "[46] Finally, regarding the administration of the central bank,
a board of directors "appointed by the government for a term of, say, five
years, and selected from the ablest and most capable persons with a tested
experience and ability, and. . . representing banking, commerce, industry,
and agriculture, would be most likely to give the best service. "[47]

Mr. Robertson. Mr. G. W. Robertson, Secretary of the Saskatchewan Wheat Pool, attributed the intensification of that province's heavy
debt burden to the "free extension of credit during periods of high prices,
followed by an entirely too drastic contraction of credit during periods of
low prices. "[48] He defined contemporary banking operations in Saskatchewan as "the business of loaning umbrellas when the sky is clear and the
sun is shining, and demanding their return as soon as it begins to rain. "[49]

Mr. Coote. Carrying over his criticism of the Finance Act into the
central bank controversy, Mr. Coote noted that, if the Act had been handled
intelligently, it would have been a very useful piece of legislation, but that
it had not been so handled. It had made possible the great inflation of bank
credit during the last years of the war and up to 1920. It had also been the
cause of the inflation which Canada experienced during 1928 and 1929. Had
the Act been administered by a national bank charged with the responsibility of maintaining stable price levels, there would have been no increase
in advances to the chartered banks in 1929 to enable them to make large
call loans in both Canada and New York. "Surely it would be worthwhile
to establish a national bank to administer the Finance Act intelligently,
if for no other reason. "[50]

The United Farmers of Alberta. The United Farmers movement was
prominent among the radical groups advocating a central bank. In its
brief, the United Farmers of Alberta[51] called the attention of the Royal

Commission to the instrumental role which it had played in bringing about, in 1923, the first parliamentary investigation into the Canadian monetary and banking system; also to the increasing support among professional economists and policy makers for the unorthodox views propounded by the U. F. A. during the previous decade. The time had come when there should be established in Canada:

> A nationalized system of currency and credit unattached to any metallic base or to any specific commodity. Its objectives should be the effective control of currency and credit; stability of the price level; regularity of production, consumption, and employment; control of foreign exchange; and generally the maintaining of a proper relationship between consumer purchasing power and the goods and services available for use. These objectives can be obtained only through a nationally-owned government bank.[52]

In addition to its generally accepted functions, the bank should act in an advisory capacity towards the government on all matters of taxation. The importance of this should not be overlooked, for "taxation should be an instrument of money policy as well as a means of raising revenue."[53]

The United Farmers of Ontario. The brief presented by the United Farmers of Ontario[54] argued, in "quantity theory" terms, that the chief responsibility for the wide fluctuations in the Canadian price level--in so far as these were due to monetary causes--rested with the chartered banks. Two extenuating claims might be urged by, or on behalf of, the banks. It might be, first, that the connection between credit policies and price levels was unknown to the bankers. Such ignorance, however, should no longer be tolerated as an excuse for error. Secondly, it might be that the bankers had been guided by a stern sense of duty to their depositors. If that were the case, they had taken a very short-sighted view of their duty, in that the bank liquidity exalted by the bankers had been obtained at the expense of continued deflation, and could not but jeopardize their long-run solvency. It was essential that depositors be protected from being used to cloak anti-social manipulations of the price level.

There should be established in Canada, the U. F. O. continued, both a central bank and a "Board of National Investment." The functions of the central bank should be:

> (1) To take over the Dominion note issue, ... and to make provision for the gradual taking-over of that part of the note issue now managed by the chartered banks; ... (2) to take over all the powers and functions now exercised by the Treasury Board, in the matter of advancing Dominion notes to the banks under the Finance Act of 1923; (3) to take over the banking business of the Dominion and provincial governments, and to act as agents for such governments in all their borrowing operations; (4) to make provision for the control and stabilization of the Canadian currency

and the foreign exchanges by establishing connections with foreign central banks [that is, adopting low and flexible statutory provisions as to minimum gold reserves], and by other appropriate measures; and (5) generally to supervise the structure, management, and operation of the Canadian banking system, so as to bring greater stability to economic development and minister to the welfare of the Canadian people.[55]

In order to prevent the nullification of effective policy by those who opposed it, the U. F. O. suggested that the management of the central bank be entrusted to a "board of banking experts, economists, and statisticians completely divorced from any financial, commercial, or industrial interests."[56] The Board of National Investment (which might or might not be merged with, but should in any event work in harmony with, the central bank) should be empowered to "co-ordinate, supervise, and rationalize investment processes so as to bring about greater economic stability and security, and should be as completely divorced from private financial, industrial, and commercial interests as the Board of Management of the central bank."[57]

The Trades and Labour Congress. A definite (though non-analytical) stand was taken also, by the substantial segment of organized labour represented before the Royal Commission by the Trades and Labour Congress. According to the Congress, the establishment of a central bank in Canada was necessary for the prevention of wide fluctuations in exchange rates, and for bringing "under state control the power to extend credits commensurate with the required needs for the development of [Canada]."[58]

The League for Social Reconstruction. There was, finally, the case argued by the League for Social Reconstruction.[59] It was essential that there should be no sudden contraction in the volume of short-term credit available. The deflation resulting from any such contraction was "a major factor in perpetuating a condition of industrial stagnation, and therefore a much more serious cause for concern than any danger which might arise from a supposed decrease in the liquidity of commercial-bank assets."[60] A conscious and deliberate monetary policy, the League contended, should aim at an approximately stable level of prices. The elimination of wide fluctuations in the general price level would mitigate those changes in purchasing power, production, and investment which were accentuated by unstable prices.

It was unreal, however, to consider the problems of monetary control independently of those of investment control; or the problems of general financial control apart from those of over-all economic planning. While it was true that price stabilization would be an important step forward "it would not, in the absence of other measures, result in the elimination of industrial fluctuations. When examining the relationship between falling prices and industrial contraction, it would be a mistake to regard a symptom for a cause. Although, once the downward trend of the business cycle has begun, the fall in prices, unless forcibly stopped is self-aggravating, the initial causes of the fall in prices may be found elsewhere".[61]

A stable American level of wholesale prices from 1922 to 1928 had not, after all, prevented the accumulation of tendencies which ended in slump conditions in the United States. In so far as the price collapse was the result of tendencies outside the sphere of operations of the banking system, only a removal of those tendencies would solve the problem. It would "be foolish to hope for industrial stability from an artificial price stability."[62] The need, therefore, was for "not only a central bank in Canada but [also] a complete social control of the machinery of finance and investment through a National Investment Board working in conjunction with a National Planning Commission."[63]

In the constitution and powers of the central bank, the League emphasized the following considerations: (1) commercial bank obligation to keep a minimum portion of liquid assets in the form of deposits at the central bank; (2) central bank power to establish branches throughout Canada, and to act as banker and financial agent to the federal and subsidiary governments; (3) capitalization of the central bank by the federal government or by the public, with the latter having no right to the election of the management; (4) government appointment of the chief officials of the central bank, who should have no direct financial or industrial interests; (5) central bank power of note issue (foreign exchange being considered as virtually equivalent to gold reserves), of accepting deposits from public authorities, or rediscounting commercial paper, of engaging in open market operations (the establishment of a bond market in Canada was considered essential in this connection), and of regulating the rate of exchange between the Canadian dollar and foreign currencies.

The Economists' Crucial Contribution

The persistent and forceful agitation of the radicals during the twenties could not fail to influence the thinking of academic economists in Canada. The severe incidence of the Great Depression in Canada, and the monetary experience of other countries, must have had similar repercussions. The consequence of these factors was the economists' mass entry into the final stages of the central bank controversy. Their contribution was strongly on the side of creation of a central bank; the arguments of those few economists who opposed it were neither detailed nor convincing. Moreover, the economists' case was more confined than that of the radicals to the direct issue; there was little involvement with questions like nationalized commercial banking or interest-free financing of public works and other government expenditures. And finally, the economists, as a group, provided the greatest analytical support for, and guidance to the operation of, a Canadian central bank; this was especially true of their discussion of commercial bank policy, the Finance Act machinery, and the functions which a central bank would be able to perform in Canada.

Professor Swanson. Professor Swanson was still opposed to any central banking institution.[64] To his way of thinking, the Canadian banking system might be strengthened by an increase in the responsibility of the Canadian Bankers' Association, or by the appointment of "a Monetary

Commission composed of able men, practical bankers, to direct the financial policy of this country and to recommend advances by the banks to the Treasury."[65] It might also be worth considering "one or two possible changes in the currency."[66]

Professor Michell. Professor Michell framed his analysis largely in terms of a defence of the workings of the Finance Act against alleged misconceptions respecting its responsibility for the intensification of the domestic inflation of the twenties, and for Canada's abandonment of the gold standard.[67] Those difficulties had not been precipitated by the chartered banks, but by the Dominion government's strenuous efforts to meet its foreign obligations maturing in New York. "In what may be called 'a runaway [money] market' no [monetary] control was possible."[68] Indeed, the Finance Act had had the advantage over a central bank of not raising the rediscount rate, and so enabling "the chartered banks to obtain the funds needed to allow them to meet the demands of business."[69] Professor Michell also defended the personnel of the Treasury Board, pointing to their many years of experience in the management of the gold reserve. The Board had been "criticized mistakenly for not doing what, as a matter of fact, it is powerless to accomplish. On the contrary, the Finance Act has functioned admirably so far as it has gone."[70] In any event, central bank control would be impossible in Canada, since there was no money market and therefore no scope for the chief instrument of control, namely, open market operations.

Professors Gregoire and Montpetit. Completing the small opposition group of academic economists were Professors J. E. Gregoire and E. Montpetit of Laval University and the University of Montreal, respectively.[71] The former was the less discriminating. He simply voiced a general denial of any central bank's power to regulate the supply of money or prices, and declared that, in any case, a central bank which was able to exercise monetary control was an unnecessary risk and would be of no benefit to the Dominion as a whole. Professor Montpetit was satisfied, in the main, with the previous record of the chartered banks. He pointed, moreover, to the existence of central banks throughout the world, and to their experience as a demonstration of the fact that such an institution should not be regarded as a panacea for all Canadian ills. "Unless a country is running itself on sound business lines, the most perfect banking system in the world cannot save it from the inevitable consequences of its breaches of economic laws."[72] It was unlikely that central bank control could be achieved in Canada, owing to the limited money market, the vulnerability to international disturbances, the constitutional difficulties associated with provincial rights, and the danger of political interference. While acknowledging the inadequacy of existing machinery for monetary control, Professor Montpetit proposed, instead of a central bank, the removal from the Treasury Board of its monetary functions, and the creation, within the Ministry of Finance, of "a central body, under the name of 'The Banking Commission,' composed of experts and not exclusively of bankers, and whose duties would be to maintain control over the rediscount and to draw up the interest rates according to cir-

cumstances, to build up reserve funds in other countries with a view to
having some influence, when necessary, on the exchange rates, and lastly,
to construct, within the necessary period of time, the foundations of a
financial and monetary policy. "[73]

Professor Curtis. In the forefront of the pro-central-bank group
were the Queen's University economists, Professors Curtis, Mackintosh,
and Knox.[74] Indeed, Professor Curtis, more than any of his colleagues
throughout the Dominion, seems to have made the establishment of a central bank his special concern.[75] It was clear to him--on the basis of his
analysis of Canadian monetary developments during the late twenties--
that the Finance Act had eliminated control of credit by the chartered
banks, and that no other control agency had appeared in its place. He was
unable "to see how one can defend a monetary structure which has in it an
agency capable of performing one of the most important jobs of a central
bank--that of giving cash reserves to the commercial banks--without any
of the responsibility which central banks have".[76] There was no escaping
the fact that Canadians had grossly mismanaged their monetary system,
and that the only satisfactory permanent solution to Canada's monetary
problems was the creation of a central bank. "Such an institution would
not mean a monetary millenium, but it would at least place the responsibility for credit control with an institution developed for such purposes.
Canada will have no monetary stability until such an institution is developed. "[77]

Professor Curtis's organizational proposals are also of interest. He
envisaged a modest institution, capitalized at between $2 million and $10
million. The source of the capital was unimportant, but it was fundamental that all the directors of the central bank be governmentally appointed.
There should be no reserve requirements for the central bank, but such
requirements--subject to change by the central bank--should be stipulated
for the chartered banks. The latter suggestion was "not based upon any
idea of safety--as it used to be in the United States--but upon the necessity
for control of the commercial banks' credit expansion by the central bank."[78]
On the question of note issue, Professor Curtis was not unduly concerned
over the burden which would be imposed on the banks by their loss of the
issuing privilege; by way of compromise, however, he favoured allowing
the banks to issue notes up to their then existing paid-up capital. The central bank should be a bankers' bank, not dealing directly with the public,
or with municipal or provincial governments. He emphasized, finally,
the importance of the central bank powers of rediscounting and engaging
in open market operations; in the former case, rules for eligible paper
might be prescribed by statute, but there was much to be said for empowering the central bank to state and to change the assets eligible for rediscount.

Professor Mackintosh. Professor Mackintosh[79] prefaced his case
for a central bank with an appraisal of the development of the Canadian
banking and monetary system. Specifically, he contrasted the prewar
quasi-automatic system of control with the non-automatic system created

by the Finance Act. The essential feature of the former had been that:

> The chartered banks as a system could not increase their reserves
> from sources within the country. It was the business of each bank
> to regulate its lending in accordance with its reserves and the
> trend of its clearing debits or credit balances. Any withdrawal of
> gold from the country was a reduction of bank cash and forced ap-
> propriate curtailment of bank credit. Imports of gold increased
> bank cash and furnished the basis for increased loaning.... In all
> this, the Department of Finance performed highly important but
> purely routine functions.... In addition to its excellent record
> in other fields, the prewar banking and monetary system was singu-
> larly efficient in achieving the single objective of prewar monetary
> policy, viz., the maintenance of the exchanges. [80]

There was no criticism to be made of the Finance Act of 1914 as an emergency war measure designed to provide, within the Dominion, a source of
cash reserves for the chartered banks. Though hastily conceived and
adopted, it had fulfilled its wartime functions admirably. But the perpetu-
ation of the provisions of the 1914 Act by the Finance Act of 1923 had signified a fundamental alteration in the monetary structure that made it incompatible with the maintenance of the gold standard. For the Finance
Act had created a monetary system in which control, if effective, would
have to be deliberate rather than automatic. But no institution had been
set up for the exercise of deliberate judgment:

> It is folly to suggest that had the Department of Finance raised the
> rate charged on advances under the Act, its gold reserve would
> have been protected. This would be to require that the Department
> of Finance should assume central-banking functions which plainly
> were not contemplated in the Act, since no provision is made for
> the maintenance of any reserve against notes advanced to the banks
> under the Act. Equally it is folly to suggest that the chartered
> banks ought to have so limited their liabilities and so restricted
> their borrowings under the Finance Act that the government's gold
> reserve might have been maintained. That would be to require that
> a commercial bank should exercise central-bank functions and use
> criteria of policy quite different from those used by a commercial
> bank. The fault was in the legislation, not in the chartered banks
> or in the Department of Finance. [81]

For these reasons, Professor Mackintosh believed that Canadian
monetary machinery had demonstrated its inadequacy. He then proceeded
to note the possibility of the adoption of one of three alternative courses
of action: (1) repeal of the Finance Act and restoration of the prewar
system; (2) strengthening of the Finance Act by providing monetary control functions; and (3) establishment of a central bank. The first alterna-

tive he rejected on grounds of the permanent disappearance of those economic conditions (mainly English international dominance) which made it possible for the prewar system to work; and the second alternative because it would logically lead to a central bank "lacking in prestige, misunderstood abroad, and seriously subject to political influence."[82] His case for a central bank derived added force from his brief but convincing refutation of those objections to a central bank that were based on greater effectiveness of an improved Finance Act, the danger of serious encroachment on chartered bank operations, and the damage incurred by central bank mismanagement.

What was needed, then, was "not an elaborate, top-heavy institution designed for reckless over-ambitious experiment, but a small institution, modest in its beginnings, yet capable of growth as its experience accumulates.... It is not contended that a central bank could perform miracles; that it would restore prosperity, solve the western debt problem, or revive depressed industries. In the carrying out of sound policies to meet these problems, however, it would be a valuable, and indeed essential, aid."[83] Canadian prosperity, moreover, was dependent to a peculiar degree upon world prosperity; and effective co-operation with other countries in restoring prosperity required the existence of a central bank in Canada.

Professor Knox. The distinctive aspect of Professor Knox's case was his virtually exclusive concern with the international orientation of the Canadian economy, and with what he therefore considered to be the overwhelming importance of a monetary policy directed at the stabilization of exchange rates.[84] Canada would be continually subjected to shocks originating in economic conditions largely beyond its control, such as changes in the world price of raw materials or changes in the willingness of foreign investors to buy Canadian securities. This necessarily meant, according to Professor Knox, that "a purely domestic policy, such, for example, as the stabilization of the level of wholesale prices, is of a subordinate importance to the achievement of stability of the foreign-exchange value of the Canadian dollar in terms of the currencies of the countries with which we trade."[85]

Both long-run and short-run monetary policies required, for their implementation in Canada, a properly constituted central bank. For the immediate future, while the course of domestic monetary policies in the major countries was uncertain, it was undesirable for Canada to tie its currency to that of any other country. It was, nevertheless, vital that restrictive control be imposed upon "the possibly wide fluctuations in the value of the Canadian dollar which the working out of plans in other countries may involve."[86] Looking further ahead to a relatively stable world environment, Professor Knox envisaged a new gold standard which would remain intact by causing a minimum of domestic disruption in member countries. The new standard would provide for a widening of the gold points, allowing Canadian dollar fluctuations within 2 per cent of par either way. Minor adjustments could thereby be effected without requiring the sort of central bank action which operated only through changes in the volume of credit, and which therefore altered the conditions under which both the foreign and domestic business of the country were conducted. Whenever changes in the foreign exchange value of the dollar within some such range as 4 per cent proved insufficient, the central bank would be obliged to call the domestic mechanism of adjustment--rediscount rates and open market operations--into operation through influencing the volume of the reserves of the chartered banks.

But the uniqueness of Professor Knox's long-run scheme rested in his contention that its successful operation could be achieved in Canada without the use of the instruments of central banking policy; that the significance of the absence of a Canadian money market was not so much that it rendered those techniques ineffective as that it made their application unnecessary:

> The future task here suggested for a central bank in Canada is the stabilization of exchange rates with other countries, not direct operation on prices in pursuit of a purely domestic currency policy such as the stabilization of prices. That is, the Canadian problem is one of keeping the movement of prices in Canada roughly in line with price movements in the major countries. The ordinary sale or purchase of gold or foreign exchange at the gold points chosen will ordinarily effect the restriction or easing of the volume of commercial-bank reserves required for the carrying-out of such a policy.[87]

Open market operations were forced on such central banks as those in London or New York because of the large volume of short-term funds moving so readily from one international money market to another in response to conditions other than those arising directly from a changed balance-of-payments situation requiring correction. Those central banks had, therefore, to undertake open market operations to offset the effects of movements of international funds in order that the country's international trading position should remain unchanged. "The absence of a money market in Canada, to and from which funds might flow, would relieve the Canadian central bank from the necessity of undertaking these offsetting open market operations."[88]

Thus, Professor Knox centred his approach to monetary problems on Canada's position in the world economy. In terms of this position, he identified Canadian monetary policy with action designed to achieve a stable relationship between the Canadian dollar and the currencies of the world's major countries. The early restoration of national economic stability throughout the world was the implicit assumption underlying his confidence in the feasibility of exchange stabilization through a modified gold standard system. Such stabilization was considered, moreover, to be not only practical under existing institutional arrangements but also almost entirely adequate to Canada's monetary needs. That is to say, there would be few

occasions on which deliberate action by the central bank would be required
in the Dominion. "The restriction of a too rapid expansion of credit in
boom periods would probably be the most usual instance. In such times,
the simple sale of government securities to the Canadian market should
be all the open market operation needed to make the rediscount rate effective."[89]

Mr. Plumptre. This emphasis by Professor Knox on the achievement
of long-run exchange rate stability was the basis, also, of Mr. Plumptre's
written appraisal which had appeared about one year earlier.[90] However,
the latter's analysis was more broadly oriented; and his primary objective was one of clarity of exposition relating to the operations and advantages and disadvantages of a central bank.

Mr. Plumptre, after carefully distinguishing between central and commercial banks, concerned himself initially with three instruments of central
bank control: (1) moral suasion (or "propaganda"); (2) open market operations; and (3) the discount rate. The first technique depended mainly on
the prestige enjoyed by the central bank, and so achieved the greatest effect in England; in Canada, where the chartered banks had attained a position of considerable strength, at first "the tail would probably wag the
dog."[91] There were serious limitations, also, on both the second and
third techniques. Mr. Plumptre described the mechanics of open market
operations in "balance sheet" terms, noting their dependence on the size
and maturity of the money market, on the amount of securities held by
the central bank, on the co-operation of the commercial banks (that is,
their maintenance of a fixed relation between reserves and deposits), and
on the degree of international stability. The money market consideration
was paramount in the use of the discount rate--a technique which could
not operate through central bank initiative. Monetary control, then, would
necessarily be far from complete "in countries such as Canada, where
conditions have not favoured the growth of a money market and where a
tradition of stable interest rates has grown up."[92]

But both British and American monetary experience dating from World
War I had an important bearing upon Canada--the former in terms of the
need for centralized monetary control, and the latter in terms of maximizing the operating efficiency of a central bank. The relevance of British
experience lay not so much in the grave error committed by the Bank of
England in advising the return to the gold standard in 1925 at the old
dollar-pound rate of exchange, or in the ensuing abandonment of gold in
1931, but rather in the fact that in those crucial years England at least
had an agency ready to make basic decisions and to accept responsibility
for them. In Canada, by sharp contrast, there was the complete absence
of any such agency, despite the emergency of the over-riding problem of
making a choice between sterling and dollar parity for the Canadian dollar.

With respect to American experience, Mr. Plumptre advanced two
reasons for the inappropriateness of discussing a central bank for Canada
on the basis of the Federal Reserve System: (1) the original evils which
the System had set out to remedy (by the mobilization, liquification, and

distribution of the reserves of thousands of unit banks, and by the provision of an "elastic currency") were not evils which existed in Canada; and (2) the major problems which had been faced by the System since its beginnings (the flotation of government bonds, and disturbing inflows and outflows of gold) were not problems which were likely to arise in anything like the same form in Canada. However, some aspects of Federal Reserve experience were significant for Canada. First, there was the serious impediment to efficiency occasioned by unlimited publicity for central bank operations; the Bank of England was notable for both the efficiency and secrecy of its actions. Second, it was not desirable to have occupational and regional representation in the management of a central bank (as was the case with the Federal Reserve Banks and the Federal Reserve Board), because of the tendency of such management to be sectional and partial; it was desirable, of course, to have men with an intimate knowledge of all sectors of the economy. Third, the central bank should be empowered to discriminate as to when lending to the commercial banks should be carried out; American law made such lending automatic when certain conditions were satisfied. And finally, "no central bank can prevent the public cutting its own throat if the public is sufficiently determined to do so"; [93] that is to say, there existed the danger of continuous and violent changes in the public's mind as to the relative desirability of keeping its savings in the form of stocks, bonds, foreign securities, bank deposits, or hoarded currency.

Even when account of these factors had been taken, there remained the limitations arising from internal political pressure and foreign interference; [94] also from attempts to reach impossible goals (such as complete monetary control in an internationally oriented country like Canada), [95] or to combine incompatible banking duties (such as commercial and central banking functions in the French and Australian central banks). [96] What a Canadian central bank might do effectively:

> Is to use what legal and persuasive powers are at its command in order to check the inflow of foreign capital which is sucked in by, and itself aggravates, booming conditions. If it were successful in this, the backwash of a "flight of capital" and the steady undertow of debt service in depression times might in part be avoided. There can be little doubt that one, if not the chief, function of a Canadian central bank should be to supervise, if not in some degree to control, Canada's international borrowing and lending. [97]

Thus, although a Canadian central bank could not have avoided the depreciation of 1931, which had been precipitated by external changes, it could have mitigated its severity by checking the excessive import of foreign capital and so reducing the interest burden in later years, and by restraining that portion of the internal credit expansion which had been made possible by the Finance Act. That Act, in principle and practice, was opposed to Dominion Government's official policy. The Act was also opposed to the principles of scientific credit control operated in the interest

of economic stability; the Act had not been the cause of the boom and
slump, but it had "played at least a minor part in those movements."[98]
If, therefore, a central bank was not established in Canada, the minimum
requirement was that the control of Finance Act borrowings should be
vested in a more expert board, or that the chartered banks should be
charged with responsibility for monetary control. On the other hand, if
a Canadian central bank was set up, it "should be thought of, not so much
as a bank of note issue and Finance-Act rediscount, but rather as a bank
of exchange-rate control."[99]

Summarizing the pro and con views in the central bank controversy,
Mr. Plumptre cited five arguments against the control function of a central bank: [100] (1) the past experience of other countries; (2) the inability
of a Canadian central bank to initiate new policy; (3) the danger of political interference; (4) the central bank's impotence through the opposition
of the chartered banks and the absence of the conditions (such as an extensive money market) for successful operation; and (5) the excellence of
the existing banking system.[101] Against these arguments had to be set
the conviction of the proponents of a central bank that conscious monetary
control (mainly through open market operations and exchange rate policy),
however inadequate, must be instituted in Canada; that little, if any, cost
would be incurred by the central bank or the chartered banks; and that a
central bank could therefore do no harm and might do a great deal of good.

Mr. Plumptre characterized his own position by the following observations: First, the existing Canadian monetary system was unsatisfactory,
at least partly on account of the Finance Act. Second, if no central bank
was founded and the Treasury Board was not reorganized, it was to be
hoped that the chartered banks would assume monetary responsibilities.
Third, Canadian monetary policy was to be thought of in terms of the exchange rate and foreign borrowing, rather than in terms of attempts at
direct manipulation of the volume of currency and credit. Fourth, if a
central bank was established in Canada, legislation was only the first step,
and the great need was for co-operation. If, finally, such an institution
was created, it would be of little or no use in 1933, but it would be making
useful experiments by 1938, and "by 1943, if it had succeeded in attracting
into its service men of vision and ability, it might be the cornerstone of
Canadian finance, and one of the props of a more permanent prosperity
than we have been able to achieve in the past."[102] Mr. Plumptre cautiously
concluded that, "if Canadian bankers were more conscious of the existence
of currency problems, a central bank might be quite unnecessary"; and
that, "if they were less strong or less efficient in the field of commercial
banking, it might be a dangerous innovation"; but that, "on balance, it
would be possible to devise a Canadian central bank of whose foundation
[I] would approve."[103]

Mr. Creighton. Mr. J. H. Creighton's 1933 analysis is best viewed
as a critical synthesis of the events and arguments which had hitherto comprised the central bank controversy.[104] He set out to point up the inadequacy of the credit control record of the Canadian banking system; and,

on the basis of this, to refute the arguments of the leading Canadian bankers, and to emphasize the urgent need for a central control institution in
the Dominion. Mr. Creighton focussed his attention on the Finance Act.
After carefully considering the evidence with respect to its operation, he
noted that:

> In some respects, it is like a bankers' bank, particularly in that
> it provides loans for the banks, supplies emergency currency,
> and has the commercial banks as its only customers. On the other
> hand, one finds that, as a bankers' bank, it is very inadequate in
> that it does not hold the reserve funds of the banks, that it does
> not act as a clearing house for the banks, that its loaning function
> does not constitute real rediscounting, and that its administration
> has been hopelessly inefficient from the point of view of central
> banking. As a bankers' bank, then, it is only "a piece of a bank."[105]

Nor did it serve, in any sense, as a government's bank. And it was even
worse as a "people's" bank, "for it not only fails to provide any social
control whatever, but actually is a dangerous source of instability in
Canada's monetary structure."[106]

Mr. Creighton enumerated (in somewhat overlapping fashion) no less
than twenty functions which his proposed central bank might be expected
to perform. It could: (1) act as depository for the chartered banks' cash
reserves; (2) perform the functions of a clearing house; (3) conduct rediscounting operations; (4) assume the duties then performed by the
Trustees of the Central Gold Reserves; (5) take over the supervision of
the Circulation Redemption Fund; (6) carry out the work of bank inspec-
tion; (7) assume responsibility for the solvency of the whole banking
structure; (8) relieve the Department of Finance of the responsibility of
administering the Finance Act; (9) promote the development of a Canadian
money market; (10) act as the depository of government funds; (11) act
as the fiscal agent of the government; (12) represent the government at
financial conferences; (13) assume the monopoly of the note issue;
(14) serve as financial adviser to the federal, provincial, and municipal
governments; (15) investigate all currency and credit problems; (16) exercise control over foreign exchange; (17) stabilize the price level;
(18) publish financial statistics; (19) protect the money and banking system from domination by political and financial interests; and (20) exercise
complete control over money and credit in the general interest rather than
in the interest of profit. The last-mentioned function, to be undertaken by
a nationally owned and operated central bank, was, for Mr. Creighton,
the most important of all.

While summarily rejecting most of the bankers' arguments, he did
recognize the serious nature of the absence of a money market in Canada.
The supply of Treasury bills was, to be sure, neither large nor constant,
and the supply of commercial paper, while very large in over-all amount,
comprised small individual items which were not concentrated in any one

or in a few centres. Nevertheless, it was important not to over-emphasize this difficulty. Other instruments of control were available, including the rediscount rate and moral suasion; indeed, the latter might well prove to be the most effective device. It was highly probable, moreover, that the establishment of a central bank would accelerate the growth of a money market. It might well be asked "to what extent the lack of a money market... should be regarded as a result of having no central bank rather than as a good cause for not creating one."[107]

The other serious difficulty which Mr. Creighton acknowledged was that associated with Canada's position in the world economy. Admittedly, Canada was only a part of a world economic unit; and owing to world-wide influences, the central bank could not guarantee national economic welfare. "Nevertheless, by establishing such an institution to act in co-operation with other central banks and an effective world bank (which the Bank of International Settlements may become), Canada would at least be contributing a share towards ending the present anarchy in international finance."[108]

In conclusion, Mr. Creighton contended that "a central bank would not be a cure-all and end-all for Canada's troubles, but it would be of real value. It would at least mean the control of money and credit in the interest of the people as a whole rather than in the interest of private profit."[109]

Professor Day. One of the clearest of all statements of the case for a central bank in Canada was that formulated by Professor Day.[110] He reduced to four the fundamental objectives that a central bank was designed to achieve: (1) a strengthened banking system through provision of a reservoir of emergency currency; (2) economy in the use of gold through centralization of a country's gold reserves; (3) centralized control over monetary policy as a means of stabilizing the internal and external purchasing power of the monetary unit; and (4) effective international co-operation in monetary policies.[111]

With respect to the first objective, Professor Day approved of the arrangement for currency expansion during the crop-moving season, but he was highly critical of the Finance Act machinery for Dominion note advances. Because of the past rigidity of rediscount rates, as well as their tendency to be exceeded by market rates of interest, there was a real danger that rediscount facilities would lose their emergency character and become a mere engine for currency inflation. This danger of abuse could be rectified by abolishing advances under the Finance Act, and by providing for careful and flexible supervision by the central bank over all rediscounting.

The achievement of the second objective, economy in the use of gold, would, according to Professor Day, be a by-product of the achievement of the third objective, credit control. For the popular acceptance of paper money because of its redeemability in gold "is... based on an unsound foundation. The right of redemption in gold is worthless and unutilized in normal times, and in abnormal times it is rendered valueless by restrictions on the only way [gold export] in which the premium can be realized."[112] Traditionally, the public had found this difficult to believe, but experience had pointed to the truth. "The only basis of faith for trusting our paper money is the belief that our monetary authorities will so order events that its purchasing power will be maintained. If they do not, the right of redemption in gold will not help us."[113] Professor Day cited Blackett, Keynes, Kisch, and the English Macmillan Report in support of his contention that "the amount of gold we need in Canada is to be measured by the possible magnitude of the short-period adverse balance of payments that we may have to meet in gold."[114] It was in this sense of appreciation of the real function of a gold reserve, and of its consequent limitation to the performance of that function, that the concentration of federal government and chartered bank gold reserves in the central bank would permit a greater economy of gold.

Professor Day considered the control of general credit policy to be the essential purpose for which central banks were established. Examining the record of the Canadian banking system during the great investment boom of 1927-9, he found it to be "the practical demonstration of the truth which we reached on theoretical grounds: that any control of general banking policy which depends on the unco-ordinated efforts of ten competitive chartered banks is likely to prove inadequate."[115] He visualized a system in which variation of rediscount rates would serve as the major instrument for stabilization. He was not unaware of the "more or less formidable difficulties" standing in the way of effective control by a central bank. Particularly important were:

> The initial inexperience of the directorate; the absence of an
> organized money market for short loans in any Canadian financial
> centre; the fact that credit is often extended by means of over-
> drafts rather than on bills eligible for rediscount, and that it takes
> time to change the habits of borrowers or the form of borrowing.
> Furthermore, if control by means of manipulating the discount
> rate is likely to be somewhat harsh and clumsy in Canada, control
> by open market operations has also its special handicaps here.
> The central bank, if possessed of sufficient resources, could pre-
> sumably always buy suitable securities and so inject additional
> currency into the banking system to provide for easier credit
> conditions when such were desirable, but, in the opposite case
> when tighter credit conditions were needed, the sale in Canada
> of securities by the central bank might, considering the relative
> narrowness of the market, not always be so simple a matter.[116]

But by no means did it follow from these limitations that a central bank would be useless as an instrument of control in Canada, or that its establishment at that time would be premature. "If we have only a poor instrument at present, it would be foolish to refuse to accept a better one merely because the better one is not perfect. A central bank in Canada might not attain for some years a really adequate power of control, but even inadequate control is better than none."[117]

The desirability of achieving the fourth objective, maximum Canadian participation in international financial co-operation, was so obvious to Professor Day as to require little attention. On the one hand, there was no institution in the Dominion--not excluding the Canadian Bankers' Association--capable of providing for such participation. And, on the other hand--far more so than in the gold standard era--the stabilization of the international standard of value, and with it the survival of civilization, depended upon the most skilfully executed international financial co-operation.

But while attacking the rationale for the Canadian bankers' objections to a central bank, Professor Day incorporated their general opposition into his proposal for delaying the establishment of such an institution. For without the voluntary co-operation of the chartered banks, the successful functioning of a central bank in Canada would be impossible. It is true that he conceded the possible desirability, in the face of chartered bank opposition, of nationalizing the Canadian banking system. He looked to drastic reform of this kind, however, only in the eventuality that the bankers' opposition proved "unreasonable" and was prolonged "indefinitely." Furthermore, it was his view that:

> There is no reason to suppose the bankers of the country will show themselves unalterably opposed to the introduction of the central banking principle in the face of sufficient evidence to convince the majority of their fellow-citizens of its desirability.... Time must be given for the bankers' views to ripen, and the natural course of events will push them towards thinking more and more of the banking system as a whole and less exclusively of the strength, progress, and prosperity of their own particular bank.[118]

But until such time as the bankers were "sincerely and whole-heartedly converted" Professor Day favoured the setting up of a five-man "standing Advisory Committee on general credit policy" and, under it, "a small, permanent, very carefully selected, and eventually expert, secretariat, developing into an Intelligence Staff for the whole banking community."[119] If, after a fair trial of a few years, the advice of the Committee was not found useful, "the only loss would be the expense incurred in running it, but, if it was, the transition to a central bank, with powers more than advisory, might become welcome, and our present difficulty of no trained staff to run it would have been removed."[120]

Mr. Parkinson. Broader and more radical were the views expressed by Mr. Parkinson.[121] "The purpose of monetary control," he argued, "should be to stabilize the rate of economic development in Canada, to provide for the most effective use of all national and human resources, and, so far as possible, to free the economy from cyclical fluctuations in employment, wages, farm incomes, and profits."[122] This objective was far more comprehensive, and far more important, than that of a stable wholesale price level, which he considered as only one constituent element in a wider plan. Indeed, "concentration on the question of price levels, considered in vacuo, ... is both dangerous and useless; useless because stable price levels at one period give no guarantee of invulnerability to sudden disturbances, dangerous because it deflects attention from the causes which produce change to the instruments which register them."[123] Price stability, moreover, might well be achieved at the expense of an enormous volume of unemployment. It followed that monetary control, in the narrow sense in which it was usually interpreted, was inadequate to the task and had to be supplemented by the adoption of an extensive set of controls over those financial transactions subsumed under the term "investment."[124]

At the very least, therefore (that is, in addition to a "National Investment Commission"), the Dominion needed a central bank. Its absence had been responsible, to a considerable extent, for Canada's failure to take effective measures to stabilize the external and internal value of the Canadian dollar. Thus, in the former case, there existed:

> No authority able to make an independent estimate of the degree of depreciation most appropriate to a stable internal price level, and able to reach and maintain it. As it was, the conflicting economic and group interests fought out their wordy battle. Exporters, farmers, and some manufacturers called for exchange depreciation to the level of the pound sterling or thereabouts in the interest of higher prices and farm incomes in Canada. Governmental opinion, inhibited by fear of the rising cost of the foreign-debt services, and orthodox financial opinion, distressed at what it described as the decline of Canada's financial prestige, both favoured a dollar able to look the American currency in the face. In the face of this stalemate, our monetary policy became one of drift. Anxious for the best of both worlds, of higher prices and financial prestige, we got neither.[125]

As for the price collapse after 1929, one of its most conspicuous features had been the marked shrinkage in chartered bank assets, particularly commercial loans and discounts. During the period 1929-33, however, the liquid assets of the banks had risen from 32 per cent to 41 per cent of total public liabilities. The Canadian economy had paid too high a price for a liquid banking system:

> It would be demonstrated, no doubt, in defence of such a policy, that every action [of loan liquidation and absorption of government issues] had been justified by the subsequent fall in wholesale prices, profits, and collateral values, and therefore especially prudent from a banking point of view. It could not possibly occur to each of the banks separately that it was being forced to contract its lending operations because each of its fellows was doing likewise, nor could any of them have put a stop to this process.[126]

This was part of the explanation for the bank deflation. "The fault may [therefore] lie with the banking system as a whole for giving a secondary impetus to the initial deflation, even though it can be shown that the subsequent shrinkage in loans was due to the absence of good borrowers."[127]

Mr. Parkinson emphasized the following as essential prerequisites for effective central bank control in Canada: (1) comprehensive functions and powers for the central bank, including exclusive control over the Dominion note issue and over the gold reserves held against it, the right to rediscount the eligible commercial paper of the chartered banks, and the right to engage in open market operations; (2) an independent and expert management; (3) the centralization of bank reserves and gold holdings; (4) a minimum legal reserve for the central bank of not more than 30 per cent of the total note issue, or not more than $60 million; (5) consideration of the central bank's English and American holdings as equivalent to legal reserves up to an amount equal to one-half of the total reserves held against notes; (6) the commercial banks' keeping of 5 per cent of their liquid assets in the form of deposits at the central bank; and (7) central bank supervision and control over Canada's international transactions arising from trade.

Other economists favouring a central bank. Most of the major lines of pro-central bank argument sketched above can be observed, also, in the testimony of the other economists who appeared before the Royal Commission on Banking and Currency.[128] They underscored the following considerations: (1) Both the chartered banks and the Treasury Board had been unconsciously regulating the money supply and price levels, and both were, in the nature of things, incapable of effective regulation. (2) It was essential that the proposed central bank be invested with broad functions and powers--including rediscount rates, open market operations, and the Dominion note issue--by way of controlling the internal and external value of the Canadian dollar. (3) The central bank would necessarily encounter grave, but not insuperable, difficulties, such as the lack of a money market and of experienced administrators. And (4) the central bank was, consequently, not to be regarded as a panacea for all Canadian economic ills, but rather as a vital contribution to the achievement and maintenance of economic stability. There were differences of degree in the enthusiasm with which these economists sanctioned the central bank; and differences of interpretation on procedural questions, particularly those relating to central bank versus chartered bank control of the note issue, and to private versus governmental ownership and operation. The general position taken by this group was, nevertheless, quite clear and provided additional support for the more detailed cases for a central bank made out by their colleagues.

Belated Conservative and Liberal Recognition

On the basis of the available evidence, there is no reason to believe that the onset of the Great Depression altered the orthodox attitude of the eastern politicians. On the contrary, from the 1929 collapse until virtually the time of appointment of the Royal Commission on Banking and Currency, they stood firm in their conviction that a central bank was neither necessary nor desirable.

Thus, in May 1931 Prime Minister Bennett asked Mr. Coote not to press his parliamentary motion for the establishment of a central bank, on the ground that Canada was not prepared to make the change; until it became apparent that the country was so prepared, the Government was not warranted in taking such action.[129] Almost a year later, as pressure increased, the Prime Minister expressed his anxiety lest the House of Commons interpret his suggestion of an inquiry into Canadian banking problems as an expression of the view that a central bank should be set up. He was merely "pointing out that the question is well worthy of consideration, that all has not been said about it that will be said, and all that can be said with respect to the question cannot be said upon the one side." [The banking system had been the] sheet anchor [of the Dominion, for] there is not one of us who, however small or large may be his deposit in a bank, cannot with certainty draw his check upon that fund today and know that it will be paid".[130] His Minister of Trade and Commerce, Mr. Stevens, had even more definite views. He was unable to "see that a central bank would or could affect price levels to any extent.... I say this-- I said it in 1923 when the Bank Act was up for revision, I have said it many times since, and I say it again now--that we now have machinery under the Finance Act almost, if not quite, as flexible and effective as that of a central bank."[131]

Not until February 1934, when central bank legislation had actually been drafted, did the Conservatives--perhaps more by way of rationalization than conviction--begin to incorporate the then familiar supporting arguments into their programme. The chief spokesman was Mr. Rhodes, the Minister of Finance.[132] The Government, he declared, had come round to recognizing the advantages of a Canadian central bank, largely for controlling the total volume of credit and so indirectly influencing the general price level. A measure of control had previously been exerted through the Finance Act and the chartered banks, but the former lacked the powers, and the latter the motivation, traditionally associated with central bank action. The proposed institution would meet the new externally inspired demands for increased co-ordination and control of Canada's financial structure.[133]

There was the same combination of apathy and opposition within the Liberal party, although the change apparently occurred somewhat sooner there. It was Mr. Mackenzie King who, in February 1933, placed the Liberals squarely (if ambiguously) behind the establishment of a central bank:

> The Liberal party believes that credit is a public matter, not of interest to bankers only, but of direct concern to the average citizen. It stands for the immediate establishment of a properly-constituted national central bank, to perform the functions of

discount, and the control of currency issue, considered in terms of public need. A central bank is necessary to determine the supply of currency in relation to the domestic, social, and industrial requirements of the Canadian people, and also to deal with the problems of international commerce and exchange.[134]

With the major parties, then, it was hardly a case of action dictated by understanding. It can, indeed, be legitimately asked whether a central bank would have been created at the time if pure economic reason had prevailed. The policy-making authorities operated, rather, as the passive-- and, on the whole, reluctant--servant of a national state of mind which had crystallized only partly through economic analysis and even more through popular revulsion against the severe economic and social hardships induced by the Great Depression. By 1934 the establishment of a central bank had become a political necessity which no politically responsible group could afford to ignore.

Central Bank Thought and the Royal Commission Report.[135]

Such was the social-political-economic setting in which the Report of the Royal Commission on Banking and Currency was framed. More specifically, however, this Report--recommending the immediate establishment of a central bank in Canada--must be regarded, as the successful culmination of the central bank thought which had been formulated during the previous decade, in the first instance by the radicals and secondarily by the academic economists.

The organizational provisions of the Report are not without interest-- in terms of comparison with suggestions made before its publication and with the arrangements embodied in the resultant legislation.[136] Particularly worth noting are the provisions involving: (1) privately financed capitalization; (2) private management for the bank;[137] (3) the gradual retirement of the chartered bank note issue over a period of years; (4) the 5 per cent minimum reserve ratio against chartered bank deposit liabilities; (5) the concentration of the country's gold holdings in the new institution; and (6) the maintenance of a 25 per cent reserve in gold and foreign exchange against central bank note and deposit liabilities.

But the most significant aspect of the Report is its reiteration of the sentiments previously expressed throughout the Dominion regarding: (1) the commercial bankers' excessively narrow conception of their role in the economy; (2) the inadequacy of the chartered banks and the Finance Act as over-all instruments of control; (3) the importance of rediscounting and open market operations as central bank powers for stabilizing the external value of the monetary unit and mitigating domestic fluctuations in the level of economic activity; (4) the money market limitation on central bank control in Canada; and (5) the general limitations on the remedial functions of central bank action. Significant also was the Report's rejection of the Administrative Board proposed by the Canadian Bankers' Association;[138] and of the bankers' arguments pointing to the lack of

Canadian skill for central bank management and the high costs of operating a central bank. Resting its case on these considerations and on the fact that Canada had abandoned the gold standard, the Commission concluded that a central bank was highly desirable, and that it should be established without delay.

But by way of critical comment, it should be noted, in the first place, that the Report indiscriminately applied British banking theory and practice to Canadian conditions.[139] Secondly, the Report tended to identify price stability with economic stability, and to ignore the volatility of private investment and the machinery through which monetary policy might be supplemented in stabilizing this component of aggregate expenditure. And thirdly, the one crucial recommendation made by the Report--the creation of a central bank--received the approval of the narrowest possible majority of Commissioners, three to two: of the three in favour, two were British (Lord Macmillan and Sir Charles Addis), and the only Canadian was Mr. J. E. Brownlee, the radical Premier of Alberta;[140] both dissenters, Sir Thomas White and Mr. B. Leman, were prominent Canadian bankers (the former having served also as wartime Minister of Finance), and both echoed the "delay-futility" arguments repeatedly raised by their professional colleagues.[141]

Thus, but for the grace of two Englishmen and a Canadian radical, there would have been no recommendation of a central bank in Canada. As a matter of fact, the general contribution of the Report to Canadian monetary thought suffers by comparison with the Proceedings on which it was based. And it is to be doubted whether, in the light of those Proceedings and of the contemporary economic crisis, a negative conclusion by the Report on the central bank issue would have materially affected the course of the legislative action which followed.

II. FURTHER DEVELOPMENT TOWARDS MONETARY MATURITY, 1935-9

It was inevitable that the addition of the Bank of Canada to the Canadian institutional structure would serve not only to change the character of monetary policy but also further to clarify thinking on monetary problems. It is not as though misconceptions were entirely dissipated; some of them died particularly hard among the banker and social credit groups. But what does seem striking is the growing insight into monetary questions shown by virtually all groups in the Canadian economy; this was nowhere more pronounced than among government leaders, civil servants, and economists.[142]

Money, Credit, and Prices

The ideas which continued to be formulated in connection with the credit creation process are a case in point. Most of the bankers and politicians either did little to resolve the extremes of misunderstanding or contributed to it themselves.[143] But an increasing number of respon-

sible individuals and groups began to take exception to the orthodox position, and to advance reasonable interpretations of the crucial loan-deposit
relationship. Especially noteworthy, in this connection, are the contributions made by the League for Social Reconstruction, and by the Governor
of the Bank of Canada, Mr. Towers.[144] The former pointed clearly to
the logical fallacies of the cases argued by the extreme groups in the
credit creation controversy; while the latter probed deeper into the credit
mechanism, illustrating--in terms of bank balance sheets and simplifying
assumptions--the general process through which credit actually is created,
as well as the important limitations to which this process is subject.

Both the League and Mr. Towers also had interesting comments to
make about the general relationship between money and prices--even while
the bankers were still fluctuating between the view that there was no such
discernible relationship and that it was the reverse of the relationship
postulated by monetary theory. The League held the firm conviction that:

> In the absence of compensatory influences, [changes in the supply
> of money] give rise to a change in the general level of commodity
> prices, or in the rate of interest and the amount of borrowing and
> new capital expenditure, or in the external value of a country's
> currency--or a combination of all of them. In particular, a con-
> traction in the quantity of money may, by deflating commodity
> prices, produce a state of economic dislocation; a sharp increase
> in the volume of purchasing power will produce the equally drastic
> state of economic dislocation of somewhat different character,
> which we associate with inflation.[145]

Between those two extremes, there were "a number of intermediate positions, varying with the monetary policy pursued at the time."[146]

The theme of Mr. Towers' comments was similar, though he was
more concerned lest changes in the supply of money be invariably identified with changes in purchasing power:

> Expansion of the volume of money in Canada tends to produce a rise
> in the level of prices by increasing the potential demand for goods
> and services. In general, however, an increase in the volume of
> money will increase the total amount of buying only if there has
> been previously an actual shortage of money. There may be impor-
> tant factors offsetting the effect of an increase in the volume of
> money, as the amount of spending is almost entirely a matter of
> individuals' decisions which are influenced by many other factors
> than the volume of money.[147]

Another significant factor limiting the price effects of internal monetary
expansion was "the importance in the Canadian price structure of export
and import prices which are chiefly determined in world markets, and,
as long as we maintain existing currency adjustments, are almost entirely

outside the control of internal policy."[148]

Meanwhile, top policy-makers like the Minister of Finance, Mr. Dunning, were becoming more and more impressed with "the great advances made in monetary theory and central banking practice during the postwar years."[149] Concentrating on the concept of money velocity, he realized that the process of influencing the price level through monetary action was "not nearly as simple as some would have us believe. Under certain conditions, the price level will rise even if there is some decrease in the amount of cash in the country. Under other circumstances, the price level will fall even though the cash is increased."[150]

Problems of Monetary Policy

One of the significant facts to be recorded in connection with the Bank of Canada is the relative ease with which it came to be accepted throughout the Dominion as an integral part of the financial structure. In consequence, much of the monetary debate during the second half of the decade centred, not upon the economic issue of the policy implications of central banking, but upon the political issue of where ownership and control of the new institution should reside.[151] However, the wide range of economic problems opened up by this institutional change did not go unheeded.

Professor Plumptre. Among economists, the discussion took the form of renewed examination of the machinery of central banking, and of the setting in which Canadian monetary policy had operated in the past and would operate in the future. Professor Plumptre's analysis--more thorough and more technical than any of his previous efforts--again merits special attention.[152]

He acknowledged that, to the extent that open market operations were dependent upon an adequate security market, they would be successful in Canada, because, contrary to common expectations during the central bank controversy, "the [Canadian] bond market has been sufficiently broad not only for the central bank's operations but also to allow the commercial banks to respond by purchasing securities in substantially larger amounts."[153] Moreover, central bank control over long-term security markets might be particularly important in relation to the better established and less risky enterprises in the secondary industries, which, by recourse to the open capital markets, increasingly sought emancipation from the banks or from the limits set by their own profits; also in relation to the borrowing operations conducted by central and subsidiary governments and government agencies.

But, Professor Plumptre argued, there was a second important factor upon which the success of open market operations depended, namely, the maintenance of a fairly stable cash reserve ratio by the commercial banks; for this was the determinant of the action taken by the banks in response to the change effected in their reserves by central bank purchase or sale of securities. That the Canadian chartered banks should at that time be maintaining their customary 10 per cent ratio, despite the extent to which they had had to alter their business to do so, was the most remarkable

fact associated with the contemporary open market operations of the Bank
of Canada. However, it would be wrong (because of uncertainty as to
their attitude towards the central bank) to assume, without question, that
the banks would continue to maintain this stability of cash proportions.
And the ironic aspect of this "reserve ratio" factor was that, if stability
were assumed, there might well be serious unfavourable repercussions
on the security market: first, the large bank holdings of government
securities through which the stability probably would be maintained, would,
because of government costs, reduce the upward flexibility of the interest
rate structure, that is, would necessitate some degree of central bank support of bond yields and so impede open market sales of government securities; and secondly, those large holdings of securities would mean the in-
sulation of chartered bank policies regarding commercial loans from the
influence of the central bank's restrictive operations. On balance, economic circumstances pointed to the diminishing effectiveness of open market operations in achieving their objective of altering the cash reserves
and the lending and investing policies of the commercial banks.[154]

The limitations became even more severe when consideration was
given to the broader question of the effects of such variations in interest
rate as could be induced upon the general level of economic activity. In
short-run terms, there were four lines of argument supporting this conclusion:

> First, because Canadian banks have apparently been [unwilling]
> to extend long term agricultural credit they do not occupy [a stra-
> tegic] position in regard to the development or organization of
> agricultural areas. Secondly, the relatively advanced state of the
> Canadian security market must in some degree free Canadian in-
> dustries from dependence upon the banks, while at the same time
> giving to the banks a field for... liquid... investment.... Thirdly,
> the Canadian economic and financial system seems to have reached
> that stage of development already reached in the United States and
> Britain, where a long run decline in demand for bank credit has
> set in.... Fourthly, some Canadian borrowers have access to
> bank credit in neighbouring American cities.[155]

In long-run terms, the increasing uncertainty of economic conditions and
the growing rate of obsolescence of specialized machinery appeared to be
of increasing significance to those who considered raising funds; consequently, the interest rate and current security prices were likely to become progressively less important. "This being so, the central bank may
have to rely ... chiefly on personal persuasion, either over the would-be
industrial borrowers or over the financial groups which take up or float
securities."[156] And finally, unique to countries like Canada, there were
the international repercussions of central bank policy which might greatly
mitigate its efficacy. Chief among these were: under an easy money policy, the immunity of export incomes from control, and the tendency towards

import pressure on the balance of payments through high income levels and capital outflow; and, under restrictive conditions, the possibility of resort to foreign borrowing, with consequent easing of the immediate position in the capital and foreign exchange markets, at the expense of intensified difficulties of repayment at a later date.[157]

It was in this context of serious obstacles to effective central banking in Canada that Professor Plumptre undertook his analysis of the case for exchange depreciation. This inquiry--together with those of Professors Inman, Knox, and Allely[158]--typified Canadian economists' growing interest in the international economic problems then confronting the Dominion.[159]

The radicals. The three strands into which radical thinking had come to resolve itself were clearly in evidence during the second half of the decade. That is to say, one can distinguish between the views on monetary policy advanced by the C.C.F., by the Social Crediters, and by those who gave their support to neither of those two groups. Despite the broad theoretical cleavage, all had this much in common: they were convinced of the inadequacy of the traditional techniques of central banking, and of the urgent need for expansionist monetary measures aimed at raising levels of income and employment.

(1) The C.C.F. Of the three groups, the C.C.F.--through its intellectual arm, the League for Social Reconstruction--achieved the greatest degree of analytical clarity; though, again, its appraisal was coloured and somewhat distorted by its preoccupation with socialist, as distinct from purely economic, considerations.[160] The League, fully aware of the potentialities of central bank policy,[161] envisaged an institution in which governmental control (not necessarily ownership) was complete; and which was under no commitment to maintain the gold standard, and, therefore, to subordinate the Dominion to the possible adverse influences of British or American monetary policy. The maintenance of gold reserve and gold convertibility requirements of the currency at all times was "out of line with intelligent monetary policy even in a capitalist world."[162] With those difficulties removed, one vital objective of monetary policy would be the maintenance of an approximately stable level of prices, in so far as monetary policy could attain this end. "We do not claim that the achievement of a stable price level alone will eliminate depressions. It is nevertheless true that economic stability and waste will never be eliminated as long as price levels show violent fluctuations."[163] The acceptance of this objective implied that the volume of bank loans should be: (a) expanded to the extent that the part of the national income set aside as savings was not invested; (b) expanded in times of unemployment, such expansion tending to stimulate production rather than to raise prices; and (c) varied directly with the total volume of goods and services. The other major objective of monetary policy was the maintenance of the Canadian dollar at a stable value in terms of foreign currencies.

It was obvious, the League pointed out, that these two objectives, stable internal prices and a stable exchange rate, might at times be incompatible:

If the general level of prices in other countries were rapidly rising or falling, it would be impossible to maintain both a stable purchasing power of the Canadian dollar and a stable rate of exchange with other currencies of unstable purchasing power. There is room for an honest difference of opinion as to which is the better policy in any particular instance; whether it is preferable to keep the level of prices stable and let exchange rates fluctuate, or to keep exchange rates stable and let the price level fluctuate. We favour the view that the balance of advantage will usually be on the side of a stable internal price level. Especially is this true on occasions of violent deflation abroad such as has occurred during the last six years.[164]

In such circumstances, a policy of controlled exchange depreciation would be a desirable method of minimizing the effects of a depression in Canada. "But such a policy is not inconsistent with the avoidance of wide fluctuations in exchange rates over short periods. Frequent fluctuations from day to day should be avoided, and long-period changes introduced in an orderly way."[165]

The League refused, however, to place complete reliance on monetary policy. Taken by itself, it was inadequate to the task of stabilizing the level of activity under any economic system. But the limitations were particularly severe under capitalism because of: (1) the central bank's inability directly to raise the volume, or to determine the direction, of lending by commercial banks; (2) the vulnerability of the central bank to strong private group pressures (whether governmentally owned and operated or not); and (3) the inevitable maldistribution of credit arising from the close identification of bank directors with the control of the dominant industrial and financial institutions of Canada. A truly effective Canadian central bank, therefore, would not closely resemble the central banks then operating in other countries. "It would not be an advisory or persuasive body which, through certain manipulations of interest and discount rates, and of the volume of its security purchases, tried to influence the more or less irresponsible policies of competing, profit-seeking, and often-recalcitrant, commercial banks. Rather it would simply be the 'head office' of the unified [i.e., socialized] Canadian banking system."[166]

(2) The Social Crediters. The Social Credit politicians continued to state their position with varying degrees of crudeness. Some were convinced that all that was required for Canadian prosperity was "not commissions, not export markets, not an extensive scheme of public works which will increase our national debt, but a major operation, nothing short of... making available to the people at all times sufficient purchasing power to enable them to purchase the total price values."[167] Others showed an awareness of inflationary dangers, of the public-works aspects of an increased money supply, and of the fact that support for their policy proposals could be found in the writings of such economists as Fisher and Keynes.[168] But virtually all had the same distorted conception of the

processes of credit creation, savings and investment, and taxation and borrowing--with the result that the zeal with which their policy proposals were advanced was tempered either inadequately or not at all by analytical precision.

(3) The independents. The Social Credit contribution can, in fact hardly bear comparison with that of the independent radical thinkers who were apparently free of "A plus B" predilections. Of illustrative importance are the ideas propounded by the two Liberal members of Parliament, Mr. G. G. McGeer and Mr. W. A. Tucker, in the course of questioning Mr. Towers on the operations and significance of the Bank of Canada.[169] Apart from the unique Douglas theories, their misconceptions were strikingly similar to those of their social credit colleagues. Moreover, the persistence with which they, too, indulged in their inaccuracies of reasoning could not help but try the patience of other members of the House Committee on Banking and Commerce, as well as that of Mr. Towers. But this very persistence, together with the broad range of economic problems covered by the two Liberals--the implications of a 100 per cent reserve banking system, the effects of government repayment of bank-held debt, the mechanics of interest-free government financing, the limitations of traditional central bank techniques, the effects of monetary expansion and increased government spending on prices, incomes, and employment-- elicited the most painstaking economic analysis from the Governor of the Bank.[170]

Mr. Towers. On the whole, Mr. Towers handled himself with consummate skill in the role of what amounted to a teacher of economic principles. His well-reasoned answers to the questions raised by the radicals stand as a clear demonstration of the significant advances in civil service thinking which had been achieved by the end of the thirties. Three sets of excerpts from Mr. Towers' testimony will serve to support this contention.

On the 100 per cent reserve question, the Governor pointed up for Mr. Tucker the full implications of such a policy.[171] Mr. Towers showed, again through balance sheets, that two basic changes would be involved, the taxation of bank depositors, and the establishment of some new form of banking system for the purpose of making loans; both changes would follow from the fact that the chartered banks would be restricted in their lending and investing to an amount not exceeding their capital and reserve funds, and that bank earnings would decline drastically along with the banks' ability to finance the requirements of agriculture, industry, and individuals. The assumption of full control over such financing by the central bank might not constitute a net improvement over the existing system. In other words, the 100 per cent reserve proposal was to be viewed as not merely a device for softening the inflationary impact of (1) government repayment of bank-held debt or (2) financing government expenditure through currency issue-- Mr. Tucker had those policies in mind--but as a fundamental reorganization of the existing banking structure.

Another of Mr. Tucker's proposals was that providing for a tax of 1/12 per cent per month on savings deposits so as to raise the level of

consumption.[172] According to Mr. Towers, the first effect of such a proposal would, obviously, be a 1 per cent reduction (from 1 1/2 per cent to
1/2 per cent) in the annual net interest return on personal savings deposits.
Other effects would depend upon the resultant action taken by the depositors concerned:

> If savings depositors considered that, even at 1/2 per cent per
> annum net interest return, a cash balance was preferable to any
> other form of investment, then savings deposits would remain the
> same and the government would receive increased revenues of,
> say, $17 million per annum at the expense of a similar reduction
> in net interest received by depositors. If savings depositors felt
> that a net interest return of 1/2 per cent per annum was so small
> that they preferred some other uses for their funds, I think it
> would be very unlikely that they would increase their purchases
> of goods and services. In all probability, they would turn towards
> other forms of investment. The supply of corporate securities
> being quite small, ... the important avenue of investment to which
> savings depositors might turn would appear to be government se-
> curities. An increase in demand of this kind for government se-
> curities would reduce the yields on government securities which
> would force the banks ultimately to reduce the rate of interest on
> deposits.[173]

Under those circumstances, the effect of the hoarding tax would be the
same as that of an extension of the easy money policy which had been followed since 1935, and which could be continued if so desired. The Governor was also critical of the tax as a fiscal measure, on the ground that
its incidence would be particularly heavy on the small depositor, "who
would have very little, if any, chance of profitably employing his funds
elsewhere. It might lead him to withdraw his deposit and hold notes.
This would be a most undesirable development, both from a social and
financial point of view."[174]

On the scope and limitations of monetary policy, Mr. Towers made
many interesting observations, largely by way of response to the demands
of Mr. McGeer and Mr. Tucker for expansion beyond the bounds of traditional central bank action.[175] Two of these observations are worth special
emphasis. The Governor of the Bank of Canada was convinced, in the
first place, that "in no country and at no time have there been bank and
market responses to central bank... policies more complete, more full,
and more in line with anything that a theorist might have anticipated, than
have taken place in Canada."[176] Support for this view was to be found in
the enormous fluctuations of the Canadian central bank's holdings of securities relative to total assets. And secondly, he contended that the amount
of monetary expansion achieved through the Bank's easy money policy had
been sufficient, when considered in relation to actual conditions, "to offer
all the incentive to a high level of economic activity and prosperity which

monetary policy can be expected to offer in a country where non-monetary factors are so important."[177] Mr. Towers acknowledged that such expansion in Canada might not produce a marked price increase for some time because of the importance of export and import prices in the Dominion's price structure; but he proceeded to argue that:

> It [internal monetary expansion] will, however, tend to lower the rate of interest and increase the burden borne by savings depositors, policy-holders, and, in general, those who receive fixed-interest incomes. [Its] further effects depend upon when and to what extent the additional money created is actively used by the public....
> Active use of the increase in the volume of money would produce an unfavourable internal situation in which pressure on the balance of payments would result, and which would force a decision between reversing the policy of internal expansion and depreciating the external value of the dollar.[178]

Adoption of the "depreciation" alternative would increase the burden borne by recipients of fixed interest and extend it to wage-earners, who would bear a major share of the internal transfer caused by depreciation.[179]

Government and business views. This same balanced approach to monetary policy already had begun to take hold (though in less sophisticated form) at the Cabinet level of government, and even, to some extent, in private financial circles.[180] Thus, while defining the general objectives of the central bank and the government as "the maximum possible sustained level of productivity and the minimum possible level of unemployment"[181] --that in itself having been an important step forward in economic thinking-- Mr. Dunning, the Liberal Minister of Finance, was quick to add that monetary policy alone could not achieve those objectives and should not be regarded as a panacea. "It can, at best, only create conditions favourable to sound development. In a constructive program, it should merely take its place as part of a much larger whole. Fundamentally, our need is an increase in our aggregate national income."[182]

Mr. J. T. Bryden, Assistant Treasurer of the North American Life Assurance Company, warned against attaching too much importance to cheap money as an instrument for promoting business recovery and higher levels of employment:

> Looking back from the vantage point of the fifth year of recovery [1937], it is difficult to assess the part that artificially easy money has played in recovery, but it is clear that the benefits of low interest rates have been slow to work through the economic structure....
> In most cases, interest is only a minor item in the cost of production and is becoming increasingly less important as speedy transportation narrows the distance between producer and consumer....
> The mere existence of cheap money is evidently not enough to assure recovery. Confidence, or lack of it, has also played a major role.[183]

And Mr. C. H. Herbert, Economist for the Sun Life Assurance Company of Canada, was similarly convinced that the recovery period of the thirties had shown that cheap money by itself was somewhat limited in its effect as a business stimulant, though it was a valuable aid when other conditions were ripe for recovery.[184] It was also clear to him that:

> Economic theory is turning more and more towards the adoption of fiscal policy...as the most efficient mechanism for controlling booms and depressions. It would be quite incorrect to state that this mechanism has yet been nearly perfected or that it is widely accepted either by the public or by government bodies. Nevertheless, it does appear that the development of economic control over the next ten years 1939-1949 will move in this direction, and that the need for high interest rates to check unhealthy booms will diminish and may ultimately disappear.[185]

Concluding Remarks on Monetary Thought

It was logical, after all, that the new concern with the inadequacies of monetary policy should have driven home to growing numbers of Canadians the realization of the importance of fiscal techniques in giving strength, direction, and speed to the flow of expenditures influenced by both conventional and unorthodox monetary means. The other vital policy inference which could be drawn--and which was drawn--from the emphasis on monetary problems was that the extent of Canada's control over fluctuations in its income and employment levels was severely limited so long as Canadians chose to maintain the existing international orientation of their economy.

But this latter inference was hardly unique to the decade of the thirties; nor was any thorough analysis brought to bear on the degree of its validity, and on the implications of a narrowed scope for international specialization in Canada. In terms of subsequent developments, the stage had rather been set for the elaboration of fiscal concepts and instruments with a view to expanding the effective range of domestic stabilization policy. Of course, the problem of international limitations could not be dismissed. Indeed, the ensuing wartime and postwar fiscal advances in both thought and policy would necessarily hasten the acquisition of a full critical appreciation of its importance.

CHAPTER IX

CANADIAN MONETARY POLICY IN DEPRESSION
AND RECOVERY

MONETARY POLICY during the crucial decade of the thirties derived its uniqueness from, and helped in turn tb determine, the final outcome of the inflation and central bank controversies. Analysis of this policy divides logically into three parts: the first two comprise the "internal" and "external" efforts made to stabilize the Canadian economy in the depths of depression; [1] while the third involves the monetary measures undertaken by the new Bank of Canada during the latter part of the decade. The basic division, then, is between the pre- and post-central bank years, and attention is accordingly turned to the complex problems posed by each period.

I. INTERNAL MONETARY POLICY DURING THE GREAT DEPRESSION[2]

In the light of the near unanimity among those individuals and groups most directly influential in the formulation of monetary policy, as well as the widely divided counsels then being offered by professional economists, the main lines of Canadian policy actually pursued in the early thirties were almost a foregone conclusion.[3] That any deviation whatever occurred from the orthodox position must come as a matter of surprise and can be interpreted only on the basis of two important factors: (1) the looseness of the theoretical framework devised to support unqualified orthodoxy; and (2) the increasing gravity of the economic circumstances prevailing in Canada after the 1929 collapse.

Remedial Government and Bank Action

During the entire period from the beginning of 1930 to November 1932, there does not appear to have been any active monetary policy on the part of either the federal Government or the chartered banks. Little was done by way of monetary easing of the depressed conditions at that time. On October 26, 1931, the Treasury Board reduced from 4-1/2 to 3 per cent the rate of discount paid by the banks for advances under the Finance Act; a 1/2 per cent increase in the rate was made on May 21, 1932, and for almost a whole year thereafter no further reduction occurred. From time to time, during the 1930-2 period, the banks made some reductions in interest rates charged on loans and advances to individuals and business enterprises; these concessions, however, were very small.

The only development of this period which could have made a significant remedial contribution was the borrowing operations conducted by the Government with the banks. Security purchases by the banks in 1930 were insufficient to offset the reduction in deposits produced by the liquidation

of commercial loans. In November 1931, however, the Government made
its first major offering of bonds to the banks. There is little ground for
the presumption that this "Dominion of Canada National Service Loan, "
amounting to $221 million, reflected the conscious desire of the Govern-
ment to engage in a comprehensive programme of deficit financing; or
that the banks' main interest in subscribing to the loan was to support the
government bond market and thereby promote low interest rates and easy
money conditions generally. In the latter connection, bank portfolios of
securities were reduced as soon as the government issue had been subscribed, and the reduction of loans and deposits proceeded simultaneously.
The truth is that, unable to discover safe opportunities for investment in
commercial loans, Canadian banks felt compelled to increase their holdings of securities in order to maintain their earning assets at an adequate
level; this despite the prevailing philosophy favouring a strict programme
of commercial-loans. Thus, it was with considerable reluctance, and
with the aim of making it only temporary, that the banks indulged in increased security buying. Their reaction to the National Service Loan, as
well as to their $50 million purchase of one-year Treasury bills on August
1, 1932, only serves to bear out this contention.

On November 1, 1932, there occurred an unusual transaction between
the Government and the banks. The former persuaded the latter to buy
$35 million of 4 per cent one-year Treasury bills, and to pledge these
securities with the Treasury Board for an advance of Dominion notes of
a similar amount at 3 per cent under the Finance Act. The result of this
operation was that the Government obtained its money at a net cost of
1 per cent, and both bank deposits and bank reserves were increased.
The banks were thereby placed under the virtual necessity of further expanding their earning assets, and their security holdings began to rise.
This was the first substantial governmental attempt at inflation--made,
no doubt, partly as a means of implementing, without the proper central
banking machinery, the "Ottawa Agreements" to ease credit conditions
and thereby to increase prices. The effects of this expansionist policy
were not very great, however, because, as security holdings increased,
commercial loans continued to decline, and the banks--unwilling to be
permanently indebted to the currency authority--took the earliest opportunity to liquidate their previous borrowings under the Finance Act.
Moreover, the downward pressure exerted on bond prices by the sales of
Canadian securities by foreign holders strengthened the more orthodox
in their conviction that "no good could come of inflation. "

In the spring of 1933, the banks again supported the security market
prior to and during the floating of a large government loan, and once
more they reduced their investments after the loan had been subscribed.
Another significant development at that time was the 1/2 per cent reduction,
not without Government encouragement, of the interest rate paid by the
banks on savings deposits, and the 1 per cent reduction on loans to farmers
and municipalities. This action, which helped the Government to secure
funds at a low rate, constituted the first recorded general movement in

the history of Canadian short-term rates. There also occurred, in May 1933, a reduction in the Treasury Board rate on Dominion note advances to an unprecedented level, namely, 2-1/2 per cent. In 1934 the banks again bought government securities and further reduced the rate of interest on savings deposits. But none of the reductions in the interest rate were substantial; furthermore, there were inexcusable delays in making the desired reductions.

On the last mentioned occasion, the banks continued to add to their investments after the completion of government borrowing. This prolonged security buying was the consequence of the Government's second major attempt at monetary inflation--its amendment of the Dominion Notes Act on June 28, 1934. By means of the new legislation, the quantity of Dominion notes which could be issued against a 25 per cent gold backing was raised from $50 million to $120 million. The Government then proceeded to expand the fiduciary issue by the maximum of $52.5 million permitted by the amendment, and to use the new money to defray budgetary expenses, including public works.[4] All this was done, of course, in the name of orthodoxy. The Prime Minister found the necessary justification in the resolution of the London Monetary and Economic Conference recommending the provision of greater elasticity in monetary systems through the maintenance of legal gold reserves of not more than 25 per cent as coverage for national currencies.[5] Probably stronger motivating forces behind the Government's action were: (1) the apparent cessation of the downswing in Canadian business conditions in the latter part of 1933; (2) the enormous recovery of the Canadian dollar, relative to United States currency, resulting from the Roosevelt devaluation policy; and (3) the partially favourable Canadian impression of the New Deal radicalism then taking hold in the United States.

But whatever the contributory factors, the effects of the policy itself were considerably below expectations. Bank cash reserves did increase steadily from $192 million in June 1934 to $250 million in July of the same year.[6] In view of the Canadian banks' customary 10 per cent reserve ratio, this increase was large enough to support an even greater volume of loans and investments than had prevailed in boom times. As a matter of fact, the increase in total bank deposits for the one-year period beginning in July 1934 amounted to about $91 million. With their reserves greatly augmented and the demand for commercial and other loans weak, the banks felt almost compelled to buy more securities in order to increase their earning assets. The resultant rise in this type of bank credit--$181 million between July 1934 and July 1935--was offset, however, by the simultaneous decline in loans--$78 million during the same period--and by the fact that much of the credit expansion took the form of enhanced savings deposits.[7]

A useful appraisal of the limited governmental "reflationary" efforts is embodied in the conclusions reached on this matter by Professor Inman:

The government was quite successful in its attempt to increase the

supply of money. To the extent that inflation involves a more
plentiful monetary medium, the government achieved its ambition.
But if by inflation we mean a rise (or the prevention of a fall) in
prices through an increase in the monetary supply, the government's success was by no means spectacular. Something more
than the mere addition to the money available is required in order
to bring about a rise in prices; the money must be spent.[8]

Of course, the Government utilized the borrowed funds, and this exercised
a positive influence on prices. Granting that such funds would not have
been employèd by other spending units, the Government's activities in this
regard necessarily provided a stimulus. However, with this money (after
having been spent by the Government) tending to remain idle, the price
effects could not be very extensive. The Government was able to arrest
the fall in the money supply by the end of 1932, but the velocity of circulation continued to decline until the second quarter of 1933; nor did their
revival have crucially important ameliorative results.[9]

The Banking System and Economic Stability
        The negative aspects of the depression policy pursued by the chartered
banks are revealed in the above survey, while Chart 3 depicts the general
monetary outlines of economic instability between 1926 and 1934. The lack
of initiative and co-ordinated action--in general, the doing of "too little
too late"--must have seriously impeded Canadian recovery from the Great
Depression. The question now arises whether the stultifying effects of
bank action took a more positive form. The evidence is clear with respect
to the role of the banks in the events leading up to the collapse of 1929.
It has already been concluded that, despite late efforts to control the situation, the banks' easy recourse to the Finance Act as a source of cash,
their liberal financing of uneconomic commercial and speculative loans,
and the extreme rigidity of the interest rate structure, combined to exert
a strong intensifying influence on the boom, and to demonstrate fundamental weaknesses in the Canadian banking system. It is more difficult, however, to attribute major causal importance to banking policy during the
downswing phase of the cycle, when non-bank deflationary forces are so
powerful, and when so much bank action reflects the defence of shaky
financial positions brought on by these forces.
        The actual facts of the situation were approximately as follows.
First, statistical investigation shows that during 1929 the physical volume
of business declined before total bank credit (total loans and investments)
in Canada; the credit index, moreover, remained above the business index throughout the Great Depression.[10] Second, at the height of the 1929
boom, the Canadian banking system, as can be seen from Table XI, was
in a much more extended position than it had been on the occasion of the
previous boom of 1920. Thus, in the "cash" circumstances of 1929, unlike those of 1920, a moderate bank-initiated deflation of liabilities would
not have been sufficient to restore cash ratios to customary levels. In

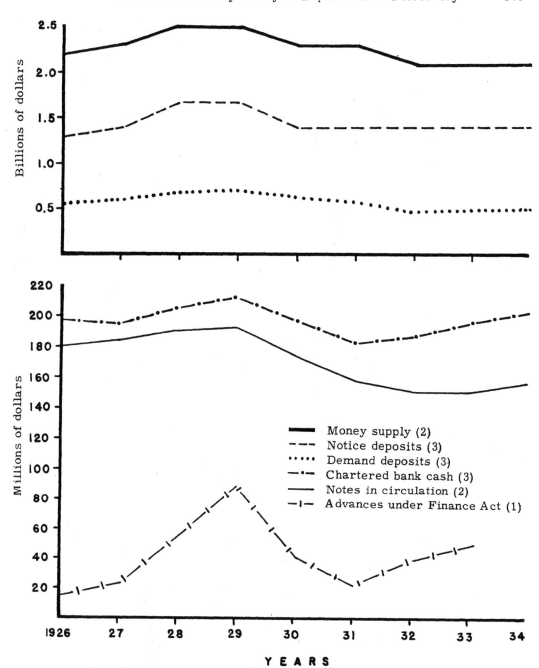

CHART 3. Selected banking statistics, 1926 - 1934.

Sources: (1) C. A. Curtis, <u>Statistical Contributions to Canadian Economic History</u> (Toronto, 1931), vol. I, p. 27; and Canada, <u>Report of the Royal Commission on Banking and Currency in Canada</u> (Ottawa, 1933), pp. 41, 42. The 1933 figure is the average of the monthly figures from January until July, inclusive. (2) <u>Canada Year Book</u>, 1947, p. 1023. (3) Bank of Canada, <u>Statistical Summary: 1946 Supplement</u> (Ottawa, 1946), p. 8.

TABLE XI

Bank Reserve Ratios October 1920 and 1929

Ratios	Percentage	
	October 1920	October 1929
Total cash[1] as percentage of notes and deposits	15.70	9.40
Free cash[2] as percentage of deposits	13.54	10.13
Net cash[3] as percentage of deposits	11.90	6.37
Total gold as percentage of notes and deposits	7.35	4.72

Source: Elliott, "Bank Cash," C.J.E.P.S., IV (Aug. 1938), p. 444.
[1]"Total cash" is defined as chartered banks' holdings of gold and Dominion notes in Canada.
[2]"Free cash" is defined as total cash, less gold and/or Dominion notes deposited in the central gold reserve.
[3]"Net cash" is defined as total cash, less advances under the Finance Act.

October 1929, for example, the restoration of the "total cash" reserve ratio to, say, 11-1/2 per cent, after repayment of advances under the Finance Act and allowing for no gold imports, would have necessitated a 50 per cent bank reduction in notes and deposits, that is, from $2,579.2 million to $1,325.1 million.[11] The third fact to be noted, in connection with the role of the banks in the depression, is the two-period aspect of the credit deflation. Between October 1929 and January 1931 there was a reduction in notes and deposits from the peak of $2,579 million to $2,187 million--a drop of $392 million, or 15.2 per cent, as compared with 14.3 per cent after the 1920 collapse.[12] The second distinct period of deflation began ten months later, in November 1931, and had spent itself by January 1933; the decline in notes and deposits amounted to 12.4 per cent, with the most severe deflation of bank credits occurring between November 1931 and October 1932.[13]

But it should not be inferred that there is a simple pro-bank solution to the problem of apportioning responsibility for the large-scale loan liquidation of the early thirties. Indeed, the operation of the whole deflationary process was quite complex. In regard to the first point mentioned above, neither the time lag of the credit index behind the business index nor the consistent excess of the former over the latter proved, as many leading bankers contended, that the banks were in no way to blame for the depressed economic conditions following the 1929 collapse. Such reasoning would have to be based on the assumption that money and credit are merely passive factors in the economic system. While it would probably be impossible to determine the exact nature of the cause-effect relationship between these two magnitudes and the numerous other economic variables, it is no longer open to question that an intimate reciprocal relationship of this kind does exist.

Secondly, in describing the over-extended position of the Canadian banks in 1929, one must agree with Mr. C. Elliott that:

> A deflation... in notes and deposits of the order of 50 per cent
> could not, of course, have been contemplated, nor was it necessary.
> The decline in speculation at home and abroad after the 1929 crash
> in prices brought some relief to the Canadian banking position, the
> quick fall in New York open-market money rates modified the at-
> traction of free balances for employment there, the decline in pro-
> duction, trade and prices, and the growing desire for liquidity
> brought its own reduction in the demand for commercial-bank
> credit, and substantial issues of securities abroad compensated
> for further deterioration in the Canadian current balance of inter-
> national payments.[14]

Nevertheless, this leaves still unexplained the general restraining effect which must have been exerted by the direct psychological impact of the banks' over-extended position upon the bankers themselves.

The third point raises the interesting question as to whether the 1929-31 period represented the swift, necessary, "business-like liquidation of extended private positions"[15] accomplished partly by bank action; and whether the 1931-3 period of deflation was merely the result of the world-shaking economic disturbances beginning with the failure of the Kreditanstalt in May 1931 and ending with Great Britain's abandonment of the gold standard in September of the same year. This was the position taken by Mr. Elliott, as expressed in his contention that, "if criticism is warranted, it is not on the basis of the post-boom policies of the banks, but on the basis of too great leniency in the boom days, when public policy was also deficient."[16] It does seem reasonably clear that, by 1931, the process of rehabilitation of internal banking positions was well advanced, and with it the general adjustment of the Canadian economy to the dislocations of 1929. The reserve position of the banks had improved, the pace of loan liquidation had slackened, and the incidence of deflation was being further offset by bank purchases of securities. In August 1931, three months before the National Service Loan, bank holdings of securities stood at $701 million, an increase of $270 million, or 63 per cent, over the figure for January 1930.[17] The Canadian dollar had returned to parity in the foreign exchange markets, and federal government bonds had attained their highest price levels since prewar days. There can be no doubt, moreover, of the severe Canadian repercussions of the 1931 international collapse--a

calamity to which the Canadian banking system can hardly be considered
to have made a significant contribution. Under such circumstances, and
in view of the Dominion's highly concentrated banking structure, "the
failure of one large bank in Canada through illiquid assets would, " as
Professor Inman pointed out, "be something akin to a national disaster. "[18]

But four questions of a more general character remain. First, was
the primary bank credit deflation of 1929-31 excessive, in terms of banker
over-concern with the liquidity of bank assets at the expense of stable levels
of income and employment? Second, did this same zeal for liquidity make
the secondary deflation of 1931-3 longer and more intense than it would
have been if only external forces had been operative? Third, granting the
need for a measure of loan liquidation, from the point of view of both the
individual banks and the economy, would formal centralized monetary
machinery have achieved such liquidation more efficiently and in combination with offsetting actions designed to keep the Canadian economy on an
even keel? And fourth, even if this machinery had existed, would Canada
still have undergone the economic privations associated with the Great
Depression?

There can be no categorical replies to such broad questions. Bearing
this limitation in mind, it would appear that all four answers must be in
the affirmative--the first two on grounds of (1) the bankers' strong expression of faith in the need for thoroughgoing "adjustments" to the excesses
of boom periods, in the commercial loan philosophy, and in the narrow
profit making role of the commercial bank in the community, and (2) their
consequent eagerness to minimize securities holdings, except under extraordinary conditions; and the third answer on the basis of the partially successful co-ordinating and stimulating functions performed by central banks
in other countries as well as the obvious imperfections of such Canadian
machinery as did exist. The fourth answer is, in a sense, the most crucial of all, since it places the whole central bank controversy in proper
perspective and demonstrates that the attempt to allocate blame for cyclical developments was misdirected to the extent that it obscured the limited
effectiveness of central bank monetary policy as an instrument for countercyclical control. A combination of experience and advances in monetary
theory has shown that this type of policy--aimed traditionally at directly
influencing the attractiveness of spending, rather than the amount, direction, or speed of the spending--has serious limitations in both the upswing
and downswing phases (particularly the latter) of the cycle.[19] And this generalization becomes even stronger when specific application is made to
countries, like Canada (in the thirties), geared to a large amount of international trade while possessing only the most primitive of money markets.

In its internal aspects, then, Canadian monetary policy of the early
thirties emerges from the foregoing appraisal as a loose, poorly co-
ordinated combination of measures taken "on the spot" and with little
understanding among policy-makers of their broad implications. The
fault lay not so much with what government leaders and bankers actually
did--the record is not clear on this issue, though the conclusion seems

warranted that the latter did, on balance, play a substantial intensifying role during the 1926-33 period--as with the long-stagnant state of their economic thinking, and their consequent failure to set up the monetary machinery which would have lessened the force of the boom and mitigated the effects of the ensuing depression; it being thoroughly understood that monetary machinery and policy would, in themselves, have been neither adequate nor (probably) of paramount importance. It is evident, therefore, that monetary developments during the early thirties--while not quite as vulnerable to criticism, or as overwhelmingly significant, as characteristically assumed in radical circles--provided little justification for the complacency of, and the general satisfaction expressed by, the more orthodox groups and individuals with respect to the working efficiency of the Canadian monetary and banking system.

II. EXTERNAL MONETARY POLICY DURING THE GREAT DEPRESSION

Fluctuations in the Canadian Dollar and Balance of Payments[20]

The intimate relationship between the Canadian dollar, on the one hand, and the British pound and American dollar, on the other, has already been described. In terms of the relative importance to Canada of the other two currencies, it was, clearly, a relationship involving one minor currency, the Canadian, and two major ones, the British and American. Upon the fluctuation of one of these major currencies relative to the other, freely operating market forces (operating through changed demand and supply conditions for exports and imports) would, therefore, cause the Canadian currency to occupy a position intermediate between the British and American.[21]

But one would have expected something quite different to occur after the de facto Canadian abandonment of the gold standard in 1929, namely, the depreciation of the Canadian dollar in terms of both sterling and the United States dollar. The pressure on Canada's foreign exchanges had already seriously depleted the government's stock of gold. Largely because of the 1928-9 change from a $132 million favourable trade balance to a $94 million unfavourable balance, the deficit on current and long-term capital account had risen to a peak of $230 million by the end of 1929.[22] And the precipitous fall in merchandise exports during 1930 was only very slightly exceeded by the decline of imports. Under such circumstances, the large and increasing interest and dividend payments on foreign investment in Canada would--in the absence of any offsetting capital movements--necessarily have imposed a crushing burden upon any process of balance-of-payments adjustment carried on within a stable exchange rate framework. As indicated in Table XII and Chart 4, however, a period of more than two years elapsed before any depreciation of the Canadian dollar took place.

The failure of the Canadian dollar to depreciate before mid-1931 is to be attributed largely to the phenomenal rise of net long-term capital imports in 1930 to $315. 7 million, "the highest net capital import of any

TABLE XII

Monthly Average Price of U.S. Dollars and Sterling in Montreal, 1929-1934

(in Canadian dollars)

Month	1929		1930		1931		1932		1933		1934	
	U.S. dollars	Sterling	U.S. dollars	Sterling	U.S. dollars	Sterling	U.S. dollars	Sterling	U.S. dollars	Sterling	U.S. dollars	Sterling
January	1.00	4.86	1.01	4.92	1.00	4.86	1.17	4.01	1.14	3.85	1.01	5.07
February	1.00	4.87	1.01	4.89	1.00	4.86	1.14	3.96	1.20	4.10	1.01	5.08
March	1.01	4.88	1.00	4.87	1.00	4.85	1.11	4.06	1.20	4.14	1.00	5.11
April	1.01	4.89	1.00	4.86	1.00	4.86	1.11	4.16	1.18	4.23	1.00	5.15
May	1.01	4.88	1.00	4.87	1.00	4.86	1.13	4.17	1.14	4.50	1.00	5.10
June	1.01	4.88	1.00	4.86	1.00	4.88	1.15	4.20	1.11	4.62	.99	5.01
July	1.00	4.87	1.00	4.85	1.00	4.87	1.15	4.07	1.06	4.93	.99	4.99
August	1.01	4.87	1.00	4.86	1.00	4.87	1.14	3.95	1.06	4.79	.98	4.95
September	1.01	4.88	1.00	4.85	1.04	4.69	1.11	3.84	1.04	4.84	.97	4.86
October	1.01	4.92	1.00	4.85	1.12	4.38	1.09	3.71	1.02	4.79	.98	4.84
November	1.02	4.95	1.00	4.85	1.12	4.19	1.16	3.79	.99	5.08	.98	4.87
December	1.01	4.92	1.00	4.86	1.21	4.09	1.16	3.79	1.00	5.10	.99	4.89
Average	1.01	4.89	1.00	4.87	1.04	4.69	1.14	3.98	1.09	4.58	.99	4.99

Sources: D.B.S., Canada Year Books, 1932, 1933, 1934-35, pp. 795, 924, 1003, respectively; and F. A. Knox, Dominion Monetary Policy, p. 3.

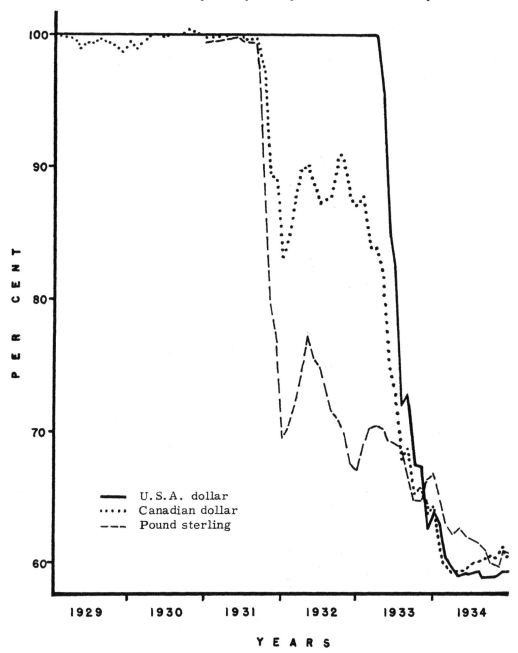

CHART 4. Currencies as percentage of former gold parities, 1929-34: monthly average quotations.

Source: League of Nations, <u>Monthly Bulletins of Statistics</u> (Geneva, 1931-6).

year since 1914 by over $100 million, and, what is more significant, $249.6 million larger than the net import of capital for the year 1929."[23] This additional credit enabled the Dominion to pay almost fully the highest current account deficit of the whole period 1928-35. The Canadian dollar returned to par because, through a rise in net capital imports, Canadians obtained a supply of foreign exchange just short of the demand for it at the going price. Table XIII sets out the important changes in the Canadian balance of payments during the crucial years 1930-4.[24]

Thus, the continued strength of Canada's foreign exchange position was largely dependent on the sustained inflow of long-term capital from abroad. The position of the Canadian dollar was made especially precarious by the fact that so great a proportion of the capital funds had been coming from the United States, a country in which the gravity of the Depression impact was second to none. The break could not, therefore, be long averted, and the balance-of-payments deterioration which occurred in 1931 was severe.

The stage was set for the exchange crisis primarily by the phenomenal 97 per cent drop in net long-term capital imports between 1930 and 1931, that is, from $315 million to $8 million. The consequence of this was a $166 million shortage of foreign exchange (in terms of the required offset for the current account deficit of $174 million). The deficiency would, indeed, have been even greater had it not been for the 40 per cent decline in the value of merchandise imports (as compared with the 32 per cent decline in the value of merchandise exports), accounting for the first favourable balance of trade since 1928.[25] It was, nevertheless, a deficiency which exerted tremendous pressure upon the Canadian dollar. The pressure increased steadily during 1931, with the continuous export of monetary gold and the sale of foreign assets, and the resultant progressive deterioration of the cash reserve position of Canada's chartered banks. In this weakened condition, the Canadian dollar was highly vulnerable to any severe shock to the international payments mechanism. Its actual depreciation in New York followed the British abandonment of the gold standard in September 1931.

For approximately two years thereafter--until the autumn of 1933-- the Canadian dollar continued to fluctuate at a premium in terms of sterling and at a discount in terms of the United States dollar. The peak monthly discount of the American dollar during the depression was 21 per cent, reached in December 1931, while the sterling premium stood at its maximum point of 23.5 per cent in October 1932.[26] This was the period during which the Canadian dollar took up, roughly, a mid-way position between the American dollar and the British pound--the "natural" position which might be anticipated for a minor currency in relation to two major currencies representative of important commercial and financial areas for the minor country.

The balance of payments in 1932 reflected both the instability of the Canadian dollar and the worsening of the depression produced by the

TABLE XIII

Canadian Balance of International Payments: Net Balances of Transactions with All Countries, 1930-1934

(millions of dollars)

Net Receipts or Credits (+); Net Payments or Debits (-)

Items	1930	1931	1932	1933	1934
Current account					
1. Merchandise	- 93	+ 21	+ 97	+164	+164
2. Non-monetary gold	+ 39	+ 57	+ 70	+ 82	+114
3. Tourist trade	+ 88	+ 82	+ 65	+ 45	+ 56
4. Interest and dividends	-289	-282	-265	-226	-211
5. Freight and shipping	- 33	- 25	- 28	- 22	- 27
6. Miscellaneous	- 49	- 27	- 35	- 45	- 28
7. Balance on current account	-337	-174	- 96	- 2	+ 68
Long-term capital account					
8. New issues & retirements of Canadian securities	+290	- 2	- 1	- 32	- 58
9. Other security transactions	- 13	- 24	- 16	+ 51	+ 9
10. Other capital movements	+ 38	+ 34	- 32	- 75	- 48
11. Balance on long-term capital acc't.	+315	+ 8	- 49	- 56	- 97
12. Balance on current & long-term capital acc't.	- 22	-166	-145	- 58	- 29
Balancing items					
13. Canadian bank assets abroad	(-0.4)	+ 28	+ 38	+ 24	- 19
14. Monetary gold	- 36	+ 33	+ 3	+ 6	- 4
15. Total	- 36	+ 61	+ 41	+ 30	- 23
16. Residual item	+ 58	+105	+104	+ 28	+ 52

Source: D.B.S., The Canadian Balance of International Payments, p. 240 and The Canadian Balance of International Payments, 1926-1945, p. 48.

world-wide repercussions of the European financial crisis which had developed in the summer of 1931. The current account deficit dropped from $174 million in 1931 to $96 million, but then only because of the continued greater decline in merchandise imports than in merchandise exports. The payments problem was aggravated, moreover, by an outflow of $49 million in long-term capital exports, the first such movement since 1928. The resultant $145 million deficit on current and long-term capital account was only about $10 million less than the corresponding figure for the previous year.

With the inception of world recovery in the latter part of 1933, the Canadian balance of payments registered more appreciable improvement. By the end of the year, merchandise exports had risen to $532 million, an increase of $37 million over 1932.[27] This was the first such increase since 1928, and, together with the $30 million decline in merchandise imports and the $38 million drop in interest and dividend payments, it was responsible for the lowest deficit on current account since 1926. The net flow of long-term capital was again outward, this time to the extent of $56 million. This export of capital, however, made for a combined deficit on current and long-term capital account of only $58 million, or less than one-half the corresponding deficit for the year 1932.

The American banking crisis of early 1933 appears to have been major factor in the series of exchange rate fluctuations which developed during the latter part of the year and restored pre-September 1931 parities between the Canadian dollar, the British pound, and the United States dollar. The essence of these fluctuations was as follows:

> The depreciation of the United States dollar during 1933 to a point, in terms of gold, below that to which the pound had already fallen, brought the pound back to par and above in New York. At the same time, the Canadian dollar again fell in terms of gold, stopping at a degree of depreciation roughly equal to that of the pound and the United States dollar. As a result of the fall of the three currencies to about the same degree in terms of gold, the former relationships between them were restored. In Montreal, the United States dollar fell to par, and the pound sterling rose to par and above. These dramatic exchange-rate movements did much to restore the position undermined by the events of the years 1931-1932. Once more pounds sterling obtained from the export of Canadian goods and services had their old weight in paying our debts in New York and yielded in Canada more dollars to the export producer.[28]

In terms of the international aspects of economic well-being, the trend for Canada was even more clearly upward during 1934. The stimulus of increased world income and employment, and of the return to dollar-sterling parity, was powerful enough--particularly by way of effecting a $116 million increase in merchandise exports which exactly matched the rise in imports--to achieve the first surplus on current account since 1926, and (despite the substantial capital outflow) the second-lowest deficit on current and long-term capital account ever recorded.[29] At no time during the year, moreover, did the discount in terms of the United States dollar and the pound exceed 1 per cent and 6 per cent, respectively, while the highest premium in the former case was 3 per cent, and in the latter, .4 per cent. This three-way, near-parity relationship prevailed, with little variation, until the outbreak of the Second World War.

An Evaluation of the Case for Exchange Depreciation

These, then, were the economic circumstances surrounding the Dominion Government's policy of non-intervention in the foreign exchange market during the Great Depression. It has already been suggested that this policy was rooted partly in the economic and financial realities of Canada's international position, and even more in the general psychological antipathy towards any radical departure from traditional practice. These two sources of motivation are, of course, inseparable one from the other, and it is to be questioned whether any balanced--not to mention "depreciation favourable"--judgment could possibly have been brought to bear upon the former, in the light of the tenacity with which the latter was held by the majority segment of Canadian public opinion. The following analysis of the depreciation problem is intended, nevertheless, as both a "hindsight" appraisal of the "realities" on their own merits and an indication of the maturing process which the writings of Canadian professional economists were undergoing during the late thirties.[30]

It should be realized, at the outset, that the fundamental question to be considered is not what "might have been" if the Canadian dollar had depreciated--for it did depreciate, in terms of the American dollar, under the influence of market forces--but, rather, what "might have been" if the Dominion Government had deliberately undertaken to increase the depreciation to the point where the Canadian dollar was no longer at a premium in terms of the pound sterling.[31] That is to say, through no intention of the Dominion Government, exchange rate fluctuations had, by late 1931, already produced a situation in which, vis-a-vis the United States, the commodity export potential was greater, and the commodity import and debt service potentials less, than before the exchange fluctuations; and the exact opposite situation with respect to Anglo-Canadian relations. Viewed in this light, a policy of deliberate depreciation of the Canadian dollar--to the extent that it had direct balance-of-payments effects--would have involved, not a clean break with what had gone before, but, in the case of the United States, a continuation of forces which already had been set in operation, and, in the case of Great Britain, a reversal of the trend which had begun with the British abandonment of the gold standard.

In its essentials, the case for depreciation rests upon the twofold contention that (1) it is an effective instrument for raising or supporting the incomes of exporting groups, by making higher domestic currency prices of exported goods and services compatible with unchanged foreign currency prices for those exports, and/or by achieving an increased volume of export sales through a combination of unchanged domestic currency prices and resultant lower foreign currency prices; and (2) it stimulates production and employment in the entire economy, not only by maintaining demand in the export sector, but also by curbing domestic expenditure on imported goods and services and diverting it towards domestically produced goods and services. In Keynesian terms, the argument may be summarized in this way:

> A depreciation of the exchange at once increases the... values received from exports in terms of local currencies, ... and diminishes the... people's propensity to import rather than to consume.... The increased value of foreign currencies tends directly to increase the incomes of exporters; and in addition, it will lower the marginal propensity to import and raise the marginal propensity to purchase home products, and thus raise the multiplier. If, by these changes, the total volume of local income is kept at a higher level than otherwise, the incentive to invest will be kept higher; and this will give further support to local incomes. [32]

With specific reference to the Canadian economy, the argument is that the depreciation of the dollar to the level of the pound would have partly offset the income losses sutained mainly by the producers of wheat and other food products, whose exports to the United Kingdom comprised over 80 per cent of total Dominion exports to that country and almost 20 per cent of Dominion exports to all countries; and that such depreciation would have fully counteracted, and possibly reversed, the decline in incomes suffered by Canadian producers engaged in selling goods to the United States, particularly the exporters of wood, wood products, and paper, and of non-ferrous metals, which accounted for approximately 60 per cent of Canadian exports to the United States and 24 per cent of Canadian exports to all countries. The stimulative effects produced in this manner would have been magnified by the continued reduction in imports from both the United Kingdom--with the importers of fibres and textiles standing as the most prominent single group to be affected--and the United States, which was supplying the widest possible variety of commodities ranging from automobiles to food products.

The favourable effects of depreciation would have been further strengthened through the operation of an additional factor not yet mentioned, namely, the increased liquidity of the Canadian commercial banking system. This would have resulted from the rise in the value in Canadian dollars of the foreign liquid assets held by the banks; and from the tendency of depreciation to encourage exports and retard imports, and so to permit the banking system to gain, instead of to lose, liquid assets. On both of these counts, the chartered banks would have been in a better position to support the level of local incomes; at any rate, they would have been relieved of the necessity, born of illiquidity, of actively promoting a deflation.

The basic assumptions. The case for depreciation can be seen to stand or fall chiefly on the argument that the effect of the changes in the prices of exported and imported commodities brought about by depreciation would be, primarily, to support the incomes and purchasing power of the exporting groups, and, secondarily, to stimulate the entire economy. This necessarily implies that higher export values and a higher marginal propensity to consume would be associated, respectively, with lower foreign currency and/or higher domestic currency prices for exports, and a lower marginal propensity to import; and that lower import values would also be the consequence of higher domestic currency prices for imports. And these effects, in turn, involve the following set of assumptions: (1) substantial domestic and foreign price elasticities of demand (with the latter being great enough to outweigh the depressing "income" effects on foreign demand for the depreciating country's goods), or inelastic domestic and foreign supply schedules[33] (in those circumstances in which domestic and foreign demand elasticities are less than unity); [34] (2) for the depreciating country, a negligible diversion, or no diversion at all, of the funds withdrawn from import consumption, into idle savings or bank balances, as opposed to expenditure on domestic goods and services; (3) the absence, or minor importance, of destabilizing expectations tending to cause further depreciation and to aggravate the conditions which the original policy of deliberate depreciation was designed to remedy; and (4) the small likelihood of retaliation by foreign countries.

None of these assumptions could be empirically validated without the greatest difficulty. A heavy burden of proof rests, therefore, upon those who would have advocated a policy of deliberate depreciation for Canada in the early thirties; therein lies the greatest source of strength in the case against such depreciation. The former position is far from completely hopeless, however, for several significant general observations can be made.

(1) Price elasticities of demand and supply. The increase in Canadian exporters' incomes postulated by the advocates of depreciation would have depended directly, for its occurrence, upon the particular market circumstances affecting each commodity. First, there was Canada's most important single export, wheat, which was usually regarded by the radicals as the major beneficiary of depreciation. The facts were by no means so conclusive, for Canadian wheat constituted an important part of world wheat exports, and this made foreign demand even more inelastic than it ordinarily must have been in the case of such a basic food product. The resultant downward pressure on world prices of wheat was intensified by the huge wheat carryovers that had been accumulated in Canada during the previous three years. On the other hand, the supply of Canadian wheat (like that of virtually all staple agricultural production) was characteristically inelastic. But most favourable of all to the case for depreciation was the fact that, throughout the period under consideration, the Canadian Co-operative Wheat Producers Ltd., with federal governmental

backing, was supporting the price of Canadian wheat in Winnipeg and Liver-
pool above normally competitive world prices. The probability is that the
restriction of the volume of wheat sales necessary to forestall any depressing effects on world prices would have been undertaken with greater thoroughness and efficiency by such a central selling agency than under conditions of atomistic wheat marketing. Summarizing all the imponderables,
the cautious conclusion seems warranted that "exchange depreciation alone
would not have automatically produced benefits for the wheat grower, but
that gains might have been secured had appropriate government wheat-
selling policies been combined with exchange depreciation."[35]

Second, there were the extremely important pulp and paper products,
most of which were marketed in the United States. In the buyers' market
created by high levels of production in the face of falling demand, it is unlikely that any price rises would have resulted from the depreciation policy.
Nevertheless, it is equally unlikely that any serious decline in Canadian
prices would have occurred since the reduced American-dollar prices of
Canadian pulp and paper would have greatly strengthened the competitive
position of Canadian exporters as against the numerous American and
overseas producers.[36]

Third, there was a large variety of important products for which direct
gains from depreciation, though no more amenable to precise measurement,
were an even likelier prospect than for the first two commodity classes.
They included: (1) meat and dairy products, whose world supply was far
from being predominantly Canadian; (2) base-metal products, the sale of
which had been consistently maintained in a strong independent position in
relation to the various world cartels; (3) manufactures, particularly the
products manufactured in Canadian branch plans of American concerns,
which would probably have been quick to take advantage of the stronger
competitive position in preferential Empire markets and in Latin America;
and (4) the wide range of highly price-elastic goods and services purchased
largely by American tourists, who, by diverting even a small percentage
of their normal traffic from Europe and/or the United States itself, would
have effected a substantial increase in Canadian export incomes.

The one Canadian group of exporters which had the greatest likelihood
of receiving the full direct benefit of any depreciation was the producers of
non-monetary gold. The world market was unlimited as long as any country remained on the full gold standard. "Since Canada possessed, in the
early years of the depression, important marginal resources capable of
rapid exploitation, the stimulus to the industry and the increase in the
gross money income of gold-producing regions would have been certain."[37]

On the Canadian import side, there were many commodities--plant
machinery and equipment, automobiles, whiskey, rolling-mill products,
coal, radios, refrigerators, jewelry, etc.--which possessed the main
properties contributing to high price elasticity of demand, namely,
(1) postponability of consumption, (2) substitutibility, and (3) minor importance as a portion of the total demanded by all countries. This situation
was most characteristic of American-supplied imports, with their heavy

concentration in capital goods, and in consumer goods of the luxury kind
or of the type to which alternative domestic sources of supply might be
found. That is to say, the highest price elasticities of demand would have
manifested themselves in the direction in which they were most needed,
for it was the outflow of goods and services to the United States, along
with the net inflow of long-term capital from that country, which underwent
the greatest decline during the depression, and which were the most important sources of dislocation in the Canadian balance of payments.

(2) Import and domestic spending. No easy answer can be given to the
question whether those expenditures no longer made on imports would have
been largely injected into the domestic payments stream in the form of increased spending on domestically produced goods and services. However,
the answer does depend, in large measure, upon the then existing state of
expectations of Canadians with regard to the future course of prices and
incomes. Thus, for example, if the downward movement of prices in late
1931 or early 1932 was expected to stop at once, or to continue with diminishing intensity and stop after a very short time, then greatly increased
domestic outlays on both consumption and investment would, in all probability, have followed the curtailment of import spending. The foregoing
analysis of the impact of the Great Depression on Canada suggests the wide
prevalence of such an optimistic business outlook. In so far, therefore,
as the state of expectations did determine consumer and business decisions
as between spending and saving, the answer to the question raised above
would seem to be in the affirmative.[38]

(3) Destabilizing expectations. Expectations must also be considered
in connection with the argument that any beneficial effects derived from
the deliberate depreciation of the Canadian dollar would have been nullified
by the two developments which would accompany such depreciation, namely,
violent capital flight, and speculative perversion of the normal tendency
for exports of goods and services to rise and imports to fall. The reply
to this criticism is that, while further deterioration in economic conditions--
and, indeed, in the foreign exchange value of the Canadian dollar--might
have occurred, such decline was by no means inevitable.

To be sure, the early inauguration of a vigorous internal policy of inflationary financing of public works projects, in the face of strong public
predilections for "sound finance," might well have had, serious destabilizing repercussions on the international position of the Canadian dollar.
But even in those circumstances, such a result might have been averted
or greatly mitigated by the net stimulative effect which might have emerged
from the support provided for the level of internal purchasing power.
Moreover, in the "thought milieu" prevailing at the time, no less within
government circles than others, there was only the remotest possibility
that deliberate depreciation would have been achieved in this way.

For this was not the only way. It would, for example, have been perfectly possible for the Dominion Government to depreciate the dollar to
the point--and maintain it there--where it stood at some given relationship to the already depreciated pound, by the Government publicly announc-

ing its intention to buy and sell sterling freely at the new fixed rate for an indefinite period of time. Such a policy would have insured both initial exchange depreciation and subsequent exchange stability. Naturally, the existence of a central bank in Canada would have added considerably to the effectiveness of the policy, in terms of over all co-ordination, and of supervision over the administration of the exchange equalization fund which would have been required. Even without a central bank, however, the policy could have been implemented with some measure of success. The opinion expressed by Professor Knox is of special interest in this connection: "It must be insisted, contrary to much current comment, that the absence of a central bank was no insuperable obstacle to the carrying-out of such a plan. Had there been a will to depreciate, a way would have been found."[39]

(4) Foreign retaliation. With respect to the possibility of retaliatory action being taken by foreign countries, at least three factors were operating in Canada's favour. One was its position of relative economic insignificance in the world--a fact underlined by the small amount of trade conducted between Canada and countries other than the United Kingdom and the United States, and by the far greater importance to Canada than to the latter two countries of the extensive trade carried on between the three.[40] A second favourable element in the Canadian situation was that the Dominion could justifiably have made it clear to other countries that its policy was one of depreciation of an overvalued currency so as to restore balance-of-payments equilibrium, rather than one of currency undervaluation designed to achieve a new equilibrium. It was, in other words, a defensive income-supporting policy, not an aggressive "beggar-my-neighbour" policy, and as such was less likely to evoke foreign retaliation. And thirdly, the success of a public declaration of this kind would have been more likely if accompanied--as it probably would have been--"by some degree of marketing control, where necessary, to prevent a demoralizing flood of export offers."[41]

It is, of course, quite true, on the unfavourable side, that governmental emphasis on the desire to minimize adverse international consequences would have been rendered less convincing by the tariff increases made, and by the failure to adopt vigorous measures for internal recovery; and that, in a world of desperate governments faced with mass unemployment and unchecked by any international regulatory agency, depreciation was likely to become almost universal (as it did in fact), and to cut deeply into the attempts of individual countries to gain the advantage for themselves. The latter probability, however, does not constitute a part of the argument against depreciation on grounds of retaliation, but rather an assertion that depreciation policies would have been pursued by foreign countries regardless of any action taken by the Dominion in the field of exchange rates. If this interpretation is valid, then the justification for a defensive policy of deliberate depreciation of the Canadian dollar was even stronger than it otherwise would have been. Moreover, the essence of the problem was time, for if enough time was allowed for internal recovery to take place, any counter-depreciation which did occur would probably have had relatively mild effects on the Canadian economy, especially if practised by countries in which sharp internal price rises were to be expected.

The "peripheral" arguments. In addition to the arguments rooted in the four assumptions enumerated above, three important sources of criticism still remain for consideration. All of these involve, primarily, questions of equity and efficiency, and all, therefore, are "peripheral" in the sense of having little direct bearing upon the income-employment-creating basis of the case for depreciation.

(1) Income transfer and decline. Both the internal "income transfer" and the external "real income" aspects of the first argument were clearly outlined by Mr. Towers of the Bank of Canada in his evidence given in 1939 before the House of Commons Standing Committee on Banking and Commerce:

> The general effect of depreciation is to transfer income between various groups within the depreciating country through a rise in prices which reduces the pressure of relatively fixed internal costs, such as wages and interest, at the expense of wage-earning and "rentier" classes. . . . Import prices, in most instances, would increase by the full amount of depreciation; in only a few cases is Canadian demand large enough to exercise an appreciable effect on import prices. Higher prices for industrial raw materials, coupled with additional protection afforded domestic producers by currency depreciation, would probably mean an advance in the prices of products fabricated from imported materials. Higher prices for imported finished goods would directly increase the Canadian cost of living. . . . [Canadians would also be paying] larger amounts for. . . debt charges and other foreign obligations.[42]

The case for depreciation does not collapse with acknowledgment of the validity of the income transfer argument. There was, after all, nothing sacred about the pre-1931 distribution of Canadian incomes. To no small extent, it reflected the crushing debt burden imposed by the 1929 price collapse upon the agricultural sector and other debtor groups within the Canadian economy. The real criteria for appraisal of the change which would have occurred were (1) whether or not the new distribution was a more equitable one, and (2) whether or not the net income-employment effect was an expansionary one. Notwithstanding the lack of concrete corroborative data, and even of universal agreement on the economic meaning of the "equity" criterion, the income transfer would probably have been justified on both counts--provided that the easing of the debt burden is assumed to be the over-riding consideration in the first case, and the net spending change in the second.

The "real income" version of the first argument is equally valid per se. Indeed, therein lay the strength of the support widely advanced, during the early thirties, for the maintenance of the median position of the Canadian dollar through a continued "hands-off" public policy. This position, in effect, did represent a rough compromise between the objectives of maximizing real income and sustaining employment and monetary income levels. The achievement of the former objective was retarded, and the latter advanced, by the premium on the American dollar; the opposite result was reflected in the discount on sterling. But the fall in Canadian real income was not the consequence of any depreciation: this decline was inherent in the lower volume of imports entailed by the drop in export values and foreign borrowing; and depreciation was actually an instrument for easing this burden on one group, the exporters, and spreading it throughout the Canadian economy by confronting most Canadians with increased costs of living and of doing business. Then, too, these cost increases could be regarded as undesirable only on the assumption that the pre-1931 level of costs was the optimum one, and that the rise in incomes reduced by depreciation would not have increased the capacity to discharge the higher living, business, and foreign debt costs. The contrary assumptions would appear to be much closer to the truth.

(2) Timing. The second peripheral argument is that a policy of deliberate depreciation raises the delicate question of timing, and that the policy would be ineffective not only in the obvious case of being applied too late, but also in the case of being applied too soon. Of course, this problem of timing cannot be uniquely associated with depreciation; it is common to all forms of stabilization policy. In so far as the problem does relate to depreciation, however, it must be recognized that deliberate Canadian dollar depreciation prior to Britain's going off the gold standard would probably have failed to achieve any sizable increase in the national money income or in employment, and might even have left them unchanged. For it was in the early part of the depression that the feeling was especially strong and widespread that "sound finance" policies were both adequate and necessary to bring about recovery. At that time, also, price expectations were probably quite unfavourable (that is, in all likelihood, further price declines were anticipated with consumer and business expenditures consequently being restrained); and the international balance on current and long-term capital account was not adverse enough to minimize foreign doubts as to the purely "defensive" nature of a Dominion policy of depreciation. These limiting factors might well have served to deprive the Canadian economy of most, if not all, of the direct benefits derived from the stabilization of exporters' incomes.[43] But this line of reasoning, even granting its validity, remains weak in the specific sense that the Dominion Government, if it had undertaken any depreciation, was not likely to have done so before allowing a "wait-and-see" period to elapse; moreover, the argument is irrelevant to the main point at issue, in the general sense that it is more of an argument for properly timed depreciation policy than against depreciation policy as such.

(3) Lack of precision. There is the contention, finally, that exchange depreciation is an over-all, non-selective, and indirect policy the precise "income-employment" effects of which are difficult to assess and impossible

to control. Admittedly, these limitations are inherent in such a policy, since it does involve, initially, a generalized change in the external and internal cost-price structures, and, subsequently, additional changes whose direction and extent depend upon the whole maze of complex inter-acting factors which have been discussed in the foregoing paragraphs. But this amounts to no more than an acknowledgment of the inadequacy of depreciation, with its attendant waste and uncertainty, as the sole in-strument for economic recovery from severe depression. It is, indeed, appropriate to concede that, under different international circumstances, other policies could have been devised instead, with a good chance of achieving the beneficial results of depreciation while avoiding its undesir-able consequences. Neither admission, however, stands as an indictment of a policy of deliberate depreciation: the former merely implies that other measures of economic stabilization were vitally necessary; while the latter is but the reflection of the unrealistic wish that all countries, including Canada, could have found ways and means to get along without any depreciation.

     Summary and conclusion. On balance, then, the case for deprecia-tion of the Canadian dollar remains intact, though on a less solid founda-tion than realized by most of those who agitated for it during the early thirties. To be sure, the appraisal made above is little more than a loose judgment built upon many generalities and few clearly demonstrated facts with specific and direct applicability to industries, groups, and in-dividuals. This is partly the result of its inherent speculative quality in terms of estimating "what might have been, " and partly the manifestation of the gaps in empirical data without which conclusive analysis is impos-sible. Against this limited background, the practical test must be the ability to show, through the most carefully reasoned economic analysis possible, the probable excess--in substantial proportions--of favourable over unfavourable factors relating to the attainment of given objectives. This test, it seems to the writer, would have been satisfied by the policy of deliberate Canadian depreciation in the early thirties.[44]

III. EXPANSIONARY MONETARY POLICY, 1935-9[45]

On March 11, 1935, the Bank of Canada formally commenced opera-tions. This was a landmark in Canadian monetary and banking develop-ment--no less notable for the concentration of all functions of monetary control in a single agency than for the climax of a controversy which had pervaded virtually every sphere of Canadian economic life. If the subse-quent policy importance of the Bank (prior to World War II) fell short of the expectations of its most enthusiastic proponents, it far exceeded the bounds of utility set for it by those who had endeavoured to exclude it from the institutional structure of the Canadian economy.

Central Bank Operations
Apart from the efficient performance of its routine functions (as

clearing house, fiscal agent, etc.), the Bank made several positive contributions to the maintenance of economic stability in Canada. Of these, the
most significant was its continuation and careful supervision of the easy
money policy which the Dominion Government, through the machinery of
the Finance Act, had inaugurated during the Great Depression. The 2-1/2
per cent rate on Finance Act advances remained unchanged, in the form of
the Bank's rediscount rate, throughout the second half of the decade. Open
market purchases of government securities by the Bank constituted the
chief instrument by means of which the general state of liquidity was
achieved.

   Between July 1935 and March 1938, total assets of the Bank of Canada
rose from $298. 2 million to $385. 4 million, an increase of $87. 2 million,
or 29 per cent.[46] Analysis of the composition of these assets shows, further, that the increase in reserves (foreign exchange and gold and silver
coin and bullion) amounted to only $12. 8 million, and that the correspond-
ing increase in securities holdings of the Bank was $77. 3 million.[47] Tak-
ing these securities, in turn, one finds that the increase in short-term
holdings of government securities ($103. 6 million) accounted almost com-
pletely for the expansion in security operations (with foreign securities
rising by $12. 3 million and other government securities actually declining
by $38. 5 million).[48] Additional indication of the scope of the easy money
policy is provided by the observation that, during the period March 1935
to December 1938, chartered bank deposits increased by $464 million, or
23 per cent; currency in circulation by $75 million, or 56 per cent; and
chartered bank reserves by $42 million, or 20 per cent.[49] There is, fin-
ally, the fact that the amount of monetary expansion in Canada was approximately in line with the increase in other countries where monetary policy
has been considered an important factor in economic recovery; comparing
1926 with 1938, the volume of Canadian bank deposits increased 23 per
cent, as against 6 per cent in the United States, 26 per cent in the United
Kingdom, 22 per cent in Australia, and 23 per cent in Sweden.[50] The
practical consequences of this policy were: (1) the promotion of economic
recovery within the limits imposed by monetary techniques; (2) the Canadian market's absorption of the bond issues of the Dominion and provincial
governments without a severe stiffening of interest rates; and (3) the
broadening of the Canadian bond market as a basis for subsequent credit
operations.[51]

   The fact remains, however, that, judged in terms of traditional conceptions of central banking, the functioning of the Canadian institution left
much to be desired. In the first place, the Bank developed a bill market
in which Treasury bills represented virtually the sole important credit
instrument; and with the Bank as their most important buyer, even these
bills could not be of great advantage to it as a means of credit control.[52]
Secondly, up to 1939 the Bank had never held any bills other than the
Treasury bills which it had purchased voluntarily, and had never done any
rediscounting for the chartered banks; [53] nor was it likely, in the nature
of things--a limited money market and abundant liquidity among the char-

tered banks--to carry out such rediscounting in the foreseeable future.
The Bank, in the third place, consistently refused to adopt a positive policy in the field of exchange rates unless so instructed by the Dominion
Government; [54] this passive attitude was in marked contrast with the approach taken by the central banks of other countries, and by those Canadians who had advanced the cause of central banking during the two previous
decades. Fourthly, despite numerous indirect overtures made by the
Bank to the provincial governments, no formal working relationships were
developed among them; in addition to its 1936 loan to Saskatchewan, the
Bank did, in 1937, comply with a provincial-Dominion request to investigate and arbitrate the financial difficulties involving the debt-ridden
Prairie Provinces and their chief creditor, the federal government, but
no province elected to use the Bank as its fiscal agent or as a depository
for its funds.[55]

Implications for Subsequent Monetary Control

But the deficiencies arising from the foregoing features of Canadian
monetary policy are not as damaging to the case for central banking in the
Dominion as they might at first sight appear to be. Three of the four features cited were not inherent in, or vital to, the execution of monetary
policy in Canada. Thus, it seemed probable to competent observers, as
early as 1939, that "holding treasury bills, and ultimately trading in them,
will gradually gain in popularity in the various Dominions...[especially]
in Canada, where there is already an active market in other short-term
government securities"; and, indeed, that "for that very reason the introduction of a treasury bill market is the less necessary for central banking
purposes."[56] As for the Bank's passive role in the field of exchange
rates:

> The tasks both of choosing and, under favourable circumstances,
> of implementing an exchange policy in Canada are difficult, and it
> is no wonder that the authorities [were] hesitant. The economy is
> one of considerable complexity and wide variety of economic inter-
> est. Positive policies and bold strokes of statemanship [were,]
> under [the then-existing] circumstances, likely to set up or aggra-
> vate centrifugal tendencies among the various groups, areas, and
> provinces that make up the country.[57]

The problems associated with exchange rate policy were, in any case,
greatly simplified by the relative strength and stability of the Canadian
dollar during the second half of the decade of the thirties.[58] It could,
moreover, be presumed (as warranted by economic events during and
since World War II) that the passiveness of the Bank in exchange rate
matters was partly the reflection of its lack of experience and would
therefore give way, in time, to more direct action. Again, the time aspect would seem to be paramount for the question of central bank co-
operation with the provinces. This was, after all, only one facet of the

larger problem of Dominion-provincial co-operation in a federal state.
The elimination of the former problem would follow, as a matter of course,
from the solution of the latter.[59]

The fourth defective aspect of Canadian monetary policy between 1935
and 1939--the impotence of the rediscount rate--did have an element of
permanence, however. Nor can it be denied that the successful application of the rediscount rate to the Canadian economy would enhance the efficacy of central bank control. It is clear, nevertheless, that this approach
proved to be unnecessary for the attainment of the easy money objective in
the late thirties; that the psychological impact of the rediscount rate on
the money market was likely to assume considerable importance; and
that, in long-run terms, the major technique of strong central bank control would probably be that of open market operations in a highly developed
government bond market.[60]

Far greater cause for concern derives from the striking fact that, at
the end of the interwar period, bank holdings of all securities, and of
Dominion and provincial government securities alone, amounted to 43 per
cent and 34 per cent, respectively, of total bank assets.[61] The federal
Government's easy money policy and the accompanying development of
the Canadian bond market underscore the successful application of open
market operations by the Bank of Canada. But it was a one-way (expansionary) success, creating the very conditions which might well be responsible for the future ineffectiveness of this instrument of monetary control.
Professor Plumptre's comments, made in 1939, on the nature of the dilemma are equally appropriate at the present time. It was, he argued,
quite possible, although paradoxical, that open market operations in Canada might never again be as effective--either in the expansionist or con-
tractionist direction--as in their first application:

> As for renewed expansion, it would be rash to foretell failure
> because of the extraordinarily co-operative way in which the
> Canadian bankers have responded in the past; but the fact that
> the horse has been led to the water and drunk one bucketful makes
> it less rather than more probable that he will drink another with
> equal obedience. The Canadian banks are already uncomfortably
> liquid; that is, if their security holdings can properly be consi-
> dered liquid assets. And from the point of view of political stra-
> tegy it is unwise for them to subsist chiefly on the interest from
> government bonds. As for contraction, there are conceivable
> circumstances in which the Bank of Canada could sell an appreci-
> able portion of its security holdings without raising too great a
> hue and cry; but the fact that so much Canadian government debt
> is now of relatively short term would mean that a hardening of
> interest rates would quickly be reflected in governmental costs.
> The political pressure to keep interest rates low has increased,
> is probably still increasing, and is unlikely to diminish.[62]

There can be no question of the inflation sensitivity of an economy whose monetary authorities give priority to the objective of stability of bond prices and whose commercial banks (as of December 1955) hold government securities amounting to about one-third of their total deposit liabilities.[63]

It remains, however, to emphasize the least tangible source of Bank influence--its advisory function in relation to both the chartered banks and the Dominion government. In terms of the highly concentrated banking structure and the monetary developments of the late thirties, "moral suasion" could even then have been viewed as one of the crucial instruments of monetary control--important in its own right, as well as being one of the major determinants of the efficacy of the positive techniques. It is also clear, with respect to central bank relations with the Dominion government, that by 1939 an expert economic agency had evolved as a top-level guide in the formulation of policy. Thus, careful evaluation of monetary policy must rest on inquiry not only into the problem of interest rate limitations, but also into the direction and intensity of chartered bank and governmental response to general advice tendered by the Bank of Canada.

PART IV

FISCAL CHANGE IN THE THIRTIES

CHAPTER X

FISCAL THINKING IN CANADA - OLD AND NEW

TO NO SMALL EXTENT, the development of Canadian fiscal thought during the thirties, particularly in the first half of the decade, constituted
but one aspect of the inflation and central bank controversies which have
already been analysed. The truth is that, whether Canadians were discussing monetary or fiscal problems, their orientation was almost invariably monetary, in terms of major concern with such factors as the monetary and banking structure, the supply of money, and price levels.
Thus, fiscal observations took on meaning, for the most part, in a monetary context; indeed, this is an important reason for both the immaturity of fiscal thought and the inadequacy of fiscal policy during the depression and recovery periods.

But out of these monetary roots a system of ideas pertaining to fiscal
problems was beginning to evolve. A similar pattern of development had,
after all, occurred in countries like the United States and Great Britain;
and it was to be expected, in view of their economic and social ties with
Canada, that a similar trend would be experienced in the Dominion.
Moreover, as in the American and British cases, Canadian fiscal change
can be most clearly traced through the attitudes and misconceptions of
monetary thinkers forced, by economic circumstances, to cope with issues beyond their traditional range of interest. The result was the attainment, by the end of the decade, of a degree of sophistication which made
easily apparent the separateness (despite their close relationship) of the
fiscal and monetary approaches to economic stability.

I. THE CONCEPTUAL APPROACH TO FISCAL POLICY, 1930-4

As in the monetary field, the regional-occupational cleavage in fiscal
thinking was not unique to the decade of the thirties. But from the Great
Depression this division, too, acquired a sharpness and a degree of arti-
culation which it had at no time previously possessed. And while the year
1934 does not provide as clear a line of demarcation as in the case of the
central bank controversy, yet in view of the changing fiscal outlook partly
fostered by the establishment of the Bank of Canada, it does not grossly
misrepresent the actual thought pattern.

Fiscal Orthodoxy in Government and Business
    Cabinet views. At the official level, the attitude of the Conservative
Administration towards fiscal operations was keynoted, and consistently
upheld, by Mr. E. N. Rhodes, Minister of Finance during the most intense years of the Great Depression.[1] According to Mr. Rhodes, the
Government would be recreant in its duty if it failed to face its problems

with determination, and, at whatever sacrifice, fully meet its financial
obligations, balance its budget, and preserve the "national credit" in the
eyes of an observant financial world. "This course may result in hardship.
It may entail sacrifice. But in the long run it will call for less sacrifice
than that which would flow from a policy less courageous. Furthermore,
the preservation of our national credit is an indispensable prerequisite to
the return of prosperity."[2]

The economic rationale for all of Mr. Rhodes's budget speeches was
the aim of maintaining high tax rates in the face of heavy and unavoidable
government expenditures, and so minimizing additions to the national
debt. Especially on the national debt issue he received the strongest support from his Cabinet colleagues. Prominent among the latter was the
Minister of Trade and Commerce, Mr. H. H. Stevens, who frequently
expressed his conviction that governments should cease living beyond
their means and going into debt.[3] All debt was deemed, ordinarily, to be
a burden upon the debtor, and it was only in unusual circumstances and
periods of rapidly rising prices that the debtor could afford to borrow at
high rates of interest and remain in a satisfactory financial position.
"For the nation or for the municipality, as for the private corporation
and the individual, debt is inherently objectionable and to be avoided.
And to be out of debt is the greatest possible advantage in a period like
the present."[4] Here was a typical case of erroneous identification of private with public debt; and of the failure to recognize the possibility of
government incurring additional debt while reducing the debt burden
through raising income and employment levels.

Opposition views. In terms of general party sentiment, there was
hardly any need for those government officials to justify their fiscal orthodoxy. Nor, for that matter, was there any such need--in the light of the
approach taken by the Liberal Opposition. Mr. Mackenzie King set forth
his party's views in 1930. It would attempt to remedy the unemployment
problem "by retrenchment of public expenditures, by reduction of principal and interest on the public debt, by a reduction in taxation, and by increasing revenues through the encouragement of trade."[5] In 1932 Mr.
W. D. Euler was "still old-fashioned enough to believe in the principles
of thrift and the policy of spending a little less than we earn or than we
receive, and that applies to governments as much as it does to individuals."[6]

Such fiscal opposition as the Liberals did provide took the form of
dissatisfaction with the allegedly excessive expenditures then being made
by the Government; and with the Conservative "blank cheque" spending
technique of not specifying the precise amount, duration, and manner of
allocation of funds requested from Parliament. Thus, according to Mr.
J. L. Ilsley:

> To those of us who sat in the last Parliament and listened to the
> budgets presented by the late Mr. Robb and by Mr. Dunning, bud-
> gets which year after year disclosed large surpluses, large de-

creases in the public debt, and large reductions in taxation, the
three budgets which have been presented by this Administration
since the elections of 1930 are nothing more or less than fiscal
nightmares.... It was bad enough [moreover] in the emergency
session of 1930 to ask for a vote of $20 million for works which
were not specified; it was worse in the session of 1931 to get
from this Parliament a blank cheque and legislation which set up
a dictatorship between sessions; but it is infinitely worse for the
government to have the temerity to come before this House and
seek to perpetuate that dictatorship while Parliament is in session.[7]

Mr. Mackenzie King was similarly outspoken in denouncing the fiscal policy carried out by the Bennett Government.[8] Every single canon that existed with respect to the control of Parliament over expenditure of public
money was, he contended, being violated by the Conservatives. They
were taking away from Parliament the power of appropriating public money;
they asked for blanket authority to legislate and spend; and in addition,
even when they did come to Parliament and did ask for money, they did
not put in an estimate and give to the House of Commons the reasons on
which their estimate was based. During the preceding four years (1930-3)
there had been heavy expenditures, looting of the federal Treasury by provincial and municipal agencies, autocratic administration, and financial
favouritism for corporations. At the end of its term of office, the Government had nothing to show for its efforts but "this vast expenditure and
waste."[9]

Business orthodoxy. Widespread support for fiscal orthodoxy was
provided, also, by the financial and industrial community. For the banking and business leaders, annual budget balancing, drastic curtailment of
government expenditure, and primary reliance on taxes as a source of
government revenue formed a necessary complement to the general antipathy towards monetary expansion and exchange depreciation. Thus, Mr.
S. H. Logan, General Manager of the Canadian Bank of Commerce, characteristically expressed the view that Canadians' ability to justify other
people's strong faith in them, as well as to meet maturing external obligations, depended largely upon the success which they achieved in balancing government revenues and expenditures; economy in government expenditures should be the watchword of public finance.[10] According to Sir
Thomas White, the maintenance of economic stability did not require a
fundamental change in the economic system, but "simply a new recognition of those old and homely truths which we all know so well, namely...
that old-fashioned thrift is a virtue, and that wanton extravagance is a
vice."[11] In the course of a review of economic events during the year
1932, Sir E. W. Beatty, Chairman of the Board and President of the
Canadian Pacific Railways, wrote:

Nothing that the troubles of the past year have brought into public
recognition is so outstanding as the need for curtailing public

expenditures and co-ordinating and reorganizing public activities
so that they may be placed upon a basis such as this country... can
well afford. Courageous effort has accomplished real progress
along this line, but much remains to be done before our national
affairs are on a sound economic basis.[12]

The Canadian Manufacturers' Association, while recording its appreciation of efforts made to reduce expenditures, repeatedly urged all government agencies to restrict still further their expenditures "as far as possible consistent with maintaining necessary efficiency"; and strongly requested that all members of the Association, their employees, and the
public refrain from asking for public expenditures, excepting those which
were immediately necessary.[13]

Such illustrations of individual and group expression could easily be
multiplied.[14] For the mass of Canadian public opinion--and especially
for those segments most influential in the formulation and execution of
government policy--the only appropriate fiscal policy was that which conformed to the tenets of orthodox public finance.

Business radicalism. There were, nevertheless, several noteworthy
instances of advanced fiscal thought in the industrial and financial spheres.
One of the earliest of these was provided by the Canadian Bank of Commerce, in its advocacy of a "public works reserve" to be accumulated in
prosperity and spent in depression.[15] While acknowledging administrative
and forecasting difficulties, the Bank stressed the importance of advance
planning and accurate timing in public works policy. If the money raised
by taxation and set aside in prosperity proved inadequate for depression
spending, additional funds could be raised by governmental short-term
borrowing; such debt would be retired out of the increased tax revenues
received during the following upswing of the cycle. The Bank estimated
the construction multiplier at 2, and regarded its own "purposeful plan"
as a far more satisfactory method of obtaining that stimulative effect
than the "haphazard system of public construction work" in operation in
1932.[16]

Mr. W. D. Black, Vice-President of the Otis-Fensom Elevator Company, set forth a more detailed plan for stabilizing the Canadian construction industry.[17] He argued that the most pressing national and international
need for the future was the planning and stabilization of economic affairs;
and that national depression was, in effect, durable-goods depression, and
this, in turn, was essentially construction depression. The solution of
Canada's unemployment problem was largely dependent, then, upon the
stabilization of the building industry. Thus, if the expenditures on public
works of all Canadian governments had been reduced to the minimum during the boom of the twenties, when private investment was rampant, total
construction would have exceeded the "mean economic line"[18] by only
about $80 million; and the contraction of public works undoubtedly would
have resulted in a contraction in other forms of construction expenditure.
Moreover, the consequence of such a withholding policy would have been

the accumulation of a public works reserve of approximately $500 million for use during the depressed thirties; in comparison with that reserve, the probable public works expenditure of $50 million in 1934 seemed feeble indeed. Mr. Black made two concrete proposals: (1) the establishment of a Federal Stabilization Board--representative of governmental, financial, building, and labour interests--with direct control of government building at all levels, and with authority to make tax concessions and grant subsidies to private builders, and to regulate production, working hours, financing, and unemployment insurance throughout the construction industry; and (2) the creation of a Federal Commission of Investigation--composed of an economist as chairman, and representatives of the building industry, the Canadian Manufacturers' Association, labour, and finance--"empowered to investigate the entire circumstances of the construction industry, to consider opinions and suggestions, and to bring in recommendations for its present improvement and future stabilization."[19]

The tariff issue. However, in the over-all picture, such expressions of business views are to be regarded as exceptions to the general rule of fiscal orthodoxy.[20] Only on the tariff issue was there, in fact, any sharp division in the thinking of the orthodox East. From the very beginning, the Administration was committed to the use of the tariff as a means of "blasting a way into the markets of the world."[21] The Prime Minister's justification of the upward revision of 1930 provided the basis for Conservative tariff policy throughout the first half of the decade:

> Our tariff measure is not a general revision of the tariff, but deals only with such items in the tariff as it is believed will ensure additional employment to a large number of men and women in Canada. . . . What we have done is to take those industries that we believe are, in a sense, the key industries of this country, where activity may be stimulated and employment ensured to the greatest possible extent. . . . We are going to endeavour to induce our fellow-Canadians, without increasing the prices they pay for the implements of production, to buy in Canada the products of Canadians, so that the purchasing power created by their effort will remain in this country to add to its wealth and make it what it should be.[22]

The conventional protectionist aspects of tariff policy were to be subordinated then, to the supreme effort aimed at raising domestic employment and incomes through drastic reduction of the import leakage in aggregate demand.

From the Liberals came strenuous and persistent opposition to the tariff policy enunciated by the Government. Mr. Mackenzie King clearly summarized the attitude of his party when he stated:

> In the long run, exports must be paid for by imports. That is something which is well understood. What ought to be equally obvious is that, world competition being what it is today, in the

interest of the home market itself it behooves us to see that in
every way possible the cost of production and the cost of living
which enter into the cost of the articles which are exported from
the country, are kept at as low a figure as possible. This [tariff]
legislation will increase the cost of production; it will also increase the cost of living, and it will tend vitally and materially to
restrict the trade of the country. It will tend to destroy the home
market. Instead of expansion we will have stagnation.[23]

Just as the Conservatives were bypassing the traditional protectionist
arguments, so too were the Liberals de-emphasizing the long-run case
for free trade in an attempt to demonstrate the adverse stability effects
of a high tariff policy.

But neither the two major political parties nor the divided business
and financial groups whose views they reflected thereby deviated from the
philosophy of fiscal orthodoxy. On the contrary, the special appeal which
high tariffs had for the Administration--apart from their compatibility
with the historical pattern of Conservative policy--lay in their use as an
instrument for alleviating mass unemployment without increasing government expenditure or the national debt. And the crux of the Liberal objections to high tariffs--apart from their violation of long-standing party
notions--was exclusive preoccupation with the upward distortion of the
cost-price structure which would presumably occur, and with the "unsound" fiscal measures which might therefore be implemented for remedial purposes. In their zeal for their chosen cause, the advocates of
high tariffs were ready to overlook the possibility of unfavourable repercussions of such factors as foreign retaliation and price-inelasticity of
domestic demand for external goods; while the proponents of low tariffs
were reluctant to consider the possibility of stimulative effects through
a net increase in domestic purchasing power.

Fiscal Radicalism in the West
The tariff controversy of the early thirties continued to produce the
anomaly of the Western radicals taking an even more "classical" stand
than that of the Liberals and other low-tariff groups. The radical position was argued in terms of the long-run balance of trade, the tendency
being to neglect or ignore the short-run employment aspects of tariff
policy.[24] Admittedly, the radicals were impressed with the war hazards
and the inherent (pressure group) expansiveness of protectionist policy;
and they were most anxious that no argument should detract from the
monetary remedies which formed the essence of their recovery programme.
But it is difficult, nevertheless, to explain their failure to give serious
consideration to short-run tariff effects without recourse to the hard political and social fact of their status as representatives of--and in many
cases co-workers with--the traditionally low-tariff farmers of the West.
There is no question, however, as to the fiscal radicalism of the
C. C. F. -Progressive group in the sphere of domestic policy. The con-

tention that theirs was a monetary radicalism, pure and simple, contains a considerable amount of truth. For the Western radicals, more than for any other "thought class, " the fundamental problems were those of creating credit, expanding the supply of money, and raising prices.[25] Influencing the level of aggregate demand without manipulating the money supply was a procedure which few of them understood or even contemplated; while planned use of the budgetary process had little importance for them beyond its capacity for facilitating the implementation of a policy of monetary expansion. But enough was being said about expenditure, taxation, and debt to give unprecedented impetus to the evolution of a separate body of fiscal doctrine.

Compensatory spending. The chief object of radical criticism was the policy of economy of expenditure and high tax rates in depressed times.[26] To Mr. Woodsworth, for example, it was clear that the Bennett budgets revealed the Government's complete failure to understand the grave economic problems which called for immediate solution.[27] Private corporations had some excuse for curtailing their expenditures and withholding credit; but the Government had adopted a policy of retrenchment at the very time when a government should increase its expenditures and so supplement the expenditures being made by private individuals and business firms.[28] Such public policy was in direct conflict with the principles then being formulated by the world's leading economists.[29] Thus, the Government's attempts to balance its budgets by cutting expenditures, as well as by raising tax rates, had reduced individual incomes and so had made it more difficult for the Canadian people to balance their own private budgets.

Mr. Spencer[30] and Mr. Irvine[31] were similarly perturbed over the Government's approach to budgetary problems. In the former's opinion, the federal budget statement would be incomplete until it presented a quantitative comparison of "the total annual production and the total annual consumption of goods in Canada."[32] On the output side of his crude but significant national income statement, total production would be supplemented by "total appreciation" and total imports; and, on the expenditure side, to total consumption there would be added "total depreciation" and total exports.[33] From such a statement the truth would emerge that, if the Government was trying to balance its budget at the cost of the people of the country by taxing them heavily and by reducing public expenditures when the Dominion needed more purchasing power instead of less, then it was not sound policy to balance the budget:

> The government should alter its policy with regard to public works and taxes.... It is a wrong process to tax heavily when times are bad; taxation should be heavy when times are good and people have the money to pay. On the other hand, public works should not be encouraged when times are good, when business is active, but should be carried out on a large scale when times are bad and business generally is frozen.[34]

Mr. Irvine, too, emphasized the compensatory aspects of governmental spending policy. During times of severe depression and great prosperity, he contended, most governments tended to spend less and more, respectively, than at other times. This was the natural reaction to general public feeling, but it was poor policy. The governments of Canada--federal, provincial, and municipal--together exerted a greater degree of control over capital expenditure than did any other sector of the Dominion economy. If all those governments would undertake to carry on advance planning, "and to engage in capital expenditure to the greatest extent in times of depression and to husband their resources in times of prosperity, that would have a regulating effect upon the boom and slump cycle."[35]

Public works. For the radicals, the concrete embodiment of increased spending was public works.[36] They repeatedly called attention to the enormous potentialities of public works in terms of housing, roads and bridges, parks, hospitals, public buildings, harbours and canals, reclamation of waste lands, and reforestation. The basis for this preference is not far to seek; it lay in their underconsumptionist misconceptions involving the aggravation of depression difficulties by any form of spending which increased the production of consumer goods and services.[37] Public works, they reasoned, would not have this effect, but would merely increase purchasing power and so bridge the gap between total production and total consumption.

New money. By way of further mitigating the downswing, the radicals almost unanimously advocated the financing of the public works through government issue of new currency. Both taxation and government borrowing from the public were regarded as inappropriate financing techniques-- the former because it could provide no net stimulus to the economy, and the latter because it would add materially to the burden of the national debt. Mr. Irvine's analysis of the tax-financing procedure adopted by the Government was representative of the radical approach.[38] The Consolidated Revenue Fund, from which the public works money was to be taken, was maintained, he pointed out, by general taxation. Consequently, there could not possibly be any increase in purchasing power, for every farmer who paid a portion of the taxation would be compelled to buy much less in goods than he would otherwise be able to purchase. All that was being accomplished, then, was that something was "being taken from the people who have already too little, and being given to assist people who now have nothing."[39] The public works and relief legislation would, therefore, not even be a palliative if financed out of tax revenues. Moreover, if the necessary funds were raised by means of government borrowing, "the people of Canada would be paying tribute perhaps for all time."[40] That being the case, the only sensible way for the Government to finance its depression expenditures was by the issue of money on the strength of the "national credit."[41] Subsequently, as economic conditions improved, this money could be withdrawn through taxation over a period of years.[42]

General evaluation. But despite the fallacious reasoning on which, in no small measure, the radicals' case for currency-financed public

works was based, it had considerable validity.[43] Not even the most confused theoretical analysis, or the greatest neglect of the international orientation and vulnerability of the Canadian economy, could alter the simple truth that, in a severely depressed industrialized country with a rapidly expanding capital structure, governmental injection of new investment
funds would exert a strong ameliorative influence which, at least in the
initial stages of recovery, might well outweigh considerations of price
and balance-of-payments instability. Moreover, the case for such injection derived added force from the fact--clearly recognized by the radicals
themselves--that its income-employment effects were likely to be not the
equivalent, but some multiple, of the original public spending.[44]

Nor, indeed, was it necessary that the income-generating expenditure
should be directed solely to the capital goods industries. Money spent in
the form of direct relief--however objectionable on non-economic grounds--
was likely to have similar multiplier effects, as was any stimulus to private consumption spending in the lower income groups. It is against this
background that the renewed radical agitation for a comprehensive system
of social insurance is here worth noting.[45] For although they continued
to be motivated primarily by long-run welfare objectives, the radicals
were not oblivious to the stabilizing potential of such a system. At any
rate by the early thirties social insurance, partly through their persistence, had virtually ceased to be a controversial issue in the federal field.[46]

Fiscal Views of the Economists

Up to the middle thirties, Canadian economists had not developed a
distinctive pattern of thought on the question of economic stabilization
through fiscal techniques. This was in marked contrast to the fundamental
contribution which they had made to the central bank controversy. Problems of fiscal theory were beginning, nevertheless, to engage their attention.

Mr. Plumptre. Mr. Plumptre, of the University of Toronto, was
again in the forefront of the discussion.[47] Writing towards the end of 1930,
he argued that the crux of the unemployment difficulty in Canada was excessive saving and inadequate spending on the part of the upper income
groups; and that the public authorities should endeavour to tap those savings (through borrowing) and spend them:

> By far the most effective method of alleviating unemployment would
> be to build things like roads and bridges and power stations which
> would employ men in all parts of the Dominion, and, by putting
> money into their empty pockets, would augment... purchasing pow-
> er.... This would be more certain, and more effective, at least
> at first, than trying to persuade private manufacturing interests
> to construct new plants, because they might begin to produce too
> much goods too soon, and thus force prices down again.... It
> would be better to allow ordinary manufacturing concerns to in-
> crease their operations gradually, as the new purchasing power
> made itself felt in an increased demand. [48]

By 1934, Mr. Plumptre had come to express a more guarded approval of public works policy.[49] This was the reflection of his growing conviction that, "in a raw-material exporting country, the chief source of variation in the national level of prosperity is likely to be the fluctuating incomes received by the producers of such materials"; and, therefore, that "the foreign exchange rate is and must be the monetary key to the level of prices and prosperity in a country such as Canada."[50] Unless the primary industries were reasonably prosperous, the outlook for secondary industries and for general economic buoyancy was unlikely to warrant any widespread or enduring programmes of private or semi-private construction. "Thus, in Canada especially, public works must be regarded more as a 'palliative' than as a 'priming of the pump' which is hoped to start the stream of purchasing power flowing in a normal manner."[51]

But it was important to Mr. Plumptre that his approach should not be construed as agreement with the contention that direct relief was preferable to public works in time of depression; or that public works would, in any case, serve to aggravate the distortion of the domestic price structure by further raising the prices of manufactures in relation to primary goods prices. In refutation of the latter argument, he emphasized that such distortion was of secondary causal importance in depression, as compared with reduced agricultural incomes and purchasing power; and that, owing to excess productive capacity and unemployed labour, the prices of manufactured products were not likely to be raised substantially by a public works programme. As for the relative merits of public works and direct relief, it was clear that the case for the former "would gain weight if it became necessary to revise the Canadian debt situation, and particularly if it appeared likely that, instead of undermining a large number of towns with unwanted sewers, a public works policy could be directed towards improving the housing conditions of the least fortunate Canadians."[52]

Professor Cassidy. Early in 1932, Professor H. M. Cassidy, of the University of Toronto, made a similarly cautious appraisal of public works as a stabilizing device.[53] Basing his judgment on the experience of Ontario during 1930 and 1931, he noted the following beneficial effects for that province: (1) the provision of employment for upwards of 50,000 men; (2) the maintenance of the morale of the unemployed, as contrasted with direct relief; (3) the creation of many useful public improvements; and (4) the provision of a stimulus for the entire economy through the secondary effects of heavy capital expenditures. On the "liabilities" side of the public works "balance sheet," however, he listed: (1) their failure to keep pace with the mounting tide of unemployment; (2) their provision of only one class of work, namely, pick-and-shovel labour; (3) the dubious value of a substantial portion of the work projects; (4) the wastefulness and inefficiency of relief methods of construction, as compared with ordinary commercial practice; (5) the 40 per cent non-wage component of every dollar of public works expenditure; (6) the inequities characteristically associated with municipal administration, such as the lack of uniform treatment for the unemployed, and the uneven distribution of the financial burden among the various authorities; and (7) the shrinkage in the borrowing and tax potential of the municipalities at the very time when the need for governmental action was at its height. "The weight of this argument, " Professor Cassidy concluded, "is definitely against relief works as they have been conducted in Ontario during the past two years. Certainly it may be said that Ontario has not found relief work a very successful remedy for unemployment. "[54]

But the fact remained that the works programme had displayed some degree of usefulness; that it had been "much better than nothing at all, or better than a bad alternative. "[55] Furthermore, many of the deficiencies pointed up by the Ontario experiment could be avoided in the future--particularly if the projects were planned well in advance, that is, during the years of prosperity. With such planning, they would cease to be relief works; they would become useful undertakings which were postponed until the period of depression, and which could be constructed as efficiently as works done in good years. That is to say, there were strong indications that:

> A public construction program of this sort would do a good deal to counteract the fluctuations of private business. Relief works of the kind we have had may have failed, in large measure, but that does not say that the idea of provision of work by the public authorities in time of crisis is false. It is fatal, I believe, for us to give up the idea of setting the unemployed to work and to relapse into acceptance of direct relief--our Canadian "dole".[56]

Mr. Parkinson. As already noted, Mr. J. F. Parkinson, of the University of Toronto, regarded investment control as the necessary supplement to monetary policy in the approach to economic stabilization.[57] Thus, the purpose of the National Investment Commission which he recommended was the substitution of a comprehensive system of national control for the inadequate and biased investment authority then being exercised by closely integrated industrial and financial groups. That "would extend to the processes of long-term investment a system of federal controls at least as far-reaching as those to be imposed by the establishment of a central bank. "[58] In specific terms, the Commission (1) would attempt to stabilize the rate of private capital investment, and "would supervise the undertaking of all programmes of governmental capital construction so as to provide a counterpoise of its own making to the fluctuating character of private investment";[59] (2) would co-operate with other government agencies in providing detailed statistical information relating to investment activity within Canada and between Canada and other countries; (3) would promote, directly and indirectly, public capital enterprises (such as slum clearance) which, while socially desirable, had been neglected or postponed largely for financial reasons; (4) could act in an advisory capacity to governments with respect to their borrowing and debt-retirement operations; (5) could exercise strict supervision and control

over the new foreign borrowing of public and private authorities;   (6) might
formulate, and assist in the execution of, plans for the rationalization of
the entire process of municipal and provincial borrowing;   (7) might con-
tribute towards the extension and co-ordination of the contemporary inadequate machinery for the financing of the intermediate and longer-term
needs of agriculture;   and (8) would assist in co-ordinating provincial
security-fraud prevention, while strengthening those national safeguards
already in force.[60]

Here, then, was one of the early far-seeing approaches to stabilization policy. Mr. Parkinson, very much in keeping with his advanced
business-cycle theory, had stepped clearly beyond the narrow monetary
confines of his time to formulate a concept of counter-cyclical fiscal--or.
more accurately, expenditure--policy which would make a vital contribution to Canadian economic stability.

Mr. MacGregor. For Mr. D. C. MacGregor, of the University of
Toronto,[61] the major fiscal problem centred around the fact that, "while
financial obligations of governments have increased due to long-term
trends beyond human control, the powers of government to control and
divert the flow of the national income have not increased proportionately."[62]
Concretely stated, the inflexible and primitive Canadian tax structures had
failed to keep pace with the increasing public expenditures stemming from
technical progress and the demand for higher living standards. The result
had been a steady accumulation of public debt and a substantial rise in the
governmental outlays required for servicing that debt. What Mr. Mac-
Gregor found particularly disturbing was the deflationary impact upon the
Canadian economy of heavy taxation designed to finance these servicing
operations; his assumption being that the rentier class was generally reluctant to invest its interest receipts in new business ventures. He recognized "the more or less inflationary influence of public borrowing whenever it puts in motion savings deposits which would not otherwise have been
invested through private enterprise."[63] But government borrowing per se
could not restore, or even maintain, the domestic price level in the face
of depressed export prices. There was "no good reason to believe that we
can either borrow our way or squander our way into prosperity by public
agency alone."[64]

The public debt problem, therefore, could not easily be dismissed.
Its solution could be achieved by government through either (1) the introduction of financial flexibility in terms of control over debt charges, salaries, and other categories of rigid public expenditures, or (2) the maintenance of national income stability; or through (3) some compromise
between those two extremes. While the procedure of financial adjustment--
necessitating, as it would, the disappearance of fixed-interest-bearing
securities--"would arouse stubborn opposition from the courts, from the
whole legal profession, and from many of the less intelligent financial
interests, it would probably be the simplest and least harmful form of
government intervention which could be devised in our present troubles."[65]
This choice reflected Mr. MacGregor's scepticism regarding the "stability"

alternative. The adoption of the latter course of action, he argued, would involve the subjection of the whole of Canadian economic life to "an unpredictable amount of regulation and experiment."[66] The technique of cyclical control was only partly understood at that time, and it was not even known whether stabilization was possible at all under private capitalism. As for those countries, such as Canada, which were largely dependent upon exports of primary products, it was "not likely that their incomes could ever be stabilized in a dynamic world."[67]

In conclusion, Mr. MacGregor described as follows the ultimate fiscal objective which the Dominion and all other debt-vulnerable countries should strive to attain:

> As rapidly as the present transfers from poor to rich, which result from the debt service, can be eliminated by reduction of interest payment and by heavier progressive taxation, just so rapidly should all further capital expenditures be paid for out of current revenue, and a policy of orderly collective saving and investment be adopted. If past tendencies and present indications are at all significant, the ratio of socially-controlled capital to total capital will continue to increase. It is essential that it be socially owned and not socially mortgaged, if the transition to a more fully collectivized economy is to be made by peaceful means.[68]

The special interest of the MacGregor analysis lies in this combined adherence to orthodox and radical concepts in the fiscal sphere--in the former case, its rejection of deficit financing, and of vigorous governmental stabilization policy; and in the latter case, its acknowledgment of a permanently high level of public expenditure, and its preference for drastic downward adjustment of fixed-interest obligations.

Other views. Attention should be drawn, finally, to the brief fiscal commentaries made, in the early thirties, by Professors C. A. Ashley and G. E. Jackson and Mr. F. W. Burton, all of the University of Toronto.[69] Professor Ashley was impressed by the fact that, "under our present system, government taxation and public works both tend to accentuate the booms and depressions of the business cycle."[70] This was equally true of federal, provincial, and municipal governments, and the total influence which they exerted was very strong. The cyclical difficulties were inherent in the year-to-year planning of Canadian budgets, but remedial action was feasible "if the fear of losing votes is not too strong to allow a long view to be taken."[71] Referring to the increasing burden of taxation in Canada during the Great Depression, Professor Jackson cautioned that "the most stringent measures of governmental economy are urgently needed, and all new financial adventures should be discouraged."[72] Mr. Burton was less optimistic about large-scale government expenditures than about exchange depreciation:

> Such expenditures will relieve unemployment temporarily, but

can only bring about a general recovery if the increase of profits
which results from inflation provokes a new flow of private investment sufficient to continue the stimulating effect of the expenditures after they have ceased.   There would be no reason to expect
such a flow of private investment in Canada, since, in our case,
investment, whether in primary or secondary industry, must wait
upon the prosperity of our primary industry--in other words, upon the state of our markets abroad.[73]

Mr. Burton was arguing, in effect, that the Dominion could, by itself, restore equilibrium through exchange depreciation, but that further expansion was dependent upon rising foreign demand for Canadian goods, rather
than upon any policy which the federal Government might carry out.

II.   THE CONSOLIDATION OF FISCAL THOUGHT, 1935-9

For the radicals and the economists, the second half of the decade
was largely a period of consolidation of ideas previously expounded--with
the former elaborating upon the fallacies of protectionist policy, balanced
budgets, and debt accumulation, and applying their government-spending
arguments to economic conditions which provided somewhat less justification for such policy than had been the case during the early thirties;
and the latter pursuing their eclectic line of thought, while drawing increasingly upon the Keynesian framework in support of their positions.
For other groups, in and out of government, it was a period of slow and
partial absorption of the new fiscal doctrines towards which the less conservative "thought classes" seemed to be groping.

Further Elaboration of the Radical Approach
      The C. C. F. views restated.   Recognition must again be accorded
the League for Social Reconstruction for its comprehensive exposition of
the C. C. F. approach,[74] in terms of: (1) governmental creation of a
National Investment Board charged with responsibility for channeling all
savings into desirable investment outlets, eliminating inequities in the
investment structure, stabilizing the level of aggregate expenditure, and
ultimately operating "the entire machinery of investment in co-operation
with the socialized banking system and the Planning Commission";[75]
(2) debt-free financing of emergency public works through credits provided
by this socialized banking system;   (3) drastic reduction in both the over-
all amount of, and the interest on, the public debt, by means of a "debt-
redemption levy"[76] supplemented by increased inheritance taxation and
skilfully conducted conversion operations;   (4) substantial economizing
in government expenditure through railway unification;   and (5) financing
of a national non-contributory system of social insurance through increased progressive income taxation at the source and minimum reliance
on consumption or sales taxes.[77]
      The Social Credit position.   On the Social Credit side, there was the

argument repeatedly advanced, for example, by Mr. Quelch,[78] that, under the orthodox Canadian financial system, neither of the two remedies for large-scale unemployment, namely, increased exports and government spending, was sound: that it was impossible for all countries simultaneously to increase exports, and undesirable for any country to subject itself to foreign destabilizing influences;   and that spending policy was "impracticable, ... because it means an increase in debt until eventually our fixed debt charges will exceed our total revenues. " The only sensible alternative was for government to issue money based on the national credit and designed to provide a national dividend as well as developmental projects--to the point of filling in the inherent "A plus B" gap between production and consumption.[79]

   And the "independent" radicals.   There was, finally, the interesting mixture of confusion and enlightenment best typified by the arguments of political independents like Mr. G. G. McGeer.[80] Noting the lessons of English experience during the twenties, Mr. McGeer emphasized the mid-decade shift from orthodox deflation to expansionary policy, as well as the general discovery that "the old idea of regulating the flow and withdrawal of bank credit by the bank rate and open market operations is utter non-sense."[81] England had been compelled to resort to a system of managed currency and public spending, among other techniques, in order to effect economic recovery.   That is to say, it had been necessary to abandon the classical orthodox concepts of stabilization, and to substitute the new approach then being advanced by Keynes.   Unless Canada proceeded along similar lines, it would continue to "slough along, picking up only the crumbs that fall from the tables of other countries where expansion and public works are going forward, and doing nothing to secure for our own people those great benefits which have come to the people of other nations through governmental action."[82] The "absurd and impossible situation of being taxed into a depression" had been created simply through Canada's adherence to the "thoroughly unsound proposition that sovereign governments have no access to public spending power other than by collecting taxes from, and making other levies on, the people, and by borrowing from accumulated savings.   That this proposition is thoroughly unsound, is no longer open to question."[83] The obvious route to increased aggregate demand, Mr. McGeer concluded, was large-scale government expenditure financed by either borrowing or direct creation of money;[84] and the fear of resultant inflation was wholly unjustified so long as widespread unemployment prevailed and the public spending added to the nation's productive capacity.

Continued Development of the Economists' Views

   The major stimulus to the clarification of fiscal thinking among Canadian economists came at the very end of the decade, under the inspiration of the chaotic economic and financial situation which had been precipitated by the Great Depression.   This stimulus received formal expression mainly through the economic studies prepared in 1939 for the Royal

Commission on Dominion-Provincial Relations.[85]

Before 1939. Numerous pre-1939 attempts at fiscal analysis could, of course, be cited. But these appear to have been both superficial and narrowly orthodox. Professor Michell, for example, admitted that as late as 1938 much remained to be done by way of alleviating the unemployment situation. To his way of thinking, however, the expense of stabilization measures was so great as to be almost prohibitive. More specifically, the inauguration of a large-scale public works programme was beyond the bounds of practical policy for the Dominion. Like everything else that was desirable, progress had to be paid for, and could be attained only "by the labour of our hands, and not by some magical cure-all which social reformers imagine will lift us out of the troubles that beset us."[86] Mr. C. Elliott was similarly impressed with the financial burden which would be imposed by public spending.[87] Canada already had a substantial overhead of fixed charges, and, in view of the great importance of the export industries, any government spending which increased that fixed burden would endanger Canada's competitive, as well as financial, position.

Among the few exceptions to this early generality of approach was Professor D. C. MacGregor's renewed treatment of Canada's public debt problem.[88] He demonstrated--by careful argumentation in terms of the depressing and monopolistic effects of taxation on business, the redistributive effects of interest payments on the public debt, and the need for a minimum level of welfare expenditure--that, in the circumstances of the middle thirties, orthodox budget balancing, while technically feasible, would prolong depression and unemployment, especially in the construction industries, and would sustain the standard of living of an already favoured group, namely, the rentiers. "It would be hard to find a combination of forces more harmful under present conditions, or more likely to render the economy vulnerable in the future."[89] But Professor MacGregor continued to associate the inadequacy of orthodox public finance with the problem of interest reduction rather than the urgency of effective fiscal stabilization policy. He was, in fact, quite explicit in his assumption that wide and unpredictable fluctuations in national income would persist as a characteristic feature of Canadian experience. On the basis of this reasoning, the only solution to the debt problem was the examination of the many devices for interest reduction ranging from simple conversion to repudiation; and the utilization, despite bitter rentier opposition, of the one deemed appropriate to Canada's debt position.

Later writings: Professors Bates and Plumptre. The orientation of the Royal Commission on Dominion-Provincial Relations was, as already noted, primarily long run, in that its basic concern was with the optimum division between taxing powers and expenditure functions in a federal state. But the Commission's staff studies--particularly those dealing with the measurement of national income, the financial and economic history of Canadian governments, and housing policy--clearly reflected the realization that the long-run problem of equitable and efficient financial operations was inseparably linked to the short-run problem of economic stabilization through federal and subsidiary fiscal machinery.

This realization was elaborated with the greatest care by Professor S. Bates of Dalhousie University.[90] Through his study of federal and provincial finance, he was able to point up both the lack of fiscal integration among those governments and the serious destabilizing role of their passive approach to fiscal problems throughout the interwar period. Admittedly, he argued, fiscal controls in most countries had by 1939 only entered the stage of "trial and inquiry". But even this primitive stage was impossible of attainment in Canada, for the Dominion was "the only remaining political federation attempting to operate a completely unco-ordinated fiscal system."[91] Moreover, since World War I, Canadian governments had passively accepted their financial position as it had been determined for them by the economic exigencies of the time. This outlook had especially severe repercussions during the Great Depression:

> On the expenditure side, the great curtailment of new capital works, the failure to maintain existing equipment, the reduction in current expenditures on health, education, public domain, and highways, and the increased charges for debt and relief, all reflected the passive role of government expenditures in face of the depression.
> On the taxation side, the increases in tax rates, almost regardless of the effects of this action on depressed private enterprise, and almost regardless of the equity or justice of the tax system as a whole, also reflected the negative attitude towards economic development.[92]

In combating depression, the vital function of public finance was "to direct government expenditures as a whole so as to stimulate investment, and to reallocate taxes in a way that will least deter private enterprise."[93] Intergovernmental fiscal relations formed a part of this wider issue, and the basic question was whether the constitutional distribution of powers and revenues among the different governments could be so arranged as "(1) to increase the efficiency of expenditures and taxation, ... and (2) to provide, when necessary, a national fiscal policy as an additional instrument of economic control, to be used together with banking, tariff and transport policy when severe disturbances are about to affect the Canadian economy."[94] The most important single sphere through which such fiscal action would be channeled was investment. "Public investment should be 'timed' so as not to conflict but rather to move inversely to the ups and downs of private investment."[95]

But Professor Bates's countercyclical fiscal approach can hardly be regarded as having been fully representative of the views of, or adequately understood by, Canadian economists. And the same general observation could justifiably be made with respect to the fiscal views set forth by Professor Plumptre in 1939, even though the latter was--as he had been previously--more skeptical regarding the efficacy of countercyclical public investment policy.[96] His skepticism derived from: (1) the complex dif-

ficulties of forecasting, which were not unique to private business;
(2) the erosive influence exerted by pressure groups struggling for self-
improvement in the political field;   (3) the likelihood of increased import
pressure on a country's balance of payments;   and (4) the failure, in an
open economy like Canada, of government outlays on capital goods to go
to the root of the depression, namely, the export industries.   "In some
measure, however, a better timing of public works is probably possible;
and if possible, it seems desirable."[97]

Because of its novelty in the contemporary Canadian economy, Professor Plumptre's thinking on long-run trends is no less significant.   What
he did was to raise the interesting question as to whether the "secular-
stagnation thesis" had any validity for Canada.   His judgment on this issue
tended towards the affirmative.   In any case, the fact was that government
expenditures, taxes, and debts would probably continue to grow;   and, in
terms of high-income, high-revenue possibilities, that was "a matter to
be contemplated without heart failure."[98]

Changing Fiscal Thought in Government and Business

The National Employment Commission.   To a great extent, the advances in governmental thinking during the 1935-9 period were the product
of ideas developed by Canadian economists and financial experts working
increasingly in a governmental or quasi-governmental capacity.   It is in
this light that the 1937 and 1938 Reports of the National Employment Commission should be viewed.[99]   On the basis of its causal analysis of the
Great Depression, the Commission made two series of recommendations,
namely, the short-run group designed to improve the immediate situation,
and the long-run group intended as a comprehensive attack on economic
instability.   The former comprised the following measures: (1) a broad
housing policy of financial assistance embracing the Home Improvement
Plan and the stimulation of low-rental housing;   (2) thorough modernization and extension of the Employment Services under unified Dominion
administration;   (3) revision of the haphazard and wasteful system of federal grants-in-aid;   (4) an extensive Dominion-provincial programme of
rehabilitation and training aimed at increasing the general employability
of all workers;   (5) curtailment of public works outlays at that late stage
of recovery;   and (6) a farm placement plan for relieving the winter problem of concentrations of single homeless adults in urban areas.[100]   For
the long run, the Commission also envisaged a wide variety of techniques:
(1) governmental curbing of expenditures and debts in buoyant periods of
rising revenues;   (2) financial and administrative preparation for unemployment relief (through contributory unemployment insurance and supplementary aid) during the initial period of readjustment to depression;
(3) provision for expansion of public expenditures at the end of this period;
(4) further reorganization and modernization of Employment Services;
(5) planned use of projects for maintaining and increasing workers' employability;   and (6) co-ordination of this entire programme with the monetary policy implemented by the government and the Bank of Canada.[101]

The Commission's comments on budgetary policy are of particular importance. Singling out for criticism the fiscal policy of Canadian governments after 1930, it argued that:

> Dangerous debt increases cannot be avoided during a depression unless adequate financial preparation has been made by all governments during the periods of rising revenues. Such financial preparation cannot be considered adequate unless it includes such control of expenditures as will make possible substantial debt reduction in periods of prosperity, and the expansion of expenditures, combined with unimpaired credit and tax reductions rather than increases, during depressions.[102]

There was, then, "sound economic ground for urging a policy under which public expenditures might be expanded and contracted to offset fluctuations in private expenditures";[103] that is, a policy under which the fluctuations in public expenditures might make total expenditures (public and private) more stable. Such a programme, however, would probably be dangerous and ineffective unless the most careful advance planning and timing were provided--the former to ensure debt control, maximum absorption of unemployed, minimum interference with the private sector, and a high degree of flexibility; and the latter to ensure launching of the programme "not at the onset of a crisis, but after necessary adjustments have been made, and before a secondary depression, based on fear, the prospect of further declines in prices and investment, and general panic, develops."[104] In the selection of projects, it was essential that consideration also be given to their "value in promoting the competitive strength of Canadian industry, and in improving the conditions of life in the Dominion."[105] This criterion would be satisfied by such undertakings as highway building, slum clearance and low-rental housing, public health and safety projects, the development and maintenance of tourist regions, reclamation and conservation projects, and land clearance and settlement projects. Measures should, moreover, be taken by way of stimulating private expenditures (for example, through housing policy), and encouraging large corporations to follow the timing of the government programme in so far as this was consistent with efficient operation. For provision, finally, of the employment data and analysis governing expenditure decisions, the Commission proposed the creation of an "inter-departmental committee of officials... so constituted as to ensure the most careful consideration by the government of its findings."[106]

Mr. Towers. The fiscal views expressed in the late thirties by Mr. Towers of the Bank of Canada possess similar analytical clarity.[107] It was idle, he pointed out, to suggest that government budgets should be balanced during a depression. "Theoretically, such a result might be achieved by a heavy increase in taxation. In fact, the imposition of additional taxation of this order would probably defeat its own object by intensifying the depression."[108] The truth was that substantial increases in debt were inevitable during depressed years, and it followed that debt reduction in prosperous periods was essential. The test which Canadian governments faced was their ability not only to balance budgets but to achieve surpluses in good years for the purpose of reduction of debt incurred in bad years.

But Mr. Towers called into question the advisability of vigorous pursuit of countercyclical fiscal policy. He was dubious as to not only the long-run "secular-stagnation" case for deficit spending, but also the short-run "stability" case for such policy. His comments in the latter connection are especially instructive. The basis of his criticism rested in what he considered the relatively minor applicability of the fiscal approach to a country vulnerable to violent fluctuations in foreign demand for its goods and services. Deficit spending in Canada could have "little direct influence upon the course of foreign demand for our products."[109] Moreover, because of the specialized nature of Canadian production, it was "unusually difficult to meet a decline in foreign demand by creating domestic demand for new things which [Canada] can produce at a reasonable cost."[110] And the concomitant labour and capital shifts--even if practicable--might be clearly wasteful if the decline in export demand proved to be of short duration. There was the further external consideration that, if government expenditure necessitated--as it would--increased imports without producing correspondingly larger exports, the currency would eventually depreciate, and prices would rise regardless of internal excess capacity; and, finally, the possibility of increased price-cost rigidity and of adverse effects upon private confidence and spending.

The onus, Mr. Towers argued, was, therefore, "on the advocates of any government expenditure, in the ordinary as well as in the special or capital categories, to demonstrate that it definitely will add to the strength and balance of our economy."[111] And there was even less ground for optimism with respect to the use of the tax instrument for purposes of economic stabilization: "reducing taxes to promote recovery is not a plan which is likely to be widely effective in raising private spending, and at the same time has disadvantages from the viewpoint of flexibility."[112]

Cabinet views: Mr. Dunning. But the process of thought clarification on fiscal problems was not unique to the "expert" sphere. The new ideas were gradually beginning to penetrate the cabinet level of government. To be sure, the principles of "sound finance"--with special emphasis on balanced budgets and the adverse effects of government spending on private investment--remained very much in vogue during the second half of the decade of the thirties; and this was no less true of the incoming Liberal Administration than of the outgoing Conservatives.[113] The growing appreciation of stability problems in general and investment activity in particular was, nevertheless, accompanied by increasing recognition of the broad scope for fiscal action.

This recognition is best exemplified by the policy declarations made by Mr. C. A. Dunning, the Liberal Minister of Finance during the late thirties.[114] With respect to the 1937-8 recession, he notes the Government's intention to budget for a moderate deficit so as not to impose additional burdens on the economy; indeed, the object of the tax changes then being proposed was, "in the first place, to eliminate certain anomalies and inequities, and, in the second place, to make certain important adjustments designed to accelerate the forces making for business recovery."[115] In his 1939 budget speech, Mr. Dunning added:

> If business will not spend, government must.... We dare not, we cannot contract our expenditures until our industries and our people generally are spending more freely.... In the world of today, governments must act to relieve distress and prevent cumulative deflation, and, speaking generally, the magnitude of governmental expenditures in democratic countries is likely to be a rough measure of the failure of private enterprise to do its full duty.[116]

The new business approach. Evidence of absorption of the new fiscal doctrine manifested itself even in the industrial and financial sectors of the Canadian economy, where orthodox thought continued to be expressed with the greatest vigour.[117] Nor was it merely a case of a few individual businessmen, like Mr. W. D. Black, contending that governments should refrain from making expenditures on public works in good times and should set aside the funds saved for useful public works during periods of depression.[118] Both the Canadian Chamber of Commerce and the Canadian Manufacturers' Association were undergoing significant changes in fiscal outlook.[119]

The Chamber of Commerce remained convinced of the crucial need for balanced governmental budgets; but it did recognize the difficulty of achieving this balance annually, and the consequent appropriateness of budget balancing "averaged over a period of good and bad years."[120] The Manufacturers' Association argued, in greater detail, that, during the period 1919-35, Canadian governments had simply followed the prevailing economic trend, increasing their expenditures on public undertakings as general business expanded, and reducing them as business contracted.[121] Such isolated and hasty attempts as had been made to stem the downswing through emergency relief works had been so inadequate in volume, as compared to the public outlays of prosperous years, that their stabilizing influence was barely perceptible; furthermore, no attempt had been made, during the period in question, to withhold public projects in anticipation of the succeeding unemployment crisis:

> Had public works expenditures been retarded even to the level of $80 million (not to say the irreducible minimum of $40 million) during the five years 1926 to 1930 inclusive, coincident with a policy of debt reduction in anticipation of future borrowing needs, there would have been available, for the immediately succeeding years of intense depression, a reserve volume of works and credit to the extent of some $320 million. The value of an economic stimulant of these proportions during the more critical years of the recent depression would have been incalculable.[122]

Thus, public works projects had actually been carried out "in a manner which could hardly be better calculated to precipitate and intensify the problems of depression by inflating the preceding boom." What was required was "a preconceived, long-term, and consciously planned system of public works control, designed to continuously adjust the volume of public works inversely to the fluctuations of private activity." A large proportion of the resultant depression spending would necessarily be financed by borrowing, which would, in turn, be preceded by a "compensatory and preparatory" programme consisting of curtailment of borrowing and reduction of debt during prosperity. Timing was the essence of such a "regulatory or stabilizing public works policy," for "it is by the timely and adequate adjustment of the volume of public works that their potential influence can be most effectively and beneficially exercised." And one of the most important features of such premeditated planning and control of public works was that its beneficial influence would, by the very nature of these projects, "be exercised upon that department of the national economy which most requires and can best disseminate the resulting stimulation, that is, upon the capital--or durable--goods (and particularly construction) industries." The entire programme, concluded the Association, presupposed the existence of "a permanent, specialized, and technically and financially competent agency for its proper execution."

Concluding Summary

Here, then, was the meaningful demonstration of the broadened scope and re-oriented approach which Canadian fiscal thinking had achieved by the end of the thirties. On the basis of the foregoing analysis, the conclusion is unavoidable that, throughout the decade, the main currents of thought retained their rudimentary qualities; and that the time lag between the economic fact of depression and such change in fiscal outlook as did occur was so great as to deprive that change of any immediate practical significance. It seems reasonably clear, nevertheless, that two reciprocal factors--economic circumstances and radical thinking among politicians and economists--had meanwhile propelled Canadian fiscal thought beyond its monetary confines; and had produced a system of ideas which would improve the policy treatment of, and in turn be strengthened by, ensuing stability problems.

CHAPTER XI

CANADIAN FISCAL POLICY
IN DEPRESSION AND RECOVERY

AS IN THE MONETARY FIELD, the Dominion Government waged its anti-depression struggle on two fiscal fronts--externally and internally. The external approach, through the tariff structure, represented the only positive and comprehensive attempt made to raise Canadian employment and income levels during the early thirties.[1] At best, it served as an instrument for blunting the deflationary impact which would have been produced by the depression losses of those industries dependent upon domestic markets; and, at worst, as a means merely of redistributing a shrinking national income by intensifying the regional incidence of the depression. As for the internal approach, it involved--at least in the vital early stages--the piecemeal emergency implementation of tax and spending policies which could scarcely have had more restrictive effects if they had been consciously used by the Government for the purpose of achieving such results. Both approaches were, in turn, largely the consequence of oversimplified and fallacious reasoning in regard to the operation of fiscal techniques.

I. PROTECTIONIST POLICY IN THE GREAT DEPRESSION[2]

The protection afforded Canada's manufacturing industries between 1930 and 1933 embodied the most important upward tariff revisions since the National Policy of 1879-87.[3] Despite the sustained vigour of the tariff controversy and the great number and variety of specific tariff changes, there had been no significant general increase in the tariff for upwards of forty years. As a matter of fact, "such net change as there had been, was probably downward. It improved, rather than worsened, the position in which the export industries and regions had grown up."[4] The tariff legislation enacted by the Bennett Administration marked the first complete reversal of this trend--and with it the first substantial reallocation of Canadian productive resources in terms of foreign and domestic markets.

Scope of the Tariff Changes
There were three routes through which tariff changes could have been effected: (1) simple rate revisions; (2) changes in administrative procedure; and (3) changes in the weight of specific and compound duties resulting from fluctuating prices. The first two types of change were subject to government control; the third merely reflected the operation of market forces throughout the world price structure.[5] In any case, all three change routes were followed during the early thirties. "Tariff rates were greatly increased, the number of specific duties was increased, sharply falling

221

prices increased their weight, and administrative changes were in the direction of increases in the effectiveness of protection."[6]

The most direct upward revisions were those made in tariff rates. The budget proposals of September 1930 and June 1931, together with the crucial Ottawa Agreements of 1932, provided the machinery through which the major alterations were worked out.[7] In the budgetary framework, the rate changes were confined largely to the "general" and "intermediate" schedules; while the Ottawa Agreements operated more through the denial of entrance to foreign products than through the reduction of intra-Empire tariffs. The net result was that, by the end of the year 1932, substantially higher duties had been granted to every important secondary industry in Canada. Thus, during the first three years of the decade, general and intermediate rates--applying to over 80 per cent of total Canadian imports--were raised, on the average, by nearly 50 per cent. The average of preferential rates on textiles rose by about 25 per cent, and there was a two-thirds increase in the general and intermediate schedules. Rates on wool and artificial silk were approximately doubled. A 50 per cent increase was made in the duties on furniture, boots and shoes, and petroleum products, and virtually every branch of the iron and steel industry received added protection from increases of about one-third in the general and intermediate rates.[8]

This raising of tariffs proceeded in conjunction with greatly intensified administrative restrictions. So thoroughly was the latter course of action pursued during the early thirties that consideration of the customs duties power exclusively in terms of its legislative aspects becomes meaningless for that period. "Tariff-making by 'administration' was, perhaps, carried further in Canada at this time than in any other country."[9] The Minister of National Revenue was empowered to make--and did so extensively--artificial valuations on a wide variety of commodities entering the Dominion; also to fix arbitrarily, for tariff purposes, the exchange rate of any foreign currency which had depreciated. Thus, "after September 1930, through the exercise of new powers related to valuation--by levying special dumping duties and by making administrative rulings on commodity classifications--new and subtle impediments were placed in the path of imports to Canada without recourse to legislative approval."[10]

As regards the burden of specific duties, this was no less real than the other two forms of increased protection. To be sure, as late as March 1931, specific duties applied to only about 30 per cent of all Canadian imports subject to tariff regulation.[11] But in subsequent months, substantial new duties were added--both independently and in combination with the prevailing or augmented ad valorem rates. Viewed in relation to the sharp and prolonged decline in world prices, these changes necessarily strengthened the protective position of the Dominion's secondary industries while aggravating the adjustment difficulties thrust upon the consumer and export industries.

In summary, the decade of the thirties had begun on a note of tariff retaliation against American exclusionist policies and attempted achievement of wider British preferences. The moderate approach adopted by the outgoing Liberal Administration gave way, however, to Conservative schedules of duties designed to limit Canadian imports to non-competitive commodities. The policy emphasis shifted from the use of the tariff as a bargaining device (to gain concessions for Canada's exports abroad) to its use as an instrument for stimulating income and employment levels in the depressed Canadian economy. "The principle of selective protection, sponsored by both parties since 1879, was, in 1930-31, to a substantial degree superseded by all-out protection to all industries capable of producing in the Dominion."[12]

An Appraisal of the Protectionist Policy

There are insuperable obstacles confronting the precise evaluation of the stimulative importance of any single factor in a setting of the most complex economic circumstances. It is quite impossible to separate such an influence from the multiplicity of other forces operating in the same setting. Against the background of contemporary thought, however, certain useful factual observations can be made, and from them significant general inferences can be drawn with respect to the protectionist approach to economic stability.

The empirical basis. Perhaps the most striking change effected by the new tariff policy was the great diversion of Canadian purchases from imports to domestic production. Between 1928 and 1933, the value ratio of manufactured imports to total Canadian manufacturing production declined from 25 per cent to 13 per cent.[13] The reduction "was particularly pronounced in the case of textiles, automobiles, electrical apparatus, gasoline, furniture, implements, and machinery--all of which are important items either in the cost of living or the cost of production of primary producers."[14] Concrete evidence of the magnitude of this domestic-foreign reallocation appeared in the form of the materially smaller employment and income shrinkage in the protected manufacturing industries than in other branches of production; and, regionally, in the form of the concentration of this relative improvement in the central provinces and in the coal and steel industries of Nova Scotia.

But in terms of the Canadian economy as a whole, there is only the hard fact that the income-employment drop which set in late in 1929 was among the most severe downswings in the world. It can, of course, be contended that, in the absence of the protectionist policy, the deflationary shock would have been even stronger. There is, however, no empirical basis for such reasoning--either in the downswing itself or in the recovery which began in 1933. That recovery was so closely associated with rising world (particularly American) incomes as to preclude the assignment of any vital causal role to the "tariff revolution." It is doubtful whether the course of depression and recovery in Canada was substantially different than it would have been in a freer trading economy.[15] The sole clearly warranted conclusion is that "the increased restrictions to imports added considerably to the wide disparities in the incidence of the depression on the various industries and regions"; [16] and that consequently there occurred important shifts in the distribution of Canadian national income. [17]

Analytical evaluation. Theoretical analysis lends support to the narrowness of this appraisal. The basic argument involves the comparative weighing of gains and losses in terms, respectively, of reduced import leakage from aggregate domestic purchasing power, and higher rigid prices for home products. That is to say, in so far as home products could be obtained only at higher prices than those charged for imports, Canadian buyers--unless their incomes had been increased--had no alternative but to curtail their purchases of goods and services in general. Even if the result was increased aggregate monetary expenditure, the initial net income-employment stimulus would have been less than the import leakage by the amount of funds transferred from import consumption into idle balances. In the extreme case of unchanged or reduced aggregate monetary expenditure, the stimulus could have been achieved only on the assumption of improved expectations in the protected industries, or of the greater share of total sales proceeds accruing to those industries and regions with the higher inducement to invest. In the light of these imponderables, it is at least "questionable whether, on balance, the gain in employment from concentrating almost the whole demand on the domestic producers was greater than the loss through the restriction of employment by the maintenance of high prices." [18]

The remaining aspects of the theoretical "stabilization" argument can, perhaps, be best emphasized by a comparison of tariff policy with exchange depreciation. Obviously, the two approaches have much in common. Both involve taking advantage of the "openness" of an economy in order to raise depressed levels of domestic income and employment. Both are designed to change the structure of prices--tariff policy through duty-raised import prices, and exchange depreciation through reduced foreign currency prices for home-produced exports. Both have secondary price effects--the former largely in terms of higher domestic prices for protected goods, and the latter in terms of higher domestic prices for home-produced goods in general. Both approaches are consequently concerned with the degree to which the reduced import leakage in demand is reflected in increased domestic purchasing power; with the possibility of foreign retaliation; with the problems posed by the need for accurate timing; and with the real-income losses sustained from distorted price patterns.

There are three important differences to be noted, however. First, there is the fact that tariff policy operates through the budgetary process; this implies, among other things, the possibility of achieving greater selectiveness and precision than in the case of exchange depreciation, together with the absence of foreign debt complications and the probable absence of the destabilizing expectations frequently precipitated by monetary manipulation. There is, in the second place, the quality of permanence associated only with tariff policy; the implications of this difference are the greater vulnerability to foreign retaliation, and the long-run reallocation of productive resources. But the third point of distinction is, for

stabilization purposes, the most important. It relates to the failure of
tariff policy, in itself, to effect the increase in exporters' incomes which--
assuming substantially price-elastic (and low income-elastic) foreign de-
mand--is the essence of exchange depreciation.[19] Thus, in the "depreciation" case, the derivation of a net gain in employment does not require
the analyst to postulate, on the one hand, minor diversion of import funds
into idle balances; or, on the other hand, either an industry differential
in investment expectations or a shift in the consumption pattern for home-
produced commodities. The increase in aggregate money expenditure
produced through the exporting groups provides the initial stimulus; the
ultimate magnitude of the export multiplier will be governed by the market response to the higher domestic prices, and by the force of, and direction of influence exerted by, the other factors which have here been cited.

Restating the argument it seems reasonable to conclude that, in the
economic circumstances of the early thirties, the Dominion Government
implemented the external policy which had the lesser prospect of success.
The deliberate depreciation of the Canadian dollar in terms of foreign
currencies probably would have combined an export stimulus with other
results which, all things considered, would not have been adverse enough
to offset it. In contrast, the tariff policy actually carried out was, despite
certain advantages over depreciation, probably inappropriate to the task
of providing a net stimulus powerful enough to make the policy worthwhile.[20]

II. INTERNAL FISCAL POLICY IN DEPRESSION AND RECOVERY[21]

The Dominion Government's internal fiscal approach to economic
stabilization divides itself logically into two periods, corresponding to
the depression and recovery phases of the 1929 collapse. The policy pattern for the 1930-3 period will be found to comprise, in the main, the
perverse application of budgetary techniques; while the remainder of the
decade witnessed the belated introduction of stimulative measures for
which the need became progressively less urgent as the Canadian economy
continued to experience the effects of improving world conditions.

Fiscal Retrenchment, 1930-3

The fiscal policies implemented by the Government during the early
depression years have been appropriately termed "the most extreme variety of cost-cutting, tax-raising, budget-balancing orthodoxy.'[22]

Tax policy. The truth of this observation can be most readily demonstrated by an examination of the tax changes which occurred in the federal
sphere. In absolute terms, there was a $142 million decline in total tax
revenues between 1929 and 1933, that is, from $396 million in 1929 to
$254 million in 1933.[23] But this decline was not the result of reduced
tax rates; on the contrary, it occurred despite substantial rate increases
and in response to the unprecedented drop in national income. In the latter connection, the ratio of total taxation to gross national product rose,

during the same period, from about 6. 4 to 7. 2 per cent.[24]

The nature of the Government's tax policy stands out more clearly in regard to rate changes.[25] Relatively minor downward revisions were made in 1930. The general rate of the sales tax was reduced from 2 to 1 per cent; while income tax exemptions were granted co-operative organizations, charitable donations, and government annuities; and the then prevailing $500 exemption for children was extended to cover certain physically or mentally handicapped dependent relatives. The only significant change effected in 1931 was the increase in the sales tax rate to 4 per cent. It was the years 1932 and 1933 which brought the marked rate increases. In 1932 the sales tax was increased from 4 to 6 per cent; a variety of special excise duties was imposed, and numerous increases were made in the old rates. The corporate income tax was raised from 8 to 11 per cent. In the case of personal incomes: (1) a surtax of 5 per cent was levied on net incomes of over $5, 000; (2) the exemptions were reduced from $3, 000 to $2, 400 for married persons, and from $1, 500 to $1, 200 for single persons; and (3) the 20 per cent deduction formerly allowed from the tax payable under the established rate schedule was repealed. All the 1932 income tax changes were made retroactive to 1931 incomes. In 1933, the Government increased the corporate income tax to 12 per cent and removed the $2, 000 exemption. For personal incomes: (1) a higher rate schedule was applied to the entire range of taxable income; and (2) the $2, 400 and $1, 200 exemptions for married and single persons were reduced to $2, 000 and $1, 000, respectively, along with a $100 reduction (from $500 to $400) in the exemption for dependent children. The 6 per cent sales tax remained unchanged, "though with a view to additional revenue an adjustment of the exempt and partly-exempt lists was made";[26] at the same time, further increases were effected in, and new taxable commodities added to, the special-excise group.

There can be no doubt as to the cyclical, rather than countercyclical, pattern traced out by this tax policy. In the face of shrinking incomes and employment, it served to maintain almost unchanged the revenues yielded by the major internal tax instruments of economic stabilization. Both personal and corporate income tax collections were actually higher in 1933 than in 1929--the former having risen from $24. 8 million to $26 million, and the latter from $34. 6 million to $36. 1 million;[27] sales tax receipts declined very slightly from $83 million to $82. 2 million.[28] In 1933, the combined yield from those taxes amounted to 56 per cent of total tax revenues, as compared with the 36 per cent ratio for 1929. The over all drop in tax receipts was chiefly accounted for by the 57 per cent decline in customs and excise duties.[29]

Spending policy. The federal expenditure pattern is similarly striking. Total expenditures rose annually between 1930 and 1933, but these increases were, in reality, "unavoidable depression minima" incurred despite the most drastic economy measures directed towards the routine functions of government. Especially noteworthy, in this connection, are the disbandment of the Air Force and the large-scale reductions of salaries throughout the civil service.

"Unemployment relief" was, quite naturally, the expenditure sphere in which the major efforts were concentrated. The Government's relief activities were embodied in the Unemployment Relief Act of 1930, the Unemployment and Farm Relief Act of 1931, the Continuance and Relief Acts of 1932, and the Relief Act of 1933. In all of this legislation, formulas were devised for Dominion-provincial-municipal sharing of the costs of both "public (or relief) works" and "direct relief."[30] Moreover, in every year but 1932, when complaints of inefficiency and waste became particularly intense, the attempt was made to carry out a substantial number of works projects. But, as shown in Table XIV, the greater proportion of unemployment funds was, in fact, appropriated for purposes of direct relief. During the 1930-3 period, the combined federal expenditures on direct relief and relief works amounted to about $93 million (excluding some $22 million for which there is no breakdown by type of spending); of this total, some $54 million, or 58 per cent, was devoted to direct relief.[31] It is also apparent that annual expenditures on direct relief became progressively more important, and expenditures on relief works (with the exception of the 1930-1 change) increasingly insignificant, during the most severe depression years; by 1933, the latter had declined to the point where they totalled approximately 7 per cent of the former. The same sharp downswing can be found in the data pertaining to direct federal outlays on public investment, which fell continuously from their 1930 peak of $99 million to $36 million in 1933; relative to total federal expenditures, public investment dropped from 28 per cent in 1930 to 9 per cent in 1933.[32]

The budgetary deficits which appeared between the fiscal years 1931 and 1934 must, therefore, be regarded as having been purely involuntary-- the result of the Dominion Government's failure to achieve its clearly stated objective of increased tax revenue and reduced expenditure and debt.[33] There are the further unfavourable considerations that: (1) the most "income-oriented" tax instruments were applied in strong restrictive fashion; and (2) the outlays actually made were varied in the manner, and were frequently of the type, least calculated to offset the volatility of private investment or to produce the maximum income-employment effects.

Provincial-municipal policy. This inadequacy of federal stabilization efforts would have been serious enough in combination with a countercyclical fiscal pattern in the provincial-municipal sphere. The fact is, however, that no such pattern can be discerned for the early thirties. On the contrary, the fiscal policies pursued at the subsidiary governmental levels reflected, with remarkably few exceptions, the same set of changes in the direction of rising deficits incurred despite the most strenuous tax-raising and expenditure-reducing measures. The clearest demonstration of these changes is again provided by the public investment data. The direct investment outlays of both the provincial and municipal governments shrank continuously from their 1930 peaks--from $112 million to $47 million in 1933 in the former case, and from $111 million to $61 million in the latter; relative to total expenditures at each level of government, the decline was from 43 to 21 per cent and from 35 to 20 per cent, respectively.[34] Such action by the subsidiary governments could serve only to aggravate further the depressed conditions in which the Canadian economy found itself during the early thirties.[35]

TABLE XIV

Federal Stabilization Expenditures, 1930-3

(millions of dollars)

Year	Expenditures		
	Direct relief[1]	Relief works[1]	Direct public investment[2]
1930	.4	2.8	98.7
1931	10.0	22.0	79.6
1932	17.6	12.5	48.3
1933	26.2	1.8	35.9
Total[3]	54.2	39.1	262.5

(1) Report of Royal Commission on Dominion-Provincial Relations, book III, pp. 98-115.

(2) Department of Trade and Commerce, Private and Public Investment in Canada, 1926-1951, p. 186.

(3) The totals for relief expenditures exclude the following items: $16.9 million spent through Dominion (as contrasted with provincial-municipal) agencies; and $5.3 million spent on "agricultural aid" to Saskatchewan and Alberta (the latter having received only $18,000 of this amount). There is no available breakdown, according to type, of federal relief expenditures through Dominion agencies. It seems reasonable to assume that such figures would not differ materially, in relative terms, from those presented for expenditures through provincial-municipal agencies.

Fiscal Expansion, 1934-9

A full appreciation of Canadian fiscal experience in the recovery period which set in during 1934 necessitates analysis on the basis of both its "broad" and "narrow" aspects. In the broad sense, measures were taken which, for the most part, had little direct bearing upon the contem-

porary stability problem, and whose implications were of the longer-run
welfare type. These are to be contrasted with the specific quantitative
efforts made to raise levels of income and employment through fiscal
means. The latter fall more properly within the scope of this inquiry;
but it is important to make preliminary reference to the former because
of their function of having materially hastened the process of change in
the institutional and theoretical frameworks within which Canadian fiscal
stabilization policy would subsequently operate.

The Bennett "New Deal." The so-called "Bennett New Deal," implemented during the Conservative Administration's last eighteen months in
office, comprised a series of legislative enactments which, in scope and
speed of execution, had no peacetime precedent. New ground was broken
in virtually every major sphere of economic activity--labour, agriculture,
industry, and finance--by such far-reaching laws as: (1) the Natural Products Marketing Act and amendments, authorizing a Dominion Marketing
Board (and those local boards to which it might delegate power) to regulate
the marketing of the great variety of natural products, and to carry out
investigations into prices, wages, production costs, and trade practices
in the regions where such goods were produced; (2) the Minimum Wage
Act, empowering the Minister of Labour to fix minimum wage rates and
to confirm such rates when they were established by collective bargaining;
(3) the Limitation of Hours of Work Act, setting a legal maximum of eight
hours per day and forty-eight hours per week; (4) the Weekly Rest in Industrial Undertakings Act, providing for one rest day in every week;
(5) the Employment and Social Insurance Act, setting up a three-member
Commission to administer an employment exchange system and an unemployment insurance fund; (6) the Dominion Trade and Industry Act, establishing a Federal Trade and Industry Commission with numerous functions, including the administration of the Combines Act and the investigation of unfair trade practices; (7) a group of amendments to the Criminal
Code and to the 1934 Dominion Companies Act (as well as the latter Act
itself), designed, respectively, to eliminate price discrimination and other
monopolistic practices, and financial speculation in business; (8) the Economic Council Act, creating a sixteen-member body to study social trends,
to co-ordinate private and governmental economic research in Canada,
and to publish its own reports; (9) the Canadian Wheat Board Act, setting
up a three-member agency empowered to buy wheat from producers, to
sell, store, or transport it, and to operate elevators; and (10) the Dominion Housing Act, authorizing the government, from a $10 million loan
fund, to advance to approved lending institutions or local authorities 20
per cent of the cost or appraisal value (whichever was lower) of the proposed loan when the lending institution itself added 60 per cent.[36]

The merits of the individual legislative components of this programme
are of no special interest here.[37] Nor, in the present context, is there
cause for concern on account of: (1) the 1937 constitutional invalidation
of the basic measures dealing with the marketing of natural products,
wages and working conditions, and social insurance; and (2) the impossi-

bility of precisely evaluating the relative importance of radical agitation, American proximity, approaching elections, and genuine reforming zeal, in promoting the Conservatives' legislative upheaval.[38] The crux of the matter is that--despite its tardiness, the lack of political astuteness in its execution, and its conceptual ambiguity--"the 'New Deal' was of great historical importance, for it constituted both a comprehensive approach to the problems of the new postwar Canada and a frontal attack upon the limitations of the constitution."[39] There can be no question of the strong pro-government shift in popular economic thinking which the Bennett legislative upheaval reflected, or of the tremendous impact which it had on both thought and policy in the post-depression period.

Stabilization policy. But meanwhile, in the narrower sphere of fiscal policy, the cyclical pattern of federal government operations persisted throughout the recovery period. The "New Deal" was neither timely enough nor clear enough in its conceptual basis to affect the fiscal approach to the stabilization problems immediately at hand. The result was the continued appearance of budgetary deficits in the face of sustained high expenditure levels and the use of the major tax instruments without regard for their stability effects.

(1) Taxes. For the early recovery years, 1934-6, a policy of reduced tax rates--or, at the least, of no substantial rate increases--would have been the appropriate course of action.[40] The rate changes made in 1934 were relatively minor, comprising small excise tax reductions and an offsetting 25 per cent tax on gold deposited at the Mint for sale. But several important changes were made in 1935, including: (1) an increase in the corporate income tax from 12-1/2 to 13-1/2 per cent (and on consolidated returns to 15 per cent); (2) a surtax, ranging from 2 to 10 per cent, on investment income included in any income over $5,000 (all incomes in excess of $14,000 being considered investment income for tax purposes); and (3) a gift tax, with rates ranging from 2 per cent on amounts up to $25,000 to 10 per cent on gifts exceeding $1 million (an annual exemption of $4,000 being stipulated, along with specific exemptions for gifts to educational or charitable institutions or to governments). And important upward changes were again brought into effect in 1936, including: (1) an increase in the corporate income tax from 13-1/2 to 15 per cent (and from 15 to 17 per cent for consolidated returns); and (2) an increase in the rate of sales tax from 6 to 8 per cent.[41]

The buoyancy of tax receipts from virtually all sources and the gradual uninterrupted rise in total revenue during this three-year period are not to be attributed to the rate increases--which must have had deflationary repercussions--but rather to the 32 per cent increase in the gross national product which a combination of internal and external recovery factors achieved between 1933 and 1936.[42] Thus, while in the downswing of the Great Depression income changes had served to reinforce the deflationary tax rate changes in producing falling revenues, the stimulative effects of the former more than offset the depressing influence of the latter to produce rising tax yields during the early recovery years. Under Conservative

and Liberal Administrations alike, tax policy was geared overwhelmingly
to the balanced budget objective; tax collections did vary, but mainly in
response to spending and income fluctuations.

By 1937 the Canadian economy had reached the recuperative stage
where there was no longer ground for approaching downward tax revision
with the same sense of urgency.   Although a considerable gap persisted
as between 1929 and 1937 income-employment levels, gross national product, domestic investment, and exports had risen from their 1932-33 minima to the highest values since their 1929-30 peaks.[43]   The smoothness of
the recovery process was broken only by the 1937-8 recession, which, in
turn, had already been dissipated by early 1939.   Critical comment on the
maintenance of relative tax rate stability between 1937 and 1939 must,
therefore, be restricted to its inaccuracy in timing, and to its motivation
by declining budgetary deficits rather than by effects on economic stability.
The single noteworthy exception to this general rule was Mr. Dunning's
introduction of an important sales tax change in the 1938 budget--the exemption from this tax of the major products used in housing construction; the
purpose of the tax reduction was clearly stated to be the revival of the crucial construction industry, whose lagging improvement was being further
weakened by the 1937-8 recession.[44]

In structural terms, the tax policy had one redeeming feature.   As
shown in Table XV, it projected into the thirties the basic revenue trend
which had become apparent by 1929.   The result of the heavy reliance
placed on income and sales taxes during the Great Depression was that,
by 1939, these revenue instruments had come to yield about 67 per cent
of total tax receipts, as compared with 9 per cent in 1919 and 36 per cent
in 1929.   For those years, the corresponding ratios in the case of customs
and excise duties were 30, 76, and 63 per cent respectively.   On the eve
of World War II, then, prime importance rested with those taxes which--
apart from adverse equity and resource allocation effects notably with respect to sales taxes--would exert the most direct and most powerful internal
influence on Canadian levels of employment and income.

(2) Expenditures.   The strongest observation to be made in favour of
federal expnditure policy during the recovery period is that the vital stabilization outlays rose substantially between 1933 and 1934 and were thereafter consistently maintained at the higher levels.   Dominion spending continued to be carried out under the unemployment relief legislation, particularly: (1) the Relief and Public Works Construction Acts of 1934, the latter
authorizing a $40 million federal works programme (as contrasted with
federal contributions to the provinces under the former); (2) the Relief
and Supplementary Public Works Construction Acts of 1935, the latter
again providing for a federal works programme, not to exceed $18 million;
(3) the Unemployment Relief and Assistance Act of 1936, extending the arrangements for tri-governmental sharing of relief costs; (4) the Unemployment and Agricultural Assistance Act of 1937, with its renewed sharing
procedure, together with the "youth training schemes" and the Home Improvement Plan introduced in accordance with the recommendations of the

TABLE XV

Canada's Changing Federal Tax Structure, 1919, 1929 and 1939[1]

Revenue	1919		1929		1939	
	Amount ($000)	Percentage of total taxes[2]	Amount ($000)	Percentage of total taxes[2]	Amount ($000)	Percentage of total taxes[2]
Customs duties	147,169	63.0	187,206	47.3	78,751	18.1
Excise duties	30,342	13.0	63,685	16.1	51,314	11.8
Income taxes:						
Individuals	7,973	3.4	24,793	6.3	46,591	10.7
Corporations	1,377	.6	34,629	8.7	85,186	19.5
Business profits tax[3]	32,970	14.1	455	.1	-	-
Sales taxes[4]	11,889	5.1	83,007	21.0	161,711	37.1
Miscellaneous taxes	1,969	.8	2,146	.5	12,154	2.8
Total taxes	233,689	100.0	395,921	100.0	435,707	100.0
Total revenue	312,947		460,151		502,171	

Sources: Canada Year Books, 1941 and 1947, pp. 754 and 759, and p. 966, respectively. (Income tax figures can also be found in Department of National Revenue, Taxation Statistics, Ottawa, 1946, p. 11.)

(1) Fiscal years ending March 31.
(2) Figures rounded to total 100 per cent.
(3) The business profits tax was abolished as of December 31, 1920, but it continued to yield belated revenue until 1933.
(4) The item, "sales taxes," includes the general sales tax and the excise taxes levied under the "war tax legislation" (of World War I). The general sales tax--which from its inception constituted the bulk of the "sales taxes" as here defined--was first levied in 1920.

National Employment Commission;[45] and (5) the National Housing Act of 1938, repealing the Act of 1935 and empowering the government (a) to make a 25 per cent contribution--the total not exceeding $14.5 million--to low-cost-housing loans made by lending institutions, (b) to grant 20-25 per cent guarantees on those loans, and (c) to make loans to local housing authorities--not exceeding $30 million--also for the construction of low-cost dwellings.[46]

But the facts presented in Table XVI tell an unimpressive story. To be sure, the $286 million total of federal relief spending between 1934 and 1937 was more than double the amount spent during the preceding four-year period. There was, secondly, not a single year in which the combined ex-

TABLE XVI

Federal Stabilization Expenditures, 1934-7

(millions of dollars)

| Year | Expenditures | | |
	Direct relief[1]	Relief works[1]	Direct public investment[2]
1934	39.3[3]	4.0	40.5
1935	31.1[3]	10.0	48.6
1936	36.4	11.5	40.7
1937	35.5	7.6	45.4
Total[4]	142.3	33.1	175.2

(1) Report of Royal Commission on Dominion-Provincial Relations, book III, pp. 98-115.

(2) Department of Trade and Commerce, Private and Public Investment in Canada, 1926-1951, p. 186.

(3) The 1934 and 1935 totals for direct relief include one item for which no division is available as between direct relief and agricultural aid. This item is the "Dominion grant" to the province of Saskatchewan, amounting to $5.0 million in 1934 and $4 million in 1935.

(4) The over all totals for relief expenditures exclude the following items: $95.3 million spent through Dominion agencies; and $15.1 million spent on "agricultural aid" to the Prairie Provinces ($13.1 million of this sum having been received by Saskatchewan). See Table XIV for comment on the classification of federal relief expenditures through Dominion agencies.

penditure on direct relief and relief works through provincial and municipal agencies fell below $41 million, which, in turn, exceeded by about $9 million the peak year (1931) of relief spending during the Great Depression. And thirdly, the volume of direct investment outlays made by the Dominion Government gradually approached pre-depression levels, and by 1939 they had reached $61 million, or $25 million above the 1933 low.[47] But these considerations are of minor importance in comparison with the following facts: (1) The heaviest relief expenditures were made in the upswing, rather than the downswing, of the Great Depression. (2) Budgetary deficits were incurred throughout the recovery period and tended to be smaller in the later years, not because of deliberate tax-expenditure policy, but through expanding economic activity.[48] (3) The great bulk of relief expenditures took the form of direct relief representing neither careful planning nor tangible addition to productive capacity. (4) And in no single year during the upswing did the ratio of federal public investment to gross national product exceed the 1.2 per cent figure attained in 1938.[49]

Provincial-municipal operations. Meanwhile, the fiscal policies of the provincial and municipal governments were proceeding along parallel lines. The general position was one of buoyant revenues, high expenditures, annual deficits, and little appreciation of the countercyclical potentialities of fiscal operations. Especially prominent among the statistical indicators of recovery developments are the approximate trebling of provincial public investment between 1933 and 1937, and the 25 per cent increase in municipal public investment during those years; the former stood at $146 million in 1937, as compared with $47 million in 1933, while the latter rose from $50 million to $63 million.[50] With provincial investment comprising about one-third of total public investment in 1933,[51] the enormous increase in this component of provincial spending must have contributed materially to the general economic improvement.

At the same time, however, the grave problem of heavy obligations in the face of limited revenue sources was growing progressively more acute at the subsidiary levels of government--particularly in the municipal sphere, where the share of relief expenditures and public investment by all governments had been, of necessity, reduced from 23 per cent and 42 per cent in 1933 to 11 per cent and 25 per cent, respectively, in 1937.[52] That is to say, emerging with unprecedented clarity from the Great Depression was the two-sided fiscal problem of a federal state, namely, the optimum pursuit of stabilization policy, and the most efficient and most equitable allocation of spending and taxing powers among the various governments. To the extent that the allocation issue involved infringement of the freedom of the subsidiary governments to undertake the appropriate stabilizing measures at any given time, it was, of course, inseparably linked with the problem of countercyclical fiscal policy.

Concluding Appraisal

The conclusion seems warranted that, granting the stimulus provided by governmental efforts, "Canadian recovery was more the result of an improving world situation than of the domestic policies pursued by the Dominion, provincial, and municipal governments. "[53] There are two supporting general observations--pointed up by the foregoing analysis-- which overshadow all others. The first relates to the quantitative inade- quacy of governmental action during the Great Depression; it is under- scored by the fact that the combined 1930-7 relief expenditures of $965 million and the corresponding public investment outlays of $1,769 million represented annual averages amounting to $121 million and $221 million, respectively, or 2.0 per cent and 3.6 per cent of the gross national pro- duct in 1929.[54] The second observation is illustrated in Table XVII and Charts 5 and 6; it involves, for the entire interwar period, an almost completely uniform fiscal pattern of governmental conformity with, rather than divergence from, the upward and downward swings of the business cycle; that is, a pattern of policy which coincides clearly with analytically sound procedure only in the "early recovery" phase of the cycle--and which even then conforms only in "expenditure" terms and is largely involuntary in its execution.

Implicit throughout this study has been the author's view that a Cana- dian interwar policy of economic stabilization by fiscal techniques would have materially reduced the violence of cyclical fluctuations in the Dom- inion. It seems beyond doubt, moreover, that such policy would have been most productive during the Great Depression, --characterized as it was by a general collapse in purchasing power and extremely low levels of activity in the capital goods industries.

Unlike the case of monetary policy, there are no complex issues aris- ing from the question as to whether stimulative or contractive effects would have followed immediately and directly from the broad implementation of internal fiscal measures. To that extent, the problem of appraisal is con- siderably simplified, so much so, indeed, that, for closed industrial eco- nomies (like the United States), the economic feasibility of achieving im- portant stability effects is no longer a matter of debate among economists. The major issues are rather: (1) given the stability objective, how to ob- tain the optimum combination of fiscal instruments for the realization of that objective; and (2) how to define the limits of the fiscal approach in terms of the relationship between the stability objective and other objec- tives--economic and non-economic--of public policy.

It is clear, from even the most casual analysis of "fiscal mechanics," that all internal fiscal instruments have both advantages and disadvantages in common, and that each has such features unique to itself. The obvious need, therefore, is for the acknowledgment of stability limitations on the fiscal approach as a whole; and for a judicious policy admixture of all in- struments. The nature of the combination will be dependent upon the com- parative evaluation, for any given situation, of quantitative employment- income effects, flexibility and timing potentialities, and resource alloca- tion effects.

It is also evident, from any appraisal of fiscal instruments, that this procedural problem bears closely on the issue of viewing the stability objective against the background of such other goals of public policy as efficiency, growth, and freedom. That is to say, the problem of the relationship between social objectives is relevant and common to all variants of the fiscal approach. Nor is there any question as to the abundance of scope for both harmony and conflict between the stability objective and others. It is not the author's intention to explore these analytical possibilities. For purposes of this study, it is sufficient to note that there is nothing in the nature of things which makes social goals compatible with each other; that the need consequently arises for frequent review of the stability objective in the light of its impact upon other objectives; and that this need is nowhere more pressing than in regard to the interaction between short-run cyclical and long-run growth problems, and between anti-inflationary controls and the exercise of private volition.

But these problems of techniques and objectives should not obscure the significant truth that the reality of the contribution made to stability by the fiscal approach has ceased to be the prime contentious issue in macro-economic analysis. This generalization has validity for closed and open economies alike. To be sure, it must be tempered, in the latter case, by considerations of relative immunity from control characterizing foreign demand for exports and domestic demand for imports; and, for a particular open economy, Canada, by considerations of substantial factor immobility within the Dominion, as well as the complexities introduced into the operation of the multiplier process by sharp regional discrepancies throughout the country.[55] The gravity of these added limitations is a matter for empirical investigation which the author makes no attempt to pursue further--his findings having established the importance of such factors as domestic investment and government policy during the interwar years. In the present context--the appropriateness of countercyclical fiscal policy in Canada at that time--no broader supporting basis is necessary, unless it be assumed that other internal stabilization techniques would have been adequate, or that the machinery was then available for the minimization of Canada's stability problems by international means. Neither of these assumptions would appear to be in accord with the facts of the interwar period.

TABLE XVII

Gross National Product and Investment in Canada, 1926-39[1]

(millions of dollars)

Year	Gross national product[2]	Private investment[3] New investment[4]	Private investment[3] New investment and maintenance[5]	DIRECT PUBLIC INVESTMENT[3] Dominion New[4]	Dominion New and maintenance[5]	Provincial New[4]	Provincial New and maintenance[5]	Municipal New[4]	Municipal New and maintenance[5]	Total public utility investment[6]
1926	5,294	747	1,088	33.5	45.5	28.1	49.1	44.7	72.8	156
1927	5,647	860	1,223	45.5	61.5	36.0	60.2	54.8	87.8	187
1928	6,105	1,033	1,423	50.5	68.7	46.9	75.0	60.1	94.8	209
1929	6,166	1,176	1,579	58.5	79.9	56.5	87.4	66.7	103.5	260
1930	5,546	923	1,276	78.8	98.7	77.1	112.2	72.6	111.3	225
1931	4,560	593	893	59.7	79.6	67.9	105.7	55.5	98.4	183
1932	3,767	327	576	35.8	48.3	44.6	73.8	46.1	82.8	100
1933	3,552	217	450	26.3	35.9	27.8	47.1	32.8	60.8	84
1934	4,034	286	550	29.1	40.5	52.5	86.1	27.2	49.8	88
1935	4,345	346	623	34.8	48.6	57.9	89.2	32.4	56.8	99
1936	4,701	423	729	27.8	40.7	58.7	85.1	33.0	59.9	124
1937	5,355	579	924	31.2	45.4	112.0	146.4	34.0	63.0	150
1938	5,233	539	873	42.3	61.2	81.6	120.2	36.1	69.4	145
1939	5,707	547	898	44.7	61.3	72.6	111.4	38.9	73.6	139

(1) Figures for gross national product apply to calendar years, and investment figures to fiscal years ending nearest to December 31.

(2) D.B.S., National Accounts: Income and Expenditure, 1926-1950, pp. 26, 27.

(3) Department of Trade and Commerce, Private and Public Investment in Canada, 1926-1951, pp. 145, 148, 152, 166, 186, 190, 198. "Private investment" is here defined as the excess of total domestic investment over investment by government departments at all three levels, federal, provincial, and municipal.

(4) "New investment" comprises all outlays (private or public, as the case may be) on new durable physical assets (including outlays made to replace existing assets).

(5) "Maintenance" represents all expenditures (private or public) made to maintain the existing stock of durable assets in a normal state of repair.

(6) "Total public utility investment" refers to the "new investment and maintenance" outlays of utilities owned by the Dominion, provincial, and municipal governments.

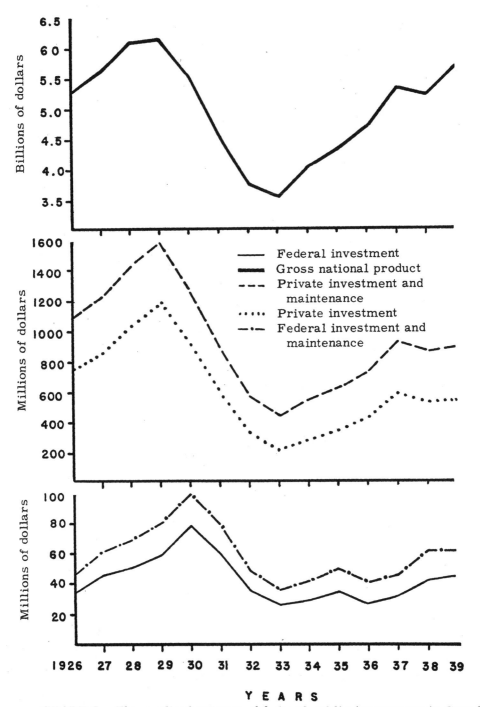

CHART 5. The cyclical pattern of federal public investment in Canada, 1926-39. All investment figures are in "gross" terms; that is, they include allowances for depreciation or obsolescence of existing capital facilities.

Source: Figures taken from Table XVII.

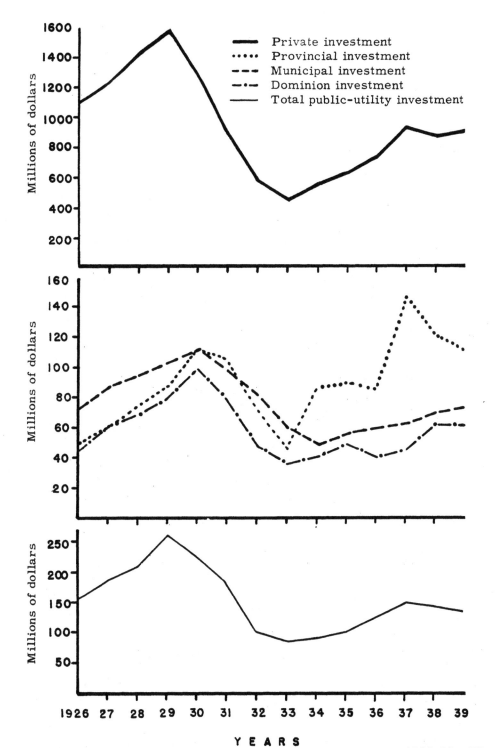

CHART 6. Canadian public investment, all governments, 1926-39. All figures apply to "new investment and maintenance," as defined in Table XVII. Source: Figures taken from Table XVII.

CHAPTER XII

THOUGHT AND POLICY IN RETROSPECT

EXCLUSIVE CONCERN with either the thought or policy aspects of Canadian interwar fluctuations would have imparted a degree of precision to this study which it has not achieved. But either approach, taken by itself, would have had serious shortcomings for purposes of providing a broad understanding of the dynamic forces governing policy evolution in the stability sphere. This is not meant to imply the total adequacy of the combined approach which has been followed, but rather its closer approximation to economic truth.

There is no intention here to retrace ground already covered. The attempt has been made throughout to draw from the analytical survey those general inferences which shed the most light on a particular phase of Canadian economic development. The brief concluding comments which follow--on the nature of, and relationship between, the thought and policy processes--are aimed at separating out these crucial observations from the mass of technical and historical detail.

With reference to Canadian economic thinking, strong empirical support has been found for the following: (1) The prevailing interwar pattern was one of reluctance and inability to cope with those problems arising out of income-employment fluctuations. (2) This immaturity of approach was most clearly reflected through an overwhelming faith in the automatic self-adjusting powers of the economic system, and in the non-controllability of those destabilizing forces impinging upon the economy. (3) To the extent that policy issues were projected into the forefront of discussion, the prime concern was with monetary problems--but only in the restricted sense of rationalizing the existing institutional structure, and acknowledging only those arguments which implied either negligible alteration, or none at all, in that structure. (4) General awareness of the stabilizing potentialities of fiscal techniques did not manifest itself until the final stages of the interwar period--and then only as an appendage of monetary analysis. (5) Permeating the entire thought fabric were fully articulated radical notions of income determination, monetary management, and budgetary policy--usually lacking in sophistication and often erroneous in reasoning--which provided a continuing check upon rigid national adherence to classical economic doctrine. And (6) through the expanding group of professionally trained economists, a new element of balance--which for the interwar period played its most fruitful role in the central bank controversy--was gradually being incorporated into the thought pattern; and simultaneously beginning to bridge the gap between government policy and the careful formulation of economic guides to action.

The central object of the policy investigation has been to appraise the federal government's use of compensatory instruments against the background of both contemporary thought and subsequent refinements in the

tools of economic analysis: (1) In the face of the gravest stability problems
such stabilizing efforts as were made derived largely from expediency and
lacked any comprehensive or unifying approach. (2) As for the policy actually implemented, there was but minor deviation from monetary and fiscal
orthodoxy--and then typically when the particular emergency had subsided.
(3) In consequence, there was, for the most part, a policy intensification
of the upward and downward swings of the business cycle. (4) This intensification was striking in the fiscal field--especially during the Great Depression, characterized, as it was, by emphasis on strict economies in government expenditure and high rates of taxation. And (5) from the interwar experience there emerged, with unprecedented clarity, the Canadian failure
to solve the fiscal problems of federalism--a vital defect in its own right,
but also in terms of the added limitations which it imposed upon stabilization policy.

It is evident that, in general, the interwar policy carried out at the
federal level conformed closely to the dominant thinking on problems of
economic stability. But such a finding provides no answer per se to what
is surely one of the most important of all questions pertaining to the "dy-
namics" of economic policy: What kind of relationship prevailed as between
the thought and policy aspects of Canada's approach to interwar fluctuations?
In other words, to what extent, if any, was there a causal connection between these processes of economic development? For without an assumption of some degree of causal relationship, the author would be hard pressed
to defend the over-all approach followed in this inquiry. If thought were
purely the consequence of policy or bore no definable relation to it, the
separate and exclusive consideration of either could proceed with no serious adverse effects on the analyst's understanding of the problems involved.

It would be unreasonable to deny the overwhelming difficulties associated with any attempt to give precise meaning to the thought-policy relationship. Not even the most comprehensive socio-political-economic study
could provide such a solution. But something less than precision is appropriate to this type of research. And for the writer's purposes, it is sufficient to allude to three limiting factors which seem important and relevant
to the survey already made, and to appraise their impact upon his basic
"causal" assumption of interaction.

One limitation stems from the incontrovertible fact that, in an industrialized community governed by parliamentary institutions, public policy
in any sphere does not evolve in a "thought vacuum" but constitutes the
end result of a power struggle among competing pressure groups for the
achievement of conflicting objectives. In this struggle, theory often
emerges as the dominant group's instrument for identifying its welfare
with that of the community. Secondly, the inadequacies of institutional
and professional development constitute a limitation, not only in the sense
of narrowing the scope of ideas, but also in terms of precluding certain
lines of policy irrespective of the trend of thinking about major issues.
And thirdly, complex policy problems frequently make their appearance
with such rapidity as to precipitate emergency action which is only later

rationalized by the formulation of a system of thought.

These limiting factors should serve to inject an element of uncertainty into generalizations about the analytical superiority of any particular Canadian group or individuals during the interwar years; and as to the general significance of "thought" contributions to policy execution. Indeed, attention has been called repeatedly to those qualifications which would prevent the adoption of an over-simplified approach to the thought-policy relationship. Such skepticism, however, must not be carried too far. The stability problems encountered by the Dominion were, after all, susceptible in some degree to precise economic analysis which had no unique relation to pressure group interests or to the contemporary institutional framework. There were problems of income determination and monetary and fiscal theory to which reasonably satisfactory solutions could be found. To those who--borrowing freely from the analytical tools being forged elsewhere-- applied themselves, however imperfectly, to this task must be attributed at least a part of the responsibility for the gradual maturing of Canadian economic thought. Moreover, abundant evidence has been produced to show the growing tendency towards reflection of the newer and more fully expounded ideas in the countercyclical techniques being utilized.

In short, the only thought-policy conceptual framework which has meaning for the author is that of a reciprocal cause-effect relationship. The importance of each aspect of the stability problem having been established, it remains only to add that further strong confirmation of their interaction is afforded by Canadian experience during and since the Second World War.

NOTES

Chapter One

1. By this term is meant no more than (1) the analysis of stabilization problems in terms of the "receipts" and "expenditure" components of the "gross national product," and (2) the maintenance of aggregate demand at a level high enough to absorb full-employment national output. There is no intention to imply either general agreement on the "mechanics" of stabilizing aggregate demand, or lack of appreciation of the theoretical and practical limitations of Keynesian countercyclical policy.

2. For wartime and postwar governmental expression of intention of, and proposed methods for, achieving "high and stable levels of income and employment," see Canada, Department of Reconstruction, Employment and Income, with Special Reference to the Initial Period of Reconstruction (Ottawa, 1945); also Canada, Dominion-Provincial Conference on Reconstruction, Proposals of the Government of Canada (Ottawa, 1945).

3. See, for example, D. C. MacGregor, J. B. Rutherford, G. E. Britnell, and J. J. Deutsch, National Income, A Study Prepared for the Royal Commission on Dominion-Provincial Relations (Ottawa, 1939). For a historical and analytical account of the development of techniques of national income measurement in Canada, see S. A. Goldberg, "The Development of National Accounts in Canada," Canadian Journal of Economics and Political Science (henceforth contracted to C. J. E. P. S.), XV (Feb. 1949).

4. Among the studies alluded to above are the following: J. H. Creighton, The Bank of Canada (Vancouver, 1933); H. A. Innis and A. F. W. Plumptre (eds.), The Canadian Economy and Its Problems (Toronto, 1934); D. C. MacGregor, "The Problem of Public Debt in Canada," C. J. E. P. S., II (May 1936); M. K. Inman, "Experience in Canadian Banking, 1929-1934," unpublished Ph. D. thesis (Harvard University, 1938); Canada, Final Report of the National Employment Commission (Ottawa, 1938); C. Elliott, "Bank Cash," C. J. E. P. S., IV (Aug. 1938); M. L. Stokes, The Bank of Canada (Toronto, 1939); W. A. Mackintosh, The Economic Background of Dominion-Provincial Relations, S. Bates, Financial History of Canadian Governments, F. A. Knox, Dominion Monetary Policy, 1929-1934, and H. C. Goldenberg, Municipal Finance in Canada, studies prepared for the Royal Commission on Dominion-Provincial Relations (Ottawa, 1939); Canada, Report of the Royal Commission on Dominion-Provincial Relations (Ottawa, 1940; R. B. Bryce, "The Effects on Canada of Industrial Fluctuations in the United States," C. J. E. P. S., V (Aug. 1939; J. R. Petrie, "The Tax Systems of Canada," unpublished Ph. D. thesis (Montreal, 1940); A. F. W. Plumptre, Central Banking in the British Dominions (Toronto, 1940).

5. Typical of this group of writings are the following: J. J. Deutsch, "War Finance and the Canadian Economy, 1914-1920," C. J. E. P. S., VI (Nov. 1940); J. F. Parkinson (ed.), Canadian War Economics (Toronto,

1941); A. F. W. Plumptre, Mobilizing Canada's Resources for War (Toronto, 1941); D. C. MacGregor, "The Project of Full Employment and Its Implications, " Canada after the War, eds. A. Brady and F. R. Scott (Toronto, 1943); B. H. Higgins, "Postwar Tax Policy" (Part II), C. J. E. P. S., IX (Nov. 1943); B. H. Higgins, The War and Postwar Cycle in Canada, 1914-1923, Report Submitted to the Advisory Committee on Reconstruction (Ottawa, 1944); B. H. Higgins, Canada's Financial System in War, National Bureau of Economic Research Occasional Paper 19 (April 1944); J. R. Beattie, "Some Aspects of the Problem of Full Employment, " C. J. E. P. S., XI (Feb. 1945); M. C. Urquhart, "Public Investment in Canada, " C.J.E.P.S., XI (Nov. 1945); Department of Reconstruction, Employment and Income; Dominion Provincial Conference on Reconstruction, Proposals of the Government of Canada; Dominion-Provincial Conference on Reconstruction, Public Investment and Capital Formation, and Comparative Statistics of Public Finance (Ottawa, 1945); D. C. MacGregor, "The Problem of Price Level in Canada, " C. J. E. P. S., XIII (May 1947); R. C. McIvor, "Canadian Wartime Fiscal Policy, 1939-45, " C. J. E. P. S., XIV (Feb. 1948); Department of Trade and Commerce, Investment and Inflation, with Special Reference to the Immediate Postwar Period, Canada, 1945-1948 (Ottawa, 1949); V. W. Malach, "Internal Determinants of the Canadian Upswing, " C.J.E.P.S., XVI (May 1950); V. W. Malach, "External Determinants of the Canadian Upswing, " C. J. E. P. S., XVII (Feb. 1951); Department of Trade and Commerce, Private and Public Investment in Canada, 1926-1951 (Ottawa, 1951); Dominion Bureau of Statistics, National Accounts: Income and Expenditure, 1926-1950 (Ottawa, 1951); E. Marcus, "The Cyclical Turning Points in an Open Economy: Canada, 1927-1939, " American Economic Review, XLIII (Sept. 1953); R. C. McIvor and J. H. Panabaker, "Canadian Postwar Monetary Policy, 1946-52, " C. J. E. P. S., XX (May 1954).

There are four investigations known to the writer which pursue a broad Keynesian approach to the problems of economic instability in Canada during the interwar period: the unpublished Ph. D. thesis of A. N. McLeod, "Maintaining Employment and Incomes in Canada" (Harvard University, 1949); V. W. Malach, International Cycles and Canada's Balance of Payments, 1921-33 (Toronto, 1954); E. Marcus, Canada and the International Business Cycle, 1927-1939 (New York, 1954); and A. E. Safarian, "The Canadian Economy in the Great Depression, " unpublished Ph. D. thesis (University of California, Berkeley, 1955). However, these studies also have a rather different orientation from that of the author, in that: (1) they are not concerned, to any great extent, with the evolution of Canadian economic thinking and its relationship to policy; and/or (2) their analytical emphasis is overwhelmingly on the international, as against the national, aspects of stability problems.

6. There is no intention of conveying the impression of uncritical acceptance of such theory. The author is well aware of the fact that, when viewed historically, the apparent validity of economic doctrine has often proved to be transitory; that institutional and conceptual changes have characteristically combined to make obsolete for contemporary economic activity a theoretical framework which was appropriate to a prior stage of

social development; and that these observations are likely to be more in
point for the present than for any other time. Nevertheless, the Keynesian
system, in terms of general professional acceptance of its analytical
framework (as against its public-policy implications), would seem to be the
most reliable standard currently at hand for monetary-fiscal appraisal. It
is hoped that errors in judgment will be minimized by continual exposure
to this attitude of caution and tentativeness.

    7. One minor aspect of this occupational problem concerns the mode
of reference to economists whose occupational status changed, after the
given time of writing, from graduate student to professor, from professor
to civil servant, etc. The practice here will be to use the title which par-
allels the period under consideration.

    8. This is not meant to imply that all combined approaches to unem-
ployment, monetary, and fiscal problems were similarly confused. There
were more than a few instances, particularly in the thirties, of balanced
treatment--in most of which economists were involved. See, for example,
Innis and Plumptre, The Canadian Economy and Its Problems; Report of
Royal Commission on Dominion-Provincial Relations; and Plumptre, Central Banking in the British Dominions; also League for Social Reconstruction, Social Planning for Canada (Toronto, 1935).

    9. The analytical consequence of this division of effort will be only
passing concern with two exceedingly important groups of fiscal problems,
namely, the development of Canadian commercial policy, and the "efficiency,"
"equity," and "growth" effects of Dominion fiscal operations. Examples of
extended treatment of these problems are: Report of Royal Commission on
Dominion-Provincial Relations; Petrie, The Tax Systems of Canada;
O. McDiarmid, Commercial Policy in the Canadian Economy (Cambridge,
Mass., 1946); D. R. Annett, British Preference in Canadian Commercial
Policy (Toronto, 1948); H. E. Brazer, "Coordination in Canadian Federal
Finance," unpublished Ph. D. thesis (Columbia University, 1952); J. H.
Perry, Taxes, Tariffs, and Subsidies: A History of Canadian Fiscal De-
velopment (Toronto, 1955).

    10. The "money supply" is here defined, in orthodox terms, as the
total volume of legal tender currency (metallic coin and Bank of Canada
notes) and checking deposits in circulation at any given time. When applied
to the long pre-central bank period of Canadian development, this definition
must be modified to the extent of Dominion notes and chartered bank notes
being substituted for the Bank of Canada notes (see "The Canadian Monetary
Structure," in chapter III).

    11. The truth is, of course, that, in any real-world situation, the
chain of response to monetary manipulation is far more complex than that
implied by "money supply-interest rates-stability." That such reasoning
is basic to contemporary analytical thinking on countercyclical monetary
policy can, however, hardly be doubted.

    12. Not until June 1954 was the Bank of Canada empowered to vary the
reserve requirements of the chartered banks (2-3 Elizabeth II, 1953-4, 1st
Session, 22nd Parliament). Rediscounting has either never been controlled
in the Dominion (under the Finance Acts of 1914 and 1923) or rarely been

used (under the Bank of Canada); but see chapter IX, n. 104, for reference to recent legislative efforts to develop a commercial paper market in Canada. No mention is made in the text of such selective instruments as margin requirements and direct regulation of consumer instalment credit. These are designed to influence the composition, rather than the magnitude, of the money supply. Indeed, it is in this latter sense that the selective techniques afford potentialities for the increased efficacy of the traditional monetary instruments.

13. As far as is known to the author, Canadian governments made no use of these techniques during the interwar period. In the pre-central bank years, however, they did apply moral suasion to the chartered banks. And on two occasions--November 1932 and June 1934--the government implemented expansionary monetary policies which a central bank would have effected, respectively, through rediscounting operations and reduced legal reserves for the commercial banks (see chapter IX).

14. There may be unfavourable repercussions of rising public debt and public expenditures, dependence on foreign sources of supply and demand, errors in forecasting, etc. Many of these, however, are not unique to fiscal policy; while monetary policy, even granting a degree of effectiveness, presents special secondary problems of its own (e. g., the problem of restricting speculative activity and yet not choking off productive investment).

15. It is readily acknowledged that the Cambridge cash-balance approach, and even (indirectly) the Fisher transactions-velocity approach, discussed the liquidity function through K and V, respectively; but the tendency was either to assume that it was constant (in the long run) or that its changes were offset by equivalent changes in T (in the short run).

16. Among the interesting recent developments in fiscal theory is the demonstration of the possibility of an expansionist effect of a balanced budget with regressive taxation. In this instance, the net stimulus would be achieved, not through tapping savings without materially reducing consumption, but through the use of a portion of spending units' active funds in new or under-used spheres of employment. The stimulus would represent a change in employment, not in expenditure, so that there would be no multiplied effects on income. On this regressive tax argument, see, for example, T. Haavelmo, "Multiplier Effects of a Balanced Budget," Econometrica, XIII (Oct. 1945). But see also W. J. Baumol and M. H. Peston, "More on the Multiplier Effects of a Balanced Budget," American Economic Review, XLV (March 1955); and A. H. Hansen "More on the Multiplier Effects of a Balanced Budget: Comment," and Baumol and Peston, "Reply," American Economic Review, XLVI (March 1956).

17. For example, no change in the depreciating country's money supply would occur to the extent that the depreciation raised the marginal propensity to consume domestically produced goods and services; but the repercussions of depreciation are far more widespread than this.

18. By the same token, tariff policy is here treated as a fiscal instrument--with the analysis restricted to its stability effects, as distinct from commercial policy in general--not so much because of its implementation

through the budgetary process, as because of its greater directness and precision in achieving income-employment effects, as well as the absence of any necessary connection with changes in monetary reserve or money supply. But again, the important procedural point is that both the fiscal and monetary implications of tariff policy should be discussed.

19. For corroboration of this contention of uniformity of postwar cyclical patterns, see Higgins, The War and Postwar Cycle in Canada, 1914-1923, pp. 2-6.

20. The criterion here used for distinguishing between major and minor phases is that of the duration of the cycle, with the former applying to 8-12 year cycles and the latter to 3-4 year cycles; in Schumpeterian terms, then, account is taken of the Juglar and Kitchin cycles, respectively (see J. A. Schumpeter, Business Cycles, New York, 1939, I, chapter IV). This distinction presents difficulties, however, such as the question as to whether the first post-war (World War I) cycle should be regarded as major or minor. It would seem to be an important borderline case whose after-effects were not eliminated until 1925. The writer's justification for adopting the minor cycle classification is to be found in the rapidity of change, and the key role of inventories, during the boom and recession phases.

21. There can be nothing definite about the beginning and terminal years of each cyclical phase. On the basis of some statistical indices, for example, the peak of the Great Depression boom and the trough of the Great Depression downswing were reached in 1930 and 1932, respectively; the preponderance of statistical evidence, however, supports a 1929 peak and a 1933 trough. Similarly, the other phases set forth above appear to be the appropriate ones. Nevertheless, it should be noted, by way of further emphasizing the looseness of the author's time-series breakdown, that there are valid statistical grounds for postulating the occurrence of Kitchin cycles in Canada between 1921 and 1924, between 1924 and 1927, and between 1933 and 1937; also the occurrence of peak-to-peak building cycles from 1922 to 1929 and from 1929 to 1941 (see O. J. Firestone, "Estimate of the Gross Value of Construction in Canada, 1940," C.J.E.P.S., IX May 1943, p. 219; Dr. Firestone contrasts the 10-year-average Canadian building cycle with the 17-to-18-year-average American building cycle).

22. Higgins, The War and Postwar Cycle, p. 53.

23. Dominion Bureau of Statistics, Prices and Price Indexes, 1944-1947 (Ottawa, 1948), p. 14.

24. Ibid., p. 5.

25. See Table I. Actually, by 1933 gross investment had undergone an $11 million increase over its lowest point in 1932. When the statistical source in the above ("text") paragraph is not noted, Table I is implied.

26. The output figure was obtained from Dominion Bureau of Statistics, Economic Fluctuations in Canada during the Postwar Period (Ottawa, 1938); and the employment figure from Dominion Bureau of Statistics, Canada Year Book, 1942 (Ottawa, 1942), p. 422. (Henceforth Dominion Bureau of Statistics will be contracted to D.B.S., and the Canada Year Book to C.Y.B.).

27. D.B.S., Prices and Price Indexes, 1944-1947, p. 14.

28. The use of the ratio between government expenditure and gross investment requires elaboration. It is intended merely as an indication that any change in the most unstable component of aggregate demand (business investment) could have been offset by an opposite change in government expenditure which, in relative terms, was seldom appreciably greater, and often considerably less, than the original investment change. (This fact would be made all the more impressive by exclusion of "capital outlays of government business enterprise" from "gross domestic investment.") It is, of course, only fair to point out that, at the 1929 peak, when the greatest drop in gross investment was in the making, government expenditure amounted to only 49 per cent of it; and that expenditure of the federal government alone (in "total," and especially "investment," terms) then compared even less favourably with gross investment (see chapter IV). On the other hand, it should be borne in mind that changes in government expenditure constituted only one of many stabilizing devices available to the Dominion government during the Great Depression.

29. These "debt" figures present a sharp contrast with the corresponding ratios for the final year of, and the two years following, World War II. Thus, in 1945 and 1947 the national debt amounted to 95 per cent of gross national product; and in 1946 the ratio was 112 per cent. C.Y.B., 1954, p. 1091; and D.B.S., National Accounts: Income and Expenditure, 1926-1950, pp. 26, 27.

30. It is true that government expenditure increased during the recession year 1938. However, subsequent investigation will reveal that Canadian interwar fiscal policy was largely predicated upon past trends in the level of economic activity, and that government expenditure at any given time was designed to conform to those trends. If these observations are valid, it follows that the 1938 rise in government expenditure did not reflect any substantial preventive or remedial attempts at stabilization, but the inability to discern evidence of a downturn already begun; and that accurate appraisal of past trends might well have led to a decline in government expenditure in 1938.

31. A time lead can also be observed for gross investment in the 1920-2 downswing; the investment peak was reached in 1919, not 1920.

32. "It has become quite a commonplace statement to say that Canada is one of the largest trading nations of the world and her prosperity is greatly dependent on the volume of her exports. What is not so generally realized is that Canadian prosperity rests on many pillars, of which exports are only one, although an important one. Investment is another pillar of prosperity, which, in some respects, is even less secure than exports. This may appear, at first glance, a surprising observation, for the volume of exports is largely determined by decisions made abroad, while the volume of domestic investment is, to a great extent, determined by decisions made at home. But the observation is supported by historical records of Canadian economic fluctuations." Department of Trade and Commerce, Investment and Inflation, with Special Reference to the Immediate Postwar Period, Canada, 1945-1948, p. 45; see also pp. 46, 47.

For an appraisal of the causal role of Canadian investment and exports in the Great Depression, see McLeod, "Maintaining Employment and Incomes in Canada, " pp. 97, 98; Malach, International Cycles and Canada's Balance of Payments, 1921-33, chapter V; and Safarian, "The Canadian Economy in the Great Depression, " chapters I-III.

It should be noted (again using 1926 as the base year) that between 1919 and 1925 the index of domestic investment reached peaks of 84 and 93 (in 1919 and 1925, respectively) and a trough of 27 (in 1921); while the corresponding high and low points for the "exports" series were 94, 96, and 64 (in 1920, 1925, and 1921 respectively).

33. Cf. Mackintosh, The Economic Background of Dominion-Provincial Relations, chapters V and VI. The statement regarding Maritime stagnation must be qualified to take account of the severe incidence of the 1919-20 boom and the 1920-2 recession in Nova Scotia. In general, however, the decade of the twenties was a period of negligible expansion for the Maritimes-- indeed, the major development was a "loss of competitive strength in world markets, a worsening in the trade position of their most important exports" (ibid., p. 45). And, in consequence, the Maritimes suffered less from the effects of the Great Depression than did other Canadian regions.

34. The interwar fluctuations of the United States, taken in the aggregate, were of greater severity than those of all other industrial countries. Cf. League of Nations, Economic Stability in the Postwar World (Geneva, 1945), chapters IV and VI; also, United States Department of Commerce, The United States in the World Economy (Washington, 1943), p. 30.

35. The computations for Canada are derived from the figures presented in Table I. The American computations are based on figures obtained from United States Department of Commerce, Statistical Abstract of the United States, 1949 (Washington, 1949), pp. 285, 302, 928; in this connection, see also United States Department of Commerce, Historical Statistics of the United States, 1789-1945, Supplement to the Statistical Abstract of the United States (Washington, 1949), pp. 12, 233, 234.

36. The world figures on the incidence of the Great Depression were calculated on the basis of data provided in League of Nations, World Economic Survey, 1932-33 (Geneva, 1933) pp. 39, 57, 84, 214.

Chapter Two

1. On the scope and character of Canada's role in the first World War, see F. H. Underhill, "Canada and the Last War, " Canada in Peace and War, ed. C. Martin (Toronto, 1941).

2. Figures are derived from the article by J. J. Deutsch, "War Finance and the Canadian Economy, " C. J. E. P. S., VI (Nov. 1940). Complete reliance cannot be placed on the national-income statistics recorded for World War I (see Table I).

3. The wartime picture had its less desirable aspects. The money value of output in the construction industry had actually shrunk by 65 per cent during the 1913-18 period. The increase in real national income had been no more than 10 per cent, and this suggests the degree to which infla-

tionary developments had contributed to the rise in money incomes. As a matter of fact, almost the entire cost of the war had been met by borrowing, and the resultant legacy of expanded bank credit, inflated price levels, and increased public debt was bound to have strong adverse repercussions throughout the Canadian economy. Cf. Deutsch, "War Finance."

4. The divisive role of French Canada cannot, of course, be overlooked. It must, however, be viewed as but one aspect of a sectionalism which Canada characterized throughout the war.

5. For a general discussion of postwar social, political, and economic changes occurring in Canada at that time, see Canada, Report of the Royal Commission on Dominion-Provincial Relations (Ottawa, 1940), book I, chapter IV; also S. Bates, Financial History of Canadian Governments, A Study Prepared for the Royal Commission on Dominion-Provincial Relations (Ottawa, 1939), pp. 58-64.

6. The connotation of the terms "conservative" and "radical," respectively, is intended to be the simple and colourless one of the tendency to adhere to old established doctrine, and of susceptibility to new ideas.

7. Dominion Bureau of Statistics, Canada Year Book, 1941, p. 60.

8. A. R. M. Lower, "The Development of Canadian Economic Ideas," Supplement in J. F. Normano, The Spirit of American Economics (New York, 1943), p. 214.

9. It will be seen that, during much of the interwar period, the East-West division was synonymous with the party alignment in federal politics; that is, the Liberals and Conservatives on the "conservative" side, and the Progressives, members of the Co-operative Commonwealth Federation (C. C. F.), Social Crediters, etc., on the "radical" side.

10. An eastern group, the United Farmers of Ontario (U. F. O.), was prominent in this movement, along with the United Farmers of Alberta (U. F. A.) and the United Farmers of Manitoba (U. F. M.).

11. W. A. Mackintosh, "The General Election of 1921," Queen's Quarterly XXIX (Jan., Feb., March, 1922), p. 312. By 1922, the Progressive party, with 65 seats, had become the second largest group in the House of Commons; and farmers' governments had been returned in Ontario, Manitoba, and Alberta. Further reference to the brief history of the federal party is made in chapter VI. See also, L. A. Wood, A History of Farmers' Movements in Canada (Toronto, 1924), part V; C. Wittke, A History of Canada (5th ed., Toronto, 1941), chapter XXXI; A. R. M. Lower, Colony to Nation (Toronto, 1946), chapter XXXIII; W. L. Morton, The Progressive Party in Canada (Toronto, 1950); D. E. McHenry, The Third Force in Canada (Toronto, 1950), chapter I; S. M. Lipset, Agrarian Socialism (Toronto, 1950), chapter III.

12. J. A. Corry, The Growth of Government Activities since Confederation, A Study Prepared for the Royal Commission on Dominion-Provincial Relations (Ottawa, 1939), pp. 4, 5.

13. For an analysis of the many fallacies and misconceptions in economic reasoning during and immediately after the war, see B. H. Higgins, The War and Postwar Cycle in Canada, 1914-1923, A Report Prepared for

the Advisory Committee on Reconstruction (Ottawa, 1945).

14. Canada, House of Commons Debates (henceforth contracted to Debates), April 14, 1926, III, p. 2430.

15. Ibid., March 20, 1922, I, pp. 238, 239.

16. Ibid., April 24, 1922, II, p. 1073.

17. This is another generalization which requires qualification. It is possible, for example, to go back as far as 1919 to find in the federal realm individual instances of espousal by eastern politicians of a vigorous economic role for government. One such instance is provided by the parliamentary address made by Mr. H. C. Hocken, a Unionist (supporting the coalition administration of Sir Robert L. Borden). Referring to the government's pledge to create a "Department of Health, " Mr. Hocken made the following comments: "The phraseology might be improved; and for my part, I would like to see it described as 'The Department of Public Welfare', which term would include not only health, but many other things that ought to come within the purview of this Government. There was a time not long ago--and I think the idea persists still with some men in representative positions--that Government ought to deal solely with roads, bridges, and tariffs. That has been the idea largely in the past; but during the last decade, particularly upon this North American continent, an entirely new principle, and one which is going to be recognized more fully in the future, has been adopted by many governmental bodies. That principle is that Government is concerned not only with making roads to travel upon and providing other means of transportation, but with looking after the personal welfare of those who are left in such a position that they are unable to take care of themselves." Ibid., March 3, 1919, I, p. 156.

18. W. A. Mackintosh, "The Future Trend of Prices, " Journal of the Canadian Bankers' Association (henceforth contracted to J. C. B. A.), XXXIV (Jan. 1927), p. 151. It should be added that Professor Mackintosh had support from eminent American economists on this issue.

19. Appearing in 1923 before the Banking and Commerce Committee of the House of Commons, Major C. H. Douglas, the founder of Social Credit, declared: "I personally am convinced that, if you go along the lines that you are following at the present, and if you continue along these lines for any considerable period of time, ... you are heading for the most terrific disaster that the mind of man can conceive. " House of Commons, Proceedings of the Select Standing Committee on Banking and Commerce, 1923, p. 443.

20. As can be seen in the annual financial statements of Canadian banks, most bankers, although imbued with the general spirit of optimism pervading the country before the Great Depression, did repeatedly urge caution in view of danger signals ahead, particularly the speculative stock market orgy fast reaching a climax.

21. The World War I experience might well have justified a distrust of old theories. "With few exceptions [the Dominion government] asked and received but little aid from Canadian economists. Too often the advice offered was in the nature of a sermon on the danger of tampering with

economic law, when what was desired and needed was 'practical advice';
practical not in the sense of disregarding theory, but in the sense of linking
theories with actual complex situations, rather than with carefully-selected
groups of facts." W. A. Mackintosh, "Economics, Prices, and the War, "
Queen's Quarterly, XXVI (April, May, June, 1919), p. 452.

22. Debates, Feb. 26, 1923,· I, p. 647.

23. Although Keynes and his followers were advancing new economic
ideas throughout the twenties, those ideas did not receive clear and comprehensive formulation until the thirties--particularly with the publication of the
article by R. F. Kahn, "The Relation of Home Investment to Unemployment, "
Economic Journal, XLI (June 1931); and of J. M. Keynes, The General
Theory of Employment, Interest, and Money (New York, 1936). For the
interesting story of the origins and evolution of the "new economics, " see
R. F. Harrod, The Life of John Maynard Keynes (London, 1951).

24. A distinction should be made between two groups of economists:
(1) those in the universities and in government, whose views were expressed
on a more or less individual basis; and (2) those in the service, and active
in formulating the attitudes, of business and financial groups. This is an
over-simplification to the extent that (a) economists move from one group
to another; (b) economists in the first group formulate governmental attitudes towards policy; and (c) economists in the second group make observations which are dissociated from any particular business or financial
group. It is, nevertheless, a distinction which will be seen to have general
significance in terms of the regional-occupational analysis of Canadian economic thought.

25. Cf. W. C. Clark, Business Cycles and the Depression of 1920-21
(Bulletin no. 40 of the Department of History and Political and Economic
Science, Queen's University, Aug. 1921). Dr. Clark served as Deputy
Minister of Finance from 1932 until his death in 1952. It would be a serious
mistake to appraise his contribution to the formulation of Canadian economic
policy--particularly during the thirties--on the basis of his published writings. The demands imposed upon his time by the responsibilities of his
governmental office and by his own occupational zeal, as well as the conventional restraints associated with high-level work in the civil service,
mitigate against heavy reliance on published material as a guide to his
economic thinking and to his role in the development of public policy. For
insight into his vitally important efforts in both spheres, see: W. A. Mackintosh, "William Clifford Clark: A Personal Memoir, " Queen's Quarterly,
LX (Spring 1953), and "William Clifford Clark and Canadian Economic Policy, " C.J.E.P.S., XIX (Aug. 1953); and R. B. Bryce, "William Clifford
Clark, 1889-1952, " C.J.E.P.S., XIX (Aug. 1953).

By the same token, it would be misleading and unfair to suggest that
contemporary economic thinking of professional economists and others was
fully reflected in the published literature. Oral and unpublished written
elaboration of ideas were crucial forms of communication (as they are now);
nor had social science publication yet become a large-scale Canadian enterprise. The necessary corollary of these truths, however, is that it becomes

exceedingly difficult to present a balanced and comprehensive picture of
the interrelationships between economic thought and policy in Canada during the interwar period.

26. Clark, Business Cycles and the Depression of 1920-21, p. 5.

27. On this aspect of the war experience, see Higgins, The War and
Postwar Cycle in Canada, 1914-1923.

28. Clark, Business Cycles and the Depression of 1920-21, p. 24.
Compare Dr. Clark's economic fatalism with that expressed by the then
Prime Minister, Mr. A. Meighen, with reference to a proposal that the
government spend $50 million in the form of loans to war veterans for
their housing needs. Such a scheme would not be "strict economy; it is
not reasonable assistance, bringing results commensurate with costs or
anything like it, to enter upon programs of construction merely or mainly
for the sake of employment. To do so may relieve for a short time, but it
only arrests the necessary process of deflation. It only artificially sustains
a situation which, as long as it is sustained, merely postpones the suffer-
ings incident to deflation, which, in some form or another, must come before normal conditions return." Debates, June 2, 1921, V, p. 4362.

29. G. E. Jackson, "Wheat and the Trade Cycle," Canadian Historical Review, III (Sept. 1922), p. 265.

30. H. Michell, "Banking and the Trade Cycle," J. C. B. A., XXX
(Jan. 1923), p. 254. In more general terms, Professor Michell cautioned
as follows: "The problem of the economic cycle is... still an unsolved
mystery. We can diagnose the symptoms with exactness, we can even
prescribe certain palliatives that may, or may not, be partially successful:
but the real secret still eludes us. We know very well indeed that this so-
called cycle recurs at varying intervals; we can recognize its inception,
its course, and its end. We can, with the modern refinements of statistical
methods, measure it with accuracy. But what is the real fundamental cause
of it? We don't know." Michell, "The Business Cycle," Canadian Forum,
III, (June 1923).

31. H. Michell, "The Rate of Turnover of Bank Deposits," J. C. B. A.,
XXXVII (Jan. 1930), p. 168.

32. Debates, April 17, 1925, III, p. 2151; May 7, 1926, IV, p. 3215.

33. Ibid., Feb. 24, 1928, I, pp. 766, 767.

34. Ibid., June 5, 1922, III, p. 2502.

35. In time, Mr. Irvine came to combine the economic analysis of
Social Credit with the socialistic approach early espoused by Mr. Woodsworth.

36. Debates, March 20, 1922, I, pp. 219, 221; June 5, 1922, III,
p. 2500.

37. Haberler, Prosperity and Depression, p. 119.

38. L. R. Klein, The Keynesian Revolution (New York, 1947), p. 137.
It is of interest to note, in this connection, that the temporary maladjustment caused by the mere act of saving (disregarding the problem of investment outlets)--as elaborated, for example, in the Foster-Catchings time-
sequence analysis--really has never been adequately refuted or appraised

by professional economists. Cf. F. A. Hayek, "The Paradox of Saving, " Economica, no. 32 (May 1931).

Quite apart from such short-run stability difficulties, there is the grave possibility--ignored by Keynes and towards which the underconsumptionists may have been groping--that the long-run additions made by investment to a country's productive capacity may mean that the maintenance of savings-investment equilibrium is an insufficient condition for stability at high employment and income levels. Stated in Robertsonian terms, it may be that "it is not sufficient... that savings of yesterday be invested today, or, as it is often expressed, that investment offset saving. Investment of today must always exceed savings of yesterday. A mere absence of hoarding will not do. An injection of new money (or dishoarding) must take place every day. Moreover, this injection must proceed, in absolute terms, at an accelerated rate. The economy must continually expand." E. D. Domar, "Expansion and Employment, " American Economic Review, XXXVII (March 1947), p. 42. Cf. also: R. F. Harrod, Towards a Dynamic Economics (London, 1948); J. R. Hicks, A Contribution to the Theory of the Trade Cycle (Oxford, 1950); and R. Eisner, "Guaranteed Growth of Income, " Econometrica, XXI (Jan. 1953).

39. In response to frequent attacks, Douglas made repeated definitional changes.

40. That the retailer is the central figure in the A + B theorem appears highly probable from an examination of Douglas' writings. On this matter, see H. T. N. Gaitskell, "Four Monetary Heretics, " What Everybody Wants to Know about Money, ed. G. D. H. Cole (New York, 1933). For other sources of refutation of the Douglas fallacies, see: The Labour Party, Labour and Social Credit: A Report on the Proposals of Major Douglas and the "New Age" (London, n. d.); D. Copland, Facts and Fallacies of Douglas Credit (Melbourne, 1932); E. F. M. Durbin, Purchasing Power and Trade Depression (London, 1933); H. Belshaw, The Douglas Fallacy (Auckland, 1933); H. McQueen, six articles in the Winnipeg Free Press (beginning March 5, 1934); League for Social Reconstruction, Social Planning for Canada; S. G. Moulton, The Formation of Capital (Washington, 1935); D. A. MacGibbon, "Inflation and Inflationism, " C. J. E. P. S., I (Aug. 1935); J. F. Parkinson, "The Economics of Mr. Aberhart, " Canadian Forum, XV (Nov. 1935); Australia, Report of the Royal Commission on the Monetary and Banking Systems (Canberra, 1937), chapter V; A. H. Hansen, Full Recovery or Stagnation? (New York, 1938), chapter IV; M. G. Meyers, Monetary Proposals for Social Reform (New York, 1940), chapter IV; Klein, The Keynesian Revolution, chapter V; C. B. Macpherson, Democracy in Alberta (Toronto, 1953), chapter IV.

41. Keynes, The General Theory of Employment, Interest, and Money, p. 371.

Chapter Three
1. Cf. R. G. Hawtrey, Currency and Credit (London, 1919, 1923, 1928), and Trade and Credit (London, 1928); I. Fisher, The Purchasing

Power of Money (New York, 1922), and The Theory of Interest (New York 1930); J. M. Keynes, A Tract on Monetary Reform (London, 1924), and A Treatise on Money (2 vols., New York, 1930). Wicksell occupies a position of distinction among these writers, although his most prominent works (Interest and Prices, London, 1936, and Lectures on Political Economy, London, 1934-5) originally appeared (in German) at the turn of the twentieth century (Jena, 1898 and 1906, respectively). For comprehensive analysis of the development of monetary theory, see A. W. Marget, The Theory of Prices (2 vols., New York, 1938).

2. It was not until the early thirties that these three economists began to part company. Fisher's position remained substantially unchanged. Hawtrey's important contribution was an increased recognition of the importance of the income flow. Keynes, of course, made the greatest change of all--a drastic shift of emphasis from the monetary to the fiscal sphere. (Interestingly enough, evidence of a current reverse monetary trend is not unimpressive.)

3. No distinction is made, throughout this investigation, between Progressives and those individuals (like Mr. Irvine after 1926, and Mr. Coote) associated with semi-autonomous radical groups such as U. F. A., which retained provincial importance after the Progressive party had ceased, and the C. C. F. party had begun to be significant in federal politics.

4. For a more detailed treatment of this matter, see: B. H. Beckhart, "The Banking System of Canada," in Foreign Banking Systems, eds. H. P. Willis and B. H. Beckhart (New York, 1929); C. A. Curtis, "The Canadian Monetary Situation," Journal of Political Economy (henceforth contracted to J. P. E.), XI (June 1932); J. Holladay, The Canadian Banking System (Boston, 1938); M. K. Inman, "Experience in Canadian Banking, 1929-1934," unpublished Ph. D. thesis (Harvard University, 1938); M. L. Stokes, The Bank of Canada (Toronto, 1939), pp. 1-26.

5. The Canadian banking system had undergone a steady process of concentration, partly through failures and liquidations, but largely through mergers. Thus, between 1901 and 1913, there had been a reduction from thirty-four banks to twenty-five. In 1931, only ten banks remained. Stokes, The Bank of Canada, p. 3.

6. Legislative changes have, in fact, been made at irregular intervals, though bank charters continue to be renewed on a ten-year basis. The most recent statutory revision received parliamentary approval in 1954.

7. It should be understood, however, that common policy among the banks was basically the result of the heavy concentration of banking control in Toronto and Montreal. The true function performed by the Canadian Bankers' Association was the formalizing and strengthening of the long-existent practice of bank co-operation.

8. Cf. Stokes, The Bank of Canada, pp. 2, 4.

9. League of Nations, International Currency Experience (Princeton, 1944), pp. 98, 99.

10. It is, perhaps, more accurate to state that Canada first abandoned

the gold standard on August 10, 1914, when an Order-in-Council was decreed, suspending the redemption of Dominion notes in specie. The "suspension" provision (among others) of the Finance Act did not actually become effective until September 3, 1914; on that date, the Order-in-Council was revoked. Cf. Beckhart, "The Banking System of Canada," in Foreign Banking Systems, p. 389; and Holladay, The Canadian Banking System, pp. 188, 190.

11. As noted below, no operational content was given the Treasury Board's powers of monetary supervision. The fact is that initiative under the Finance Act was largely in the hands of the commercial banks; and, indeed, that the latter's discretion was limited by their customary attempted maintenance of predetermined ratios between primary and secondary reserves.

12. The same term was used to describe the then-prevailing Canadian outlook on international monetary relations by J. H. Creighton, Central Banking in Canada (Vancouver, 1933), p. 169.

13. The same analysis can, with some qualification, be applied to the process of multiple credit contraction.

14. Debates, May 18, 1920, III, p. 2480.

15. Debates, April 14, 1926, vol. III, p. 2416.

16. The monetary views of Dr. Clark and Professor Michell, outlined in the preceding chapter, had an important bearing on this problem.

17. Debates, June 18, 1923, V, p. 4020; April 14, 1926, III, pp. 2416, 2420.

18. Cf. ibid., May 8, 1924, II, p. 1894.

19. Ibid.

20. The following argument, made in 1926 by Mr. J. A. Robb, Minister of Finance, would seem to imply that the members of the government shared this attitude of distrust with the bankers; "I do not object to bringing gentlemen before the Committee on Banking and Commerce who are able to give us information that will be of any value, but as to our paying heavy travelling expenses for men who have simply theories to advance and who come possibly from a long distance and have heavy accounts, I submit that the ... Committee might very well pass upon that, and help the Finance Minister to keep down expenses." Ibid., April 14, 1926, III, p. 2429.

21. House of Commons, Proceedings of the Select Standing Committee on Banking and Commerce (henceforth contracted to House Banking Committee Proceedings), 1923, pp. 352, 379.

22. Ibid., p. 406.

23. Ibid., p. 325.

24. Mackintosh, The Economic Background of Dominion-Provincial Relations, p. 98.

25. House Banking Committee Proceedings, 1923, p. 541.

26. Mackintosh, The Economic Background of Dominion-Provincial Relations, p. 100.

27. See, for example, the speeches of such farseeing (pro-central

bank) men as Mr. D. R. Wilkie, a former President of the Imperial Bank of Canada and of the Canadian Bankers' Association; Mr. E. L. Pease, a former President of the Royal Bank of Canada and of the Canadian Bankers' Association; and Mr. W. F. Maclean, Conservative member of Parliament from 1892 to 1926. Probably the earliest suggestion for the establishment of a central bank in Canada was that of the Governor-General, Lord Sydenham, in 1841 (see A. F. W. Plumptre, "The Arguments for Central Banking in the British Dominions, " Essays in Political Economy, ed. H. A. Innis, Toronto, 1938, p. 193).

    28. House Banking Committee Proceedings, 1923, p. 26.

    29. Ibid., p. 325.

    30. Ibid., p. 282.

    31. Ibid., p. 511.

    32. Ibid., p. 559. Sir John Aird's point of view was substantially the same, as was that of Mr. H. T. Ross, Secretary of the Canadian Bankers' Association, who said that he "would hesitate offhand to express an opinion" as to whether there was any relationship between the amount of money in circulation and the price level. Ibid., p. 113.

    33. Ibid., p. 878. The nature and significance of these attitudes have been more thoroughly summarized by a member of the 1933 Canadian Royal Commission on Banking and Currency: "Canadian bankers ... placed an exaggerated and unwarranted emphasis on the automatic action of the gold standard in regulating the volume of currency and the internal price level and disclaimed for their part any responsibility for their control.... This was not, they held, a banking function at all. These were matters which might safely be left to the play of supply and demand without any interference on the part of the banks. The proper functions of a bank began and ended with receiving deposits from one section of the community and lending them out to another. The truth, of course, was far otherwise. The Banks had no choice in the matter.... [They] had in fact been managing the currency all along.... They could not help themselves. Consciously or unconsciously, whether they liked it or not, it was the banks who, by their daily operations, were responsible for regulating the volume of credit by which the stability of the price level ... was largely determined." Sir C. Addis, "Canada and Its Banks, " J. C. B. A., XLII (Oct. 1934), p.42.

    34. House Banking Committee Proceedings, 1923, p. 298.

    35. Ibid., p. 558

    36. Ibid., p. 363.

    37. Ibid., 1924, p. 278.

    38. Ibid., 1928, p. 22.

    39. That American bankers were similarly impressed is evident from the opinion expressed in 1924 before the Banking Committee by Mr. J. W. Pole, Chief National Bank Examiner of the United States, that the Finance Act provided Canada with practically every facility that the Federal Reserve System offered the United States, and at far less cost. Ibid., 1924, p. 139. Appearing four years later before this Committee, Mr. W. P. G. Harding, Governor of the Federal Reserve Bank of Boston, stated: "I have

never heard any criticism of the Canadian banking system in the United States. We have always regarded it as a system that, under your conditions, was adequate." Ibid., 1928, p. 90.

40. House Banking Committee Proceedings, 1928, p. 52.

41. Ibid., p. 1.

42. There is a strong presumption in favour of this generalization--and it is hardly more than that, since, as already noted, there were important exceptions, such as Mr. W. F. Maclean, who had been espousing the central bank idea since 1913. The presumption is based partly on the fact that the two Finance Acts received less parliamentary consideration than any other major change previously made in Canadian monetary legislation. The discussion of the 1914 Act occupies only half a dozen pages in the debates of the House of Commons; the discussion of the 1923 Act about three pages. It is to be doubted if the government or the public ever adequately realized the significance of these Acts. In the second place, it is highly probable that the following opinion of Mr. H. Marler, Liberal member of Parliament in 1924, typified the approach of rank-and-file Liberals and Conservatives: "Our Finance Act as it is now and our branch bank system as it is now fully cover all the necessities of elasticity of credit and banking in this country, and our Finance Act as it exists is quite sufficient to meet the requirements without any question of a federal reserve bank being taken into consideration at all." Debates, July 2, 1924, IV, p. 3945.

43. Ibid., June 19, 1923, V, p. 4092. In 1926, the next Minister of Finance, Mr. J. A. Robb, was more to the point in supporting the bankers' judgment that the banking system of the Dominion was quite suited to the country's requirements. Ibid., April 14, 1926, III, pp. 2427, 2428.

44. Cf. W. A. Mackintosh, "Doctoring the Gold Standard," J. C. B. A., XXXI (Oct. 1923), pp. 67, 69.

45. G. E. Jackson, "The Gold Standard (III)," Canadian Forum, IV (April 1924), p. 22.

46. Dr. Shortt had been a federal civil servant since 1908, when he had resigned as Professor of Political Science at Queen's University. However, he was, unlike most contemporary civil servants, a professional economist--in fact one of the first economists that Canada produced. For this reason, his views are considered here. It should be added that Dr. Shortt was also one of the first Canadians to forge what was to become a vital link between academic economists and civil servants, and so to render unrealistic any rigid separation of these two groups.

47. Professor Fisher had explained to the Banking Committee that his proposal was designed to eliminate cyclical fluctuations by making statutory changes in the gold value of the dollar commensurate with changes in the level of prices.

48. House Banking Committee Proceedings, 1923, p. 682.

49. Ibid., p. 693.

50. Ibid., p. 776.

51. Ibid., p. 798. It could be argued that this view was not inconsis-

tent with the contention that unsound banking policy was not the primary, independent causal factor in the 1921 breakdown. It remains open to question, however, whether this was the interpretation that Professor Swanson wished to be made; and, in any case, whether it would have clarified all the ambiguities and conflicts in his testimony.

52. Ibid., p. 795.

53. Ibid., p. 783.

54. Among the members of the Progressive group who made motions in favour of central and national banking were (dates and pages of Hansard in parentheses): Mr. Irvine (May 1, 1922, p. 1289; Feb. 26, 1923, p. 627); Mr. J. T. Shaw (May 21, 1924, p. 2371); and Mr. Woodsworth (March 4, 1925, p. 753; April 14, 1926, p. 2416; Feb. 13, 1928, p. 387). As already noted, the term "Progressive group" is here broadly interpreted. Thus, in the present instance, it comprises one Independent (Mr. Shaw) and two Labour representatives.

55. In 1923 Mr. Bevington, an Alberta farmer and articulate monetary reformer, told the Banking and Commerce Committee (as did Major Douglas) that financial credit should be based, not on the traditional types of collateral, but on the number, intelligence, and industry of the people, plus the capital equipment and natural resources of the country. His particular proposal would have resulted "in the Dominion government supplying a constant stream of legal tender notes, a definite and continuous redemption of which was not contemplated, and which ultimately would lead to dangerous inflation." Stokes, Bank of Canada, p. 46.

56. This is not to deny the contributory importance of other forces in the eventual creation of Canada's central bank. Of particular interest, in this connection, is the fact that the timing of, and at least part of the rationale for, the establishment of the Canadian Macmillan Commission were closely associated with the monetary conclusions reached at the Ottawa Conference of 1932, where expanded central banking was recommended as a significant prerequisite to the resurrection of the gold standard.

57. Notable contributions to the central bank debate were also made by Mr. Garland, Mr. Shaw, and Mr. L. J. Ladner (a western Liberal-Conservative). Their views, as well as those of the entire radical group, were well represented in the proposals advanced by the three men cited in the text.

58. Debates, Feb. 13, 1928, I, p. 393.

59. Ibid., 1924, IV, pp. 3938, 3939.

60. Ibid., pp. 3949, 3950.

61. Ibid., p. 3951.

62. Cf. Higgins, The War and Postwar Cycle in Canada, 1914-23; Canada, Report of the Royal Commission on Dominion-Provincial Relations (Ottawa, 1940); Mackintosh, The Economic Background of Dominion-Provincial Relations.

63. Higgins, The War and Postwar Cycle in Canada, 1914-23, p. 40.

64. C. A. Curtis, Statistical Contributions to Canadian Economic History, (Toronto, 1931), I, pp. 27, 46, 50, 51, 53.

65. Cf. Higgins, The War and Postwar Cycle in Canada, 1914-23, p. 58.

66. Cf. C. A. Curtis, "Canada and the Gold Standard," Queen's Quarterly (Winter 1931), and "The Canadian Monetary Situation," J. P. E., XI (June 1932); A. F. W. Plumptre, "Our Glittering Monetary Standard," Dalhousie Review, XI (Oct. 1931); C. Elliott, "Bank Cash," C. J. E. P. S., IV (Aug. 1938); A. N. McLeod, "Maintaining Employment and Incomes in Canada," unpublished Ph.D. thesis (Cambridge, Mass., 1949), chapter VII.

67. Curtis, Statistical Contributions to Canadian Economic History, I, pp. 27, 51, 53.

68. Plumptre, "Our Glittering Monetary Standard," p. 305.

69. Curtis, "The Canadian Monetary Situation," p. 324.

70. Ibid. The fact of relative stability in the volume of chartered bank cash should not, of course, obscure the inflationary effects of operations under the Finance Act.

71. Stokes, Bank of Canada, pp. 23, 24.

72. F. A. Knox, Dominion Monetary Policy, 1929-1934, A Study Prepared for the Royal Commission on Dominion-Provincial Relations (Ottawa, 1939), p. 57. The convertibility of Dominion notes into gold was not formally suspended until April 10, 1933. Ibid. (But see Holladay, The Canadian Banking System, p. 190, for the view that Canada's second abandonment of the gold standard occurred in May 1932. This discrepancy may result simply from the use of different criteria of abandonment-- legislation in one case, and administrative decree in the other.)

73. Elliott, "Bank Cash," C. J. E. P. S., IV (Aug. 1938), p. 442.

74. There are undoubtedly those who would deny the possibility of "errors of commercial bank policy" on the ground that the monetary policy of a country is not the responsibility of the commercial banks. In the writer's view, this line of reasoning misses the main point at issue, namely, whether the successful execution of monetary policy, especially within the structural framework of an economy like Canada's, is not exceedingly difficult, if not impossible, in the absence of an "economics-enlightened" commercial banking community.

75. No attempt was made to use the rediscount rate for control purposes. From 1914 until November 1924, the rate stood at 5 per cent. From November 1, 1924, to November 1, 1927, it was 4 1/2 per cent. On November 1, 1927, it was reduced to 4 per cent, and one month later it was further reduced to 3 3/4 per cent, where it remained until June 8, 1928, when it was increased to 5 per cent. On September 1, 1928, the rate was lowered to 4 1/2 per cent, where it remained until October 26, 1931, when it was reduced to 3 per cent. It would appear from these figures that no very specific reasoning actuated the Treasury Board in changing the rate. The evidence given before the House Banking and Commerce Committee in 1924 and 1928 corroborates this view. The only criterion of rate-setting which did receive mention was the general position of money rates in New York. However, a comparison of the Finance Act rate with that of the Rederal Reserve Bank of New York, or the commercial paper

rate in New York, shows no close connection. Cf. Curtis, "The Canadian Monetary Situation, " pp. 326, 327.

Chapter Four

1. J. B. Say, Treatise on Political Economy, translation from 4th French edition (Boston, 1824), book III, p. 195. Actually there were always exceptions to this rule. By the end of the nineteenth century, there had arisen a widespread acceptance of a subsidiary function of government expenditure, and of taxation, as an instrument of social policy. It was generally admitted that expenditure on social objects such as health, education, and--particularly in the young, expanding economies like Canada--public services (including railways and the generation of power), was beneficial and "socially productive." Moreover, there was a marked trend--reinforced by the war--towards the substitution of the principle of ability to pay for that of equal sacrifice, and this led to increasingly progressive and redistributive tax structures.

2. League of Nations, Economic Stability in the Postwar World, part II of the Report of the Delegation on Economic Depressions (Geneva, 1945), p. 163.

3. Among these basic factors were: (a) the declining rate of population growth; (b) the rising demand for luxury goods of all kinds, for durable consumer goods, and for capital goods; (c) the increasing institutional rigidities in the form of concentration of control in industry and aggressive trade unionism; and (d) the repercussions of war. Cf. League of Nations, Economic Stability in the Postwar World, pp. 25-40.

4. Cf. Dominion Bureau of Statistics, Canada Year Book, 1924; S. Bates, Financial History of Canadian Governments, A Study Prepared for the Royal Commission on Dominion-Provincial Relations (Ottawa, 1939); J. J. Deutsch, "War Finance and the Canadian Economy, 1914-20, " C.J.E.P.S., VI (Nov. 1940); J. H. Perry, Taxes, Tariffs, and Subsidies: A History of Canadian Fiscal Development (Toronto, 1955), I, chapters IX-XII.

5. Canada, Report of the Royal Commission on Dominion-Provincial Relations, Book III (Ottawa, 1940), p. 30.

6. The trebling of the rate of profits during the war suggests that this view may have been carried too far. As a matter of fact, the anti-inflationary powers of taxation were not generally understood--either before or during the war, or throughout the twenties.

7. The following figures illustrate the magnitude of this expansion: wholesale prices rose 99 per cent, and cost of living 49 per cent, between 1914 and 1918; export prices, 95 per cent; wage rates, 47 per cent; currency in the hands of the public (subsidiary coin, bank notes, and Dominion notes), 92 per cent; public bank deposits (demand and notice), 65 per cent; total bank loans, 32 per cent; and total bank holdings of government securities, 1,270 per cent. Deutsch, "War Finance and the Canadian Economy, 1914-20, " C.J.E.P.S., VI (Nov. 1940), pp. 541, 542; C. A. Curtis, Statistical Contributions to Canadian Economic History (Toronto, 1931), I,

pp. 24, 47, 48, 50.

8. C.Y.B., 1938, pp. 848, 851.

9. Ibid.

10. Although not adopted until 1920, the federal sales tax was also really a war tax, in that it was primarily designed--at its inception at least--to defray a substantial portion of the obligations incurred in connection with the war.

11. These percentages were computed from the national income figures provided in Deutsch, "War Finance and the Canadian Economy, 1914-20," p. 538.

12. C.Y.B., 1941, p. 772.

13. Ibid., p. 752.

14. Among the important federal per capita increases, during the 1914-19 period, were the following: ordinary expenditures, from $16.2 to $28.0; total expenditures, from $23.6 to $83.9; total net national debt, from $42.6 to $189.5; interest paid on the debt, from $1.6 to $9.3. Total Dominion expenditures for fiscal 1919 amounted to 19 per cent of the national income, as against 8 per cent in 1914. Ibid. pp. 752, 755, 772; and Deutsch, "War Finance and the Canadian Economy, 1914-20," p. 538.

15. Report of Royal Commission on Dominion-Provincial Relations, Book III, p. 23; Deutsch, "War Finance and the Canadian Economy, 1914-20," p. 540. These figures include Dominion advances to the Canadian National Railways.

It is essential to distinguish the new "national income" approach from that used in compiling statistics of public finance. The definition of "capital" and "current" (there are only minor differences between "current" and "ordinary") expenditures used in the "public finance" approach varies for different governments and different years, despite the fact that this procedure presumably confines the term "public investment" to outlay on capital account. "Public investment" now usually denotes the total expenditure by government for the purpose of either maintaining or expanding the productive equipment of the nation, and the net changes of government holdings in inventories and foreign assets. But on the one hand, items that do not conform to this modern concept of public investment often have been included in capital account; while on the other hand, many truly "investment" items are charged to current account. The "national income" approach has not yet been extended back beyond 1926. Consequently, the older approach, with all its limitations, must be used for the war period. Cf. Dominion-Provincial Conference on Reconstruction, Public Investment and Capital Formation (Ottawa, 1945), p. 14; and Department of Trade and Commerce, Private and Public Investment in Canada, 1926-1951 (Ottawa, 1951).

16. A detailed analysis of provincial and municipal fiscal structures and policies is beyond the scope of this inquiry. The general treatment accorded them here is intended merely as background for the interpretation of (1) fiscal thought and policy in the federal sphere, and (2) the issue which was already approaching the crucial stage during the twenties,

namely, Dominion-provincial fiscal relations. The statistical data available for World War I and the interwar period are, in any case, neither complete nor fully comparable.

Among the useful sources for more intensive treatment of the provincial and municipal fields are: C. Y. B., 1914 and 1920; H. L. Brittain, "Municipal Taxation in Canada, " Annals of the American Academy of Political and Social Science, CVII (May, 1923); Canada, Comparative Statistics of Public Finance, 1913, 1921, 1925-1939, Public Accounts Inquiry of the Royal Commission on Dominion-Provincial Relations (Ottawa, 1939); Report of Royal Commission on Dominion-Provincial Relations, books I and III; W. A. Mackintosh, The Economic Background of Dominion-Provincial Relations; S. Bates, Financial History of Canadian Governments; H. C. Goldenberg, Municipal Finance in Canada, Studies Prepared for the Royal Commission on Dominion-Provincial Relations (Ottawa, 1939); J. R. Petrie, "The Tax Systems of Canada, " 2 vols., unpublished Ph. D. thesis (McGill University, 1941); Dominion-Provincial Conference on Reconstruction, Public Investment and Capital Formation; D. C. MacGregor, "The Problem of Price Level in Canada, " Appendix, C. J. E. P. S., XIII (May 1947); Department of Trade and Commerce, Private and Public Investment in Canada, 1926-1951; H. E. Brazer "Coordination in Canadian Federal Finance, " unpublished Ph. D. thesis (Columbia University, 1952); Perry, Taxes, Tariffs, and Subsidies, I, parts IV-VI.

17. This is not to argue that the Dominion government had no revenue problems. They did not, however, involve structural limitations, but the central question as to how best to utilize the many revenue sources available.

18. Although Progressive thought often tended towards the other extreme of dismissing tariff questions as unimportant, the Progressives did show an understanding of balance-of-payments analysis which was not widely shared. Mr. Coote, for example, criticized the Dominion government for placing too much emphasis on the concept of a "favourable balance of trade. " This concept, he pointed out, "may mean much or little because there are so many invisible factors entering into it. If we are just entering on a period of great prosperity and a large influx of foreign capital is beginning, we are likely to have a decrease in our favourable trade balance, largely due to the fact that this inflow of capital comes mainly in the form of goods. I think this statement is proved by a study of our trade balance with the United States, and the large increase of American capital invested in Canada during the years 1914 to 1923. " Debates, February 21, 1927, I, p. 500.

Mr. Woodsworth took issue with Mr. R. B. Bennett--later to become Conservative Prime Minister--on the latter's concern over the fact that Canadian trade with various countries did not always balance, and that in some particular instances Canadian imports were greater than exports. Mr. Woodsworth argued that: "Trade is not always direct, and we have all sorts of three-cornered, four-cornered, and six-cornered trades. We all know the place the clearing house has in ordinary banking affairs, and I submit that in the world's great clearing house it is a matter of comparative indifference on what bank my cheque is drawn. In our analysis of [trade] figures, we must take into account the larger and more compli- cated relations, not simply the figures which relate to the direct traffic between one nation and the other.... Some of those who seek protection as the cure-all for our social ills ... have not realized fully that we can export only as we import; ... the one process is absolutely dependent on the other. If we hinder importation, we hinder exportation, and if we in- crease the one, we are liable to increase the other, indeed, we must ulti- mately increase it. " Ibid., p. 526. It would, perhaps, be unreasonable to expect Mr. Woodsworth, at that early stage, to have made the important distinction between short-run, export-balance, employment policy on the one hand, and long-run, trade-maximizing policy on the other.

19. O. J. McDiarmid, Commercial Policy in the Canadian Economy (Cambridge, Mass., 1946), p. 271.

20. Cf. ibid., pp. 265-8.

21. Ibid., p. vi.

22. Debates, May 9, 1921, IV, pp. 3116, 3117. That in other respects Sir Henry was a keen monetary and financial observer, is shown both in the preceding chapter and later in this chapter.

23. Ibid., May 23, 1922, III, pp. 2104, 2106, 2116.

24. Ibid., May 18, 1926, IV, p. 3498; March 13, 1928, II, p. 1290; April 9, 1929, II, p. 1404.

25. Ibid., May 13, 1921, IV, p. 3345.

26. Ibid., May 17, 1923, III, p. 2842.

27. Mr. J. L. Ilsley, Canada's Liberal Minister of Finance during World War II, dissented, at least by implication, from some of these majority views. It was his opinion early in 1929, that "the policy of ... budgeting for large surpluses, and applying those surpluses to the reduc- tion of the national debt in these periods of prosperity, is the proper policy for the national welfare"; that the sales tax was rightly being reduced in- stead of the income tax; and that the former should be reduced by degrees and eventually eliminated. Ibid., March 15, 1929, I, p. 996.

Mr. Ilsley's remarks on the sales tax was the argument that the anti- inflationary effects of the sales tax were more than offset by its regressive income effects; though this may be attributing to him a greater measure of sophistication in economic outlook than he actually possessed at that early stage. In approving the sales tax reduction, he may have been completely overlooking the resultant inflationary danger in a boom year.

28. Debates, March 26, 1925, vol. II, p. 1580; April 28, 1925, vol. III, p. 2561.

29. Ibid., June 5, 1922, III, pp. 2496-9.

30. Even before the Progressive group assumed national importance, there were individual instances of the advocacy of social security legisla- tion by parliamentarians associated with the orthodox political parties. One such instance is afforded by Mr. H. C. Hocken, a Unionist (see chap- ter II, n. 18), who, as early as 1919, expressed himself in favour of a comprensive system of unemployment insurance, old age pensions, and

mothers' allowances. Debates, March 3, 1919, I, pp. 156, 157.

31. Mr. Woodsworth's first parliamentary request for an extensive system of unemployment insurance was made in 1922. Debates, April 24, 1922, II, pp. 1069-72. This he followed up with discussions of social-security issues throughout the decade. Mr. Heaps entered the controversy in 1926, and by 1929 he had thrice advanced the motion--carried (though not put into effect) on the third occasion--"that, in the opinion of this House, the committee on industrial and international relations be instructed to investigate and report on the establishment of a system of insurance against unemployment, sickness, and invalidity." Ibid., March 16, 1927, I, p. 1262; see, also, ibid., Jan. 19, 1926, I, pp. 276-8; Feb. 16, 1928, I, pp. 561-5; Feb. 14, 1929, I, p. 145.)

32. In 1922 Mr. Woodsworth suggested that "the government should go into the matter of unemployment and establish a system of unemployment insurance. Not that such a system would provide work, but it would give immediate and definite relief to those who are out of work, and in the effort to provide for their immediate needs we would find ourselves driven to do something along constructive lines." Ibid., April 24, 1922, vol. II, p. 1072.

33. Concrete examples cited by the radicals were: the Liberal and Conservative party platforms of 1919 and 1927, respectively; and the social security recommendations of the Conservative-appointed Royal Commission on Industrial Relations (cf. Canada, Report of the Royal Commission on Industrial Relations, Ottawa, 1919, pp. 8, 19).

34. In 1927 the Liberal Administration did take action in one social security field. The Old Age Pensions Act authorized the nation-wide establishment of non-contributory pension systems, co-operatively financed by the Dominion and the provinces, and contingent upon complementary legislation by each province.

35. Debates, June 5, 1922, III, p. 2506. In general, the Progressives placed greatest reliance on direct taxation, particularly the personal income tax.

36. Ibid., May 8, 1924, II, pp. 1897, 1898.

37. Ibid., May 15, 1924, III, p. 2156.

38. Ibid., March 6, 1928, I, pp. 1075, 1076.

39. Ibid., March 7, 1929, I, pp. 760, 761.

40. Ibid., March 14, 1929, I, pp. 965-967.

41. Ibid., Feb. 20, 1928, I, p. 639.

42. Quoted in S. E. Harris, The National Debt and the New Economics (New York, 1947), p. 68.

43. The idea of this super sales tax originated with Sir Edmund Walker, President of the Canadian Bank of Commerce. In 1927 it was advanced by Mr. R. B. Bennett as best complying with the accepted principles of taxation: "It is simple, it is universal, it is convenient, it is equal, it is easily collected--it has all the qualifications that were mentioned by the late Adam Smith, and, in addition to that, it meets with modern conditions, and will help solve many of the difficulties that we have in this country today." Debates, Feb. 17, 1927, I, pp. 403, 404. The Progressives were quick to

point out the highly restrictive aspects of such a tax, in terms of its effects on private consumption expenditure.

44. H. R. Kemp, "The Sales Tax," Canadian Forum, III (July 1923), pp. 288, 289. The following comment made by Mr. Kemp in the same year provides a clear indication of the attitude of Canadian business interests towards the sales tax: "The sales tax has been favourably received in Canada (so far as any new tax can be said to be welcome), and it seems to be regarded, at least by the business community, as the most promising instrument for abolishing the national deficit. Unlike the customs duties, it does not offend the free trader; its ease of collection, its dependability, its elasticity, render it satisfactory from the administrative point of view; and it receives further influential support from the belief that it is entirely shifted to consumers, does not constitute a fresh burden upon "business," and does not check the accumulation of capital. In public discussions, not much has been heard with regard to its final incidence, its justice, or its probable remote effects." H. R. Kemp, "Dominion and Provincial Taxation in Canada," Annals of the American Academy of Political and Social Science, CVII (May 1923), p. 217.

45. W. A. Mackintosh, "Canadian Politics," Queen's Quarterly, XXXI (Jan., Feb., March, 1924), p. 330.

46. W. B. Hurd, "The Trend of Federal Taxation and Expenditure," J.C.B.A., XXXVI (Oct. 1928), p. 27.

47. J. B. Alexander, "Business Depressions," J.C.B.A., XXXIV, (July 1927), p. 447.

48. All references regarding changes in revenue yields and expenditures are to fiscal years.

49. C.Y.B., 1924, pp. 742, 744.

50. Ibid., p. 744. Business men and financial leaders generally were opposed to the business profits war tax, and this opposition undoubtedly had much to do with its reduction and eventual abandonment. Cf. Higgins, The War and Postwar Cycle in Canada, 1914-23, p. 47.

Custom duties were also adjusted downward in terms of (1) repeal of the 5 per cent levy on British goods and the 7 1/2 per cent duty on other commodities, and (2) reduction of the tariffs on cement and agricultural implements. The latter change may have contributed considerably to the intensification of the construction boom, and the expansion of acreage and employment devoted to field crops. On the other hand, the tariff reductions may well have mitigated the inflationary tendencies by channeling domestic demand into foreign sources of supply. Partly because of such uncertainties, but even more so because (as already noted), the "stability" implications of tariff policy were then largely ignored, it is not incorporated into the taxt of the fiscal-policy survey made above.

51. C.Y.B., 1924, p. 744.

52. Higgins, The War and Postwar Cycle in Canada, 1914-23, p. 39.

53. C.Y.B., 1941, p. 754.

54. Ibid., p. 754.

55. Ibid., p. 744.

56. The "luxury" taxes, with minor exceptions, were abolished in December 1920, but by that time the downswing was well under way.

57. Sales tax increases were enacted in 1921.

58. C. Y. B. , 1924, p. 744.

59. Ibid.

60. Ibid. The yield from customs and excise duties fell very little (5 per cent) between 1920 and 1921, rates having remained substantially unaltered; falling national income was primarily responsible for the greater drop (29 per cent) in 1922. Ibid. , p. 742.

61. Higgins, The War and Postwar Cycle in Canada, 1914-23, p. 57.

62. C. Y. B. , 1941, pp. 753, 754.

63. Ibid. , p. 753.

64. Deutsch, "War Finance and the Canadian Economy, " p. 540; Report of Royal Commission on Dominion-Provincial Relations, book III, p. 23; C. Y. B. , 1941, p. 753.

65. It should be noted, by way of qualification of the above appraisal of Canada's fiscal policy, that, although careful study of the statistical evidence relating to the immediate postwar period has since shown that deflationary disturbances had already begun in the early months of 1920, such knowledge can hardly be expected to have prevailed among those actually witnessing the postwar changes as they were taking place. Even with the aid of hindsight, present-day economists have found it difficult to determine the upper turning point in the Canadian postwar cycle (see chapter I, n. 32). Indeed, this statistical uncertainty is one of the most serious general obstacles to effective countercyclical fiscal policy.

The policy enunciated by Sir Henry Drayton, in his Budget Speech of May 1920, was apparently based on the conviction that the postwar inflationary boom was still in progress. This was particularly true of the tax policy. In proposing the sharp upward revision in excise and sales taxes, he stated the twofold objective of greater revenue and the drastic curtailment of extravagant consumer expenditure. When viewed in this light, such changes seem to make far more economic sense. By the same token, however, the 1920 reduction in the business profits tax and the 1921 increase in excise taxes represent policy shortcoming.

But despite this mutual inconsistency of tax changes--together with a strong faith in the principle of annual budgetary equilibrium which beclouded his whole approach to the problem of a combating deflation--Sir Henry did reveal a substantial measure of economic understanding. Not only was he able (as indicated in chapter III) to grasp some of the fundamentals of the monetary process, but he was also one of the few responsible public officials of his time to appreciate the economics of inflation, and to acquire some notion of the role of fiscal policy in such a situation. (Cf. Higgins, The War and Postwar Cycle in Canada, 1914-23, p. 49; also, Debates, May 18, 1920, IV, pp. 2486-9.)

66. C. Y. B. , 1941, p. 754.

67. A variety of customs-tariff reductions--notably for sugar, agricultural implements, textiles, and boots and shoes--was effected in 1922.

68. In all fairness to the then Minister of Finance, Mr. W. S. Fielding, it should be noted that, in framing his 1923 tax policy, he subordinated the balanced-budget objective to that of easing the tax burden on a depressed economy, though it was only with the greatest reluctance that he took this action. Debates, May 11, 1923, III, pp. 2641-3.

69. Mr. Fielding's successor, Mr. J. A. Robb, had much the same outlook, expressing the conviction that the tax reductions of 1924 "will give such impetus to trade that it will result in greater development and prosperity to all the provinces of Canada." Debates, April 10, 1924, II, p. 1218.

70. There were also substantial reductions in the customs duties on instruments of production used in agriculture, mining, forestry, and fishing, and on materials used in the manufacture of such instruments.

71. C. Y. B., 1941, p. 753.

72. After their great drop in 1921, those expenditures continued to play a minor role in the federal-spending sphere until the outbreak of the Second World War.

73. C. Y. B., 1941, pp. 752, 753.

74. Ibid., pp. 754, 796.

75. Customs duties on certain commodities were also slightly reduced.

76. Many important cuts were made in the customs tariff in 1926, special attention having been paid to food and automobiles.

77. Widespread reductions were also made in the 1928 customs-tariff schedules.

78. C. Y. B., 1938, pp. 848, 851.

79. Ibid., 1941, p. 753.

80. The meaning of this concept and the availability of figures pertaining to it, were discussed earlier in this chapter (n. 22). Each fiscal year to which these figures apply ends on March 31 of the following calendar year. Thus, for example, "fiscal 1926" means "the fiscal year 1926-7" and "fiscal 1930" means "the fiscal year 1930-1." Cf. Dominion-Provincial Conference on Reconstruction, Public Investment and Capital Formation; and Department of Trade and Commerce, Private and Public Investment in Canada, 1926-1951.

81. Department of Trade and Commerce, Private and Public Investment in Canada, 1926-1951, pp. 166, 187. For reconciliation of the minor differences between these figures on total expenditures, and those compiled in the Public Accounts (from which the Canada Year Book figures are taken), see Dominion-Provincial Conference on Reconstruction, Comparative Statistics of Public Finance (Ottawa, 1945), p. 68.

The second half of the fiscal year 1929-30 was, of course, a recession period. On the face of it, this fact would seem to justify the high outlay on direct investment made at that time. But the Dominion government's expenditure programme was largely devised during, and on the basis of, the early months of 1929, when the budget was brought down and discussed. It was, therefore, by conception, a cyclical, not a countercyclical, programme. That public investment was proceeding at a high rate when deflation set in was probably not the manifestation of conscious policy, but of the inflexibility of federal administrative machinery and observational capacity in the fiscal sphere. It is entirely possible that, had the government been able to resort to frequent fiscal revision during 1929, the level of expenditure in fiscal 1930 would have been considerably lower. (Compare with the case of increased federal expenditure in 1938, chapter I, n. 30).

The sustained expenditure rise in fiscal 1931 is less easily fitted into this cyclical pattern, in the light of the public works and relief expenditures appropriated during the Special Session of Parliament at the end of 1930. But even in this case, it can be assumed--not implausibly--that by early 1930 the government had not yet recognized the gravity and generality of the 1929 collapse, and was raising its expenditures accordingly.

82. All figures in this paragraph are derived from Department of Trade and Commerce, Private and Public Investment in Canada, 1926-1951, pp. 167, 190, 198.

83. Bates, Financial History of Canadian Governments, p. 13. (See, also, Higgins, The War and Postwar Cycle in Canada, 1914-23; and Mackintosh, The Economic Background of Dominion-Provincial Relations.)

Chapter Five

1. The nature and implications of this vulnerability have long been widely recognized. Further analysis along these lines may be found in: J. E. Lattimer, "The Economic Aspects of the Agriculture Problem," and "Economic Nationalism and Canadian Agriculture," Papers and Proceedings of the Canadian Political Science Association, III (1931), and VI (1934), respectively; H. A. Innis, "Introduction," and K. W. Taylor, "A Summary," The Canadian Economy and Its Problems (Toronto, 1934); W. A. Mackintosh, "Some Aspects of a Pioneer Economy," A. F. W. Plumptre, "The Nature of Political and Economic Development in the Dominions," and R. B. Bryce, "The Effects on Canada of Industrial Fluctuations in the United States," C. J. E. P. S., II (Nov. 1936), III (Nov. 1937), and V (Aug. 1939), respectively; M. K. Inman, "Experience in Canadian Banking, 1929-1934," unpublished Ph. D. thesis (Harvard University, 1938), chapter III; F. W. Burton, "Staple Production and Canada's External Relations," Essays in Political Economy, ed. H. A. Innis (Toronto, 1938); W. A. Mackintosh, The Economic Background of Dominion-Provincial Relations, chapters V and VI, and F. A. Knox, Dominion Monetary Policy, 1929-1934, Studies Prepared for the Royal Commission on Dominion-Provincial Relations (Ottawa, 1939); Canada, Report of the Royal Commission on Dominion-Provincial Relations (Ottawa, 1940), book I, chapters V-VII; A. F. W. Plumptre, Central Banking in the British Dominions (Toronto, 1940), part IV; D. R. Annett, British Preference in Canadian Commercial Policy (Toronto, 1948), chapter I; J. D. Gibson (ed.), Canada's Economy in a Changing World (Toronto, 1948); A. N. McLeod, "Maintaining Employment and Incomes in Canada," unpublished Ph. D. thesis (Harvard University, 1949), chapters V and VI; V. W. Malach, International Cycles and Canada's Balance of Payments, 1921-33

(Toronto, 1954); E. Marcus, <u>Canada and the International Business Cycle,</u> <u>1927-1939</u> (New York, 1954); A. E. Safarian, "The Canadian Economy in the Great Depression," unpublished Ph. D. thesis (University of California, Berkeley, 1955).

2. "The market situation for the two leading exports, wheat and news-print, was especially weak. The unusually large world and Canadian wheat crops of 1928 created a burdensome surplus which threatened a slump in prices even before the depression began. By 1928 Canadian newsprint cap-acity was over-extended, and the price situation was very unstable. Since Canada supplied 40 per cent of the world exports of wheat and 65 per cent of the world èxports of newsprint, she would suffer the full impact of unfa-vourable developments." <u>Report of Royal Commission on Dominion-Provin-</u> <u>cial Relations,</u> p. 144.

3. Taylor, "A Summary," <u>The Canadian Economy and Its Problems,</u> p. 182.

4. <u>Report of Royal Commission on Dominion-Provincial Relations,</u> book I, p. 146.

5. The increased importance of the automobile and construction indus-tries provided two new sources of rising income which were liable to sharp contraction in the face of economic depression. Indeed, this was only one aspect of the general trend towards Canadian expansion in the capital goods field, a trend which bore both a causal and consequential relationship to the one-third increase in average per capita national income between 1920 and 1929. <u>Report of Royal Commission on Dominion-Provincial Relations,</u> p. 126.

6. Cf. Canada, <u>Report of the Royal Commission on Price Spreads</u> (Ottawa, 1935); also L. G. Reynolds, <u>The Control of Competition in Canada</u> (Cambridge, Mass., 1940).

7. <u>Ibid.</u> The role of monopoly in cyclical fluctuations is not easily ap-praised. There are, on the one hand, the intensifying effects of inequality of income distribution; of serious restrictions on factor mobility; and of downward price rigidity and the consequent distortions of the entire cost-price structure. But it is also necessary to take into account the stabilizing effects of upward price rigidity, and of inelastic expectations with respect to falling prices. The complexity of business behaviour and the intangibility of psychological influences preclude any categorical solution to the problem, although the consensus of professional opinion would seem to favour the "intensification hypothesis." See, for example: H. S. Ellis, "Monopoly and Unemployment," <u>Prices, Wages, and Employment,</u> Postwar Economic Studies no. 4, Board of Governors of the Federal Reserve System (Wash-ington, May 1946); E. V. Rostow, "Market Organization and Stabilization Policy," <u>Income Stabilization for a Developing Democracy,</u> ed. M. F. Mil-likan (New Haven, 1953); F. Machlup, "Monopoly and the Problem of Eco-nomic Stability," <u>Monopoly and Competition and Their Regulation,</u> ed. E. H. Chamberlin (London, 1954).

8. <u>Canada Year Book,</u> 1941, p. 753; and Department of Trade and Commerce, <u>Private and Public Investment in Canada, 1926-1951</u> (Ottawa,

1951), pp. 148, 152. This proportion applies to the fiscal year 1928-9; compare with the corresponding 64 per cent ratio for fiscal 1939. Dominion-Provincial Conference on Reconstruction, Comparative Statistics of Public Finance (Ottawa, 1945), p. 44; and Department of Trade and Commerce, Private and Public Investment in Canada, 1926-1951, pp. 148, 152.

9. Department of Trade and Commerce, Private and Public Investment in Canada, 1926-1951, pp. 148, 152; and Dominion Bureau of Statistics, National Accounts; Income and Expenditure, 1926-1950 (Ottawa, 1951), p. 26.

10. C.Y.B., 1941, pp. 752, 753; and Department of Trade and Commerce, Private and Public Investment in Canada, 1926-1951, p. 187.

11. C.Y.B., 1941, p. 759.

12. Ibid., p. 754.

13. Ibid.; and Department of Trade and Commerce, Private and Public Investment in Canada, 1926-1951, pp. 148, 152. These proportions present a striking contrast with the 30 and 49 per cent ratios, respectively, for the fiscal year 1939. C.Y.B., 1941, p. 754; and Department of Trade and Commerce, Private and Public Investment in Canada, 1926-1951, pp. 148, 152.

14. League of Nations, Review of World Trade, 1932 (Geneva, 1933), p. 27.

15. D.B.S., National Accounts: Income and Expenditure, 1926-1950, p. 26.

16. The United Kingdom's share of world imports was 15.2 per cent, and of world exports 10.7 per cent, in 1929. The corresponding figures for the United States were 12.2 per cent and 15.6 per cent. This gave the latter 13.8 per cent, and the former 13.0 per cent, of total world trade. League of Nations, Review of World Trade, 1932, p. 27.

17. Board of Trade, Statistical Abstract for the United Kingdom, 1924-1938 (London, 1940), pp. 370, 372, 378, 380. All figures in section II are stated in value terms.

18. Department of Commerce, Statistical Abstract of the United States, 1931 (Washington, 1931), pp. 510, 511.

19. Unless otherwise specified, the figures cited in this section are taken from Tables V-X.

20. It is these items which account for the one instance--Canadian exports to, and total credits with, the United States--in which the two sets of ratios do differ substantially.

21. The figure for fibres and textiles was computed from information contained in C.Y.B., 1930, pp. 528, 544.

22. Ibid., pp. 507, 513.

23. Cf. J. Viner, Canada's Balance of International Indebtedness, 1900-1913 (Cambridge, Mass., 1924). As a near-full-employment economy before and after World War I, Canada's alternatives to rapid economic development through foreign borrowing were twofold: (1) gradual, internally financed expansion through improved productive techniques, increased labour efficiency, etc.; and (2) rapid, internally financed expansion through

drastic curtailment of consumer spending in favour of enormous capital outlays. It seems hardly open to question that the latter course would have been beyond the bounds of practical policy.

24. D. B. S., The Canadian Balance of Internal Payments (Ottawa, 1939), pp. 175-6; and Gibson, Canada's Economy in a Changing World, p. 250.

25. Gibson, Canada's Economy in a Changing World, p. 282.

26. The settlement of world trade was far from being a simple triangle: "Europe did not obtain the United States dollars required to settle her accounts with Canada through a trading surplus with the United States. Actually, Europe ran a large deficit in her accounts with the United States-- much larger than with Canada. She earned the necessary dollars--and to some extent she drew on her investments or borrowed to obtain them-- largely through her earnings in other countries, particularly in the East, which had a trading surplus with the United States. Moreover, even this process was partly indirect, since some European countries paid for their purchases from North America through a trading surplus with Britain, who in turn earned dollars from her investments and trade in Asia and Africa. So behind the North Atlantic Triangle lay a world-wide mechanism, of settlement. The system through which Canada was able to settle her accounts was in reality many-sided or multi-lateral. Canada's ability to sell to Europe was intimately associated with Europe's ability to sell to Asia and to Africa, with Europe's, and particularly Britain's, investments in those continents, and with the ability of the Dutch East Indies, Malaya, and such African countries as the Gold Coast to produce large trading surpluses with the United States." Ibid., p. 283.

Chapter Six

1. Canada, Report of the Royal Commission on Dominion-Provincial Relations (Ottawa, 1940), book I, p. 126.

2. It can, of course, be argued, in terms of psychological and other effects, that such action would have made the impact of the Great Depression even more severe. The implication throughout this study is that, in the light of actual policy carried out and results achieved, the burden of proof rests on those who would advance the case for extreme caution.

3. Some reference to the Canadian political framework was made in chapter II. But the whole range of political factors is integrated here, because it was during the thirties that the reflection of party division in economic thought and policy attained its greatest significance.

4. Cf. R. MacG. Dawson, The Government of Canada (Toronto, 1947), p. 496. During the thirties, this position continued to be accepted by most Canadian writers, but not by all. See F. H. Underhill, "The Party System in Canada," Papers and Proceedings of the Canadian Political Science Association (henceforth contracted to Papers and Proceedings), IV (1932), pp. 210, 211.

5. This analysis of the Progressive movement is based on the interpretation of F. H. Underhill, "The Canadian Party System in Transition,"

C. J. E. P. S., IX (Aug. 1943), p. 308. See, also, H. McD. Clokie, Canadian Government and Politics (Toronto, 1944), p. 80; and W. L. Morton, The Progressive Party in Canada (Toronto, 1950).

6. For a detailed analysis of the evolution of the C. C. F., see D. E. McHenry, The Third Force in Canada (Toronto, 1950); and S. M. Lipset, Agrarian Socialism (Toronto, 1950).

7. In January 1932, some of those intellectuals had formed the League for Social Reconstruction (L. S. R.). The League continued to maintain its separate identity, though functioning, in effect, as the "intellectual research arm" of the movement. In 1935 the League published Social Planning for Canada (Toronto), a comprehensive book on Socialism as applied to the Dominion.

8. Regina Manifesto, adopted at First National Convention (Regina, Sask., July 1933). Reaction of the major parties (both of which the C. C. F. regarded as "the instruments of capitalist interests") to the Manifesto is of interest, because it reflects the state of mind of many Canadians during this crucial period in Canadian economic history. Speaking at Winnipeg on July 22, 1933, the Liberal leader, Mr. Mackenzie King, characterized the Manifesto as "revolutionary" and declared that it would destroy liberty. Dr. R. J. Manion, Conservative Minister of Railways and Canals, speaking at St. Eustache, Quebec, on July 30, 1933, stated that the C. C. F. system was the system which existed under the name of Communism in Russia-- "a system based upon tyranny and oppression and the outlawing of personal and religious freedom." A. C. Hopkins (ed.), Canadian Annual Review of Public Affairs, 1934 (Toronto, 1935), p. 52.

9. Regina Manifesto.

10. D. Lewis, "Revelation According to Hansard," Canadian Forum, XVI (May 1936), p. 5. This is not to imply that the C. C. F. politicians committed no errors of reasoning, or that the two major parties had no highly competent representatives in the House of Commons. Such a contention would have no basis in fact. The point which does stand out, however, is that, in terms of sustained interest in economic issues and readiness to apply the methods of economic analysis to economic problems, the C. C. F. radicals won for themselves, during the thirties, a unique place in the evolution of mature economic thought and policy in Canada. That the same contention could be made concerning the Progressive and Labour radicals of the twenties is a striking commentary on Canadian economic development during the interwar period.

11. Canada, like other countries, had its experiences with revolutionary Socialism or Communism. Communism had been of little importance before 1929; its adherents had been mostly foreigners, and the country had been too prosperous to take much notice of extreme doctrine. But: "After the depression began, it found its opportunity among a few English-Canadian leaders.... The pertinacity of its members and obliging persecution on the part of the federal authorities [further] strengthened it. R. B. Bennett, while Prime Minister, abetted by the then Commissioner of the Royal Canadian Mounted Police, undertook rigorous measures against

it, invoking a law that had been put on the books during the postwar excitement of 1919, and securing the imprisonment of several men for no better reason than that they were Communists. To Mr. Bennett and the men about him, Canadian Communism owes a debt of gratitude." A. R. M. Lower, "The Development of Canadian Economic Ideas," Supplement in J. F. Normano, The Spirit of American Economics (New York, 1943), p. 237.

　　12. For brief reference to the Bennett-Stevens dispute, see A. R. M. Lower, Colony to Nation (Toronto, 1946), chapter XXXIV.

　　13. The Price Spreads Report published in 1935, has been generally regarded as a pioneering research document in the field of Canadian business competition. It was one of many examples of increasing governmental readiness, during the thirties, to base policy decisions on carefully conducted economic analysis.

　　14. Lower, The Development of Canadian Economic Ideas, pp. 237, 238. See also Morton, The Progressive Party in Canada, pp. 285-8; and C. B. Macpherson, Democracy in Alberta (Toronto, 1953), pp. 142-9.

　　15. The Social Credit party assumed power in Alberta in 1935, and in the federal election of the same year it sent to the House of Commons only seventeen representatives--fifteen from Alberta and two from Saskatchewan. Clokie, Canadian Government and Politics, p. 80.

　　16. In this connection, see F. R. Scott, Canada Today (Toronto, 1938), pp. 61-5; Clokie, Canadian Government and Politics, pp. 73-81; Dawson, The Government of Canada, pp. 501-7.

　　17. Dawson, The Government of Canada, p. 506.

　　18. Cf. Canada, House of Commons Debates, April 3, 1930, II, pp. 1221-43.

　　19. Ibid., April 3, 1930, II, p. 1223. Compare with the King statement on unemployment cited in chapter II, p. 28.

　　20. As the depression grew more severe, Mr. King's thinking on this problem became bolder, though no clearer. In 1933 he was still busily engaged in attacking his successor's recovery programme on the ground that the executive branch of the government had usurped the constitutionally established powers of Parliament--even while Mr. King himself was making the following declaration: "If a man is able and willing to work and cannot get work, or find work, it seems to me that it is the state's business to endeavour to provide work for him, and if necessity demand it, to look after him until he gets work. Anything short of that signifies some malorganization of the affairs of state." Debates, Feb. 24, 1933, III, p. 2469.

　　21. The mass of regulatory legislation, Royal Commissions, and special parliamentary investigations virtually forced on both the Bennett and King administrations during the thirties implied grudging tacit acceptance by Canadians generally of at least the principle of ad hoc planning. But by the time--late in the thirties--that general recognition of the need for more comprehensive planning was revealing itself, internal and external changes had combined to remove much of the economic chaos against which this recognition was presumably directed. Moreover, such recogni-

tion was even then by no means unanimous, particularly among business and financial groups longing for a return to the "good old days."

22. Cf. O. D. Skelton, "Is Our Economic System Bankrupt?" Papers and Proceedings, III (1931).

23. Ibid., pp. 85, 86.

24. Cf. A. Brady, "An Economic Council for Canada," Papers and Proceedings, V (1933).

25. Ibid., p. 76.

26. S. B. Leacock, "The Economic Analysis of Industrial Depression, Papers and Proceedings, V (1933), pp. 23, 24.

27. For other contemporary statements of the general case for economic planning, see, in particular, the writings of Professor F. R. Scott and Mr. E. A. Forsey of McGill University; also, L. S. R., Social Planning for Canada, chapters VII and VIII.

28. F. H. Underhill, "The Party System in Canada," Papers and Proceedings, IV (1932), pp. 211, 212.

29. See, especially, the 1930-3 parliamentary addresses of Mr. Alfred Speakmen, Mr. Garland, Mr. Woodsworth, and Mr. Irvine. The rationale for the Progressive approach found direct expression in Mr. Woodsworth's contention--made at the very onset of the depression--that "we have been told again and again that unemployment is primarily a municipal or provincial responsibility.... This was true sixty years ago, but the situation is entirely changed today.... As long as the Dominion government so largely controls the country's fiscal and immigration policies, --[it] cannot avoid responsibility for ensuing depression." Debates, April 1, 1930, II, p. 1150.

There were several "independent" politicians, among the two major parties, who voiced similar ideas on the urgent need for economic planning by government. One of these was Mr. Humphrey Mitchell (Liberal Minister of Labour during and after World War II), in whose judgment the state had to take the lead. "We find today that the leaders in finance and industry have fallen down. They are busy handing out advice and at the same time putting on the brakes on any governmental action. I am firmly convinced that so great is the drive of circumstances and events that the impetus to collectivism cannot be checked." Debates, Feb. 9, 1933, II, p. 1980.

30. A notable exception was the thoroughgoing analysis of planning carried out by the League for Social Reconstruction in the above-cited volume, Social Planning for Canada, chapters VII-XI.

31. While radical in its own unique way, Social Credit theory did not embrace the radicalism of national economic planning by a Socialist government. There were, indeed, many social credit theorists in the new C. C. F. movement, and concessions of C. C. F. principle had, therefore, to be made. One of these was probably the "woolly" talk, in the Regina Manifesto, about the debt-creating character of public finance in the past, and the financing of future public works by credit based on the national wealth (see page 81 above, and the Canadian Forum, XIII, Sept. 1933, p. 444). As time passed, differences between the two radical groups became more apparent,

and were increasingly emphasized on both sides (see, for example, the
L. S. R. critique of Social Credit outlined on pp. 96, 97; also pp. 93, 94;
and the comments of Mr. M. J. Coldwell, who succeeded Mr. Woodsworth
as C. C. F. leader in 1940, in Debates, Jan. 21, 1937, I, pp. 157-61, and
in House of Commons, Proceedings of the Standing Committee on Banking
and Commerce [henceforth contracted to House Banking Committee Pro-
ceedings], 1939, pp. 503, 504).

    32. Speech at Hamilton, Ontario (April 28, 1931), quoted in Debates,
July 29, 1931, IV, p. 4297.

    33. Debates, April 6, 1932, II, p. 1768.

    34. Address at Annual Convention of Canadian Manufacturers' Asso-
ciation, Industrial Canada, XXI (July 1930), p. 111.

    35. Address at Annual Convention of Canadian Manufacturers' Asso-
ciation, Canadian Annual Review, 1930-31, p. 748.

    36. Industrial Canada, XXII (Feb. 1931), p. 99.

    37. Ibid., p. 101.

    38. Address at Annual Shareholders' Meeting, Canadian Annual Review,
1932, p. 706.

    39. Ibid., p. 702.

    40. Address at Annual Shareholders' Meeting, Industrial Canada, XXXII
(Feb. 1932), p. 77; Canadian Annual Review, 1933, p. 598. The radicals,
on the whole, seem to have gauged more accurately the severity of the Great
Depression, though their judgment was as often the reflection of superficial
observation of prevailing conditions and doctrinaire dissatisfaction with the
capitalist system, as of careful analysis of the actual situation.

    41. At the same time, certain Canadian economists were themselves
advancing suggestions for the creation of a National Economic Council.
In this connection, see W. B. Hurd, "Planned Economy," and A. Brady,
"An Economic Council for Canada," Papers and Proceedings, IV (1932), and
and V (1933), respectively.

    42. Debates, Feb. 10, 1932, I, p. 102.

    43. Cf. ibid., Feb. 2, 1933, II, p. 1727.

    44. Cf. F. H. Underhill, "Democracy and Leadership," Canadian
Forum, XIII (July 1933), pp. 366, 367.

    45. Debates, March 18, 1935, II, p. 1809.

    46. Ibid., March 19, 1935, II, p. 1850; Feb. 17, 1936, I, pp. 266,
267. Mr. G. R. Geary, a Conservative member of Parliament during the
Bennett Administration (and appointed Minister of Justice in 1935), had
this to add to the general attitude of contempt towards (and ignorance regarding the institutions associated with) economists: "Someone acquainted
with the doings of these people in England told me that there is a body of
them numbering five who meet in Oxford quite often, and that, from every
conference they hold, there emerge six diametrically-opposed opinions, of
which as a rule Keynes holds two." Ibid., Feb. 7, 1934, I, p. 358.

    47. Ibid., Feb. 27, 1936, I, p. 578. On the other hand, Mr. King,
for several years prior to that time, had been advocating the appointment
of a National Employment Commission, staffed by economic experts,

among others, for the purpose of attacking the problem of unemployment. This Commission, finally set up in May 1936, as well as the many other investigative organizations which functioned throughout the thirties, symbolized the deep "back-door" penetration of economists and economic analysis into the sphere of public policy.

48. <u>Debates</u>, April 26, 1932, III, p. 2390.

49. <u>Ibid.</u>, Sept. 10, 1930, Special Session, p. 61.

50. <u>Industrial Canada</u>, XXXI (Oct. 1930), p. 63.

51. <u>Debates</u>, Feb. 27, 1933, III, p. 2502.

52. Cf. <u>ibid.</u>, June 1, 1936, IV, p. 3259.

53. The members of the Department of Political and Economic Science at Queen's University had raised this fundamental question four years previously, and had supported the latter alternative, "having in mind the number and distribution of our population, and the character and disposition of our resources.... There may be countries, large enough in population and varied enough in resources, to which the highly-sophisticated arguments of Mr. Keynes in favour of economic nationalism may apply, but Canada is not one of them." Department of Political and Economic Science, and Course in Commerce, "Canadian Trade Policy in a World of Economic Nationalism," <u>Queen's Quarterly</u> XLI (Spring 1934), p. 98.

54. <u>Debates</u>, Feb. 25, 1937, II, p. 1216; June 16, 1938, IV, pp. 3897-9. Compare with the interesting, though less incisive, explanation offered in 1932 by Dr. R. J. Manion, the Conservative Minister of Railways and Canals, to the effect that the unemployment in Canada was due to a world situation over which Canadians had no control, and which was, in turn, due "to the aftermath of war; to the demands for reparations by various countries...; to the pocketing of gold by two great countries...; to the competition of Russia, which is on a cheaper economic plane than any of the so-called advanced countries of the world, and, finally, to a great extent to the decrease in the selling price of the commodities of this country." <u>Ibid.</u>, March 9, 1932, I, p. 971.

55. Canada, <u>Final Report of the National Employment Commission</u> (Ottawa, 1938).

56. <u>Report of Royal Commission on Dominion-Provincial Relations</u>. This Report was not published until May 1940. However, most of the work leading to publication of the Report, and of the auxiliary Appendices and Studies, had been done during the late thirties. Furthermore, although the Royal Commission reviewed its recommendations after the outbreak of war, no changes were made. In reality, then, the Report was a product of the thirties, and is therefore examined in the present context.

The question arises here as to whether the two reports cited above-- and other official documents of a similar nature--can be legitimately considered as representing the viewpoint of Government leaders. The facts presented thus far would seem to suggest a negative reply. Even if the Government leaders had thought through the unemployment problem carefully--which was seldom the case--they could not be expected to construct the sophisticated kind of economic analysis for which the university economists and civil servants connected directly or indirectly with the Commissions must have been largely responsible. The Commissions, nevertheless, were established, and the Commissioners approved, by the party in office, and to that limited extent their reports may be associated with party policy.

57. An Interim Report was published in July 1937.

58. Cf. L. C. Marsh, "Reports of the National Employment Commission," C. J. E. P. S., V (Feb. 1939).

59. See chapter X for treatment of the fiscal aspects of the two reports cited here.

60. National Employment Commission, Final Report, p. 21.

61. Some depressions, the Report added, had been communicated to Canada through drastic reductions in capital imports, but at the time of the crisis of 1929-30 Canadian capital imports had not been large and, as they had expanded rather than contracted in 1930, they had eased rather than intensified the shock. For further reference to the behaviour of capital imports during the Great Depression, see chapter IX.

62. National Employment Commission, Final Report, p. 23.

63. For a critical appraisal of the Report, see H. A. Innis, "The Rowell-Sirois Report," C. J. E. P. S., VI (Nov. 1940); also, B. S. Keirstead, "National Policy," Canada after the War, eds. A. Brady and F. R. Scott (Toronto, 1943). For reviews of the Studies and Appendices, see C. J. E. P. S., VII (Feb. 1941); and VII (May 1941).

64. The prime consideration was the working out of an equitable and efficient allocation of tax powers and expenditure functions among Canada's three governmental levels.

65. Cf., for example, H. A. Innis and A. F. W. Plumptre (eds.), The Canadian Economy and Its Problems (Toronto, 1934).

66. See, especially, Report of Royal Commission on Dominion-Provincial Relations; S. Bates, Financial History of Canadian Governments, and W. A. Mackintosh, The Economic Background of Dominion-Provincial Relations (Ottawa, 1939). It seems worth mentioning, in connection with the similarity of approach noted above, that Professor Mackintosh had been a member of the National Employment Commission.

67. Debates, April 2, 1930, II, p. 1212. Eight years later, Mr. T. L. Church was still advancing his pet notion that "a right application of the doctrine of protection brought up to date [would] solve all the economic ills of the country." Ibid., March 30, 1938, II, p. 1857.

68. Mr. Young subsequently became a member of the National Employment Commission.

69. Ibid., June 12, 1931, III, p. 2595.

70. Later, in the 1930 general election, Mr. Campbell was elected as a Progressive.

71. Debates, April 4, 1930, II, pp. 1293, 1294.

72. Ibid., April 25, 1932, II, p. 2338.

73. Ibid., April 10, 1933, IV, p. 3890.

74. Ibid., March 8, 1937, II, p. 1585.

75. Ibid., March 4, 1937, II, pp. 1502, 1503.

76. Ibid., March 14, 1938, II, p. 1311. Mr. Deachman's remedy for this condition was the restoration of "free competition, " or the "free play of natural forces. "

77. Address at the Annual Shareholders' Meeting, Canadian Annual Review, 1930-31, pp. 701-6.

78. Ibid., p. 703.

79. Address at the Annual Shareholders' Meeting, Canadian Annual Review, 1934, p. 619. Meanwhile, the Royal Bank, through its Monthly Letter (July 1934), was stating that "overproduction of capital goods constitutes the boom, underproduction of capital goods constitutes the depression. "

80. Canadian Annual Review, 1930-31, p. 712.

81. J. P. Bell, "Socializing the Banks, " J. C. B. A., XLI (Jan. 1934), pp. 167, 168.

82. J. M. Keynes, The General Theory of Employment, Interest, and Money (New York, 1936).

83. The position taken on the employment issue by the Canadian industrial community--to the limited extent that it was articulated in the proceedings of the Canadian Manufacturers' Association and the Chamber of Commerce--did not differ sufficiently from that of the bankers to merit separate treatment. For reference to some "business" exceptions, see chapter X.

84. Sir Thomas had been Minister of Finance during World War I. In 1933 he served as a member of the Royal Commission on Banking and Currency.

85. Address at a meeting of the Toronto Bankers' Educational Association, J. C. B. A., XL (July 1933), p. 442.

86. Mr. Noble has been General Manager of the government-owned Industrial Development Bank since its inception in 1944.

87. Discussion on "Gold and the Decline in Prices, " Papers and Proceedings, III (1931), p. 113.

88. See n. 31 above, for reference to the social credit aspects of the C. C. F. Regina Manifesto. Mention should also be made here of the strong Social Credit bias within the U. F. A. movement which governed Alberta immediately before the Social Credit party; in this connection, see Morton, The Progressive Party in Canada, pp. 185-8.

89. Debates, April 1, 1930, II, p. 1149. During the course of the Great Depression, this idea was being advanced by more and more of Mr. Woodsworth's colleagues. Miss Agnes Macphail, for example, believed, that "the essence of the depression is falling prices, caused by deficiency of purchasing power.... That being so, we must seek to evolve policies, taxation, financial and trade policies, which will increase the consumption of goods.... The only thing that people with accumulated capital know what to do with it is to invest it in plant and equipment to produce goods of which there are already too much. " Ibid., Feb. 1, 1933, II, pp. 1696, 1697. A considerable part of Miss Macphail's case rested, also, on the Douglas

"A plus B" argument that, since "dividends, salaries, and wages paid out in any industry are never sufficient to buy back at the ticketed price all goods produced by that industry, there certainly is a gap, and it will have to be bridged by methods which we have not used before. I believe the solution of the agricultural and unemployment problems lies in this new theory of money." Ibid,, April 3, 1935, III, p. 2393.

But not all the radicals committed the "underconsumptionist savings-investment error." Mr. R. Gardiner, for example, contended that in early 1932 there was more money on deposit in Canadian banks than ever before in the history of the country, "because the people who in the past made profits or who saved from their salaries or wages cannot under present conditions find profitable investment for those savings. . . . Just as long as those savings remain in our banking institutions, and as long as they are not used for the purpose of providing new plant and equipment in the development of . . . our capitalist system, . . . there will be no improvement in the depression now existing." Ibid., April 12, 1932, II, p. 1952.

90. Ibid., Sept. 9, 1930, Special Session, p. 50.

91. Mr. Irvine repeatedly directed the attention of the House of Commons "to the analyses and the mathematical demonstration of Major Hugh Douglas, . . . who I think has shown more completely and more thoroughly than any other economist of his time the scarcity of money and the causes of that scarcity." Ibid., April 2, 1935, III, p. 2324. Moreover, Mr. Irvine, like others among the radicals, showed little discrimination in identifying the views of Douglas with those of Foster and Catchings, Keynes, and McKenna; though he did, quite appropriately, emphasize that all of those writers were making important contributions to what he called, interestingly enough, "the new economics." Ibid., April 3, 1930, II, p. 1262; April 2, 1935, III, p. 2324.

92. Ibid., March 1, 1932, I, pp. 706, 707.

93. Ibid., Feb. 2, 1933, II, p. 1740.

94. Ibid.

95. Cf. ibid., March 2, 1932, I, pp. 737-41; April 11, 1933, IV, p. 3907; May 6, 1936, III, pp. 2569-76.

96. Ibid., March 2, 1932, I, p. 741; April 11, 1933, IV, p. 3907.

97. There is no doubt that Mr. J. C. Landeryou, for instance, was giving expression to the official Social Credit view when he told the House of Commons, in 1936, that he did not believe that the unemployment problem could be solved by socializing the means of production. Instead, he favoured the "socialization of the products of the machines" through provision of sufficient purchasing power "to equate the selling price of the goods and services for sale. I believe that in doing that we shall solve the problem of adequately distributing the goods that are produced and the services that we can render." Debates, Feb. 24, 1936, I, p. 485.

98. Ibid., March 8, 1937, II, p. 1571.

99. In the words of Foster and Catchings, "money that is once used to bring about the production of goods, is again used to bring about the production of goods, before it is used to bring about the consumption of

goods. . . . And thus used twice in succession to bring goods to market, it creates a deficiency in purchasing power." W. T. Foster and W. Catchings, Profits (Boston, 1925), pp. 279, 284, 285.

100. Mr. Jaques was one of many Social Crediters who allowed themselves to be carried away by the achievements of Douglas. The former's highly exaggerated, not to say inaccurate, comments follow: "Major Douglas is one of the greatest and most original thinkers of all time. . . . It is true that Douglas was not a professional economist; he was an engineer and a thinker. Newton was not an astronomer; he was a philosopher, and so is Douglas. . . . Douglas is the Newton of economics, because as Newton discovered or established the proof that the earth goes around the sun, Douglas has provided the proof that no longer does our economic system revolve around production, but that it revolves around consumption, and that if we look after consumption, production will look after itself, but the reverse process will not work, because modern science and modern production methods have made that impossible." Debates, Jan. 21, 1937, I, p. 164.

101. Ibid., Jan. 21, 1937, I, p. 162; March 4, 1937, II, pp. 1479 and 1480. Clearly expressed in the above ("text") quotation is the Foster-Catchings concept of the "dilemma of thrift" (see Foster and Catchings, Profits, p. 296). Testifying in 1939 before the House of Commons Standing Committee on Banking and Commerce, Mr. G. F. Towers, Governor of the Bank of Canada, pointed out to Mr. Jaques that savings did not necessarily cause a shortage of purchasing power. Only "when there is a desire to save but insufficient opportunities for employing those savings" would there be a tendency towards depression. House Banking Committee Proceedings, 1939, p. 474. The Liberal member of Parliament, Mr. Deachman, applied a similar correction to Mr. Jaques's savings-investment argument (ibid., p. 748).

102. Debates, Jan. 21, 1937, I, p. 179. Mr. Quelch erroneously included Keynes among those economists who regarded the investment of savings as one of the causes of the deficiency of purchasing power. Cf. House Banking Committee Proceedings, 1939, p. 565.

103. L. R. Klein, The Keynesian Revolution (New York, 1947), p. 140.

104. See, also, the statements of Mr. E. J. Garland, Mr. H. E. Spencer, and Mr. G. G. Coote, respectively, in Debates, April 2, 1930, II, p. 1205; March 20, 1935, II, p. 1896; March 26, 1935, II, pp. 2135-8.

105. Cf. L.S.R., Social Planning for Canada, chapter XII. See, also, the analysis of Mr. C. McKay (a correspondent of the International Labour Press), "Rationing Investment," Canadian Forum, XII (July 1932), pp. 372-4.

106. These latter aspects of the League analysis are treated in chapters VIII and X.

107. L.S.R., Social Planning for Canada, p. 310.

108. See chapter X for discussion of these proposals.

109. L.S.R., Social Planning for Canada, p. 316.

110. Ibid., p. 319.

111. Ibid.

112. Ibid., p. 320.

113. Ibid., pp. 321, 322. In the 1938 session of Parliament, Mr. Dunning, the Liberal Minister of Finance, presented a strong case against the Social Credit analytical system. He pointed out that: "The statement that there was a chronic shortage of purchasing power because the consumer was never paid the full cost of production ignored the obvious fact that Major Douglas' B payments went to pay those wages, salaries, and dividends in other industries that supplied raw or semi-raw materials. In addition, this plan ignored the great bulk of capital goods which the consumer was never required to buy, but in the manufacture of which he acquired wages and salaries. If purchasing power ... were issued to the full extent of production costs in any industry, the result would obviously be inflation. The third factor that was ignored was the velocity of money, the actual turnover of the dollar, the effect of which was more important even than the number of dollars in circulation." Canadian Annual Review, 1937 and 1938, p. 73.

Of course, neither the L. S. R. critique nor those which followed it in the late thirties could alter the fact that, despite the confused thinking, a contribution had been made to the theory of employment and to stabilization policy, particularly by those individuals for whom the Social Credit system was only one approach to the analysis of economic problems. Nevertheless, in popular terms, with the lack of concern for sophisticated reasoning, the salutary economic aspects of Social Credit thought were bound to become submerged in a sea of "painless falsehoods."

114. The high calibre of the Royal Commission reports, written largely by economists, was alluded to earlier in this chapter.

115. It should be borne in mind that the "thought lag" of professional economists behind the "heretics" was not a uniquely Canadian, but a world, phenomenon, and that the development of Canadian "macro-economics" was little more retarded than that of other branches of the science.

116. A. B. Balcom, "The Automatic Gold Standard and the Necessary Modifications," Papers and Proceedings, IV (1932), pp. 133, 134. The very same "economic fatalism" had a wide following in Canadian newspaper circles. Thus, Mr. W. Headley, Associate Editor of the Montreal Gazette, commented in representative terms: "As the other depressions have passed, so this [Great Depression] will, in due course, give way to recovery. Economic crises are features of current business cycles, and, as Mr. Andrew Mellon said a quarter of a century ago, ... they are "as certain as the tides." Prosperity is bound to stretch the lines beyond the breaking point, and dull times are needed to restore them. The best that can be hoped, in the circumstances, is that the world, if sadder, is also wiser for these recurrent experiences. They are great tests of national stamina." "Commercial and Financial Review for the Year 1932," Gazette (Montreal, Jan. 4, 1933), p. 38.

117. Cf. Leacock, "The Economic Analysis of Industrial Depression," Papers and Proceedings, V (1933).

118. Ibid., p. 18.

119. Cf. I. M. Biss, Discussion on "The Economic Analysis of Industrial Depression," Papers and Proceedings, V (1933).

120. Ibid., p. 42.

121. Canada, Proceedings of the Royal Commission on Banking and Currency (Ottawa, 1933), III, p. 1360.

122. Cf. ibid., VI, pp. 2875-85.

123. Ibid., p. 2875.

124. Ibid., pp. 2875, 2876.

125. Ibid., p. 2879.

126. Cf. F. W. Burton, "The Business Cycle and the Problem of Economic Policy," The Canadian Economy and Its Problems (Toronto, 1934).

127. Cf. J. A. Schumpeter, The Theory of Economic Development (Cambridge, Mass., 1934).

128. Burton, "The Business Cycle and the Problem of Economic Policy," pp. 144, 145.

129. Ibid., pp. 147, 148,

130. Mr. Burton's views on monetary and fiscal policy are outlined in chapters VII and X, respectively.

131. For further treatment by Mr. Burton of this destabilizing factor, see "Wheat in Canadian History," C.J.E.P.S., III (May 1937); and "Staple Production and Canada's External Relations," Essays in Political Economy, ed. H. A. Innis (Toronto, 1938).

132. Cf. M. K. Inman, "Experience in Canadian Banking, 1929-34," unpublished Ph.D. thesis (Cambridge, Mass., 1938), chapter XI.

133. The "relative inflation" would be measured by the additional extent to which wholesale prices would have fallen had money supply and velocity remained unchanged. Most Canadian and American economists, in their preoccupation with price changes, seem to have missed the significance of the "relative inflation" in the years immediately preceding the 1929 collapse. Theirs had been a false sense of security which rested on their being deeply impressed with the relative stability of wholesale prices, and ignoring the very real danger signals arising throughout the economy.

134. These are Wicksellian concepts, the "money" or "market" rate being defined as the rate which actually prevails in the market, and the "natural" or "equilibrium" rate as the rate at which the demand for and supply of savings are equal. Cf. K. Wicksell, Lectures on Political Economy (London, 1935), II, pp. 27, 193.

135. Inman, "Experience in Canadian Banking, 1929-34," p. 235.

136. By this term, Professor Hayek apparently meant that the methods of production become more direct, less "roundabout," and less "capitalistic," in that a smaller amount of capital goods was used per unit of output of consumer goods. In the case of the "elongation of the structure of production" identified with the upswing, the opposite would be true. Cf. F. A. Hayek, Monetary Theory and the Trade Cycle (London, 1933); Prices and Production (London, 1935); The Pure Theory of Capital (London, 1941).

137. See, in this connection, the analysis contained in: A. H. Hansen, Full Recovery or Stagnation? (New York, 1938), chapter III; R. J. Saulnier, Contemporary Monetary Theory (New York, 1938), part III, pp. 215-300; Harberler, Prosperity and Depression, pp. 29-72, 481-91; Klein, The Keynesian Revolution, pp. 50-2.

138. Cf. A. F. W. Plumptre, Central Banking in the British Dominions (Toronto, 1940), chapters XV and XVI; also "The Distribution of Outlay and the Multiplier in the British Dominions," C.J.E.P.S., V (Aug. 1939).

139. Serious doubts have since arisen, among economists, as to the validity of Keynes's simple consumption function. See, for example, J. H. Williams, "An Appraisal of Keynesian Economics," Papers and Proceedings of the American Economic Association, XXXVIII (May 1948); also R. P. Mack, "Economics of Consumption," A Survey of Contemporary Economics, ed. B. F. Haley (Homewood, Illinois, 1952), II. But see A. H. Hansen, A Guide to Keynes (New York, 1953), chapter III.

140. In this instability of investment, Professor Plumptre found the solution to what he referred to as the "hen-and-egg" problem of income and expenditure. He felt justified, that is, in regarding changes in the general volume of incomes as being the consequence of variations in investment expenditures, and not vice versa--at least as far as changes originating domestically were concerned. For changes originating outside a country, it was the volume of incomes (among the exporting groups) which deserved causal pre-eminence. Plumptre, Central Banking in the British Dominions, pp. 346, 347.

141. But "if changes of incomes are chiefly generated by the fluctuating values of exports, a high marginal propensity to import will be a factor eliminating difficulties in the exchange market." Ibid., p. 349.

142. Ibid., p. 350.

143. Professor Plumptre realized that the increase in aggregate demand could be derived not only from exports but also from budgetary deficits, investment outlays, tariffs, etc.

144. Plumptre, Central Banking in the British Dominions, p. 356.

145. Professor Plumptre was quick to add that the concentration on domestic borrowing might not be desirable under all circumstances: "if ...it merely obviates the necessity for easing the financial situation by the creation of new money, that--in this day and age of 'intelligent monetary management'--is not necessarily a great virtue. And we must not forget that accumulating titles to wealth has its seamy side; for, in the absence of an adequate incentive to issue titles, to raise funds and invest them, the propensity to accumulate titles may simply produce a state of chronic underconsumption and depression." Ibid., p. 360.

146. Ibid.

147. Ibid., p. 361.

148. In 1939 Mr. R. B. Bryce of the Department of Finance also approached the problem of Canada's international economic vulnerability in Keynesian terms. Cf. R. B. Bryce, "The Effects on Canada of Industrial

Fluctuations in the United States, " C. J. E. P. S., V (Aug. 1939). His chief concern was with the influence of interwar American cycles on the export and investment components of Canadian national income. On the basis of his analysis, he came to the conclusion that: "The effects by way of trade are real and substantial, but not so preponderant that they could not be outweighed or substantially counteracted by movements in our trade with other countries. On the other hand, the influences by way of investment are more indirect and intangible, but no less effective. In part, they rest on a belief in themselves, on a belief that the dependence of Canadian business and finance on the United States is more complete than really is the case. The similar course of business in the two countries during the past fifteen or twenty years affords some basis for that belief. But I suggest that in part this similarity has been, if not accidental, then at least a result of unusually universal conditions, and that it is not at all impossible to picture a fair divergence between the course of business in the two countries. If that should not come about, it might itself reduce somewhat the dependence of our investment on American conditions, and thus reinforce itself. " Ibid., p. 386.

Chapter Seven

1. B. K. Sandwell, "Ideas of Banking Must Be Revised, " Saturday Night, December 30, 1933, p. 17.

2. The notion that the credit mechanism was a purely passive element in the monetary process had many eminent supporters in government and business. Among them was Prime Minister Bennett, who frequently went on record as stating emphatically that commercial banks lend only the money of their savings depositors. Canada, House of Commons Debates, Feb. 29, 1932, I, p. 649. Most of the radicals, on the other hand, continued to push their arguments to the other extreme. In this connection, see, especially, the views expressed by Mr. H. E. Spencer (Debates, Feb. 13, 1933, II, p. 2050; March 27, 1933, III, p. 3433; Feb. 4, 1935, I, p. 455; and Canada, House of Commons, Proceedings of the Select Standing Committee on Banking and Commerce--henceforth House Banking Committee Proceedings--1934, pp. 344-53); and by Mr. G. G. McGeer of Vancouver (Canada, Proceedings of the Royal Commission on Banking and Currency, 1933--henceforth Banking Commission Proceedings--II, pp. 508, 509).

3. See, in particular, the comments of Mr. Plumptre of the University of Toronto ("The Point of View of a Central Bank, " Canadian Forum, XIII Jan. 1933, p. 132); Mr. J. P. Bell, on behalf of the banks of Ontario (Banking Commission Proceedings, VI, pp. 3128, 3129); Mr. W. C. Good, representing the United Farmers of Ontario (ibid., V, pp. 2657, 2658); Mr. J. H. Creighton of the University of British Columbia (Central Banking in Canada, Vancouver, 1933, pp. 144, 145); and Dr. C. F. Wilson, a Canadian economist then teaching economics at Wellesley College ("Social Credit: Our Next Panacea, " Saturday Night, Toronto, Oct. 27, 1934).

4. The bankers seldom made reference to the quantity theory as such, their objections being implicit throughout their discussion of the monetary process. For a clear statement of the radical position--with its consequent assignment of responsibility for economic fluctuations to changes in credit volume induced by the commercial banks--see the remarks of Mr. R. Gardiner, Debates, Sept. 9, 1930, Special Session, pp. 44, 45. The cautious and on the whole sound, approach of Canadian economists is exemplified by the analyses of Professor Mackintosh of Queen's University ("Gold and the Decline of Prices, " Papers and Proceedings of the Canadian Political Science Association--henceforth Papers and Proceedings--III, 1931); Dr. D. M. Marvin, Economist for the Royal Bank of Canada (Discussion of L. D. Edie's "Business Forecasting, " Papers and Proceedings, III, 1931); Professor Balcom of Acadia University ("The Automatic Gold Standard and the Necessary Modifications, " Papers and Proceedings, IV, 1932); Mr. Parkinson of the University of Toronto (Banking Commission Proceedings, VI, p. 2875); and Mr. Creighton of the University of British Columbia (Central Banking in Canada, pp. 37, 38).

5. Debates, Feb. 29, 1932, I, p. 647.

6. The mechanics and effectiveness of this transaction, as well as of the 1934 legislation mentioned above, will be discussed in chapter IX.

7. Canadian Annual Review, 1933, p. 325.

8. Ibid.

9. Cf. Debates, June 19, 1934, IV, pp. 4085, 4086.

10. Cf. ibid., Feb. 6, 1933, II, p. 1832; and March 21, 1933, III, pp. 3205, 3208.

11. Ibid., March 21, 1933, III, p. 3208.

12. Ibid., Nov. 25, 1932, II, p. 1642.

13. Cf. ibid., June 16, 1931, III, pp. 2669, 2670.

14. Ibid., p. 2669.

15. Ibid., p. 2670. There were some notable Liberal dissenting voices. One of these was raised by Mr. I. Mackenzie. It was his view, in early 1932, that one of the great necessities was a comprehensive system of "controlled inflation": "I would advocate that earnest consideration be given to modifying our financial policy by the issue of Dominion currency. It was done during the War. Why not do it now in the war against poverty, misery, and unemployment which we are waging today. . . . We are living in changing times. I am sure that if [the Prime Minister] would give up his attachment to the fallacy and fiction of 'sound money' and deal immediately and fearlessly with the tremendous problem of meeting our debt and interest obligations, he would have the grateful regard of the Canadian people." Ibid., Feb. 29, 1932, I, p. 644; Feb. 13, 1933, II, pp. 2054, 2055. For a similar approach to recovery policy, see the argument put forward by the Liberal, Dr. F. W. Gershaw. Ibid., Feb. 6, 1933, II, pp. 713-16.

Mr. McGeer, though nominally a Liberal, could hardly be classified as anything but a radical. Consistently and loquaciously throughout the thirties, he set forth his programme for internal monetary expansion, free of interest obligations, by the central monetary authority. For procedural and other details during the early thirties, see Banking Commission Proceedings, II, pp. 448-607; also House Banking Committee Proceedings, 1934, pp. 645-706.

16. Cf. Canadian Annual Review, 1932, p. 714.

17. In 1933 Mr. Leman served as a member of the Royal Commission on Banking and Currency.

18. Address at the Annual General Meeting of the Canadian Bankers' Association, J. C. B. A., XXXIX (Jan., 1932), p. 166. Sir John Aird, President of the Canadian Bank of Commerce, also looked hopefully to the restoration of the gold standard as the basis for a revived world trade. Address at the Annual Meeting of Shareholders, Saturday Night, Jan. 13, 1934, pp. 26, 27. He regarded it, "under good management, not only as necessary to the life of international trade, but also as a safeguard against the tragic monetary disequilibrium of today." Ibid., p. 26.

Frequent expression was given during the thirties, to this argument that the gold standard was not inherently defective--that the monetary difficulties of the thirties arose because the gold standard was "badly worked," not because it "worked badly." This is a valid characterization of the past refusal of many countries to follow the "rules of the gold-standard game," particularly when such compliance involved drastic internal deflationary adjustments. It is true that international economic stability may have resulted from compliance with the "rules"--though even this was far from certain, in view of the severity of the cyclical disturbances at that time (a severity for which the classical economists had not allowed in their formulation of the international "price-specie" adjustment mechanism). The important point that the staunch advocates of the gold standard failed to grasp, however, is that during the thirties the amount of adjustment required came to exceed the bounds of practical policy within the social context of the countries concerned. The justification for the restoration of the pre-1914 gold standard should have been sought, not in the nicety of operation of the theoretical framework on which it was based, but rather in the extent to which this framework accorded with the "socio-economic facts of life."

19. Financial Post (Toronto), Jan. 21, 1933.

20. Address before the Winnipeg Board of Trade, J. C. B. A., XL (April 1933) p. 312.

21. Banking Commission Proceedings, VI, pp. 3165, 3175, 3176. Among the very few bankers who apparently showed, in some degree, a receptiveness to unorthodox monetary policy in the early thirties, was Mr. G. F. Towers, then Assistant to the General Manager of the Royal Bank of Canada. The view of Mr. Towers at that time are of special significance in the light of his subsequent appointment as Governor of the Bank of Canada. On the "depreciation" issue, he had this to say: "A connection with the pound sterling would, at the moment, tend to restore in Canada a level of prices nearer to that which prevailed during the years 1922-29, and would undo a certain portion of the damage created by the events of the subsequent years. The prewar gold standard, which I think

we all respect, was in effect a standard controlled very largely by England, and by English experience and financial guidance, and to me it appears that the pound sterling has better prospects for the maintenance of stability in the future than any other currency in the world." Discussion on J. P. Day's "Empire Currency Proposals," Papers and Proceedings, IV (1932), p. 160. Mr. Towers' confidence in the pound, as the bedrock of future international financial stability, was no more excessive than that of most financial observers throughout the world.

22. "Commercial and Financial Review for the Year 1932," Gazette (Montreal), Jan. 4, 1933, p. 24.

23. "Review for the Year 1933," Gazette, Jan. 3, 1934, p. 3.

24. Cf. Banking Commission Proceedings, V, pp. 2799-830.

25. Ibid., p. 2799.

26. Actually Canada had abandoned the gold standard de facto at the end of 1928, and legally in 1931 (see chapter III). In a sense, the attack made against the gold standard by the Economic Reform Association and others, notably the radicals, was an attack against the persistence of the "gold-standard mentality." It was more than that, however, for the gold standard could be appropriately regarded, on two special counts, as not having been fully abandoned: (1) in terms of the retention--apart from two reluctant deviations--of a substantial gold backing for Dominion currency, Canada was still very much on the gold standard;   and (2) the depreciation of the Canadian dollar after 1931 was not the result of deliberate governmental policy, but of merely permitting the dollar, largely through indecision, to fluctuate in response to the interplay of market forces.

27. Banking Commission Proceedings, V, p. 2813.

28. The radical position taken on the depreciation issue by Mr. M. Fisher, a Montreal importer of textiles, is noteworthy, not so much because he was an importer of British goods rather than an exporter to British markets--though this fact is of considerable interest--as because in his comments one gets a fleeting but nonetheless--in historical terms--important glimpse of the concept of the "multiplier." Thus, according to Mr. Fisher, "had the Canadian dollar been pegged to the pound sterling at par when the Bank of England suspended gold payments in September, 1931, the primary producers of western Canada would have received millions of dollars more internal purchasing power from their exports to England, than in fact they did receive, and the same is true of other exporting groups which do their foreign business in sterling.... Such purchasing power would have multiplied itself throughout the country." Ibid., p. 2450.

29. Ibid., p. 2815.

30. Ibid., V, pp. 2816, 2817.

31. Another interesting statement of the radical case for exchange depreciation can be found in the series of articles written for Saturday Night by Mr. B. K. Sandwell (Dec. 27, 1930; Jan. 24, 1931; April 11, 1931; Nov. 28, 1931; March 26, 1932; April 23, 1932; April 29, 1933).

32. There was no a priori reason why this should be so. "Export prices in Canadian dollars might not be increased by the full amount of depreciation either because of an attempt to enlarge the volume of exports by selling at a lower foreign price or as a result of competition." G. F. Towers, Memoranda and Tables Respecting the Bank of Canada, Extracted from Evidence Given before the House of Commons, Standing Committee on Banking and Commerce (Ottawa, 1939), p. 39.

33. G. G. Coote, Discussion on W. A. Mackintosh's "Gold and the Decline in Prices," Papers and Proceedings, III (1931), p. 120. Mr. Coote's estimate of the increase in the cost of living following depreciation probably was not high enough. No account, apparently, was taken of the price increases which would have resulted from the protection afforded domestic producers by currency depreciation. This qualification, however, would not materially affect the "reflationary" aspect of the case for depreciation.

34. Ibid., p. 122.

35. Debates, Feb. 29, 1932, I, p. 638.

36. Banking Commission Proceedings, Addenda, p. 53.

37. Cf. Debates, March 24, 1933, III, p. 3392.

38. Banking Commission Proceedings, Addenda, p. 59.

39. Ibid., p. 60.

40. Debates, June 17, 1931, III, pp. 2749, 2750. See also the statements of Mr. Garland (ibid., June 18, 1931, III, p. 2795), Mr. M. N. Campbell (ibid., Feb. 29, 1932, I, pp. 657-9), and Mr. Irvine (ibid., Oct. 11, 1932, I, p. 81).

41. See, for example, the evidence of Mr. H. C. Boyd and Mr. Bevington, of Alberta, and Mr. C. A. Bowman, editor of the Ottawa Citizen, before the Royal Commission on Banking and Currency (Banking Commission Proceedings, III, pp. 1205, 1236-9; and VI, pp. 3391-409); also the ideas of Mr. McGeer, cited in n. 15; and Mr. E. S. Woodward's proposal, on behalf of the Free Economy League of Canada, for the elimination of hoarding through the stamp-scrip system originally advocated by Gesell and later approved by Irving Fisher (House Banking Committee Proceedings, 1924, pp. 722-35).

42. Banking Commission Proceedings, IV, p. 1824.

43. Ibid., II, p. 820. The issue of exchange rate stability vs. internal price stability was later fully defined before the Banking Commission by the League for Social Reconstruction: "As a general rule, the stability of foreign exchange rates is desirable for short periods, and for long periods when conditions throughout the world are reasonably stable and prosperous. Such stability is of great assistance to exporters and importers in the safeguarding of long-period contracts and the maintenance of stable prices and costs in relation to all articles entering into foreign trade. But when, in the national interest, the balance of advantage lies with the depreciation of the exchange rate in the interests of a stable internal price structure, we consider that it would be a mistake to attempt to maintain the Canadian dollar at a high exchange value. On occasions of violent de-

flation abroad, as has occurred during the last four years, we suggest
that a conscious policy of controlled exchange depreciation would have been
a desirable method of mitigating the effects of this deflation." Ibid., VI,
pp. 2948, 2949.

44. Mr. Plumptre defined "monetary policy" in an interesting and--
for the early thirties--unusual manner. He took the phrase to mean any
course of action designed to affect the general flow of income through the
use of monetary or fiscal machinery: "Such action may be taken along a
variety of lines, of which four are the most usual. The volume of money
available for use, as incomes or for other purposes, may be varied. The
interest rates at which money is borrowed and lent may be changed. The
foreign exchange rate may be varied in one direction or another. The existing flow of money may be redirected by special fiscal measures of taxation, borrowing, and expenditure. The mention of the last of these four
lines of action immediately discloses the fact that the problems and policies
of public finance and of monetary management are inseparable." A. F. W.
Plumptre, "Canadian Monetary Policy," The Canadian Economy and Its
Problems, eds. Innis and Plumptre (Toronto, 1934), p. 159.

45. Many of the exchange-rate issues raised by Mr. Plumptre at
that time will be subjected to further analysis in the critical appraisal of
depreciation made in chapter IX--an appraisal based partly on the views
expressed by Mr. Plumptre himself at the end of the thirties.

46. Cf. A. F. W. Plumptre, "Currency Management in Canada,"
Papers and Proceedings, IV (1932); and "Canadian Monetary Policy,"
The Canadian Economy and Its Problems.

47. Plumptre, "Currency Management in Canada," Papers and Proceedings, IV (1932), p. 148.

48. Ibid., p. 149.

49. Ibid.

50. Ibid., p. 150.

51. Cf. Plumptre, "Canadian Monetary Policy," The Canadian Economy and Its Problems.

52. Ibid., p. 166.

53. Ibid.

54. While advocating exchange depreciation as a temporary anti-
depression policy for Canada, Mr. Plumptre recognized the "beggar-my-
neighbour" and destabilizing aspects of such a policy when used over appreciable periods of time and in haphazard fashion. It was clear to him
that "What one country gains, the rest must lose--for when we say that
the American dollar [for example] has "gone down," it is the same thing
as saying that all other currencies have "gone up." They cannot all go
down in terms of each other. And thus exchange depreciation is no way
out of a world depression. What one country gains by depreciation of its
own currency, the rest will lose through the appreciation of theirs. Indeed, haphazard depreciation is certain to cause such risks and uncertainties in international trade and finance that recovery must be retarded.
Fluctuating currencies have always been a fruitful source of trade-wars

and tariffs." A. F. W. Plumptre, "Do We Need Inflation?" <u>Canadian Forum</u>, XIV (Jan. 1934), p. 130.

55. <u>Ibid.</u>; and "Canadian Monetary Policy," <u>The Canadian Economy and Its Problems</u>.

56. Plumptre, "Do We Need Inflation?," <u>Canadian Forum</u>, XIV (Jan. 1934), p. 131.

57. See, for example, C. F. Drummond, "The Real Task of the Conference," and "Price Raising and Gold Buying," <u>Saturday Night</u> (Toronto), June 3, 1933, and Jan. 13, 1934, respectively.

58. <u>Banking Commission Proceedings</u>, VI, p. 2860.

59. <u>Ibid.</u>, pp. 2859, 2860.

60. Article in <u>Canadian Business</u>, VI (Jan. 1933), p. 11. For Professor Jackson's statement on fiscal policy in the same context, see chapter X.

61. Cf. Creighton, <u>Central Banking in Canada</u>, chapter VII.

62. <u>Ibid.</u>, pp. 171, 172.

63. <u>Ibid.</u>, p. 172.

64. Cf. H. C. Goldenberg, "Money and Depression," <u>Canadian Forum</u>, XIV (June 1934), p. 338.

65. <u>Ibid.</u>

66. Cf. F. W. Burton, "The Business Cycle and the Problem of Economic Policy," <u>The Canadian Economy and Its Problems</u>.

67. <u>Ibid.</u>, p. 153.

68. <u>Ibid.</u>, p. 156.

69. Cf. F. A. Knox, Discussion on J. P. Day's "An International Gold Standard" <u>Papers and Proceedings</u>, VI (1934); and "The Nation's Money," <u>Queen's Quarterly</u>, XLI (Autumn 1934).

70. Knox, Discussion on "An International Gold Standard," <u>Papers and Proceedings</u>, VI (1934), p. 274.

71. Knox, "The Nation's Money," <u>Queen's Quarterly</u>, XLI (Autumn 1934), pp. 305, 306.

72. Cf. J. P. Day, "Empire Currency Proposals," and "Canadian Monetary Policy--An International Standard," <u>Papers and Proceedings</u>, IV (1932), and VI (1934), respectively.

73. Apparently, though, Professor Day was not adverse to a limited degree of internal inflation. On at least one occasion known to the author, he observed that "a reasonable general inflation might easily be justified now [1931] as merely correcting the excessive deflation of values which is giving us so much trouble." <u>Gazette</u> (Montreal), Feb. 28, 1931.

74. Day, "Canadian Monetary Policy," <u>Papers and Proceedings</u>, VI (1934), p. 265.

75. <u>Ibid.</u>, p. 266. Professors Curtis and Knox and Mr. Plumptre voiced strenuous objections to Professor Day's position. <u>Ibid.</u>, pp. 272-5. According to Professor Curtis, he was "quite unreasonable in his strictures on American banking policy and his panegyrics on British monetary policy. I think there are abundant facts to show that the United States had done much to further international co-operation--with little thanks to themselves--and

that the abandonment of the gold standard by Great Britain was a direct result of her own monetary policies.... [Mr. Day's advocacy of a sterling exchange standard] leaves out the most significant factor in the whole set-up between Canada and the United States--that is the financial relationship between these two countries." Ibid., p. 272.

Mr. Plumptre believed that Professor Day's approval of the gold standard sprang not so much from a desire for its restoration as from a desire to regain the type of economic system in which the gold standard had functioned effectively. "But that world is gone for good. It is to be hoped that Canada's central bankers will have no gold-standard complex; and that their actions will be based upon appreciation of the present and perspicacity regarding the future, rather than upon hopes of resurrecting the past." Ibid., pp. 273-4.

In the opinion of Professor Knox, it was particularly inopportune, at that time (1934), to make any definite decision on the exchange rate problem. "The long run trend of events is too burdened with the debris of depression to be discernible. If a large measure of international trade is recovered, if the nations move to restore a world economy, the establishment of exchange stability on the basis of gold or the pound sterling may be possible and advisable. If present tendencies are continued, even with some mitigation as business recovers, it will be wise for Canada to preserve complete freedom of action in these respects." Ibid., p. 275.

76. This was, in essence, the technique of the exchange stabilization funds then being put into operation by Great Britain and the United States.

77. Cf. H. Michell, "The Gold Standard," Industrial Canada, XXXII (Nov. 1931), p. 42.

78. Banking Commission Proceedings, III, pp. 1367-70, 1388, 1389. In closer proximity to the truth would have been the following arguments: (1) both the abandonment of the gold standard and the unprecedented decline in international trade were the results of more fundamental developments, such as world-wide postwar structural maladjustments and the economic collapse of the United States; (2) high and stable levels of international investment could be regarded as incompatible with a non-gold standard only on the very dubious assumption that no such standard could consistently provide exchange stability; and (3) there was little theoretical or empirical justification for associating the gold standard with either short-run or long-run price stability.

79. Banking Commission Proceedings, III, p. 1389.

80. Ibid.

81. Cf. Balcom, "The Automatic Gold Standard," Papers and Proceedings, IV (1932).

82. Ibid., p. 130.

83. Ibid. It seems clear, by way of critical comment, that the validity of Professor Balcom's long-run case, at least in its theoretical aspect, depends upon the assumption of a consistent equivalence between productivity increases and price declines; and that the soundness of the contention that the business cycle is not solely a monetary phenomenon does not change the fact of the growing tendency of countries to refuse to engage in the restrictive activity called for by the gold-standard "rules" once the severe

cyclical disturbances have occurred, from whatever cause or combination of causes.

84. Balcom, "The Automatic Gold Standard, " Papers and Proceedings, IV (1932), pp. 134-5.

85. Cf. Banking Commission Proceedings, IV, pp. 2026-34.

86. Ibid., pp. 2031-2032. Apart from the neglect of reciprocal demand elasticities as a basis for the determination of the effects on exports and imports, three points of criticism should be noted in connection with Professor Clark's analysis. First, it was not likely, at least in the short run, that currency expansion would appreciably affect prices in that sector of the economy sustained largely through exports to world markets. In the second place, even assuming the opposite to be true, the stimulus to imports would, after all, come about as a result of the rise in incomes throughout the Dominion, and any tendency towards increased imports and reduced exports might be offset by further external depreciation (as noted by Professor Clark) and/or other adjustments. (The real danger was, of course, that Canada's economic position might deteriorate through large-scale capital flight and perverse speculation-induced movements of goods and services into and out of the Dominion.) In this sense, the vital question was not whether imports and exports were stimulated or checked, but whether any rise in incomes was effected; an unfavourable balance of payments on current account would not have been incompatible with domestic prosperity if it had sprung from rising domestic incomes. The third point is that, in terms of the situation with which Canada was confronted in the early thirties, the transitional nature of the changes flowing from depreciation was almost totally irrelevant; what did matter was the contribution being made to Canadian economic recovery while the balance-of-payments equilibrating process was in operation.

87. Banking Commission Proceedings, IV, p. 2029.

88. Ibid., p. 2032.

89. Ibid., p. 2033.

90. Cf. ibid., V. pp. 2603, 2611, 2615.

Chapter Eight

1. Canada, Proceedings of the Royal Commission on Banking and Currency (Ottawa, 1933), I-VI, and Addenda (henceforth contracted to Banking Commission Proceedings).

2. For a detailed account of this Royal Commission, see M. L. Stokes, The Bank of Canada (Toronto, 1939), chapter V. The Proceedings are here reappraised in terms of their contribution to Canadian monetary and fiscal thought, and in the light of the changes which have come about in general economic thinking since the publication of Professor Stokes's book.

3. See, for example, the comments of Mr. H. F. Liggins, Superintendent of the Saskatchewan Branches of the Canadian Bank of Commerce ("The Relationship of Bank Deposits and Loans, " J.C.B.A., XLI, Oct. 1 1933, p. 87); also of Mr. S. H. Logan, General Manager of that Bank (Address at Annual Meeting of Shareholders, Saturday Night, Toronto, Jan. 13, 1934).

4. Canada, House of Commons, Proceedings of the Select Standing Committee on Banking and Commerce (henceforth contracted to House Banking Committee Proceedings), 1934, p. 281.

5. Ibid., p. 286. See the similar line of reasoning followed by Mr. B. Leman, General Manager of the National Canadian Bank (Canadian Annual Review, 1932, p. 461); by Sir Charles Gordon, President of the Bank of Montreal (ibid., 1933, p. 575); and by Mr. H. F. Patterson, General Manager of the Bank of Nova Scotia (House Banking Committee Proceedings, 1934, pp. 374, 375).

6. Cf. Banking Commission Proceedings, VI, pp. 3150-381.

7. Ibid., p. 3230.

8. Ibid., p. 3231.

9. Ibid.

10. Ibid., p. 3380.

11. Ibid., p. 3232.

12. When it had become obvious--from government pronouncements and the publication of the Report of the Royal Commission on Banking and Currency--that a central bank was to be set up in Canada despite all the opposition which the bankers could muster, their position shifted to one of grudging acceptance accompanied by serious misgivings in terms of administrative inefficiency, political domination, and detrimental effects on the profitability of chartered bank operations. For expression of the new "co-operative" attitude, see the views advanced by Mr. Wilson of the Royal Bank of Canada (Canadian Annual Review, 1933, p. 599), and by Sir John Aird of the Canadian Bank of Commerce (Annual Report to the Shareholders, Canadian Business, VII March 1934, p. 40).

There were, however, a few leading bankers who favoured a central bank before its establishment became a certainty; one of these was Mr. G. F. Towers, serving at that time as Assistant to the General Manager of the Royal Bank of Canada (see Canadian Annual Review, 1934, p. 87); another was Dr. D. M. Marvin, economic adviser to the same institution (see Discussion on "Business Forecasting," Papers and Proceedings of the Canadian Political Science Association (henceforth contracted to Papers and Proceedings), III, 1931, p. 61).

13. Among the few critical references made to this relationship were those involving the efficacy of open market operations in Canada. Even if such operations could have been carried out, "there is reason to doubt whether they could have positive effect of such importance. So many of Canada's major products sell on an export basis that, so long as the exchange rate is stable, our index of wholesale prices closely reflects changes in world prices over which we have no control. The discount or premium on Canadian exchange in relation to the currencies of other countries is the major factor in any discrepancy between the Canadian and world price levels." Banking Commission Proceedings, VI, p. 3163. Emphasizing further the international basis of the Canadian economy, the bankers argued that "an open-market policy designed to produce conditions of 'easy' money in Canada might well, by leading to heavy importations of bonds

from the United States, cause a pressure on the foreign-exchange market, an outward drain of gold [assuming, of course, a restoration of the gold standard], and a consequent diminution of the credit base in Canada." *Ibid.*, p. 3162.

14. *Ibid.*, p. 3213. The bankers did acknowledge two cases, those of Britain and Sweden between 1931 and 1933, in which central banks did seem to have stabilized price levels. But they were careful to point out that in both instances there was a local explanation for the success that had been achieved: "In the case of Britain, the structure of the money market is such as to give the central bank an unusually close control of fluctuations in credit, and this control has been supplemented by the Exchange Equalization Account.... In the case of Sweden, the central bank appears to have achieved its object almost wholly by means of operations in the foreign-exchange market; but these were simplified by the fact that Sweden is, on balance, neither a debtor nor a creditor country; and so faces neither the problem of making regular payments of interest abroad, nor the problem of receiving such payments at home." *Ibid.*, VI, p. 3355.

15. *Ibid.*, p. 3161. The bankers might justifiably have added that the heavy structural concentration in Canadian banking gave rise to both aggravating and ameliorative influences in the achievement of effective moral suasion. In the former case, there was the danger of the preponderance of power resting with the commercial banks rather than with the central bank; in the latter case, there was the possibility of establishing closer and more direct contact between the central and commercial banks. The net effect would, of course, depend upon the relative strength of these opposing factors, which would, in turn, reduce itself to the psychological question as to the attitude of the commercial banks towards the central bank. In these terms, the prospects for effective moral suasion, at least in the early stages of Canadian central bank operations, were not overly bright.

16. *Ibib.*, p. 3161.

17. *Ibid.*, p. 3162.

18. *Ibid.*, p. 3163.

19. *Ibid.*, p. 3372.

20. *Ibid.* The bankers cautioned, quite appropriately, that: "It is not easy to determine, at any given time, the fact that business is becoming over-expanded; and even when this has been realized, the task of checking an over-expansion, without at the same time causing business to contract sharply, is one of extreme delicacy.... It is [moreover] as difficult to determine, at an early stage in its development, the fact that a general deflation is under way, as to form a judgment with regard to the possible over-expansion of domestic business; and the task of initiating an adjustment of conditions in the domestic market to the facts of deflation abroad, would be just as difficult as that of checking over-expansion at home without causing a sharp reaction." *Ibid.*, pp. 3370, 3371.

21. The bankers pointed repeatedly to the primitive state of the Canadian money market: "Canada has no bill market and no market for bankers'

acceptances. Bills of exchange bought from their clients by the banks are not subsequently negotiated in this country. The Canadian exchange broker is an intermediary, pure and simple between the banks. Outside the banks, there are no portfolios of acceptances or commercial bills in Canada." Ibid., p. 3157. However, they did not, as they well might have done, associate this condition with the ineffectiveness of the rediscount rate in Canada. For them the association was rather with open market operations, which they apparently interpreted to include the commercial paper market.

22. One of the prime concerns of the bankers was the danger of central bank monopolization of the note issue: "For all of these reasons-- because the cancellation of the present bank-note issue would penalize small settlements; because it would penalize the commercial banks themselves, by lessening their earnings; and because its retention would not give to the commercial banks (as it has not done in the past) an independent discretion inconsistent with sound monetary policy--it is maintained that, whatever may be done in regard to the Dominion Notes Act and the Finance Act, and whatever institution may be created for the control of credit and currency, the sole right of note issue should not be vested in the new institution." Ibid., pp. 3374, 3375.

23. Ibid., p. 3371.

24. Ibid., p. 3381. The prevailing sentiment among Canadian investment bankers--apart from their resentment of the commercial banks' encroachment upon their activities--tended to support that group on the central bank issue. Thus, Mr. J. M. Robinson, appearing before the Royal Commission on behalf of the investment bankers of Saint John, contended that under the Finance Act the federal Department of Finance had been occupying a position roughly equivalent to that of a central bank--a position which had been operated to the general good of the Dominion. The need for a central bank in the larger sense had not yet arisen. Moreover, the establishment of such an institution was undesirable in the Canadian confederation which embraced a political partnership of provinces with strong special interests. When and as further activities became necessary or advisable, the functions of the Department of Finance could readily be extended to meet the needs. Ibid., IV, pp. 2196, 2197.

25. Attention should be drawn here to the series of articles written by "A Canadian Banker" on the central bank question. His over-all attitude was the typical one of opposition to a Canadian central bank on grounds of the adequacy of the chartered banks and the grave problems posed by central bank operations. In concrete terms, he argued that the chartered banks could in no way be considered responsible for the 1931 depreciation of the Canadian dollar, or for the intensification of the depression through loan liquidation; and that a Canadian central bank would be impotent because of the absence of a money market and the minor importance of the cost of money as a component of business costs. Financial Post (Toronto), Dec. 10, 17, 24, 31, 1932. See, also, the anti-central-bank article of the Secretary of the Canadian Bank of Commerce, Mr. F. C. Biggar, "Canadian Bankers and a Central Bank," Papers and Proceedings, V (1933).

26. The attitude of Western businessmen was rooted largely in their dissatisfaction with the relative stringency of credit conditions in the West, and with the dominant industrial and financial position which had been attained by the business community in the East.

27. The statements made by provincial government leaders and the press usually proceeded in parallel fashion. See, especially, the pro-central-bank views expressed by Mr. J. Bracken, Premier of Manitoba, and Mr. W. J. P. Macmillan, Acting Premier of Prince Edward Island (Banking Commission Proceedings, IV, pp. 1690, 1691, and Addenda, pp. 1-9, respectively); also the contrary approach taken by Mr. G. H. I. Cockburn, President of the Executive Council of New Brunswick, and Mr. P. Bilkey, Editor-in-Chief of the Montreal Gazette (ibid., IV, pp. 2167-9, and "Commercial and Financial Review for the Year 1932, " Gazette, Jan. 2, 1932, p. 2, respectively).

28. The relationship between the proposed central bank and the federal government was the subject of heated debate, and of numerous organizational changes, throughout the decade of the thirties (cf. Stokes, The Bank of Canada, chapter VII). On present reflection, the issue of a nationalized central bank (in Canada as well as elsewhere) would appear to have received a disproportionate amount of attention--probably because of the strong English tradition of private central banking. It should have been realized, as English experience had shown, that the ownership aspect of central banking was of secondary importance; that central bank policy, if it was to be effective, could not be carried out in a political vacuum, free of governmental co-ordination with other economic policies; and that, in the absence of any private institution with a long tradition of social responsibility (such as the Bank of England), ultimate control powers would have to be invested in the government.

29. Banking Commission Proceedings, V, pp. 2362-5.

30. Ibid., p. 2365. A wide variety of minor amendments was put forward by the conservative businessmen. For example, Mr. M. Marois, President of the Quebec Shoe Manufacturers' Association, suggested, instead of a central bank, "the establishment of a Bureau of Information which would keep in touch with the different branches of industry through the Board of Directors of their Associations, in view of studying the particular conditions of each industry, and advising the banks as to their needs." Ibid., p. 2319.

31. Ibid., pp. 2433-53.
32. Ibid., pp. 2820-6.
33. Ibid., p. 2439.
34. Ibid., p. 2440.
35. Ibid.
36. Ibid., p. 2445.
37. Ibid., p. 2451.
38. Ibid., p. 2453.
39. Ibid., p. 2823.
40. Ibid., p. 2824. The Association was arguing, in effect, that the

only type of control institution worth setting up in Canada was one in which were combined both monetary and fiscal functions.

41.   There were a few instances of radical uncertainty on, and even opposition to, the establishment of a central bank. For example, Mr. E. Hebert, a Manitoba farmer, believed that the Canadian banking system was functioning properly, although interest rates were high, and that a new central bank would give rise to inefficiency and political corruption. Cf. Banking Commission Proceedings, IV, pp. 1870, 1871. Mr. J. B. Reed, representing the Quebec Branch of the United Farmers of Canada, told the Royal Commission that "we are willing to leave it to you and the government to decide whether or not we need a central bank." Ibid., V, p. 2399.

42.   This observation should be qualified. The issue of nationalization, for example, underlay the radicals' growing skepticism regarding the efficacy of a central banking institution superimposed upon the existing structure. Such an institution would be "a technical improvement in our banking system," and it was "a potential instrument for bringing about desirable social changes"; but it would not automatically bring about those changes, "and so long as our present politicians and financiers are at the wheel, we may be sure that a central bank will not be used for any such purpose." Editorial, Canadian Forum, XIV (Nov. 1933), p. 44.

43.   Banking Commission Proceedings, II, pp. 918-31.

44.   Ibid., pp. 922, 923.

45.   Ibid., pp. 928, 929.

46.   Ibid., p. 929.

47.   Ibid., p. 930.

48.   Ibid., III, p. 1640.

49.   Ibid.

50.   Banking Commission Proceedings, Addenda, p. 61. Mr. Coote had been concerned, earlier, lest the Royal Commission be rendered useless by the appointment of orthodox Canadian bankers. He had suggested that the Government appoint "men of the type of John Maynard Keynes, Lord Macmillan, or Reginald McKenna, and with these a few Canadians, some of whom could be found capable and unbiased and not in any way connected with our banks." Canada, House of Commons Debates, March 24, 1933, III, p. 3391.

With the actual appointment of the Royal Commission, the worst radical fears were apparently realized. Taking an even stronger position than Mr. Coote, the Canadian Forum declared editorially that: "The colonialism which makes us in Canada so liable to be dazzled by the names of prominent Englishmen, has kept most of our newspapers from pointing out that Mr. Bennett has pretty thoroughly packed his Banking Commission. Only one of his five Commissioners (Mr. Brownlee) represents anything but the most orthodox banking opinions. The original Macmillan Commission in England made its remarkable report not because of the personality of its chairman (Lord Macmillan), who is a rather commonplace industrious lawyer, but because it included two elements in its membership who are completely unrepresented in Mr. Bennett's selection (the unorthodox banker like Mr. McKenna, and the academic economist like Mr. J. M. Keynes and Professor T. E. Gregory)." Canadian Forum, XIII (Sept. 1933), p. 445.

Professor Gregory did give evidence before the Commission, expressing himself strongly in favour of a central bank, even while acknowledging the absence of a Canadian money market, the great Canadian dependence on international economic change, and the existence of quasi-central-banking powers under the Finance Act. See Banking Commission Proceedings, VI, pp. 2976-3049; also Stokes, The Bank of Canada, pp. 100-5. Mr. Coote's motion that Keynes be called to give evidence before the House Banking and Commerce Committee in 1934 was rejected. Cf. House Banking Committee Proceedings, p. 106.

51. Banking Commission Proceedings, II, pp. 815-33.
52. Ibid., p. 825, 830.
53. Ibid., p. 831. The "government bank" would, among other things, presumably facilitate the embarkation, by the Dominion government, on a "substantial program of useful public works financed by direct use of the national credit to provide employment and place purchasing power in the hands of consumers." Ibid., p. 833. In other words, the U. F. A. was proposing a rather comprehensive monetary-fiscal programme--with government expenditures, to the extent necessary, financed through social credit means.
54. Ibid., V, pp. 2656-73.
55. Ibid., pp. 2670, 2671.
56. Ibid., pp. 2671, 2672.
57. Ibid., p. 2672.
58. Ibid., Addenda, p. 12. Because of the tax burden which the payment of interest involved, the central bank would presumably be the source of new currency based on non-interest-bearing government certificates and used to finance a large-scale programme of public works; a percentage of this issue would be withdrawn from circulation each year proportionate to the decreased value of the asset created. Ibid., pp. 12, 13.
59. Ibid., VI, pp. 2933-53.
60. Ibid., p. 2945.
61. Ibid., pp. 2947, 2948.
62. Ibid., p. 2948.
63. Ibid.
64. Ibid., III, pp. 1357-95.
65. Ibid., p. 1391.
66. Ibid., p. 1393.
67. Ibid., V, pp. 2737-45.
68. Ibid., p. 2738.
69. Ibid., p. 2739.
70. Ibid., p. 2741.
71. Ibid., pp. 2337-45, 2549-79.
72. Ibid., p. 2554.
73. Ibid., p. 2577.

74. Dr. W. C. Clark, before his appointment as Deputy Minister of Finance in 1932, had been a prominent member of the Queen's group and its earliest advocate of a Canadian central bank. For a common expression of views by the Queen's economists, see "The Proposal for a Central Bank," Queen's Quarterly XL (Aug. 1933).

75. See C. A. Curtis, "Credit Control in Canada," Papers and Proceedings, II (1930); "Canada and the Gold Standard," Queen's Quarterly XXXVIII (Winter 1931); "The Canadian Monetary System," Canadian Forum, XII (March 1932); Discussion on "Banking and Currency," Papers and Proceedings, V (1933); Banking Commission Proceedings, VI, pp. 3067-76; "The Bank of Canada," Canadian Forum, XIV (May 1934). Early in 1932, Professor Curtis, pointing to the need for overhauling the whole structure of banking and monetary legislation, had suggested the appropriateness of a "Canadian Macmillan Report." "The Canadian Monetary System," Canadian Forum, XII (March 1932), p. 209.

76. Discussion on "Banking and Currency," p. 246.

77. "The Canadian Monetary System," p. 209.

78. Banking Commission Proceedings, VI, p. 3069.

79. Ibid., pp. 3052-59a.

80. Ibid., pp. 3053, 3054.

81. Ibid., p. 3056.

82. Ibid., pp. 3057, 3058.

83. Ibid., pp. 3058, 3059a.

84. Ibid., pp. 3060-66.

85. Ibid., p. 3062.

86. Ibid., p. 3066.

87. Ibid., p. 3065.

88. Ibid.

89. Ibid., p. 3066.

90. A. F. W. Plumptre, a series of seven articles on "A Central Bank for Canada," Financial Post, Oct. 8, 15, 22, 29, 1932; Nov. 5, 12, 19, 1932. Mr. Plumptre served subsequently as Assistant Secretary to the Royal Commission on Banking and Currency.

91. Ibid., Oct. 15, 1932, p. 3.

92. Ibid.

93. Ibid., Oct. 29, 1932, p. 8.

94. Mr. Plumptre pointed out that the stability of Canadian government, as well as Canada's membership in the British Empire, made it most unlikely that the great creditor powers would exert on a Canadian central bank the strong and direct influence that they had exerted on the central banks of other debtor countries. The dangers from internal political interference through a board of directors appointed by the government were more serious for Canada. There were three such dangers: "The first is that one political party might, unless the tenure of office on the board were sufficiently long, be able to "pack" the board with puppets who would use the central bank for party purposes. This danger is fortunately remote. Secondly, the party in power, either from a desire to distribute

rewards among its supporters or from a lack of knowledge of the type of man necessary, might appoint incompetent men. Thirdly, political appointees are probably more susceptible to political pressure than men who have been raised to office through other channels." Ibid., Nov. 5, 1932, p. 3.

95. "Countries whose economic system is bound up closely with the export of one or two commodities of highly variable prices and production are clearly not countries whose economic conditions are easily influenced by control of the volume of money and credit. If harvests are good and world prices are high, attempts to contract bank loans would probably not check a boom materially. Nor would efforts to pump money into circulation be likely to be very effective in alleviating a depression caused by short harvests and low world prices." Ibid.

96. The probable, though not necessarily desirable, taking-over of the chartered bank note issue by the central bank would not have constituted, according to Mr. Plumptre, an additional source of disturbance. In any event, the chartered banks' case for government compensation for income losses was strong, and there was no reason to believe that such compensation would not be forthcoming. Ibid.

97. Ibid.

98. Ibid., Nov. 12, 1932, p. 8.

99. Ibid.

100. For Mr. Plumptre, the immediate gain from the other central bank functions (including note issuance, serving as a bankers' bank, being a depository of government funds, etc.), considered alone, would hardly have been worth the cost of establishing such an institution. Ibid., Nov. 19, 1932, p. 9.

101. Mr. Plumptre regarded the fifth argument as irrelevant, on the ground that to prove that the banking system was perfect was not to prove that change in the monetary system was unnecessary. Ibid., p. 15.

102. Ibid.

103. Ibid.

104. Central Banking in Canada (Vancouver, 1933). Mr. Creighton made a similar analysis, in abbreviated form, before the Royal Commission, on behalf of the British Columbia Teachers' Federation. Banking Commission Proceedings, II, pp. 658-73. See, also, "Finance Act as Substitute for Central Bank," Saturday Night (Toronto), Sept. 2, 1933.

105. Central Banking in Canada, p. 124.

106. Ibid., p. 125.

107. Ibid., p. 141.

108. Ibid., p. 182.

109. Ibid..

110. J. P. Day, Considerations on the Demand for a Central Bank in Canada (Toronto, 1933).

111. Brief mention was accorded a fifth purpose, that of providing a fiscal agent for the government. But for Professor Day one of the prerequisites to sound monetary policy was central bank freedom from govern-

ment control; otherwise, there could be no independent policy judgment based on economic analysis.

112. Day, <u>Considerations on the Demand for a Central Bank in Canada</u>, p. 21.

113. <u>Ibid</u>.

114. <u>Ibid</u>., p. 23.

115. <u>Ibid</u>., pp. 29, 30.

116. <u>Ibid</u>., p. 32.

117. <u>Ibid</u>., pp. 32, 33.

118. <u>Ibid</u>., pp. 34, 43.

119. <u>Ibid</u>., p. 44. The Advisory Committee would be composed of two bankers, one economist, and two representatives of industry and agriculture. Professor Day suggested that this agency be established as a Standing Committee of the Canadian Bankers' Association; for him this was the only alternative to governmental control of banking policy, "which every international Conference has agreed always subordinates sound finance to political expediency." <u>Ibid</u>., p. 45.

120. <u>Ibid</u>.

121. <u>Banking Commission Proceedings</u>, VI, pp. 2855-927.

122. <u>Ibid</u>., p. 2873.

123. <u>Ibid</u>., 2874, 2875.

124. It would be virtually impossible, according to Mr. Parkinson, to extend monetary control to investment activity. "For Canadian purposes, there is a huge field of operations covered by the generic title of investment which is not capable of being influenced by the rate of interest." <u>Ibid</u>., p. 2925.

125. <u>Ibid</u>., p. 2860.

126. <u>Ibid</u>., p. 2861.

127. <u>Ibid</u>.

128. They were, in the order of their appearance: Professor W. A. Carrothers representing the Economics Department of the University of British Columbia (<u>Banking Commission Proceedings</u>, I, pp. 352-403); Professor H. W. Hewetson of the University of Alberta (<u>ibid</u>., III, pp. 1052-73); Professor W. B. Hurd of Brandon College (<u>ibid</u>., IV, pp. 1718-52); Professor A. B. Clark of the University of Manitoba (<u>ibid</u>., IV, pp. 2026-34); Mr. A. J. Glazebrook and Professor G. A. Elliott of the University of Toronto (<u>ibid</u>., V, pp. 2593-651, and Addenda, pp. 22-30, respectively); and Professor W. R. Maxwell of Dalhousie University (<u>ibid</u>., Addenda, pp. 45, 46).

129. <u>Debates</u>, May 13, 1931, II, p. 1562.

130. <u>Ibid</u>., Feb. 29, 1932, I, pp. 649, 650.

131. <u>Ibid</u>., March 28, 1933, IV, p. 3471.

132. <u>Ibid</u>., Feb. 1934, I, pp. 823-30.

133. Mr. Rhodes was careful to defend the existing system of monetary control and he sought to forestall any impression that the new institution was necessitated by the deterioration of the Canadian banking structure. The changed conditions requiring governmental attention were to be regarded

as largely of external origin, in the sense of reflecting serious postwar maladjustments throughout the world.

134. Debates, Feb. 27, 1933, I, p. 2511.

135. Canada, Report of the Royal Commission on Banking and Currency in Canada (Ottawa, 1933); henceforth contracted to Banking Report. For purposes of this study, only the impact of Canadian thinking on the Report will be considered. A systematic outline of the Report itself can be found in Stokes, The Bank of Canada, chapter VI.

136. Banking Report, Appendix, pp. 98-100.

137. The first Board of Directors of the new bank was to be appointed by the government, and subsequent appointments of the Governor and Deputy Governor were to be subject to government approval.

138. This rejection was based on the contention that it would be difficult to safeguard adequately the Board's freedom from political interference; that it would be difficult, if not impossible, for the Board to win the necessary prestige; that the Board would find it impossible to establish satisfactory relations with central banks in other countries, or with the Bank for International Settlements; and that, "insofar as an Administrative Board attempted to overcome these difficulties, it would be found, we think, that it would require powers and an organization so essentially similar to those of a central bank as to make it natural to inquire why a central bank should not from the outset have been established." Banking Report, p. 67.

139. To no small extent, the Report reflected the influence of English institutional experience. This is to be expected in the light of the fact that two of the five Commissioners were from Great Britain, and that two officials of the Bank of England were closely associated with the Commission. Concerning this English advice, which was also prominent in the establishment of the central banks in the other British Dominions, Professor Plumptre had the following critical remarks to make: "The advice was obviously given in good faith and with the best intentions; and those who gave it could claim to be experts regarding the operations of the Bank of England. But they failed, clearly and consistently, to give good advice. They recommended the introduction, through rigid legislation, of the accepted practices of the Bank of England; either ignoring the peculiarities of the local capital markets or else asserting, without proof, that these markets would after the introduction of a central bank assimilate themselves to London. ... There is nothing to indicate that the advisers were aware of the anachronisms and anomalies attaching to the Bank of England, which they naturally used as their model; and the illogic of some of their advice suggests that they did not fully understand the technical implications of the accepted form of central banking which they were inviting the Dominions to adopt. If they were aware of the peculiarities of economic development in young countries, they made little allowance for them. And finally, they seem to have been unfamiliar with the political temper of the Dominions." Plumptre, Central Banking in the British Dominions (Toronto, 1940), pp. 188-9.

140. As one would expect, Mr. Brownlee, in a separate Memorandum, dissented from the suggestions in the Report aimed at private ownership and control of the central bank. He recommended that the capital be subscribed by the Dominion government, and that all directors and executive officers be government appointed. The latter proposal he regarded as the more important, adding that in normal times the operating efficiency of the central bank management would not be impeded by the government, and in times of stress the policies of the government must prevail, whatever may be the constitution of the central bank. Ibid., p. 93.

141. See ibid., Memoranda of Dissent, pp. 85-91, 95-7.

142. With the publication of the Royal Commission Report in September 1933, the advisability of establishing a central bank ceased to be the focal point of Canadian monetary discussion. In the ensuing eighteen months, attention was devoted almost exclusively by the federal Government to the form which such legislation should take; and by non-governmental observers to appraising the legal machinery being devised, and evaluating the contribution which a central bank would make to the Dominion's monetary and financial structure. Both the economists and radicals retained their positions of prominence--the former through clarity of exposition, the latter through the vigour of their attack upon existing institutions.

For the analyses by economists, see especially A. F. W. Plumptre, "Central Banking Machinery and Monetary Policy," J. C. Elliott, "The Importation of Capital into Canada," and G. E. Jackson, "The World in Which Our Central Bank Will Work," The Canadian Economy and Its Problems, eds. Innis and Plumptre (Toronto, 1934); also A. K. Eaton, "A Central Bank for Canada," Dalhousie Review, XIII (Jan. 1934). For the verbal battle waged between the radicals (mainly Messrs. Coote, Irvine, Spencer, and McGeer) and the general managers of four of Canada's chartered banks (Mr. Dodds of the Bank of Montreal, Mr. Logan of the Canadian Bank of Commerce, Mr. Patterson of the Bank of Nova Scotia, and Mr. Wilson of the Royal Bank of Canada) over the banks' culpability during the economic fluctuations which had occurred since the First World War, see House Banking Committee Proceedings, 1934. See also the series of interesting articles on central banking written for Saturday Night by Mr. H. E. Crowle: "The Bank of Canada and Credit Control," Aug. 11, 1934; "The Bank of Canada," Sept. 15, 1934; "Central Banking Prospects," Dec. 15, 1934.

But by that time it mattered little what economists, radicals, or any other group had to say. The pressure of economic circumstances and near-unanimous public opinion had removed the question from the realm of controversy. It remained only for actual experience to broaden understanding of central bank operations; and to drive home the realization that the most effective policy was a necessary, but not sufficient, condition for economic stability.

143. See for example the credit analyses made by Mr. J. Dodds of the Bank of Montreal (Address at the Annual General Meeting of the Cana-

dian Bankers' Association, J.C.B.A., XIII, Jan. 1936); Mr. S. G. Dobson of the Royal Bank of Canada ("Commercial and Financial Review for the Year 1938," Gazette, Montreal, Jan. 4, 1939); and Mr. R. B. Bennett, the Conservative party leader (Debates, March 22, 1938, II, pp. 1609-11). For exceptional instances of banker-politician understanding, see the comments of Mr. J. L. Ilsley, then Liberal Minister of National Revenue (Debates, March 29, 1938, II, p. 1814); and Mr. B. G. Gardner, then Assistant General Manager (and now President) of the Bank of Montreal ("Bank Credit and Its Relation to Bank Reserves," Canadian Banker, XLVI, July 1939).

144. Cf. League for Social Reconstruction, Social Planning for Canada (Toronto, 1935), pp. 287-90; and G. F. Towers, Memoranda and Tables Respecting the Bank of Canada (Ottawa, 1939), pp. 30-4.

145. L.S.R., Social Planning for Canada, p. 288.

146. Ibid.

147. Towers, Memoranda and Tables, p. 38.

148. Ibid., p. 39.

149. Debates, Feb. 25, 1937, II, p. 1216.

150. Ibid., June 11, 1936, Vol. IV, p. 3613.

151. For a review of the controversy over nationalization of the central bank between 1935 and 1938, see Stokes, The Bank of Canada, chapter X; also E. P. Neufeld, Bank of Canada Operations, 1935-54 (Toronto, 1955), chapter I. It is of interest to note the catalyzing role played by the "pro-nationalization" members of the C.C.F. party during this period leading to nationalization by "half-public, half-private" Liberals over the objections of the "private" Conservatives.

152. See A. F. W. Plumptre, Central Banking in the British Dominions, chapters VIII-XI, XVI, XVII; also, "Why We Have a Central Bank," Saturday Night, Dec. 7, 1935.

See also J. S. M. Allely, "How Much Re-employment Can Be Hoped For?," Saturday Night, Aug. 8, 1936, in which reference was made to the Keynesian substitution of "full employment" for the older objectives (the gold standard, stability of exchange rates, and stability of internal prices) of monetary policy--along with the warning that the indiscriminate pursuit of easy money policy might lead to inflation even before full employment was reached; J. F. Parkinson, "Trends in Canadian Banking," Economist (London), Dominion of Canada Special Review, Jan. 18, 1936; C. Elliott, "Bank Cash," C.J.E.P.S., IV (Aug. 1938); M. K. Inman, "Experience in Canadian Banking, 1929-1934," unpublished Ph.D. thesis (Harvard University, 1938); and F. A. Knox, Dominion Monetary Policy (Ottawa, 1939).

153. Plumptre, Central Banking in the British Dominions, p. 231.

154. Professor Plumptre realized, also, that the chartered banks' 5 per cent legal minimum reserve provided in the Bank of Canada Act "is not likely to play an important part in giving effect to the operations of the Bank of Canada. As a rule the [Canadian commercial] banks keep their ratios near the customary 10 per cent; and they are not likely to revise

this well-established custom sufficiently to allow the 5 per cent minimum to become operative." Ibid., p. 266. He noted, too, the possibility of the central bank supplementing open market operations by variations of the legal reserve minima of the commercial banks. "But ordinarily open market operations are preferable. They exert a primary influence upon security prices and interest rates which does not result from changes in the legal minima. Moreover, changes in legal minima probably appear even more 'artificial' and disturbing to commercial bankers than open market operations upon their cash reserves." Ibid., p. 271.

155. Ibid., p. 214.

156. Ibid., p. 226.

157. Professor Plumptre noted one additional serious, though not insuperable, difficulty characterizing central bank policy: "It is practically never possible, not even for central bankers, to be certain of the current trend of business. It is seldom unequivocally clear, except perhaps in the deepest depression, what phase the business cycle is passing through; and thus it is never certain how far the accelerator or how far the brake is required. Moreover, different people are prone to regard inflationary or deflationary policies with different degrees of dislike or affection, depending upon their personal interests, their social and economic backgrounds, and the teachings to which they have been exposed; and thus their decisions regarding the proper time to accelerate or brake will differ." Ibid., p. 227.

158. Inman, "Experience in Canadian Banking, 1929-1934"; Knox, Dominion Monetary Policy; J. S. Allely, "Some Aspects of Currency Depreciation," C.J.E.P.S., V (Aug. 1939).

159. The studies cited above, and others--both domestic and international--will, indeed, be incorporated into the critical appraisal made of Canadian monetary policy in chapter IX. To this substantial extent, Canadian monetary writings of the late 1930's have become a part of current economic thought.

160. Cf. L.S.R., Social Planning for Canada, pp. 291-307.

161. A central bank, the League argued, might well have eliminated some of the extreme consequences of the Great Depression in Canada: "By a policy of credit restriction in the pre-depression period, it might have prevented some of the excesses of the boom. By freely exercising its powers of rediscounting during the depression, it might have supplied the commercial banks with sufficient cash to satisfy their desire for liquidity without any unnecessary and rapid reduction of loans. By a policy of exchange-rate control, it might have mitigated the severity of the price-deflation of 1930-33 in a manner which gave assistance where it could be most fruitful, i.e., in the export industries. Lastly, an aggressive policy designed to reduce interest rates might have eased the burden of the debtor classes (particularly farmers), made possible a reduction in the cost of government debt, and stimulated some measure of activity in the construction industries." Ibid., p. 296.

162. Ibid., p. 298.

163. <u>Ibid</u>., p. 299.

164. <u>Ibid</u>., pp. 300, 301.

165. <u>Ibid</u>., p. 301.

166. <u>Ibid</u>., p. 298.

167. Parliamentary address of E. J. Poole, <u>Debates</u>, April 2, 1936, II, p. 1724.

168. Cf. parliamentary address of J. H. Blackmore, <u>Debates</u>, April 6, 1937, III, pp. 2608, 2609. See, also, the discussion carried on by Messrs. Landeryou, Jaques, and Quelch in the House of Commons Standing Committee on Banking and Commerce (<u>Minutes of Proceedings and Evidence Respecting the Bank of Canada</u>, Ottawa, 1939).

169. Cf. <u>House Banking Committee Proceedings</u>, 1939. For Mr. McGeer's vague rejection of social credit theorizing, see, for example, <u>ibid</u>., 1934, pp. 703, 704; also, <u>Debates</u>, June 20, 1938, IV, p. 4067.

170. For an example of other aspects of radical monetary thinking during the second half of the decade of the thirties, see Mr. Crowle's later articles in <u>Saturday Night</u>: "The Bank of Canada and Public Ownership," Jan. 11, 1936; "The Gold Standard or Managed Currencies?" Aug. 29, 1936; "The New Gold Standard and Credit Control," May 29, 1937.

171. Cf. Towers, <u>Memoranda and Tables</u>, pp. 67-71.

172. <u>House Banking Committee Proceedings</u>, 1939, XIV, p. 452. Traces of this "hoarding tax" can be found in the request made early in 1932 by Mr. R. Gardiner, the radical leader, for a federal tax on bank savings accounts held by the public. The government, according to Mr. Gardiner, could thereby have "taxed those savings into circulation," and so could have alleviated Canada's depressed economic conditions. <u>Debates</u>, April 12, 1932, II, p. 1952.

173. Towers, <u>Memoranda and Tables</u>, p. 58.

174. <u>Ibid</u>.

175. Mr. McGeer often declared that one of the great lessons in monetary reform that emerged from the Report of the British Macmillan Committee was that the rediscount rate and open market operations were "only effective in precipitating a depression, and not effective in restoring prosperity or maintaining stability." <u>Debates</u>, June 29, 1938, IV, p. 4065.

176. Towers, <u>Memoranda and Tables</u>, p. 37.

177. <u>Ibid</u>., p. 43.

178. <u>Ibid</u>., pp. 39, 61, 62. In the light of this choice between deflation and depreciation, the Governor argued, it was incorrect to describe-- as the radicals were prone to do--interest-free financing as a "costless" operation. <u>Ibid</u>., p. 62. By the same token, a policy of furnishing additional money to the depressed western agricultural region of Canada (as proposed by Mr. Tucker) would not promote a general improvement in economic conditions and would involve sacrifices for other sections of the country, because of the international nature of the Canadian economy, and the consequent rise in imports leading to the depreciation of the dollar and to the increased cost of all payments abroad and a general rise in the level of internal prices and costs. <u>Ibid</u>., pp. 62, 63.

179. *Ibid.*, p. 62.

180. The major concern of influential bankers and businessmen appears to have been emphasis on the inevitably harmful consequences of unorthodox monetary experiments, and on the Dominion's good fortune in having successfully resisted such schemes. See, for example, B. Leman, "Scarcity in a World of Plenty," Canadian Banker, XLIV (July1937), p.419; also Sir E. W. Beatty, "Commercial and Financial Review for the Year 1938," Gazette (Montreal), Jan. 4, 1939, p. 4.

181. Debates, March 8, 1938, II, p. 1148.

182. *Ibid.*, Feb. 25, 1937, II, p. 1215.

183. J. T. Bryden, "Interest Rates in Canada," C. J. E. P. S., III (Aug. 1937), pp. 438, 439.

184. Cf. C. H. Herbert, "Interest Rates in Peace and War," Canadian Banker, XLVI (July 1939).

185. *Ibid.*, pp. 428, 429. Mr. Herbert's fiscal views might be more appropriately considered with reference to the writings of Canadian economists. There is, as already indicated, little evidence to suggest that these views reflected the prevailing sentiment among Canadian financial leaders.

Chapter Nine

1. The distinction between "internal" and "external" monetary policy appears to the writer to have both conceptual validity and practical usefulness. It applies to those measures whose effects manifest themselves directly within the domestic economy, and to those which react upon the domestic economy through changes in that economy's international position. It is, of course, recognized that the pursuit of each type of policy has repercussions upon the other. One example of this is the exchange rate pressure exerted by "internal" expansionary policy. Another--the opposite side of the same coin--is the favourable atmosphere created for such "internal" policy by exchange depreciation.

2. In accordance with the definitional distinction made in chapter I between "monetary" and "fiscal" policy, the 1934 Amendment to the Dominion Notes Act, as well as the various loan transactions conducted by the federal government, are examined primarily in monetary terms. In none of these instances was there any direct, conscious, policy planning through manipulation of the budgetary process; though, to be sure, the governmental outlays involved had important fiscal implications, which will be discussed mainly in chapter XI. The same sort of criterion is used in differentiating between the "monetary" and "fiscal" aspects of Canadian economic thought during the thirties. In this context, the essence of both the inflation and central bank controversies--and, indeed, of much of the radical approach to remedial policy--was "monetary" rather than "fiscal."

3. Other analyses of Canadian monetary policy in the thirties can be found in A. F. W. Plumptre, "Canadian Monetary Policy," The Canadian Economy and Its Problems, eds. H. A. Innis and A. F. W. Plumptre (Toronto, 1934); J. F. Parkinson, "Trends in Canadian Banking,"

Economist (London), Dominion of Canada Special Review, Jan. 18, 1936;
S. R. Noble, "The Monetary Experience of Canada during the Depression,"
The Lessons of Monetary Experience, ed. A. D. Gayer (New York, 1937);
M. K. Inman, "Experience in Canadian Banking, 1929-1934" unpublished
Ph. D. thesis (Harvard University, 1938); C. Elliott, "Bank Cash, "
C. J. E. P. S., IV (Aug. 1938); F. A. Knox, Dominion Monetary Policy,
1929-1934, A Study Prepared for the Royal Commission on Dominion-
Provincial Relations (Ottawa, 1939); A. N. McLeod, "Maintaining Em-
ployment and Incomes in Canada, " unpublished Ph. D. thesis (Harvard
University, 1949), chapters VIII and X; A. E. Safarian, "The Canadian
Economy in the Great Depression, " unpublished Ph. D. thesis (University
of California, Berkeley, 1955), chapters III and V. The survey presented
here is based upon, and supplements, these sources, and is intended as a
further illustration of the policy implications of Canadian economic thinking.

4. The fiduciary issue previously had been $37. 5 million, that is,
$50 million less $12. 5 million in gold-backed notes. The new fiduciary
issue was $90 million, that is, $120 million less $30 million in gold-backed
notes. The increase in the fiduciary issue amounted, therefore, to $52. 5
million, that is, $90 million less $37. 5 million.

5. Cf. Canada, House of Commons Debates, June 1934, IV, pp. 4085,
4086. At the time of enactment of the new currency legislation, the Canadian gold reserve against Dominion notes stood at more than 40 per cent.

6. Parkinson, "Trends in Canadian Banking, " *Economist*, Jan. 18,
1936, p. 53.

7. *Ibid.*, p. 51.

8. Inman, "Experience in Canadian Banking, " p. 324.

9. *Ibid.*, pp. 326, 328, 352. Substantial economic recovery did not
set in until 1934--and then largely in response to an improving international economic situation.

10. *Ibid.*, p. 105.

11. Elliott, "Bank Cash, " *C. J. E. P. S.*, IV (Aug. 1938), p. 444.

12. *Ibid.*, p. 445.

13. *Ibid.*, p. 448.

14. *Ibid.*, p. 444.

15. *Ibid.*, p. 445.

16. *Ibid.*

17. *Ibid.*, pp. 445, 446.

18. Inman, "Experience in Canadian Banking, " p. 106. Professor
Inman, like Mr. Elliott, tended towards a conservative interpretation of
banking policy. While acknowledging that a good theoretical case could
have been made for a more liberal extension of credit during the depression, and that some of the bank actions were, in fact, defective, he believed, nevertheless, that deliberate inflation was of doubtful merit in an
economy of the Canadian type, and that the more "heroic" policy was the
banks' retention of public confidence and a sense of security in Canadian
banking institutions. As far as he was concerned, the burden of proof

rested on the more radical viewpoint which argued in favour of a "liberal" credit policy. Ibid., pp. 374-6.

19. The post-depression introduction of such "selective controls" as regulation of consumer credit and "margin requirements" for stock exchange transactions did constitute an attempt to influence the direction of spending, and much may come from further development of these techniques. See chapter I, n. 12.

20. The analysis of these "external" fluctuations is based largely on the study made by Knox, Dominion Monetary Policy, 1929-1934. See also Dominion Bureau of Statistics, The Canadian Balance of Internation Payments (Ottawa, 1939); D.B.S., The Canadian Balance of International Payments, 1926-1945 (Ottawa, 1947); V. W. Malach, International Cycles and Canada's Balance of Payments, 1921-33 (Toronto, 1954); E. Marcus, Canada and the International Business Cycle, 1927-1939 (New York, 1954); Safarian "The Canadian Economy in the Great Depression," chapter III. There are various discrepancies--for the most part minor in nature--between the Knox and D.B.S. balance-of-payments figures. To reconcile them would be to go beyond the scope of this study.

21. For a lucid analysis of the "mechanics" of such adjustment, see A. F. W. Plumptre, Central Banking in the British Dominions (Toronto, 1940), pp. 414-16.

22. See Table X above.

23. Knox, Dominion Monetary Policy, p. 8.

24. Unless otherwise stated, the figures in the ensuing paragraphs (in the text) on exchange rate and payments fluctuations are derived from Tables XII and XIII.

25. D.B.S., The Canadian Balance of International Payments, 1926-1945, p. 48.

26. The terms "premium" and "discount" as used in this chapter refer to the buying price of English and American currency in Canadian dollars.

27. D.B.S., The Canadian Balance of International Payments, 1926-1945, p. 48.

28. Knox, Dominion Monetary Policy, p. 37.

29. D.B.S., The Canadian Balance of International Payments, p. 240; and The Canadian Balance of International Payments, 1926-1945, p. 48.

30. The discussion of depreciation policy is based largely on three Canadian sources: Knox, Dominion Monetary Policy, pp. 61-82; J. S. Allely, "Some Aspects of Currency Depreciation," C.J.E.P.S., V (Aug. 1939); and Plumptre, Central Banking in the British Dominions, pp. 382-92.

For an interesting Keynesian treatment of the closely related problem of devaluation in "income-employment" and "balance of payments" terms, see S. S. Alexander, "Effects of a Devaluation on a Trade Balance," International Monetary Fund Staff Papers, II (April, 1952); and note therein (p. 263n.) the references to the literature on the traditional supply-demand analysis. It will be clear, from the analysis in the text, that the author regards a combined approach as the most fruitful one for purposes of appraising external monetary policy; and that, consistent with the generality of approach required by this study, complex theoretical issues are noted only to the extent necessary for increasing the accuracy of major observations and conclusions. In this connection, see F. Machlup, "Relative Prices and Aggregate Spending in the Analysis of Devaluation," American Economic Review, XLV (June 1955).

31. "The rise of the pound sterling to a premium in Montreal [towards the end of 1933] put an end to the agitation for the depreciation of the Canadian dollar. Rarely had anyone suggested that the dollar should be depreciated more than the pound sterling, and that suggestion had obtained no hearing even in the worst months of the depression. . . . It is not surprising, therefore, that the session of Parliament which opened in January, 1934, heard little of the old controversies." Knox, Dominion Monetary Policy, p. 42.

32. Plumptre, Central Banking in the British Dominions, pp. 385, 386.

33. An important exception is the case of the depreciating country's substitutes for products which were formerly imported. Inelastic supply schedules for these substitutes would create, through their rapidly rising prices, a partial dampening effect on the tendency towards reduced import spending. Nor should the "price" impact of export demand and supply shifts be overlooked. To the extent that a decline in world prices would impede the policy of depreciation, such shifts, where they occurred, would be most helpful (or least adverse) if: (1) substantial in the case of foreign (increased) demand for the depreciating country's exports; and (2) minimal in the case of the latter's (increased) supply of exports, and foreign (increased supply of exports to countries other than the one carrying out the depreciation.

34. More specifically, for purposes of export-import changes, supply elasticities are irrelevant (assuming positively sloped supply curves and negatively sloped demand curves) when the sum of domestic and foreign demand elasticities exceeds unity. In that case, such balance-of-payments changes are necessarily favourable to the depreciating country (though the effects are reinforced by the existence of elastic supply schedules). Otherwise, the results will be adverse unless supply schedules are inelastic enough to offset the influence of inelastic demand. (In the extreme case where supply schedules are completely elastic, demand elasticities must exceed unity if export-import benefits are to accrue to the depreciating country. And, at the other extreme, where supply schedules are completely inelastic, such benefits will result regardless of the magnitude of demand elasticities.) Cf. L. A. Metzler, "The Theory of International Trade," in A Survey of Contemporary Economics, ed. H. S. Ellis (Philadelphia: American Economic Association, 1948), pp. 225-8.

35. Knox, Dominion Monetary Policy, p. 64. The "selling policies" argument received special emphasis, also, from Professors Allely and

Plumptre. See, for example, Allely, "Some Aspects of Currency Depreciation," C. J. E. P. S., V (Aug. 1939), p. 399; and Plumptre, Central Banking in the British Dominions, p. 390.

36. The importance of Canadian lumber exports in overseas markets, together with the keen competition provided by Scandinavian and Russian exporters, created a less favourable position for Canadian lumber producers.

37. Knox, Dominion Monetary Policy, p. 65.

38. Even the most favourable expectations would have been prevented from exercising the maximum effect if the domestic industries experiencing the increased demand had been characterized by inelastic supply schedules. A similar dampening influence would have been exerted by the protectionist stimulus afforded domestic prices through the depreciation policy.

39. Knox, Dominion Monetary Policy, p. 63.

40. This same insignificance would have tended to make the effects of British or American retaliation more severe if and when they did come. Cf. Allely, "Some Aspects of Currency Depreciation," C. J. E. P. S., V (Aug. 1939), p. 402.

41. Ibid.

42. G. F. Towers, Memoranda and Tables Respecting the Bank of Canada, pp. 39, 40.

43. Professor Knox, differentiating the mild or "normal" depression of 1930 and early 1931 from the severe depression induced by the British abandonment of the gold standard and lasting until 1933, went even further in this matter. He believed that "to have depreciated the Canadian currency during the earlier or mild phase of the depression would have been unwise; it would probably have reduced the national money income." Dominion Monetary Policy, p. 71. He based his position largely on the additional belief that "the unfortunate psychological reaction of investors and those in charge of business policy to such action would, in all probability, have outweighed the stimulating effects arising from an increased gross income to some export-commodity producers." Ibid., pp. 74, 75. The rather minor difference of opinion between Professor Knox and the author turns on the appraisal of the relative strength of the opposing factors of business psychology and income. Because of the close causal connection between the two factors, much depends upon which change would have occurred first in substantial proportions, and upon which of the two factors would have had the greater intensity of response to a given change in the other. Obviously, there is no generally satisfactory answer, and one can go no further than to emphasize that the net advantage on either side, if any, would have been small.

44. Compare this with the view of Professor Knox that "depreciation at any time after September 1931 would have tended to increase the national money income; and the probability of this favourable result increased as the depression wore on." Dominion Monetary Policy, p. 71. Professor Plumptre's general anlysis, though more cautious than his earlier appraisals made during the inflation controversy, implies a qualified but sympa-

thetic attitude towards depreciation; <u>Central Banking in the British Dominions</u>, pp. 382-93. Professor Allely was less optimistic: "There are some [countries,] like the United States, for which depreciation as a price-raising move seems much less likely to succeed than others, as Australia and Argentina, while for most countries, including Canada and the United Kingdom, the principal determinants are so conflicting that any wide margin either of advantage or disadvantage is unlikely." Allely, "Some Aspects of Currency Depreciation," <u>C.J.E.P.S.</u>, V (Aug. 1939), p. 402. Mr. Towers' position was similar to that of Professor Allely; see his <u>Memoranda and Tables</u>, pp. 39, 40. See, also, Dr. McLeod's limited approval of deliberate depreciation for the early thirties, "Maintaining Employment and Incomes in Canada," pp. 193-6; and Dr. Safarian's inconclusive discussion of the pros and cons of such a policy, "The Canadian Economy in the Great Depression," pp. 140-4.

45. For additional treatment of Canadian monetary policy during this five-year period, see: Elliott, "Bank Cash," <u>C.J.E.P.S.</u>, IV (Aug. 1938); M. L. Stokes, <u>The Bank of Canada</u> (Toronto, 1939), chapters XI and XII; Plumptre, <u>Central Banking in the British Dominions</u>, chapters IX, XI, XIII, XVIII; McLeod, "Maintaining Employment and Incomes in Canada," chapter VII; E. P. Neufeld, <u>Bank of Canada Operations, 1935-54</u> (Toronto, 1955), chapter IV.

46. Elliott, "Bank Cash," p. 455.

47. <u>Ibid</u>. It follows, of course, that other Bank assets must have declined (by $2.9 million) during this period.

48. <u>Ibid</u>.

49. Towers, <u>Memoranda and Tables</u>, pp. 34, 36; and Bank of Canada, <u>Statistical Summary; 1946 Supplement</u> (Ottawa, 1946), p. 14.

50. Towers, <u>Memoranda and Tables</u>, p. 41.

51. The bank exerted not only a broadening, but also a stabilizing, influence on the bond market. "... through its day-to-day dealings in securities and foreign exchange, [it] appears at times to have provided an auxiliary market which has doubtless minimized price fluctuations that might have been accentuated by temporary changes in the chartered banks' position. In bond transactions, this compensating action was particularly evident in the autumn of 1937 when the records show Bank of Canada security purchases helped to compensate for chartered bank sales." Elliott, "Bank Cash," p. 454.

It is impossible to assess the relative importance attached by the Bank to the objectives of economic stability and absorption of government issues. "In the circumstances of the past few years [1935-9], when government borrowing has far exceeded any other type of financing on the Canadian bond market, and when the cessation of government borrowing roughly coincided with a renewed demand for commercial and speculative bank loans, it is impossible to distinguish between the evidence of a general policy of keeping bond yields low in bad times and a particular policy undertaken for the benefit of governments." Plumptre, <u>Central Banking in the British Dominions</u>, pp. 237, 238. There can, nevertheless, be little doubt of the Bank's cognizance of the objective of economic stability, as evidenced, for example, by the following statement made by Mr. Towers: "Treasury bills can be made to play an increasingly important role in our banking life, if further experience and a further widening of the market demonstrate--as I believe they will--the utility of this form of temporary investment. One should not think of such bills as being merely a means of cheap government financing and nothing more. " Governor of the Bank of Canada, Report to the First Annual General Meeting of Shareholders (Feb. 25, 1936), p. 17.

52. Referring in 1937, to the desirability of establishing an active Canadian bill market, the Governor of the Bank of Canada commented: "One must recognize that the goal is a long way off. I feel it is quite likely that, if money conditions ever become less easy than they have been in the last few years, Treasury bills may be rather neglected, and that holders may tend to allow their Bills to run off through a desire to obtain additional cash. Such a development would call for the refunding of a suitable portion-- perhaps a substantial portion--of the Bills now outstanding. The market would then be short of assets which can properly be classified as second-line reserves. I think it is probable that experience over a period of years, and of a variety of conditions in the money market, will be necessary be-fore we achieve a satisfactory bill market in Canada. " Report to the Second Annual General Meeting of Shareholders (Feb. 23, 1937), p. 13.

53. The Bank made a few loans to the chartered banks and the Domin-ion Government, and (in the summer of 1936) one loan (amounting to $3 million) to the province of Saskatchewan.

54. Mr. Towers underscored the Bank's reluctance towards independ-ent action in the exchange rate field by insisting--in the face of both banker and radical arguments to the contrary--that "during the last few years the exchange value of the Canadian dollar has been maintained in terms of other currencies by the naturally strong position on the Canadian balance of pay-ments--not because of support derived from the Bank of Canada. " Towers, Memoranda and Tables, p. 46. See, also, Banking Supplement, Economist (London), Oct. 15, 1938, p. 14; and "Central Bank Credited for Exchange Stability, " Financial Post (Toronto), Oct. 29, 1938.

55. Cf. Bank of Canada, Reports on the Financial Position of the Provinces of Manitoba, Saskatchewan, and Alberta (Ottawa, 1937).

56. Plumptre, Central Banking in the British Dominions, p. 332.

57. Ibid. , p. 420.

58. By January 1935, the Canadian dollar had gone to a slight premium with respect to the United States dollar (.18 per cent) and stood at a negli-gible discount (.35 per cent) in terms of the pound sterling. After 1935, the Canadian dollar tended to move with the United States dollar--the latter being stabilized through large-scale capital inflows--while the pound ster-ling moved speculatively with those currencies of the Continent reflecting changes in the European political outlook. Bank of Canada, Statistical Summary: 1946 Supplement, pp. 126, 127; Governor of the Bank of Can-ada, Annual Reports, 1937-40; and Plumptre, Central Banking in the

British Dominions, pp. 417-19.

59. Bearing in mind the complex problems faced by, and the frequent
failures of, Dominion-Provincial Conferences, this statement implies, not
that extensive central bank collaboration with the provinces will easily be
achieved, but merely that the potentialities of its achievement are no weaker
than those of a workable federalism in the Dominion.

60. "The Bank of Canada is now able by means of open market operations to supply the Canadian banks as a group with what it considers the
proper volume of cash reserves. There is no reason why the banks should
ever again and especially in depression, depend upon borrowing for a large
portion of their cash. In other words, a low rate on central bank loans
should never be effective unless it is meant to apply to a particular bank
in special difficulties in bad times." Plumptre, Central Banking in the
British Dominions, p. 286.

There is the further consideration that it remained open for Canadians
to strengthen their existing monetary instruments and to adopt new ones.
Just such expansion (the significance of which, obviously, cannot yet be
fully appraised) was, indeed, effected through the Bank, Bank of Canada,
and National Housing Acts of 1954--which, respectively, provided (among
other things) for: (1) a chartered bank cash reserve requirement of 8 per
cent (as compared with the previous statutory 5 per cent); (2) central bank
authority to alter this legal reserve within the limits of 8 and 12 per cent;
and (3) a broadened money market (in terms, for example, of introducing
day-to-day chartered bank loans, and empowering the chartered banks to
engage in residential mortgage lending). Cf. A. W. Rogers, "The Bank
Act: 1954 Edition," and R. M. MacIntosh, "Broadening the Money Market,"
Canadian Banker, LXI (Autumn 1954); also Neufeld, Bank of Canada Operations, 1935-54, chapter III.

61. Bank of Canada, Statistical Summary: 1946 Supplement, pp. 8, 9.

62. Plumptre, Central Banking in the British Dominions, pp. 243-4.

63. Bank of Canada, Statistical Summary (March 1956), pp. 59, 60.
It would be going beyond the scope of this study to investigate the choice
which Canada's monetary authorities have, in fact, made between bond
price and economic stability when the achievement of either goal was incompatible with that of the other.

Similarly irrelevant, for purposes of this survey, is the interesting
question--vigorously debated in both Canada and the United States since
the decade of the thirties--as to whether the substantial post-1929 reversal
in the directions of commercial loan and securities growth reflected a long-
standing and permanent tendency towards a fundamental change in the character of commercial banking operations. (For contemporary support of
this position, see Inman "Experience in Canadian Banking," p. 157; and
for a contrary view, see J. D. Gibson, "The Changing Character of Bank
Assets," Canadian Banker, XLV, Jan. 1938." Conclusive demonstration
of such a decline in the banks' commercial lending would force problems
of conventional monetary stabilization policy into the background; and the
major emphasis would shift to the structural sphere, where the broad issue

of nationalized versus private commercial banking would have to be reappraised in the light of empirical findings. In this connection, it is sufficient to note (on the basis of data presented in successive issues of Bank of Canada, Statistical Summary, 1940-55), that the long-run change in bank lending does not appear as yet to have reached the point where, taken by itself, it materially affects the case for basic structural revision of the Canadian banking system (see also Bank of Nova Scotia, Monthly Review, Toronto, Sept. 1953).

Chapter Ten

1. Canada, House of Commons Debates, April 6, 1932, II, pp. 1748-70; March 21, 1933, III, pp. 3204-41; April 18, 1934, III, pp. 2267-2306.

2. Ibid., April 6, 1932, II, p. 1768.

3. See, for example, "Commercial and Financial Review for the Year 1932," Gazette (Montreal), Jan. 4, 1933.

4. Ibid., p. 4.

5. J. C. Hopkins (ed.), Canadian Annual Review of Public Affairs, 1935 and 1936 (Toronto, 1936), p. 13. The Liberal advocacy of tax reduction in depression did represent a deviation from orthodox public finance. It must be qualified, however, by the consideration that their over-riding concern was with the maintenance of government expenditure at a minimum; and that the idea of tax reduction was not associated with increased purchasing power, but with increased revenue from expanded freer trade.

6. Debates, March 3, 1932, I, p. 754.

7. Ibid., March 8, 1932, I, p. 937; March 28, 1933, IV, p. 3492.

8. Canadian Annual Review, 1935 and 1936, p. 79.

9. Ibid. Among the few notable exceptions in the Liberal Opposition was Mr. H. Mitchell, in whose opinion government economy was "the antithesis of mass production. Every move in the direction of economy intensifies the troubles from which we are suffering. If carried too far, these economic measures which are being promoted all around us will have the power to shake the very foundations of our social structure." Debates, April 25, 1932, II, p. 2349.

10. Address at Annual Meeting of Shareholders, Industrial Canada, XXXII (Feb. 1932), p. 75.

11. Address at Annual Meeting of Canadian Manufacturers' Association, Industrial Canada, XXXIV (July 1933), p. 116.

12. "Commercial and Financial Review for the Year 1932," Gazette (Montreal), Jan. 4, 1933, p. 3.

13. Canadian Annual Review, 1932, p. 509.

14. See, for example, the speeches and writings of the following: editorial, Financial Post (Toronto), Nov. 14, 1931; Sir C. Gordon, President of the Bank of Montreal (Canadian Annual Review, 1934, pp. 602, 603); Mr. J. Dodds, General Manager of the Bank of Montreal and President of the Canadian Bankers' Association ("Commercial and Financial Review for the Year 1933," Gazette, Jan. 3, 1934, p. 7); Mr. W. H. Miner and Mr. W. C. Coulter, Presidents of the Canadian Manufacturers' Association

(Industrial Canada, XXXIII, July, 1932, pp. 139, 140, and, Canadian Annual Review, 1933, pp. 624-6); Dr. S. G. Blaylock, President of the Canadian Institute of Mining and Metallurgy, and Vice-President and General Manager of the Consolidated Mining and Smelting Co. of Canada (Industrial Canada, XXXV, May, 1934, p. 40).

15. Canadian Bank of Commerce, Monthly Letter, Aug. 1932.

16. As shown by the following quotation, Prime Minister Bennett, too, was quite aware of the multiplier process: "Economists tell us that every dollar that is put into circulation will probably lead to ten or twenty dollars being put into circulation in the communities in which that dollar is spent.... That is, if a public work is undertaken in a community where there is considerable unemployment of one class, and that class thereby finds employment, then there will be a reaction, of course, for the benefit of other classes who are also unemployed. By reason of the fact that employment is given to the workers in Class A, the workers in other classes will benefit from the result of that employment. In other words, moneys will circulate through the productive effort of those who are paid for their services, and enure to the benefit of other classes in the community.... That has been the experience of the world, ...and it is for that reason that the primary purpose of our effort is work." Debates, Sept. 11, 1930, Special Session, p. 91.

17. W. D. Black, "To Stabilize the Building Industry, " "A Plan for Building Stabilization, " and "The Joint in the Depression's Armour, " Saturday Night (Toronto), Dec. 9, 1933; Dec. 16, 1933; and Jan. 27, 1934, respectively.

18. Mr. Black defined the "mean economic line" as the average level at which the Canadian building industry might justifiably have operated during the 1919-33 period.

19. Black, "The Joint in the Depression's Armor, " p. 23.

20. It is of interest, further, to note the countercyclical fiscal programme presented by the National Construction Council to the Royal Commission on Banking and Currency (1933). Banking Commission Proceedings, V, pp. 2704-35a. See also the cautious approval given by the business research group, Technical Research Service Limited, to the Bennett Administration's public works programme: "Money will go to workmen who will immediately put it into circulation. On John Maynard Keynes' theory, the increased tax revenues will compensate the government for virtually all its expenditures. From a near-term point of view, such action must give an impetus to general business. If the stimulation from outside continues, the added exhiliration from a domestic priming of the pump will undoubtedly result in a faster business tempo. It is not within our province to comment on the dangers of such a policy. Needless to say, they can be avoided under careful management if the aroused public opinion is ignored." Technical Research Service Limited, "How's Business?" Canadian Business, VII (Feb. 1934), p. 25.

Attention should be called, finally, to the Keynesian savings-investment analysis (on the basis of The Treatise on Money), and the support for countercyclical investment control (through a National Investment Board), advanced by Mr. H. R. Jackman, President of the Debentures and Securities Corporation of Canada (H. R. Jackman, "Control of Investment and Proposals for Public Works, " The Canadian Economy and Its Problems, eds. H. A. Innis and A. F. W. Plumptre, Toronto, 1934); and to the housing plan proposed by two Canadians, an architect and a mechanical and industrial engineer--a three-year (1935-7) $400 million programme which would be financed by the sale of government securities to the Bank of Canada (J. H. Craig and J. W. Bell, "A National Self-Liquidating Housing Program, " and "The National Housing Plan, " Saturday Night, Sept. 22, 1934, and Sept. 29, 1934, respectively).

21.. Quoted by Mr. King from an election campaign speech made by Mr. Bennett (Winnipeg, June 9, 1930), Debates, Sept. 9, 1930, Special Session, p. 29.

22. Debates, Sept. 16, 1930, Special Session, p. 238; and Sept. 20, 1930, p. 567.

23. Ibid., Sept. 17, 1930, Special Session, p. 315.

24. In this connection, see, especially, Mr. R. Gardiner's criticism of the course of action set forth by the Prime Minister in the autumn of 1930 (Debates, Sept. 9, 1930, Special Session, pp. 42-4); also the comments of Mr. Woodsworth (Sept. 9, 1930, pp. 46-8), Mr. Heaps (Sept. 17, 1930, pp. 333-9), Mr. Garland (Sept. 18, 1930, pp. 389-96), and Mr. Irvine (Sept. 18, 1930, pp. 401-6). Mr. Garland's speech made reference (p. 394) to a contemporary article by Keynes in MacLean's Magazine, in which the latter wrote that "if there is one thing that protection cannot do, ... it is to cure unemployment. "

25. The differences in C. C. F. and Social Credit emphasis have already been outlined (chapter VI). While the former party was mainly concerned with problems of nationalization of industry, it did attach importance to the monetary approach to economic stability; indeed, it is often difficult to distinguish between the monetary proposals of the two groups.

26. Unlike the Liberal Opposition in Parliament, the radicals were not greatly concerned with the constitutional aspects of the Administration's "blank cheque" spending. It appeared to Mr. Woodsworth, among others, that Mr. Mackenzie King was "almost obsessed with the sense of our constitutional disabilities. He seems to think that no matter in what direction we turn there are lions in the way; there is always something to prevent action. I take it that the country expects prompt action, and I fancy that it is willing to leave a certain degree of discretionary power to anyone prepared to take that action. " Debates, Sept. 12, 1930, Special Session, p. 166.

27. Debates, June 9, 1931, III, p. 2455; Feb. 26, 1932, I, p. 576; April 13, 1932, II, p. 1995.

28. In response to Mr. Woodsworth's "purchasing power" criticism of the Administration's reduction of civil servants' salaries, the Minister of Railways and Canals, Dr. R. J. Manion, argued that "this will not lessen purchasing power at all, because you simply save collecting that amount

of taxes from someone else." Ibid., Feb. 26, 1932, I, p. 603. Dr. Manion was obviously begging the whole question of the appropriateness of balanced budgets under all circumstances. For other sources of radical objection to the salary reductions in the federal civil service, see the remarks of Mr. A. MacInnis (ibid., Feb. 15, 1932, I, p. 194), Mr. H. E. Spencer (ibid., April 19, 1932, II, p. 2166), and Mr. R. Gardiner (Canadian Annual Review, 1932, p. 41).

29. Among the authorities cited by Mr. Woodsworth was Keynes, who, in the Atlantic Monthly of May 1932, had written: "Unluckily, the traditional and ingrained beliefs of those who hold responsible positions throughout the world grew out of experience which contained no parallel to the present.... The voices which--in such a conjuncture--tell us that the path of escape is to be found in strict economy and in refraining, wherever possible, from utilizing the world's potential production are the voices of fools and madmen." Debates, May 4, 1932, III, pp. 2643, 2644.

30. Debates, June 11, 1931, III, p. 2535; April 19, 1932, II, pp. 2166, 2167; April 10, 1933, IV, pp. 3883-6.

31. Ibid., July 29, 1931, IV, pp. 4300-5.

32. Ibid., p. 2535.

33. Mr. Spencer did not elaborate on the meaning and significance of "total appreciation." Nor did he include "net private investment" among his expenditure components; the fact is that, to his social credit, underconsumptionist way of thinking, capital investment served only to intensify the deflationary pressure by increasing productive capacity (cf. Debates, June 11, 1931, III, p. 2536). This suggests, moreover, that Mr. Spencer's "total depreciation" did not refer to the replacement investment expenditure made by business firms, but rather to the actual reduction in productive capacity resulting from the wearing out of the nation's industrial plant and equipment.

34. Debates, April 10, 1933, IV, p. 3886.

35. Ibid., July 29, 1931, IV, p. 4303. For other expressions of radical opinion on budgetary policy, see the critical comments of Miss A. Macphail (ibid., June 15, 1931, III, pp. 2639-41), Mr. Heaps (ibid., April 11, 1932, II, p. 1918), Mr. G. G. Coote (ibid., April 20, 1932, II, pp. 2211-17), Mr. Garland (ibid., Feb. 1, 1933, II, p. 1710), and Mr. W. C. Good ("Monetary Control," Canadian Forum, XIV, May 1934, p. 296).

Mr. Coote often drew support for his arguments from the writings of Keynes. On this particular occasion, he cited Keynes's Essays in Persuasion, in which the latter had contended that, if a country's ability to produce goods was unimpaired and private spending was not sufficient to absorb total production, that country, taken in the aggregate, could not impoverish itself in public spending to make use of the goods which it was able to produce; on the contrary, by so doing, the nation would enrich itself. Debates, Feb. 7, 1934, I, p. 351.

36. Some of the radicals, notably those in the C. C. F. group, had their reservations about public works policy. According to Mr. Heaps, for example, public works was "not an ultimate remedy for the unemploy-

ment problem in Canada. It provides a temporary palliative to the men and women who find themselves out of employment, but perhaps when the public works are completed, with the resulting increase in the public debt, the second stage may be worse than the first.... Therefore, it has become generally recognized that by the creation of public works we do not in any way attempt to solve the unemployment situation, but we are merely prolonging the day when the problem will have to be faced in a more fundamental manner." Debates, Feb. 5, 1934, I, p. 242.

37. Thus, Mr. Garland had this to say in connection with the Prime Minister's appeal to Canadian businessmen to invest their reserve funds in production: "Why should we produce more goods which the people are not permitted to consumer or more goods which cannot be shipped abroad under the existing system? What object could be attained at this moment by investing more money in production?" Ibid., Feb. 1, 1933, II, p. 1715.

38. Ibid., Sept. 10, 1930, Special Session, pp. 77-81; July 29, 1931, IV, pp. 4304, 4305. See, also, the interpretations of financing techniques made by Mr. Woodsworth (ibid., July 29, 1931, IV, p. 4294) and Mr. Coote (ibid., Feb. 7, 1934, I, pp. 350-2).

39. Ibid., Sept. 10, 1930, Special Session, p. 78.

40. Ibid. See also, Mr. G. G. McGeer's unqualified condemnation, before the House of Commons Select Standing Committee on Banking and Commerce, of the deficit financing later carried out by the Roosevelt New Deal Administration (House Banking Committee Proceedings, 1934, p. 683).

41. The reliance on "national credit" was not unique to those radicals with strong social credit leanings. Mr. Woodsworth, for example, characteristically suggested that "we have the whole credit of the country upon which to draw"; and that the Government should therefore issue the necessary currency. (Ibid., July 29, 1931, IV, p. 4294.)

42. Mr. Coote frequently spoke for those Westerners who favoured the use of stamp scrip as a part of the note issue; that special currency would, presumably, circulate faster than ordinary money and so materially reduce hoarding. Ibid., Feb. 7, 1934, I, p. 350.

43. There were some, among the radicals, who did recognize borrowing as an alternative to currency expansion in the financing of governmental depression expenditure. (See the parliamentary comments of Miss Macphail, as exemplified in Debates, June 15, 1931, III, pp. 2640, 2641; also Mr. Spencer, ibid., April 19, 1932, II, p. 2166.) But it was a fleeting recognition which had no place in their basic approach to this problem.

44. Pointing out, in 1934, that the decline in construction activity appeared to be responsible for much of the unemployment existing at that time, Mr. Coote quoted Keynes to the effect that: "For every man given employment directly on a program of public works, two other men will find employment as a result. Large numbers of men will secure employment in making the materials which will be used in the construction of these works, and others will find employment in making consumers' goods which the newly employed men will want to purchase with the wages which

they receive." Debates, Feb. 7, 1934, I, p. 348.

45. Mr. Heaps and Mr. Woodsworth continued to guide the radicals' parliamentary efforts aimed at the establishment of a comprehensive social security system (see, for example, Debates, April 29, 1931, I, pp. 1095-9, 1107-12). Organized labour constituted a new and important factor in support of both social security and public works (see, for example, Trades and Labour Congress of Canada, Proceedings of the Forty-Ninth Annual Convention, Windsor, 1933, pp. 141-5, 173, 174).

46. As early as 1931, Mr. Bennett and Mr. Mackenzie King, the leaders of the two major federal parties, were expressing their approval, with reservations, of a broadened Canadian system of social security (Debates, April 29, 1931, I, pp. 1099-1104, 1112-16).

47. It is an interesting fact that contemporary academic fiscal discussion was virtually monopolized by University of Toronto economists.

48. A. F. W. Plumptre, "This Unemployment Problem," Saturday Night (Toronto), Sept. 13, 1930, p. 30.

49. A. F. W. Plumptre, "Canadian Monetary Policy," The Canadian Economy and Its Problems.

50. Ibid., p. 166.

51. Ibid., p. 167.

52. Ibid.

53. H. M. Cassidy, "Relief Works as a Remedy for Unemployment," Papers and Proceedings of the Canadian Polical Science Association, IV (1932).

54. Ibid., p. 31.

55. Ibid., p. 32.

56. Ibid., p. 33.

57. Cf. Banking Commission Proceedings, VI, pp. 2855-927.

58. Ibid., p. 2881.

59. Ibid.

60. Mr. Parkinson's admixture of "would," "could," and "might," in his outline of functions for the Commission, suggests that this outline was not intended to be rigid or exhaustive. What was required was: "A Board with powers not too strictly defined and delimited, able to introduce an element of flexibility into a political-economic system hampered by a wide separation of constitutional powers; and deadened by a continual struggle between regional and economic groupings. In a real sense, such a Board will come in time to write its own constitution, so to speak, if it does anything at all. It will build up its own administrative techniques, and, given competent management and working closely with the central bank, will provide the direction for the greater degree of economic planning likely to be thrust upon the state in the future." Ibid., pp. 2884, 2885.

61. D. C. MacGregor, "Outline of the Position of Public Finance," The Canadian Economy and Its Problems; also, "The Threat of Financial Crisis," and "These Insignificant Budgets," Canadian Forum, XIII (March 1933), and XIV (July 1934), respectively.

62. MacGregor, "Outline of the Position of Public Finance," p. 59.

63. Ibid.

64. MacGregor, "The Threat of Financial Crisis," p. 207.

65. MacGregor, "Outline of the Position of Public Finance," p. 60.

66. Ibid.

67. Ibid.

68. Ibid., p. 61.

69. C. A. Ashley, "Budgets: An Examination and a Suggestion,"
J. C. B. A., XXXIX (April 1932); G. E. Jackson, in Canadian Business,
VI (Jan. 1933); and F. W. Burton, "The Business Cycle and the Problem
of Economic Policy," The Canadian Economy and Its Problems.

70. Ashley, "Budgets: An Examination and a Suggestion," p. 368.

71. Ibid.

72. Canadian Business, VI (Jan. 1933), p. 24.

73. Burton, "The Business Cycle and the Problem of Economic Policy,"
The Canadian Economy and Its Problems, p. 156.

74. League for Social Reconstruction, Social Planning for Canada
(Toronto, 1935), chapters XII and XIII.

75. Ibid., p. 312.

76. This would be a tax levied on the upper income groups, payable in
cash or approved securities, and expected to wipe out about $2 billion of the
national debt and so relieve the Treasury of about $90 million in interest
charges. In support of their proposal, the League cited the comment made
in 1933 by Professor K. W. Taylor of McMaster University, to the effect
that such a scheme would be "practicable, fair, and theoretically sound."
Ibid., pp. 333-5.

77. For representative fiscal attitudes expressed by individual members of the C. C. F. party, see the comments of: Mr. M. J. Coldwell
(Debates, Feb. 26, 1936, I, pp. 550, 551, and June 21, 1938, IV, pp. 4084,
4085; and House Banking Committee Proceedings, 1939, pp. 518-525); Miss
MacPhail (Debates, May 7, 1936, III, p. 2611, and Feb. 10, 1937, p. 751);
and Mr. Heaps (Debates, April 3, 1936, II, p. 1768, and March 8, 1937,
II, pp. 1558-61). "Equity" considerations were predominant in the tax proposals made by both the League and rank-and-file C. C. F. members. The
use of taxation as a countercyclical device does not seem to have been contemplated.

78. Debates, March 9, 1937, II, p. 1638.

79. For further statement of the Social Credit position, see the comments of: Mr. Irvine (Debates, April 2, 1935, III, pp. 2324-6); Mr. W.
Jaques (ibid., May 5, 1936, III, pp. 2551, 2552); Mr. E. G. Hansell
(ibid., May 11, 1936, III, pp. 2686, 2687); and Mr. J. H. Blackmore
(ibid., June 27, 1938, IV, pp. 4281, 4282).

80. Debates, June 2, 1936, IV, p. 3333; June 8, 1936, IV, pp. 3500,
3562, 3563, 3571, 3572; June 23, 1938, IV, pp. 4192-4. See, also, House
Banking Committee Proceedings, 1939, XIX, pp. 643-51.

81. Debates, June 8, 1936, IV, p. 3562.

82. Ibid., June 8, 1936, IV, p. 3571.

83. Ibid., June 23, 1938, IV, p. 4192.

84. Mr. McGeer remained far more impressed with money creation than with borrowing.

85. The following studies are significant in the present context: W. A. Mackintosh, The Economic Background of Dominion-Provincial Relations; D. C. MacGregor, J. B. Rutherford, G. E. Britnell, and J. J. Deutsch, National Income; A. E. Grauer, Public Assistance and Social Insurance, and Housing; S. Bates, Financial History of Canadian Governments; H. C. Goldenberg, Municipal Finance in Canada. For reference to the "countercyclical" advances in fiscal thinking made in the Royal Commission Report itself, see J. H. Perry, Taxes, Tariffs, and Subsidies: A History of Canadian Fiscal Development (Toronto, 1955), I, chapter XX.

86. H. Michell, "Report of the National Employment Commission, " Industrial Canada, XXXIX (June 1938), p. 40.

87. Canadian Business, XI (July 1938).

88. Cf. D. C. MacGregor, "The Problem of Public Debt in Canada, " C.J.E.P.S., II (May 1936).

89. Ibid., p. 175.

90. Financial History of Canadian Governments.

91. Ibid., p. 27.

92. Ibid., p. 12.

93. Ibid., p. 75.

94. Ibid., pp. 75, 76.

95. Ibid., p. 16. Professor A. E. Grauer of the University of Toronto and Professor Mackintosh were also keenly aware of the stabilizing potentialities of fiscal policy. The former, for example, recognized that, "if a program of planned public works to combat depressions becomes a part of federal policy, housing projects can be admirably fitted into such a program." Grauer, Housing, p. 61a.

96. Cf. A. F. W. Plumptre, Central Banking in the British Dominions (Toronto, 1940), pp. 373-8.

97. Ibid., p. 374.

98. Ibid., p. 376.

99. Canada, Interim and Final Reports of the National Employment Commission (Ottawa, 1937 and 1938).

100. Final Report of the National Employment Commission, p. 6.

101. Ibid., p. 26.

102. Ibid., p. 25.

103. Ibid., p. 34.

104. Ibid., p. 37.

105. Ibid., p. 35.

106. Ibid., p. 43.

107. G. F. Towers, Report to the Second Annual General Meeting of Shareholders, Bank of Canada (Ottawa, February 23, 1937), pp. 14, 15; and Memoranda and Tables Respecting the Bank of Canada (Ottawa, 1939). For the most part, these views took the form of replies to questions directed

to Mr. Towers in Banking Committee hearings by the two Liberal members of Parliament, Mr. W. A. Tucker and Mr. R. J. Deachman.

108. Towers, Report to the Second Annual General Meeting of Share-holders, p. 14.

109. Towers, Memoranda and Tables, p. 49.

110. Ibid.

111. Ibid., p. 50.

112. Ibid., p. 57. Mr. Towers did believe that tax policy was "worthy of careful consideration with respect to the limited field in which it might be a practical alternative to increased government spending." Ibid.

113. See, for example, the parliamentary addresses of Mr. E. N. Rhodes, Conservative Minister of Finance (Debates, March 22, 1935, II, p. 1966), and Mr. N. Mcl. Rogers, Liberal Minister of Labour (ibid., Feb. 17, 1936, I, pp. 242, 243; and Jan. 21, 1937, I, pp. 154-7).

114. Ibid., June 16, 1938, IV, pp. 3893-926; and April 25, 1939, III, pp. 3140-97.

115. Ibid., June 16, 1938, IV, p. 3923.

116. Ibid., April 25, 1939, III, pp. 3146, 3147.

117. See, for example, the views expressed by Mr. A. B. Purvis, President of Canadian Industries Ltd. (speech before the Canadian Construction Association, Industrial Canada, XXXV, Feb. 1935; and speech at annual banquet of C. I. L., Industrial Canada, XXXVI, July 1935); Sir John Aird, President of the Canadian Bank of Commerce (address at Annual Shareholders' Meeting, Canadian Annual Review, 1935 and 1936, pp. 584-9); and Mr. J. H. Webb and Mr. F. C. Brown, Presidents of the Canadian Manufacturers' Association (President's Annual Review, Industrial Canada, XXXVI, July 1935; and XXXIX, July 1938).

Mr. Purvis subsequently served as Chairman of the National Employment Commission, and his remarks are, therefore, especially worthy of note. Cautioning the Dominion Government against the "reckless Roosevelt approach," he declared that "'spending one's way to prosperity' is a pipe-dream which has never worked yet and never will"; and that "the proper way to get out of our difficulties and so give first place to the creation of jobs is to bring our expenses within our incomes (that is, balance the bud-get)." Speech at annual banquet of C. I. L., Industrial Canada, XXXVI (July 1935), p. 114.

118. W. D. Black, speech before the Brantford Board of Trade, Industrial Canada, XXXIX (Jan. 1939). Mr. Black, nevertheless, regarded as one of the greatest fallacies the belief that a country could spend its way out of a depression. To his way of thinking, public works undertaken to relieve unemployment were economically justifiable only if they were of practial use and if they could be operated without deficits.

119. Canadian Chamber of Commerce (C. C. C.), "Submission to the Royal Commission on Dominion-Provincial Relations," Canadian Business, XI (June 1938); and Canadian Manufacturers' Association (C. M. A.), "Brief on Public Works Submitted to the Royal Commission on Dominion-Provincial Relations," Industrial Canada, XXXIX (May 1938). The briefs submitted to the Royal Commission on Dominion-Provincial Relations as well as its

hearings, were without precedent in volume and extensiveness. They therefore constitute a rich source of insight into Canadian thinking on fiscal problems. The author, nevertheless, deems their detailed analysis to be beyond the scope of this investigation, on grounds of their primary orientation towards fiscal equity and efficiency rather than economic stability.

120. C. C. C., "Submission to the Royal Commission," Canadian Business, XI (June 1938), p. 53.

121. According to the C. M. A., public works were "the only available means of publicly countering the progressive decline in employment during periods of recession." C. M. A., "Brief Submitted to the Royal Commission," Industrial Canada, XXXIX (May 1938), p. 67.

122. Ibid., p. 70. The remaining C.M.A. quotations are derived from this source, pp. 67-70.

Chapter Eleven

1. Tariff policy in the late thirties centred upon issues other than that of economic stability. It is, therefore, beyond the scope of this study.

2. In contrast to the previous discussion on monetary policy (chapter IX), the fiscal analysis begins with the external approach to stabilization policy. The justification for this procedure lies in: (a) the overwhelming importance attached to tariff policy by those in responsible public positions; (b) the fact that, with no sharp institutional break in the course of the evolution of internal fiscal policy, it is useful to interpret developments in this sphere as a unit, that is, against the background of the entire decade of the thirties; and (c) the author's desire to draw upon this treatment in synthesizing the pattern of internal countercyclical fiscal policy during the interwar period.

3. The discussion of Canadian tariff policy in the early thirties is based on the following sources: W. A. Mackintosh, The Economic Background of Dominion-Provincial Relations, A Study Prepared for the Royal Commission on Dominion-Provincial Relations (Ottawa, 1939), chapter VII; Canada, Report of the Royal Commission on Dominion-Provincial Relations (Ottawa, 1940), book I, chapter VI; O. J. McDiarmid, Commercial Policy in the Canadian Economy (Cambridge, Mass., 1946), chapters XII-XIV; D. R. Annett, British Preference in Canadian Commercial Policy (Toronto, 1948), chapter III; A. E. Safarian, "The Canadian Economy in the Great Depression," unpublished Ph.D. thesis (University of California, Berkeley, 1955), chapter III.

4. Mackintosh, The Economic Background of Dominion-Provincial Relations, p. 84.

5. The increasingly heavy relative burden of specific duties involved conscious governmental action to the extent that downward adjustment of those duties would normally have been made, and that new specific duties were introduced.

6. Mackintosh, The Economic Background of Dominion-Provincial Relations, p. 90.

7. Reliance was also placed on the Ottawa Agreements as a device

for broadening British outlets for Canada's staple-export industries; and thereby softening the Canadian competitive disadvantage in world markets occasioned by governmental refusal to engage in deliberate exchange depreciation after the collapse of sterling. Annett, British Preference in Canadian Commercial Policy, p. 57.

8. Figures on tariff rates are derived from Report of Royal Commission on Dominion-Provincial Relations, p. 158.

9. McDiarmid, Commercial Policy in the Canadian Economy, p. 306. Dr. McDiarmid estimates that the administrative controls introduced in 1930 and 1931 raised the actual tariff level by about 10 per cent. Ibid., p. 276.

10. Ibid., pp. 306, 307.

11. Ibid., p. 276.

12. Ibid., p. 304.

13. Report of Royal Commission on Dominion-Provincial Relations, p. 158.

14. Ibid.

15. There was one important respect in which the Bennett tariff must have exerted general stimulative effects. One of its objectives was the attraction of direct investment to Canada in the form of Canadian branches for American business firms. Of the 1, 350 companies in Canada controlled by, or affiliated with, American firms in 1934, about 26 per cent were established or acquired between 1930 and 1934. The establishment of a considerable majority of these firms was unquestionably prompted by the tariff. To that extent, then, expansionary forces must have been brought into operation, though here too there was probably an offsetting tendency towards higher selling prices. McDiarmid, Commercial Policy in the Canadian Economy, pp. 329, 330.

16. Report of Royal Commission on Dominion-Provincial Relations, p. 159.

17. The two greatest shifts occurred in farmers' income and salaries and wages in the naturally sheltered industries. During the 1929-32 period, the former declined from 15 per cent of national income to 5 per cent, while the latter rose from 29 to 35 per cent; there was only a 1 per cent increase for salaries and wages in the protected industries. Ibid., p. 149.

18. V. W. Bladen, "Tariff Policy and Employment in Depression, " C. J. E. P. S., VI (Feb. 1940), p. 77.

19. Through skilled tariff bargaining, broadened export outlets can be, and have been, achieved. This, however, can hardly be considered to have been the prime objective of the Bennett protectionist policy.

20. These concluding comments should not, of course, be construed as the advocacy of exchange depreciation as a permanent feature of countercyclical policy. Reference has been made, rather, to a particular set of conditions in a single country at a given time. As a matter of fact, the burden of proof rests upon those who would recommend the incorporation of either depreciation or tariff protection into the general framework of stabilization policy. Their inflexibility and the uncertainty of their stabil-

izing effects go hand in hand with implications for equity and efficiency which are frequently unfavourable. Furthermore, there are other external remedies available to a country, such as exchange control, which make it possible to minimize these shortcomings; though even in such cases, it becomes increasingly difficult to draw the line between national defence against deflationary pressures arising in depressions abroad and the unilateral raising of domestic incomes by worsening the otherwise stable income positions of foreign countries.

21. The author knows of no comprehensive analysis of fiscal stabilization policy in Canada during the thirties. The survey made here derives largely from the following sources: C. A. Curtis, "Dominion Legislation of 1935: An Economist's Review," C.J.E.P.S., I (Nov. 1935); D. C. MacGregor, "The Problem of Public Debt in Canada," C.J.E.P.S., II (May 1936); L. Gettys, The Administration of Canadian Conditional Grants (Chicago, 1938), chapter VIII; Canada Year Books, 1936-41; Mackintosh, The Economic Background of Dominion-Provincial Relations, chapter VI; S. Bates, Financial History of Canadian Governments, A. E. Grauer, Public Assistance and Social Insurance, and H. C. Goldenberg, Municipal Finance in Canada, Studies Prepared for the Royal Commission on Dominion-Provincial Relations (Ottawa, 1939), pp. 58-90, chapter II, and parts III and IV, respectively; Report of Royal Commission on Dominion-Provincial Relations, books I (chapter VI) and III (section I); Dominion-Provincial Conference on Reconstruction, Public Investment and Capital Formation, and Comparative Statistics of Public Finance (Ottawa, 1945); M. C. Urquhart, "Public Investment in Canada," C.J.E.P.S., XI (Nov. 1945); International Labour Office, Public Investment and Full Employment (Montreal, 1946), chapter XI; Bank of Canada, Statistical Summary: 1946 Supplement (Ottawa, 1946); Department of Trade and Commerce, Investment and Inflation, with Special Reference to the Immediate Postwar Period, Canada, 1945-1948 (Ottawa, 1949), and Private and Public Investment in Canada, 1926-1951 (Ottawa, 1951); A. N. McLeod, "Maintaining Employment and Incomes in Canada," unpublished Ph.D. thesis (Harvard University, 1949), chapter VIII; Dominion Bureau of Statistics, National Accounts: Income and Expenditure, 1926-1950 (Ottawa, 1951); Safarian, "The Canadian Economy in the Great Depression," chapters III and V.

22. McLeod, "Maintaining Employment and Incomes in Canada," p. 130.

23. Canada Year Book, 1941, p. 754. The figures, in this chapter, for government revenues and expenditures apply to fiscal years.

24. The figures for gross national product apply to calendar years and are derived from D.B.S., National Accounts: Income and Expenditure, 1926-1950, p. 26.

25. The outline of tax rate changes is based on the account given in C.Y.B., 1936, pp. 824, 825.

26. Ibid., p. 825.

27. Department of National Revenue, Taxation Statistics (Ottawa, 1946), p. 11.

28. C.Y.B., 1941, p. 759.

29. Ibid., p. 754.
30. These categories of expenditure were loosely distinguished in terms of whether payment was made for services performed - "direct relief" corresponding to the "dole" with no quid pro quo.
31. The fiscal expenditure years referred to in this chapter end on March 31 of the year following the one cited.
32. Department of Trade and Commerce, Private and Public Investment in Canada, 1926-1951, p. 187. The decline in federal investment in public utilities between the peak and trough years was even more extreme-- from $198 million in 1929 to $60 million in 1933. Ibid., p. 166.
33. The deficits for the years 1931-4 were $83.8 million, $114.2 million, $220.6 million, and $133.5 million respectively. C.Y.B., 1941, pp. 752-4.
34. Department of Trade and Commerce, Private and Public Investment in Canada, 1926-1951, pp. 190, 198. In the case of public utility investment, provincial spending dropped from $36 million in 1930 to $10 million in 1933, and municipal spending from $33 million to $15 million. Ibid., p. 167.
35. Among the provinces, Prince Edward Island and Nova Scotia were notable exceptions to the general investment pattern. The investment expenditure of those two provincial governments declined very little between 1930 and 1933--from $595,000 to $591,000 and from $5.6 million to $5.1 million, respectively. In 1933, public investment by the Government of Prince Edward Island comprised 39.1 per cent of its total expenditure, as compared with 42.2 in 1933; for Nova Scotia, the corresponding ratios were 46.2 per cent in 1933 and 61.8 per cent in 1930. But the far more extreme declines in the other provinces must be considered in the light of the fact that in 1930 their investment outlays amounted to 95 per cent of total provincial public investment. Dominion-Provincial Conference on Reconstruction, Public Investment and Capital Formation, pp. 66, 68-71; and Department of Trade and Commerce, Private and Public Investment in Canada, 1926-1951, pp. 190, 193.
36. In Professor Curtis' words, the Housing Act "may be regarded in part as an attempt to meet the depression and in part as a 'social' scheme." "Dominion Legislation of 1935: An Economist's Review," C.J.E.P.S., I (Nov. 1935), p. 606. For further analysis of the Act, see A. E. Grauer, Housing, A Study Prepared for the Royal Commission on Dominion-Provincial Relations (Ottawa, 1939), pp. 39-42. There were other more direct anti-depression measures associated with the "New Deal"; two of these were the Relief Act of 1935, and the amendment to the Public Works Act of 1934, providing for increased public works expenditures to the extent of nearly $18 million. Curtis, "Dominion Legislation of 1935: An Economist's Review," p. 607. Among the many other "New Deal" laws not cited in the text were: the Farmers' Creditors' Arrangement Act; the Exchange Fund Act; the Prairie Farm Rehabilitation Act; the Patent Act; the Canadian Fisherman's Loan Act; and the amendments to the Combines Act, to the Live Stock Act, and to the Weights and Mea-

sures Act. Ibid., pp. 602, 606. The first Bank of Canada Act was, of course, also a product of this period of feverish parliamentary action.

37. For such individual analyses, see, for example: R. G. H. Smails, "The Dominion Companies Act, 1934: An Appraisal," and R. McQueen, "The Farmers' Creditors' Arrangement Act, 1934," C.J.E.P.S., I (Feb. 1935); papers on "The Employment and Social Insurance Bill," and "The Natural Products Marketing Act, 1934," C.J.E.P.S., I (Aug. 1935); F. R. Scott, "The Privy Council and Mr. Bennett's 'New Deal' Legislation," C.J.E.P.S., III (May 1937); L. G. Reynolds, The Control of Competition in Canada (Cambridge, Mass., 1940), chapters VI-IX; G. V. Haythorne and L. C. Marsh, Land and Labour (Toronto, 1941), chapter XVI.

38. On the question of American influence, it is of interest to note that Mr. W. D. Herridge, generally credited with co-authorship of the Bennett programme, was then serving as Canadian Minister to the United States. As to the reform objective, it is a fact that, at least in terms of public pronouncements, and to the dismay of many of his Conservative colleagues, the Prime Minister became steadily more radical--declaring, for example, by the end of 1934, that "the day of the robber barons is over," and that "the policy of laissez-faire is no longer sufficient" (Carl Wittke, A History of Canada, Toronto, 1941, p. 400); at the same time the Liberal leader, Mr. Mackenzie King, became increasingly conservative in his strenuous opposition to the "New Deal" on constitutional grounds.

39. C. Martin (ed.), Canada in Peace and War (Toronto, 1941), pp. 52, 53. Professor Lower's comments on the Bennett approach should be noted in this connection: "[Characteristically,] he consulted no one, he mollified no interests in advance, he asked no province to co-operate. "Blasting" seemed Mr. Bennett's favourite operation, and having failed to blast his way into markets abroad, he was now about to attempt to blast "capitalism" and provincial rights at home. The Liberals were only to glad to shout "ultra vires" without having to show their hand.... The importance of the Bennett legislation [then], lies not in its details, some of which (such as provision for marketing control) had little clarity of aim and were probably impracticable, but in the sharp turn it indicated as having been reached in the economic and social road. The laissez-faire state was coming to an end; the period of a controlled, a planned, society was beginning." A. R. M. Lower, Colony to Nation (Toronto, 1946), p. 516.

40. The survey of tax changes in the recovery period is based on the historical accounts contained in Canada Year Books, 1936, 1938, 1939, 1940, pp. 825 and 826, 837-9, 874 and 875, and 830, respectively.

41. The personal income tax structure remained unchanged, and a number of excise tax reductions were made, in 1936. C.Y.B., 1938, pp. 837, 838.

42. D.B.S., National Accounts: Income and Expenditure, 1926-1950, pp. 26, 27. The income rise was even greater in terms of domestic investment and exports--167 per cent and 73 per cent, respectively. Ibid., pp. 46, 47.

43. Ibid., pp. 46. 47.

44. Cf. Debates, June 16, 1938, IV, p. 3924.

45. The Home Improvement Guarantee Act of 1937 was designed "primarily as a re-employment effort." Grauer, Housing, p. 42. Under the Act, the Dominion government guaranteed approved lending institutions against loss on home improvement loans up to a maximum of 15 per cent of the aggregate amount of each loan made. For a statistical account of the results achieved by the Act, see Grauer, Housing, pp. 42, 43.

46. The Housing Act of 1938 was the most comprehensive federal housing legislation enacted during the thirties. As such, it had both stability and social welfare objectives. A detailed analysis of the Act can be found in Grauer, Housing, pp. 43, 44b.

Reference should also be made to the federal Government's wheat stabilization policy of 1930-7. It began in the autumn of 1930, with the Government's guarantee of the initial payment set by the Pools. In 1931, this system was abandoned, and the Government paid a five cent bonus per bushel on all wheat marketed. The bonus arrangement was discontinued in 1932, and from that year until September 1935 the Government, through the Central Selling Agency, engaged in the purchase of wheat futures in order to maintain or raise the price at which Canadian farmers sold their wheat. While wheat prices were, at times, thereby maintained above world levels, they fell, nevertheless, to extremely low levels. Moreover, by the autumn of 1935, with the establishment of the Wheat Board and the termination of the buying operations, the Government had accumulated about 205 million bushels of unsold wheat. Through a conjuncture of circumstances--the continuing drought in North America, a short crop in the Argentine, and world economic recovery--the Board was able to dispose of the whole carry-over at a small net profit during the following year, while incurring a $12 million loss on the minimum prices set for the 1935 and 1936 crops. In any case, during the entire 1930-7 period, the Dominion Government spent only about $20 million or an average of less than 1 cent per bushel, on wheat price stabilization. "The drastic impact of the depression on Prairie agriculture was not significantly reduced by government assistance." Report of Royal Commission on Dominion-Provincial Relations, pp. 161, 162. See, also, Tables XIV and XVI, in which the federal wheat expenditures are subsumed under "agricultural aid."

For discussion of the federal Government's depression expenditures on subsidies to the coal industry and in meeting the huge annual deficits incurred by the Canadian National Railways, see Report of Royal Commission on Dominion-Provincial Relations, pp. 160-2.

47. Department of Trade and Commerce, Private and Public Investment in Canada, 1926-1951, p. 186. There was also a 62 per cent increase in federal investment in public utilities between 1933 and 1939, from $60 million to $97 million. Ibid., p. 166.

48. The $61 million of federal investment spending in 1938 represented a $16 million increase over 1937 and apparently reflected the government's desire to cushion the impact of the 1937-8 recession. But the investment

total for all governments declined slightly between 1937 and 1938, by virtue
of the excess of the provincial drop over the federal and municipal rise.
Ibid., pp. 186, 190, 198.

49. Department of Trade and Commerce, Private and Public Investment in Canada, 1926-1951, p. 186; and D. B. S., National Accounts:
Income and Expenditure, 1926-1950, pp. 26, 27. The maximum public
investment by all Canadian governments, relative to gross national product, was 5 per cent in 1938. Ibid. But compare with the low ratios cited
for other countries (including the United States, Sweden, and Australia) in
International Labour Office, Public Investment and Full Employment, part
IV.

50. Department of Trade and Commerce, Private and Public Investment in Canada, 1926-1951, pp. 190, 198. The spending pattern for investment by provincially owned and municipally owned public utilities should
also be noted--the former rose from $10 million to $19 million, and the
latter from $15 million to $21 million, between 1933 and 1937. Ibid.,
p. 167.

51. Ibid., pp. 186, 190, 198.

52. Ibid.; and Report of Royal Commission on Dominion-Provincial
Relations, book III, pp. 96, 97. While both provincial and municipal
spending varied in a clearly cyclical manner during the thirties, the latter
showed less instability throughout. In this negative sense municipal spending, to some extent (and probably inadvertently), may have cushioned the
destabilizing shock produced by sharply fluctuating provincial (and federal)
investment.

53. International Labour Office, Public Investment and Full Employment, p. 187,

54. Report of Royal Commission on Dominion-Provincial Relations,
book III, pp. 96, 97; Department of Trade and Commerce, Private and
Public Investment in Canada, 1926-1951, p. 146; D. B. S. National Accounts: Income and Expenditure, 1926-1950, p. 26.

55. Cf. E. Marcus "Countercyclical Weapons for the Open Economy, "
Journal of Political Economy, LXII (Dec. 1954).

Lightning Source UK Ltd.
Milton Keynes UK
UKOW05f1000090418

320676UK00013B/945/P

9 781442 652231